Public Policy in

Public Policy in Canada

An Introduction

Third Edition

Stephen Brooks

Toronto   Oxford   New York

Oxford University Press

1998

Oxford University Press
70 Wynford Drive, Don Mills, Ontario M3C 1J9
http://www.oupcan.com

Oxford   New York   Athens   Auckland   Bangkok
Bogotá   Buenos Aires   Calcutta   Cape Town
Chennai   Dar es Salaam   Delhi   Florence
Hong Kong   Istanbul   Karachi   Kuala Lumpur
Madrid   Melbourne   Mexico City   Mumbai
Nairobi   Paris   São Paulo   Singapore   Taipei
Tokyo   Toronto   Warsaw

and associated companies in *Berlin   Ibadan*

Oxford is a trade mark of Oxford University Press

Canadian Cataloguing in Publication Data

Brooks, Stephen, 1956–
    Public policy in Canada : an introduction

3rd ed.
Includes bibliographical references and index.
ISBN 0-19-541272-9

1. Political planning — Canada.   I. Title.

JL75.B75 1998   354.7107'2   C98-931502-9

Cover Design: Brett Miller

Contents

List of Tables   vi

List of Figures   vii

Preface   ix

PART I   UNDERSTANDING PUBLIC POLICY

1   Basic Concepts in the Study of Public Policy   1

2   Theories of Public Policy   19

3   The Context of Policy-Making in Canada   42

4   Policy Implementation   66

PART II   POLICY FIELDS

5   Macroeconomic Policy   86

6   Social Policy   120

7   Family Policy   152

8   Aboriginal Policy   183

9   Cultural Policy: Language and Multiculturalism   218

10   Environmental Policy   238

Notes   271

Index   289

List of Tables

2.1 Three Theoretical Perspectives on Policy Formation 38

3.1 Contextual and Proximate Influences on Policy-Making 43

3.2 Interprovincial Distribution of Corporate Head Offices and Nationality of Ownership for the 100 Largest Industrial Firms in Canada, 1991 and 1996 59

5.1 Trends in Economic Growth, Unemployment, Inflation, and Productivity Growth for the Seven Major OECD Economies, 1966–94 101

6.1 Welfare Income as Percentage of Poverty Line, 1996 127

6.2 Public Pension Programs 130

6.3 Evolution of the Unemployment Insurance System since 1971 135

6.4 The Public Share in Total Expenditure on Health, Selected Countries, 1991 141

6.5 Major Transfers to Provinces and Territories, 1994–5 and 1996–7 149

6.6 Income Distribution for Families by Quintiles, 1971–95 150

7.1 The Individual Responsibility and Social Responsibility Models of the Family 166

7.2 The Patriarchal Family: Principles and Policies 168

9.1 Top 10 Countries of Birth for All Immigrants and Recent Immigrants, 1991 234

10.1 Five Models of Environmental Management 240

List of Figures

2.1 David Easton's Simplified Model of the Political System — 24

2.2 The Policy Process Viewed from the Public Choice
Perspective: Four Interrelated Games — 30

4.1 Stages of the Policy-Making Process — 68

4.2 The Rational-Hierarchical Model of Implementation — 72

5.1 Economic Growth and Government Spending, Selected
Countries, 1950–79 — 103

5.2 The Federal Deficit, 1980–96 — 109

5.3 Public-Sector Debt as a Percentage of GDP, Canada and
OECD Average, 1980–96 — 110

6.1 Working-Age Transfers by Type, as Percentage of GDP, 1992 — 122

6.2 Per Capita Purchasing Power Parities for Top 10 OECD
Countries, 1994 — 124

6.3 Net Transfers under Employment Insurance (Dollars of
Benefits per Dollar of Contributions), by Industry, 1995 — 133

6.4 Net Transfers under Employment Insurance (Dollars of
Benefits per Dollar of Contributions), by Province, 1995 — 134

6.5 Unemployment and Social Assistance Caseloads as Percentage
of Working-Age Population, 1981–95 — 136

6.6 Health Spending ($000) per Person in Purchasing Power
Parities, 1995 — 139

6.7 Relative Importance of Various Taxes in Canada, 1951,
1969, 1988 — 146

6.8 Index of Family Income before Transfers, by Highest and
Lowest Quintiles in Constant (1995) Dollars, 1980–95 — 147

6.9 Index of Family Income after Tax, by Highest and Lowest
Quintiles in Constant (1995) Dollars, 1980–95 — 148

7.1 Labour Force Participation of Couples with Children and
Single Mothers with Children, 1971 and 1995 — 159

7.2 Low Income by Family Type, 1980–95 — 160

8.1 Registered Indian Population by Region, 1977, 1987, 1995 — 187

9.1 Anglophone and Francophone Representation in the Federal
Public Service as a Whole, in the Management Category of
the Public Service, and in the Canadian Population,
Selected Years   225

9.2 Public Service Positions Designated Bilingual Imperative,
by Region, 1996   226

10.1 Percentage of Canadians Naming the Environment/Pollution
as the Most Important Problem Facing the Country, Selected
Years   246

10.2 World Population Growth   251

Preface

When I began work on the first edition of this book, back in 1985, Canada-United States free trade was little more than a glimmer in the eye of former Prime Minister Brian Mulroney. Quebec separation seemed to be in retreat, the ramifications of the Charter of Rights and Freedoms on Canadian politics and public policy were just beginning to be felt, and the term 'globalization' was hardly known. Much has changed since then. But at the same time, much remains the same. Donald Smiley's three axes of Canadian politics—the French-English conflict, the Canadian-American relationship, and the centre versus the peripheries of this country—provide as apt a framework for analysing Canadian politics today as at any time in the past. The canvas of Canadian politics is more crowded and complicated today, and some important details have changed. Nevertheless, as Smiley argued, there are enduring characteristics of what might be called the Canadian condition, and some policy issues have proven to be hardy perennials of Canadian political life.

This book introduces the reader to the basic issues in the study of public policy in Canada. Six of its ten chapters are devoted to the examination of particular policy fields. This reflects my belief that public policy is best introduced through the study of what governments actually do and the consequences of their actions. To this end I survey a wide range of policy fields, from fiscal and trade policy to the environment. The menu that I have chosen will not satisfy everyone's tastes. I assume, however, that most instructors will use this book along with additional readings dealing with matters that they believe require a fuller treatment.

Although the principal emphasis of this third edition is on policy fields, I have tried not to neglect those more general matters that must be part of any introduction to public policy. They are the concerns of Part I of this book. Chapter 1 examines some of the fundamental concepts in the study of public policy. Chapter 2 is devoted to theoretical frameworks used to explain policy, in particular the pluralist, public choice, and class analysis models. Chapter 3 analyses what I have called the context of policy-making, focusing on how core values, Canada's ties to the United States, regional divisions, and globalization affect policy. Policy implementation is the subject of Chapter 4, the stage of the policy process that recalls Murphy's Law ('If anything can go wrong it will').

Earlier editions of this book included a discussion of the institutions of policy-making in Canada and features of the political system, such as interest groups and the mass media, that influence significantly the process of policy-making and policy outcomes. I do not include this material in this third edition for two reasons. First, I assume that most readers of this book will have taken an introductory course in Canadian politics and government, and therefore will already be familiar with the basic structures of governance and the informal processes of politics. Second, I have not attempted to replicate what I believe is done admirably well by other writers on Canadian public policy. Les Pal's *Beyond Policy Analysis* already deals with the more conceptual side of public policy and is, it seems to me, an appropriate next step for those who cut their teeth on the present text. Howlett and Ramesh's *The Political Economy of Canada* offers students quite a different take on public policy from my own, drawing on the Canadian political economy tradition. Their emphasis is on the structures and process of policy-making and the relationship of these to social and economic power, whereas my own is on the content and consequences of policy. In this sense the two books may be viewed as complementary.

In Part II of this third edition I survey several policy fields. New to this edition are the chapters on Aboriginal policy and family policy. I assume that the inclusion of a chapter on Aboriginal policy requires no explanation, but some readers may be puzzled by the choice of family policy over some of the more standard offerings, such as telecommunications, defence, industrial policy, and so on. Although family policy has been a well-established policy field in several of the Western European democracies since World War II, with the usual institutional accoutrements of a minister, bureaucracy, budget, etc., only recently has family policy come to be recognized as a distinct policy domain in North America. This recognition has dawned more quickly and had more of a political impact in the United States than in Canada. Nevertheless, recognized or not, the ramifications of family structure and change for policies ranging from such matters as education and housing to culture and morality are enormous and warrant serious attention.

It has been my good fortune to receive the advice and support of many people over the three editions of this book. Euan White and Phyllis Wilson of Oxford University Press have been models of professionalism, and very generously never reminded me that the manuscript for the third edition was later than promised. Richard Tallman has been the book's copy editor from the beginning, and has saved me from more factual inaccuracies and stylistic slip-ups than I care to think about. Professor Joseph Garcea's comments on the manuscript for the third edition were greatly appreciated, as were those of various colleagues who have used earlier editions of the book. I owe a great debt to Barbara Faria, who typed all of the manuscript, and to Lucia Brown and Diane Dupuis of the Word Processing Centre at the University of Windsor.

Finally, I would like to thank my family, Christine, Paul, Tom, and Marianne. There was sometimes more noise and less time than I might have preferred, but without my family it would not have been any fun.

Stephen Brooks
Clinton, Ontario

PART I

UNDERSTANDING PUBLIC POLICY

Chapter One

Basic Concepts in the Study of Public Policy

Introduction

Canadians are used to thinking of their country as the world's best. Indeed, politicians—or at least those in power—regularly tell them that this is so, and as authority for their immodest claim they point to the fact that Canada is regularly ranked first by the United Nations human development index. Of course, it is flattering to anyone's ego to be told that he or she is the best. Canadians can hardly be blamed if, after being told countless times that they are the envy of the world, they accept the truth of this boast at face value. But is complacent pride justified?

It depends on whom you ask. A Quebec separatist would answer no. So, too, would many in Canada's Aboriginal community. Union leaders are likely to complain that working people have seen their rights diminished in many provinces and their incomes and job security eroded across the country. Many environmentalists worry that governments' commitment to protecting the environment has been in retreat for several years. Spokespersons for the feminist movement argue that complacency is far from justified when, they say, so much remains to be done to eliminate gender inequality. And anti-poverty activists insist that the extent of poverty in Canada is reason for shame, not pride.

Canada has often been described as a society of whiners, however, so many will dismiss criticisms such as these as the predictable bellyaching of special interests and professional malcontents. Moreover, it must be admitted that by any comparative standard rooted in the real world, as opposed to some idealized Utopia, Canada is a pretty good place to live. It is not, however, perfect, and those who dare to question the best-country-in-the-world boast should not be written off as ill-mannered party poopers. Consider the following facts:

- In the Quebec referendum of 1995, just under half of those who voted cast their ballot for Quebec independence. While interpretations of this result vary, there can be no doubt that it revealed that a large share of Quebec's population was very dissatisfied with the nature of the country and their place in it.
- Official unemployment rates have been over 10 per cent for much of the time since 1980. Youth unemployment has been considerably higher, and the unemployment rates in much of Canada east of Ontario are regularly twice the national average. Regardless of how this record compares to other national economies, it clearly is a problem for the millions of Canadians and their families who experience unemployment directly and for communities that bear the social and financial burdens of unemployment.
- The federal government's indebtedness exceeds $600 billion, much of it owed to foreigners. The debt of provinces and municipalities adds about another $300 billion to this total. If this debt were to magically disappear tomorrow, federal taxes could be reduced by about 30 per cent without adding a drop of red ink to the budget. Or, if one prefers, Ottawa could increase its program spending by about 30 per cent without running a deficit.
- Canadians requiring some form of elective surgery—an artificial hip joint or cataract removal, for example—frequently have to wait several months for their operations. In some communities it can take a year or longer to see certain specialists.
- On a per capita basis, Canada is one of the world's top spenders on education. But in a 1996 ranking of countries on standardized math and science tests, Canadian students finished eighteenth on both. They were beaten by their counterparts from a number of countries, including Bulgaria, the Czech Republic, Slovenia, Hungary, and Ireland, where per student spending on education is much lower than in Canada.

Like every other country, Canada has problems. That these problems are minor alongside those of a Bangladesh or Bosnia does not make them any less urgent for those who experience them. Public policies are the actions taken by governments and their agents to address these problems. They are the subject of this book.

What Is Public Policy?

One of the most often cited definitions of public policy is that of American political scientist Thomas Dye. According to Dye, public policy is 'whatever governments choose to do or not to do.'[1] Policy involves, then, conscious choice that leads to deliberate action—the passage of a law, the spending of money, an official speech or gesture, or some other observable act—or inaction. No one would disagree that a concrete act like the passage of a law counts as policy. But can inaction reasonably be described as policy? The answer depends on the circumstances in which the failure to act takes place, and whether a condition is viewed as being problematic.

To understand this, consider the case of toxic chemicals. For decades carcinogenic PCBs (polychlorinated biphenyls) were used, stored, and disposed of without much care being taken. There was no public policy on the handling of these deadly chemicals before it was realized that there was reason for concern. When the public became alerted to their cancer-causing properties, the use, transportation, and elimination of PCBs—and the same is obviously true of other hazardous substances—became policy issues. Government inaction before then obviously had health consequences for those who were exposed to PCBs and certainly allowed the accumulation of stockpiles of what today is one of the most widely known and feared of toxic chemicals. But this was not deliberate inaction. There was no public policy on PCBs, just as there was no policy on the production and handling of many other industrial chemicals, because there was no significant level of awareness that a problem existed. It makes no sense to speak of policy where an issue has not yet been formulated in problematic terms. Once it has, however, inaction by policy-makers becomes a deliberate policy choice.

In the case of PCBs the harmful consequences of this substance for human health are not disputed, and once they became known to the public and policy-makers the question became one of what measures were appropriate to deal with the problem, not whether a problem deserving of government action really existed. It often happens, however, that there is no agreement that circumstances are problematic and deserving of government action. Consider the case of income differences between male- and female-dominated occupations. Until a few decades ago the fact that secretaries, receptionists, nurses, and child-care workers generally were paid less than men working in occupations where the necessary skills, qualifications, and responsibilities were less demanding than in those female-dominated occupations was seen to be quite normal. It was nothing other than the result of voluntary occupational choices and the laws of supply and demand at work in labour markets. But as feminist theory developed during the 1960s and 1970s, inequalities in the workplace became contested terrain. Differences that previously had been overlooked or, when acknowledged, explained as normal and inevitable were interpreted by feminist critics as evidence of systemic discrimination and gender bias in labour markets. They proposed that governments step in to close the earnings gap through pay equity policies that would require employers to pay employees in female-dominated occupations wages equal to those earned in male-dominated occupations characterized by similar skill requirements, qualifications, and responsibilities. Across North America many governments have enacted such policies for their public-sector workforces. A few have extended these policies to cover private-sector employers.

Unlike the example of PCBs, no consensus exists that differences in male and female earnings attributable to the tendency for male-dominated occupations to be better remunerated are a problem warranting government intervention. Nevertheless, the widespread awareness of these differences and the controversy surrounding them mark a significant change from the situation of a few decades ago. Today, when a government resists demands to adopt or extend pay equity policies, this must be viewed as a deliberate choice. This was not so in the days before the gender gap in remuneration was conceptualized as a problem.

Conscious choice, therefore, must be a part of any definition of public policy. But is policy necessarily what policy-makers say it is? In other words, if we want to determine what public policy is on some issue, should we direct our attention to official government pronouncements or to the actual record of what has and has not been achieved?

In politics, as in life generally, no one should take all statements at face value. Vagueness and ambiguity are often deliberate, and are always part of the recipe for political longevity in democratic political systems. The bottom line for determining what actually constitutes public policy in some field comes down to this: both official claims and concrete action should be looked at carefully, and one should be prepared to find that actions often speak louder than words.

But the determination of policy is even more complicated than this. It often happens that a government's most sincere efforts misfire, failing to achieve the goals expected of them and perhaps even aggravating the situation they were intended to improve. Consider a policy of government-controlled rents. Critics of rent controls have long argued that such a policy in fact hurts the lower-income groups it is intended to benefit because it discourages developers and investors from building new rental accommodation for the low end of the market. As the supply dwindles, prices inevitably are pushed up. If and when this happens, are we justified in saying that government housing policy favours the less affluent? But even more common than policy misfires are those frequent cases in which government action simply fails to accomplish its intended goals. In fact, a program, law, or regulation hardly ever 'solves' a problem in the sense of eliminating the conditions that inspired controversy and demands for action in the first place. When problems do disappear, this is often the result of changing societal conditions—including when they are pushed below the surface of public consciousness by other problems—rather than a direct consequence of government policy.

We have mentioned the case of official pronouncements that do not coincide with the observable actions of government or that bear little resemblance to the facts of whatever situation they ostensibly address. When this happens, and it frequently does, we should not jump to the cynical conclusion that policy is just 'sound and fury signifying nothing'. Gestures, symbols, and words are important components of the political process. They are often valued in their own right, and their capacity to reconcile and to divide should not be underestimated. Since the ill-fated Meech Lake Accord (1987), which proposed the constitutional recognition of Quebec as a 'distinct society', the issue of whether and how Quebec's distinctive character should be recognized has been a source of division in Canadian politics. This division resurfaced around the failed Charlottetown Accord (1992) and has continued to simmer as Ottawa and some of the provincial governments continue to search for a constitutional formula that will satisfy French-speaking Quebecers' demands for recognition while not offending the one-Canada, all-provinces-and-Canadians-are-equal preferences of the majority of their fellow citizens. It is not so much that non-Quebecers believe that the constitutional recognition of Quebec as a distinct society would have material consequences for which the rest of Canada would have to pay. Rather, it is the *idea* of distinct society status for Quebec, and the recognition of this special status in the constitution, that they reject. Governments influence the allocation of symbolic values in society, what Raymond Breton calls the 'symbolic order'. And as in the case of material benefits and burdens, satisfying one group's symbolic aspirations may mean denying those of another group.

The Agenda and Discourse of Public Policy

But there is another, more general sense in which the symbols, gestures, and words manipulated by policy-makers are important. They constitute the *political agenda*, defining what is relevant in public life, how issues are defined, whose views should be taken seriously, and what sort of 'solutions' are tenable. A statement by a political leader, a law, media coverage of a group's policy demands or of some situation or event all provide an affirmation of the relevance of a problem and of the values and conflicts associated with it. If we may be excused a bit of jargon here, political issues and policy problems are constructed out of the conflicting values and terminologies that different groups put forward when they compete for something that cannot be shared so as to satisfy all of them fully. These issues and problems do not exist apart from the words and symbols used to describe them. They are constructed in the sense that political issues and policy problems do not possess an inevitable, inherent character. Whether we even recognize them as political issues and policy problems, and what comes to mind when they are presented to our attention, both depend on the particular forces that shape the political agenda in a given society. These forces change over time and so, therefore, does the political agenda. As American political scientist Murray Edelman observes, 'conditions accepted as inevitable or unproblematic may come to be seen as problems; and damaging conditions may not be defined as political issues at all.'[2]

Once we accept that the political agenda is not an inevitable product of social and economic conditions, we are then confronted with the question of why some of these conditions become formulated as problems and others do not. This leads to a consideration of the various agents of cultural learning—the family, the schools, the mass media, the workplace—that together generate the ideological parameters of society. To understand the practical importance of cultural learning, consider the following examples.

In liberal democratic societies like Canada and the United States we learn (most of us, anyway) that achievement and opportunities are relatively open to those with ability and a willingness to work hard. Consequently, most people do not perceive economic inequality as a serious problem. In another ideological setting the fact that the bottom 20 per cent of Canada's population accounts for about half of 1 per cent of the country's wealth, compared to about 70 per cent in the hands of the richest fifth of the population,[3] might be viewed as a problem.

Still on the topic of inequality, until a couple of decades ago the extensive and profound differences in the career opportunities, incomes, and social roles of men and women were not generally seen to be a problem. As cultural attitudes have changed, the unequal social conditions of males and females have become a prominent item on the political agendas of virtually all industrialized democracies. Gender politics and the policy debates that surround such issues as abortion, pay equity, affirmative action for women, pornography, publicly subsidized day care, and sexual harassment are constructed out of the arguments, claims, and demands for action put forward by women's organizations and their spokespersons, and the counter-arguments, claims, and demands of others who feel compelled to respond to their definition of the problem. The same can be said of any policy issue. What emerges from such exchanges is a *policy discourse*—an unfolding tapestry of words and symbols that structures thinking and action—constructed out of the multiple definitions (or denial) of the problem.

The capacity to influence this discourse is often half the battle. Every group, organization, and individual with the least bit of political acumen know this, so that their first line of attack is often through the mass media. Governments have a distinct advantage in the struggle to shape the contours of policy discourse. Not only do they have virtually guaranteed access to the public through mass media coverage of official statements, press conferences, and other orchestrated efforts to communicate a particular message (and influence public opinion), they also are able to tell their story through paid advertisements—the federal government has for years been the largest advertiser in Canada—and through government information services directed at households and organizations.

The messages governments communicate, particularly when they touch on the controversial issues, are often greeted with cynicism by the media and the public. But even then they receive a hearing. One reason for this is the official authority of their source. Even if the government's message is not considered to be credible, its capacity to influence the outcome of an issue means that the information it disseminates is not likely to be ignored. Cynicism, vocal opposition, and unsympathetic media are not enough to close off the channels through which government can influence policy discourse. The 1989 introduction of the widely unpopular Goods and Services Tax (GST) was followed by an extensive campaign of paid advertising and information, sent directly to businesses and households, intended to increase public acceptance of the GST. Only a couple of years earlier Ottawa had spent tens of millions of dollars on brochures and other information distributed to households 'explaining' the benefits of the Canada-US Free Trade Agreement (FTA). It is never easy to determine exactly what sort of impact these policy advocacy campaigns have on public opinion. But the very fact that the problems, positions, and information contained in such campaigns are being communicated makes them automatically a part of policy discourse on an issue.

Despite the formidable information and financial resources at their disposal, governments are a long way from being able to control either the policy agenda or the particular policy discourse that develops around some issue. Indeed, much of the time governments are on the defensive, reacting to the claims, demands, and interpretations put forward by opposition political parties, by societal groups, and by the media. Whose 'problems' reach the political agenda, and whose arguments, interpretations, and proposals are taken seriously in the policy-making process, are largely determined by the social power of the interests advancing them. In fact, the capacity to influence policy discourse would seem to be one barometer by which the power of different interests could be measured.

But this is too simple. Politics in the capitalist democracies is open-ended enough that ideas and reforms that clearly are not favoured by the powerful often are woven into the fabric of policy discourse and institutionalized through public policies. One would be hard-pressed to explain the policy successes of the women's movement, and the arguments associated with gender-based differences in such matters as employment and pay, from the standpoint of dominant class interests. Or consider the entry of Aboriginal rights, visible minorities, and the handicapped into modern political discourse. These groups lie far from the epicentre of social and economic power in Canadian society. Despite this, they have been able to influence the agenda of politics and the actions of governments in this country. Moreover, some policy areas never reach the public agenda in a way that mobilizes powerful social and economic interests. Therapies for treating the mentally ill and approaches used in dealing with criminals and victims are policy domains where scientific expertise may carry greater weight than usual because the issues involved do not capture the sustained attention of the public. We should not assume, therefore, an automatic and perfect correspondence between the ideas that get onto the political agenda and become embodied in state actions and, on the other hand, the pecking order of social and economic interests in society.

Policy discourse is not, however, a wide open mêlée in which every voice has an equal opportunity to be heard. It has become popular to speak of *systemic bias*, a term intended to capture the selectiveness of the policy system. Some points of view, it is claimed, never get articulated and some policy outcomes are virtually precluded by the biases inherent in the cultural and institutional fabric of society. At one level this is obviously true. For demographic, historical, and political reasons, language has a prominence in Canadian politics that it does not have in the United States. Conversely, individual rights and freedoms occupy a more significant place in American political discourse than they do in Canada and most other capitalist democracies. Thus, in saying that any society and political system have particular biases we have not said much—or at least nothing very profound. The more interesting question is what these biases reveal about the sources and distribution of power and about the capacity of different social and economic interests to influence the actions of government.

The Pattern of Public Policy

What governments do, *how* they do it, and with *what* consequences are aspects of public policy that have changed dramatically over time. These address what may be labelled the scope, means, and distributional dimensions of public policy. Together, they provide the basis for comparing the pattern of public policy and the role of the state in different societies, and for charting—and understanding—the course of historical change within a society.

1. The Scope of Public Policy

We know that governments do more today than they did in the past. They pass more laws and regulations on a wider range of subjects than before; they spend a larger share of national income; they tax in more ways and at higher levels; and they employ more people to operate the machinery of government. The scope of their activities ranges from the municipal by-laws requiring dog owners to carry a 'stoop-and-scoop' when walking their pooch to laws affecting the more vital aspects of our lives.

Back in 1900, the Public Accounts for Canada listed only a couple of dozen separate departments and agencies of government. Ninety years later, the Public Accounts listed 120. At Confederation, total government expenditure in Canada accounted for a little more than 5 per cent of gross national expenditure (GNE). Today government spending comes to about 45 per cent of GNE. Growth in the size of the public sector has been accompanied by change in the role of the state. The chief functions of Western governments in the nineteenth century were maintaining social order, defence, and facilitating economic development through measures ranging from railroad subsidies to tariffs. By comparison, governments today are involved in a bewildering range of functions that include all of the traditional ones plus education, health care, income support for segments of the population, broadcasting, and much more. Until the early twentieth century, about three-quarters of government spending was on goods and services, what public finance economists call *exhaustive expenditures*. Today, however, about half of total government spending involves *transfer payments* to individuals, families, and organizations. This is money that government handles, but does not itself spend on goods and services. The growth in transfer payments as a share of total government spending reflects the increasing importance of government's redistributive role in society.

The redistributive function of the state is the battleground on which the ideological forces of the left and the right have slugged it out since the last century. Although it is popular today to argue that debates between the left and the right have lost their relevance, this simply is not true. If the left is understood to prefer collectivist solutions to social and economic problems and the belief that individuals achieve dignity from the communal associations that give their lives meaning, and if the right is understood to prefer market solutions and a belief that personal dignity depends on one's own efforts and tends to be undermined by collectivist policies, then the left-versus-right debate is still very much alive. The concern that governments of virtually all partisan hues have shown in recent years with public-sector deficits and debt and the conversion of most governments to trade liberalism have contributed to the erroneous belief that collectivist (i.e., left-wing) ideology is in eclipse. But the facts—from hard measures of government's presence in society, such as the share of national income it spends or the portion of personal income it takes in taxes, to softer measures of state intrusiveness, such as the range of activities that governments regulate—do not support the claim that the collectivist model of the state has gone down to defeat.

On the contrary, it is probably fair to say that the essential premise of the collectivist ethos is widely and uncritically accepted by both élites and the general population in Canada and other advanced industrial democracies. This premise is that communal goals, such as redistributing wealth, promoting economic growth, and protecting the weak, should be pursued and can only be pursued through the state. There are, quite naturally, differences over the precise character of these goals and how best to achieve them. But the belief that the clock can be turned back to the 'nightwatchman' state of capitalist democracy's youth has little more than a marginal following even in the United States, the most liberal—in the classical sense of emphasizing market and individual freedoms—of liberal democracies.

The appropriate scope of government activities is largely a matter of personal preference. Take something as mundane as the random stopping of automobiles by police to check for drunk drivers. Some people object to this practice on the grounds that it violates the individual's freedom—not the freedom to drive while intoxicated, but the freedom from arbitrary detention by the state. Others—probably most Canadians—are willing to tolerate the possibility that innocent people may be pulled over and questioned by the police, and possibly even asked to take a breathalyzer test, as a reasonable infringement on individual freedom that contributes to public safety.

There is no one right answer to the question of whether random checking of motorists is a good thing, just as there is no correct answer to the question of whether a state that spends 45 per cent of national income is better or worse than one that spends 35 per cent. The answers to such questions depend on the normative premises within which they are situated. Someone who believes that the primary role of government ought to be the promotion of social justice will certainly have a different conception of the appropriate scope of government activities from someone who believes that government's role ought principally to be the protection of individual property rights. Where matters become really complicated, and where one might expect to be able to find objective answers to questions of what policies are best, is when people agree on the goals but disagree on the means for achieving it. In other words, if judgements on the scope of government activities are unavoidably normative, surely the question of means is an essentially technical one. As it happens, however, decisions on what means will best achieve an agreed-upon goal are usually influenced by our premises and values.

2. The Choice of Policy Instrument

Ends and means are inseparable. To choose a particular goal requires that a plan of action, the means for achieving that goal, be developed and put into effect. The successful attainment of chosen goals, including the policy objectives of governments, depends on the choice of instruments for achieving them. This all sounds very rational and calculated. In the real world of policy-making, as in other realms of life, the process by which these instruments are chosen is much messier. The selection of means is influenced by how things have been done in the past—by vested bureaucratic, political, and societal interests; by chance, including the individuals involved in a decision; and by ideas and beliefs that may or may not be well founded. In addition, it appears that means sometimes precede, and determine, the ends of policy.

Before World War II, taxes on personal and corporate incomes comprised only a small share of total government revenue: about 25 per cent in 1939.[4] Taxes on consumption and property were more important sources of government revenue. Today, income-based taxes, especially those on personal income, represent the single largest source of revenue for both Ottawa and the provinces. Payroll taxes such as unemployment insurance premiums and Canada and Quebec Pension Plan contributions are also major sources of government revenue. They did not exist during the first half of Canada's history. The tax system has become one of the chief instruments for the pursuit of government's economic, social, and even cultural policy objectives.

Regulation has also increased dramatically. Most federal and provincial regulatory laws have been enacted since 1950.[5] They affect activities from product labelling and the maximum distance between the bars of a crib to Canadian content in television and radio programming and exports of energy. The post-World War II era has also seen an explosion in the number and diversity of government-owned corporations, most of which have been created since 1960.[6] These corporations are involved in activities as diverse as the production of electrical power, the provision of credit, selling wine and spirits, and mining potash. Although many of these corporations have been privatized since the 1980s, there continue to be hundreds of such enterprises owned by Ottawa or the provinces, including such important organizations as Ontario Hydro, Hydro-Québec, and the Canadian Broadcasting Corporation.

In recent years controversy has surrounded all of the most common tools of public policy. Sometimes the issue has been whether the goals associated with a particular policy instrument—Canadian culture and the CBC; Canadianization of the petroleum industry and Petro-Canada; telecommmunications regulation and the CRTC—are worth pursuing. More often, however, debate has centred on whether there is a better, less costly way of achieving given policy objectives. This debate has been fuelled by the arguments of economists, some political journalists, and business organizations about the alleged inefficiencies of publicly owned businesses and the economic distortions produced by regulations. Taxation, subsidies, and spending programs have also come in for heavy criticism for the same reasons—that they do not accomplish the goals they ostensibly are supposed to promote.

The evaluation of how well a particular policy instrument achieves what is expected of it is not a simple task. To begin with, the government's goals may not be terribly clear, and may even be confused and contradictory. Even assuming that we can identify these goals with some precision, the only readily available standard for measuring how well they are being achieved is an economic one. It is fine to talk about 'justice', 'equity', 'national identity', 'the quality of life', and other such non-economic values. But the fact that these values do not carry price tags—indeed, the very reason governments involve themselves in the promotion of these things is often because the unregulated marketplace does not produce them at politically acceptable levels—creates a problem in assessing their worth.

The choice of means is not just about effectiveness. It is also about values. Some policy instruments, such as taxes and state-owned companies, are more intrusive than others, such as regulation or exhortation by government. Generally speaking, carrots (incentives) are less intrusive than sticks (commands and prohibitions) and are more likely to be preferred by those who are predisposed towards smaller government and greater scope for individual choice.

3. Who Benefits and Who Pays?

Entire books are written on this subject without there being any consensus on the distributional impact of public policy. The very term 'welfare state' implies that wealth is to some degree transferred by the state from those who can afford to pay to those in need. And there is no doubt that the various taxation and spending policies of governments affect the distribution of wealth. How much and to whose advantage are disputed issues.

Contrary to popular belief, the tax system does not redistribute income from Canadian society's more affluent classes to its most impoverished ones. This is because several important taxes, notably sales and property taxes and capped payroll taxes, are regressive. They take a larger share out of the incomes of lower income-earners than they do from higher income-earners. Although the personal income tax is progressive—the rate at which one is taxed increases with one's income—and governments typically rebate part of the personal cost of regressive levies like the sales and property taxes to lower income-earners, the regressive impact of total taxation is far from eliminated. On the other hand, the total effect of the money transfers received under income security programs and public spending on education, housing, health care, transportation, and a host of other programs favours the poor. The bottom fifth of income-earners in Canada account for about 1 per cent of earned income but about 5 per cent when all sources of income are taken into account.[7] The difference is due to such redistributive transfer payments as social assistance, GST rebates, and the Child Tax Benefit.

Governments in Canada also act in ways that affect the distribution of wealth between regions. These regional subsidies take three main forms:

1. equalization payments from Ottawa to the less affluent provinces, intended to ensure 'that provincial governments have sufficient revenues to provide reasonably comparable levels of service at reasonably comparable levels of taxation';[8]
2. income transfers from Ottawa to individuals, such as employment insurance (formerly called unemployment insurance), that are a major source of income in communities where employment opportunities tend to be seasonal; and
3. federal and provincial industrial assistance programs that subsidize businesses in economically depressed regions.

As in the case of policies geared towards redistributing income among individuals, there is no agreement on the impact of these regionally targeted policies. The approximately $8–$9 billion a year that Ottawa transfers to the economically weaker provinces in the form of equalization payments certainly enable them to finance a level of services that would otherwise be beyond their fiscal means. And the fact that certain regions benefit more than others from the EI system involves regional redistribution. But some have argued that these transfers impose a burden on the national economy without solving the problems that underlie the weak economies of the provinces that benefit from them. Regional industrial assistance programs have come in for the same criticism. But one should not jump to the conclusion that Ottawa's industrial assistance pipeline has flowed only one way, transferring money from the 'have' to the 'have-not' provinces. Any calculation of the regional impact of all forms of industrial support, from tariffs to government contracts to grants and loans to particular businesses, must certainly conclude that the big winners have been Ontario and Quebec and, moreover, that their gains have been at the expense of other regions.

Government's impact on the distribution of economic well-being does not stop at individuals and regions. In all industrial societies, Canada included, the state is in the business of protecting a vast range of producer and occupational groups from the unregulated workings of the market. Canadian economist Thomas Courchene calls this the 'protected society'.[9] It is a society in which any group with political clout is able to persuade the state to protect its narrow interests—at the public's expense. Courchene's concept of the protected society recognizes that both society's privileged and its disadvantaged elements may be 'welfare recipients'. Indeed, a federal government task force once described Canadian businesses as 'program junkies',[10] addicted to the billions of dollars worth of subsidies that successive governments have been willing to dole out to them. This addiction continues unabated, despite cuts to program spending in recent years. And it is not simply business that slurps at the public trough. All manner of special interests are the recipients of government largesse. The Public Accounts of Canada include hundreds of pages listing the organizations that have received government money. Their diversity is truly staggering. A recent annual list included such different organizations as the International Fund for Ireland, the Canadian Association of Provincial Court Judges, the Association franco-yukonnaise, the Federation of Italian Canadians for Yesterday, Today and Tomorrow, Manufacturier de bas culotte d'amour, and the Canadian Manufacturers' Association. That these groups may be quite deserving of public support—although 'deserving' certainly is in the eye of the beholder—is not the point. Rather, the point is that any accounting of the benefits and costs of public policy must include the multitude of subsidies and non-cash forms of support for a vast universe of organized interests.

All of the distributive effects of policy discussed to this point have involved material benefits and burdens. But as Raymond Breton observes, 'public institutions and their authorities are involved in the distribution of symbolic as well as material resources.'[11] We need only think of the outraged reaction of Anglophone Canadians to the Quebec government's 1989 decision (Bill 178) to invoke the notwithstanding clause (section 33) of the Charter of Rights and Freedoms after the Supreme Court of Canada had ruled that Quebec's restrictions on the language of signs violated the freedom of expression guaranteed in the Charter. Or recall the backlash generated among French-speaking Quebecers by the 1990 failure of the Meech Lake Accord proposals for constitutional reform, a failure they interpreted as a rejection by English Canada of equal status for French Canada. Support for separatism in Quebec reached levels never seen before or since the death of Meech. When, during the 1997 election campaign, the Reform Party brought attention to the fact that in recent decades Quebec seems to have had a near hammerlock on the job of prime minister, regardless of whether the Liberal or Progressive Conservative Party is in power, it was criticized for anti-Quebec, anti-French bigotry (although its statement of the simple truth appeared to have scored points with the electorate in English Canada).

All of these examples have to do with the politics of recognition. It is normal for people to want to see themselves reflected in the institutions of their society, including its structures of power and its symbolic trappings. This recognition may be achieved through the participation of members of a community—ethnic, linguistic, regional, gender, etc.—with which one identifies closely, or it may be generated via forms of official status for a group. The Canadian constitution and laws confer official recognition on the French and English language communities, Aboriginal Canadians, and on non-French, non-British Canadians through official multiculturalism.

But as is true of all politics, whatever the issues and stakes, the politics of recognition is characterized by scarcity. Recognition for one community may require that the values and aspirations of others be denied or at least diluted. The struggle over constitutional recognition of Quebec as a distinct society illustrates this well. Most Francophone Quebecers believe such recognition to be a just and normal expression of their two-nations understanding of Canada. Most Anglophone Canadians have problems with such recognition precisely because they do not share this two-nations understanding of Canada. It simply is not possible to satisfy the symbolic preferences of both English and French Canada on the issue of Quebec's constitutional status. Recognition and symbols are necessarily in limited supply. Although it might be tempting to believe that the solution to quarrels over recognition is to recognize all groups, the logical and practical absurdity of this soon becomes apparent. The social-symbolic value of recognition is diluted as it is extended to more and more groups, until it becomes worthless precisely because it is so common. Moreover, demands for recognition are often mutually exclusive. Distinct society status for Quebec and the notion of the equality of all provinces are, for example, demands that probably cannot be reconciled, except by some constitutional legerdemain!

Government in Retreat?

In recent years it has become commonplace to argue that governments are less able to influence the societies and economies over which they preside than was previously the case. This argument has a number of variations, but the unifying thread that runs through all of them is that the forces of globalization have increased the exposure of all societies to the world around them and decreased the capacity of domestic policy-makers to control what happens in their back-yard. *The Economist* puts it this way:

> The tasks that governments have traditionally regarded as their most important jobs, it is argued, have moved beyond their reach, and thus beyond the reach of voters. Global markets are in charge. No longer able to do big things that matter, governments busy themselves with small things, best done locally or not at all. Economic integration thus explains the political malaise affecting many of the world's big democracies.[12]

Globalization, however, is about more than markets. It is also about information and culture in a world wired by computers and satellites. The instantaneous sharing of information and images through the Internet and satellite television has reduced the ability of governments and domestic élites to control the flow of information reaching citizens. Cultural policies that rely on the ability of the state to restrict what its citizens see, hear, and read have become less tenable. Moreover, globalization is about transnational forums such as the United Nations Environment Program, the annual G-7 summits, and the UN Committee on Economic, Social, and Cultural Rights, which define and debate policy issues, and about international institutions, such as the UN Commission on Human Rights and the World Trade Organization, which establish rules that policy-makers may perceive to be binding or at least difficult to ignore. Many of these forums and institutions are market-driven, such as those that involve trading rules, financial transactions, and production standards. Others are generated by global—although mainly Western—social and political movements, such as environmentalism and feminism. International media and knowledge élites reinforce these forces of globalization.

Globalization is important in explaining the special challenges of governance as we move into the twenty-first century, but it is not the whole story. Another factor that complicates the job of policy-makers is what Neil Nevitte calls the decline of deference.[13] It appears that citizens in many democracies, including Canada, are more cynical towards public authority than in the past and more likely to perceive themselves as having rights that should take priority over the convenience and preferences of state authorities.

The evidence of this assumes various forms. In Europe the mass protests that took place in Belgium during 1996, in reaction to what most Belgians believed to be the indifference and lack of responsiveness of that country's judicial and political system to the disappearance and murder of young girls, became a symbol across Europe for popular rejection of old ways of conducting public business.[14] In Canada, the electorate's rejection of the 1992 Charlottetown Accord on the constitution—an accord that was supported by most of the country's political and economic élites—was widely and rightly interpreted as a rejection of the élitist policy-making style that has characterized Canadian politics until recent years (indeed, it would be premature to write its obituary!). More generally, the explosion of what Mary Ann Glendon calls 'rights talk' in Canada, the United States, and internationally is argued by many to be a symptom of citizens' greater assertiveness in the face of the traditional authority of government. This new assertiveness may have roots in the cultural phenomenon of post-materialism.[15] This involves a cultural shift away from preoccupation with material concerns, as lifestyle issues and matters of identity and participation assume greater importance.

If modern governments seem less able to steer the ship of state than their predecessors, part of the explanation may involve simple hubris. 'Hubris' is a Greek word that signifies arrogance arising from pride or passion. In retrospect, much of what was believed possible and expected of governance during most of the twentieth century may simply have been a hubristic error. Keynesian economic policy is a major case in point. During the 1940s, governments in the Western industrialized democracies, including Canada, became converts to the belief that they could and should assume responsibility for the maintenance of steady economic growth and full employment. The buoyant economies of the 1950s and 1960s suggested to many people that the policies proposed by the British economist John Maynard Keynes, which spread throughout the Western world by a generation of economists and policy-makers trained in Keynesian macroeconomics, did what they were supposed to do. Governments quickly became used to taking credit for what went right in the economy, at the same time as citizens came to expect policy-makers to promise economic growth, jobs, and rising incomes.

When the bubble burst in the 1970s, the optimistic interventionism on which Keynesian was premised came in for some hard scrutiny. And although Keynesian economics and policies still have their defenders, many argue that governments were given too much credit for prosperity that was fuelled by market factors. In retrospect, the brave assumptions of Keynesianism appear to have been overly optimistic, and the image of the state as manager of the economy flawed by hubris.

Inflated and probably unrealistic expectations for public policy were generated from other quarters as well. The intellectual movements known as *progressivism* in the United Sates and *Fabian socialism* in the United Kingdom both held high expectations for governments. They believed that the knowledge and insights of trained policy specialists could be used to improve the effectiveness of public policy and ultimately to solve social and economic problems. The *policy sciences movement* that emerged in the United States after World War II had as its goal the integration of social scientific knowledge and its application to public policy. In common with progressivism and Fabian socialism, the policy sciences faithful saw experts as the priesthood of a rational, knowledge-driven approach to resolving policy problems. And like these other intellectual movements, the policy sciences were inherently optimistic about the ability of government to act deliberately and effectively.

All of these ideas percolated into Canada, reinforcing the optimistic expectations for state management of society that Keynesianism encouraged in the realm of economics. Pushed to their limit, they led to visions of a brave new world whose shape was described by former Liberal Prime Minister Pierre Trudeau in the late 1960s: 'We . . . are aware that the many techniques of cybernetics, by transforming the control function and the manipulation of information, will transform our whole society. With this knowledge, we are wide awake, alert, capable of action; no longer are we blind, inert pawns of fate.'[16]

If the state sometimes seems a rather puny and helpless creature today, part of the reason surely involves the sheer breadth of the expectations held for public policy in the past. But if the scale of these expectations was unrealistic, the fact remains that governments in Canada and elsewhere continue to play a major role in society. The share of national wealth either consumed directly by the public sector or that passes through the state's hands in the form of transfers to individuals and organizations is today about what it was two decades ago. Proportionally fewer workers are employed in the public sector than in the past, and many programs have been scaled back or even eliminated at all levels of government. Nevertheless, the scope of the state's involvement in society remains vast and in recent years has actually increased in certain fields. Human rights is perhaps the major example of such expansion, as domestic and international forces have combined to raise the profile of such issues and to inject rights considerations into domains that previously were free of these concerns.

It is quite simply wrong, therefore, to suggest that policy-makers have become the helpless pawns of forces over which they have little or no control. The truth is far less dramatic. Big new initiatives of the sort that were common in the 1960s and 1970s have become rare, but the shadow cast by the state is not much shorter today than in the past. The chief exception may be in economic policy, where globalization and international trade liberalization pull the rug out from under the possibility of an autonomously determined trade or monetary policy.

The Relevance of Studying Public Policy

As the scope of state intervention in Canada has become increasingly large and the forms of state action have grown more complex, it has become more difficult for laypersons to understand public policy. On the other hand, the importance of such understanding has never been greater. Today, the state quite literally accompanies one from the cradle (and before, given today's reproductive technologies) to the grave. But it is not always easy to make sense of what governments do and why. Confusion is a natural enough response to the enormous range of government programs, the Byzantine complications introduced by bureaucracy and multiple layers of government, and the information overload that seems to await anyone intent on actually sorting out what it all means. Retreat into apathy or uninformed cynicism (not the same as informed cynicism) is a common, if unhelpful, reaction.

Public policy is not, however, something that only specialists can grasp. Those who are motivated to understand what governments do, why they do it, and what the consequences are of their actions and inaction need not despair. This book is addressed to them. Its modest aim is to help bring some meaning to the profusion of information about public policy that is daily conveyed by the mass media. Like a map, it seeks to identify important places a traveller might wish to visit and to show the connecting routes between them. It does not presume to suggest what destination is most desirable.

Chapter Two

Theories of Public Policy

Introduction

A theory provides an explanation of why things happen the way they do. When we move beyond a statement like '10 per cent of engineering students are female' to say that '10 per cent of engineering students are female *because* of learned social attitudes that discourage young females from pursuing courses in maths and sciences', or that 'Only 10 per cent of engineering students are females *because* of the lower incidence of left-brain dominance in females as compared to males', we have moved from the mere apprehension of fact to the realm of theorizing. Theory is not simply a formulation of what we know by experience. For example, to say that the sun will appear to rise over the horizon tomorrow because, so far as we know, it has always done so, is to state a scientific law based on repeated observation. For this to be elevated to the status of theory it would be necessary to explain this prediction not in terms of past experience but in terms of the laws of motion that govern bodies moving through space. Theoretical explanation is more abstract than learning and, therefore, can be generalized. Our theory of why the sun appears to rise above the earth's horizon each day should allow us to predict sunrises on other planets without ever having experienced them.

The nature and role of theory are the same whether one is seeking to understand the physical world or human behaviour. To develop theoretical laws about a phenomenon, whether the movement of celestial bodies or gender inequality, we need to describe things in symbolic terms. Thus, the nature of theory is abstract. It departs from the facts in order to establish their meaning. The role of theory is to make sense of the facts by explaining how they are connected.

People in all civilizations have sought to provide explanations for why things happen the way they do. Whether we call this the search for 'truth' or give it some other name, and whatever the impulse behind it is, the urge to theorize appears to be a part of the human condition. It is revealing that the word 'theory' derives from the Greek word *theoria*, meaning contemplation, and that it is frequently contrasted to practice (from *praxis*, meaning action). This distinction between theory and practice, a distinction reflected in everyday expressions like 'That's all right in theory, but it won't work' and 'It's just a theory', often carries with it a disdain of the theoretical in preference for practical knowledge. But this disdain both undervalues theory by treating it on a par with opinion ('You have your theory, but I'll stick to mine') and fails to recognize the practical value of theoretical knowledge.

One theory is not as good as another. We have no difficulty rejecting Lamarck's theory of trait inheritance (i.e., that acquired traits can be passed on to one's offspring) in preference for Mendel's theory of genetic inheritance. Of course, the uncontested dominance of a single theory is not always the case, even in the physical sciences. It still is true, however, that some theories will be considered more plausible than others, as making better sense of the facts. To provide plausible explanations of the facts a theory cannot be merely a statement of personal preference and self-interest dressed up in the garments of science. A theory may, however, be powerful in terms of its consequences, while being demonstrably weak in intellectual terms. Nazi theories of racial superiority are probably the best example from this century of the gap that may exist between a theory's impact and its plausibility. But in the realm of science a theory ultimately must stand or fall by its ability to explain the facts, not by the strength of the political and professional interests ranged for and against it.

The practical value of theoretical knowledge is nowhere better illustrated than in the case of nuclear weapons. Before these instruments of mass destruction could come into existence various theoretical breakthroughs had to be made in atomic physics, revealing how the energy contained in an atom could be released in a 'controlled' explosion. Such stark examples of theory being turned to practical ends are rarer in the realm of social behaviour, but less dramatic illustrations certainly exist. For example, the adoption by Western governments of responsibility for maintaining full employment and economic stability required the conversion of political élites to Keynesian economics. Indeed, Keynes himself appears to have ascribed fundamental importance to the ideas of theorists as the motor of history. He wrote:

> . . . the ideas of economists and political philosophers, both when they are right and when they are wrong, are more powerful than is commonly understood. Indeed the world is ruled by little else. Practical men, who believe themselves to be quite exempt from any intellectual influences, are usually the slaves of some defunct economist. Madmen in authority,

who hear voices in the air, are distilling their frenzy from some academic scribbler of a few years back.[1]

Keynes certainly overstated the influence of theorists, failing to acknowledge the extent to which their ideas follow events. Nor did he explain why some theories, and not others, dominate intellectual and public debates at certain times and in particular societies. Part of the answer lies in the fact that theory has political significance, a truth that is most dramatically epitomized in Socrates's trial and his decision to drink the cup of hemlock offered by the state rather than recant his views. To have political significance it is not necessary that theory determine the actions of people. More often, theory is enlisted to provide intellectual support for the interests of some segment of society. In its role as 'scientific' justification for some group's interests, theory is very much a part of political controversy. This may sound like a corruption of theory into political ideology, but the reality is that scientific debate is not immune from politics. This is particularly true of the social sciences.

Theories of Public Policy Formation

Theory is as indispensable to political analysis as a map or compass is to a traveller crossing unknown terrain. A theory serves to direct one's attention to particular features of the world, thus performing the essential task of distinguishing the significant from the irrelevant. Consider the case of a city council meeting at which councillors are debating a developer's proposal to build luxury condominiums on a piece of waterfront property that has long been used for recreational purposes by local property owners. One person reflecting on the debate and its outcome may focus on the ideological and personal motives of individual councillors. For this person the primary unit of analysis is the individual, and policy explanation is in terms of the forces that motivate individual behaviour. Another person may focus on contextual features of the policy process. These might include the increasing demand for waterfront residences by high-income professionals, the scarcity of available land for residential development, the profitability for developers of such a project, and the shrinking supply of recreational land accessible to the local population. For this person, the primary units of analysis are the economic and social forces that form the context for the deliberations of the councillors and influence their actions. A third person examining this debate on private development versus public conservation may view it in terms of conflicting class interests. Individual participants in the debate are important only to the extent that they represent these collective interests. Thus, the issue may be viewed as a conflict between a part of the capitalist class that has a material interest in the development of the waterfront and local middle-class property-owners whose support for conservation is no less self-interested, being based on their desire to protect the privacy and recreational amenities that they benefit from more than others as a result of living near the undeveloped waterfront. For this third person, the primary unit of analysis is class, and the policy process is understood in terms of conflicts and alliances between different class interests.

While these three theoretical perspectives are not mutually exclusive, each conceptualizes the policy process in a distinct way. Each one directs our attention to different features of the situation we seek to understand. The first perspective analyses policy at the level of the individual, while the second and third focus on larger social and economic forces. Thus, theories can be distinguished from one another by their *level of analysis*. But they may also be distinguished in terms of their *world-view* and the *methods* they typically employ in studying policy.[2]

'World-view' encompasses the fundamental assumptions about political life that are taken for granted by those working within a theoretical perspective. For example, we will see that Marxist approaches to public policy start from the premise that the relations between classes are necessarily antagonistic and that these relations (and politics generally) are determined by the mode of production that exists at any point in time. According to the Marxist worldview, harmonious social relations and political stability cannot coexist with a capitalist economic system. Those who work within what is often labelled the pluralist perspective are generally much more sanguine about the possibilities for peaceful coexistence. They tend to treat economic factors as only one of the sources of political conflict, along with cultural and ideological differences and social divisions. Moreover, they are inclined to view society and political conflict in terms of both individuals and collectivities, typically using the language of 'groups' and 'group interests', 'élites' and 'mass publics', instead of class. In short, pluralists do not see politics as simply a reflection of conflicts created by a society's mode of production. Because they do not view society as being comprised of antagonistic classes whose real interests are determined by whether or not they own or control the means of economic production, pluralists are more likely to see politics and the policy process as forums for bargaining, compromises, and even consensus (though this consensus may be fragile, temporary, and comprised of shifting alliances).

The fact that disputes between theoretical 'camps' sometimes have the acrimonious flavour of ideological conflicts can be explained by the differences in fundamental assumptions, or world-views, between theories. A theory based on the premise that the key to understanding politics is the 'dominance of one class and the subjection of another by the appropriation of [its] labour', and that therefore 'the social relationship is a *contradictory* one, entailing the potential of antagonism, of conflict, between the classes',[3] is more likely to arrive at negative conclusions about democratic politics and institutions in capitalist societies than a theory that does not start from the view that society is organized along the lines of hostile classes.

Despite Marx's claim that he was developing a scientific analysis of society and historical development—in the way that Charles Darwin was attempting the same thing in the realm of natural history—Marxist theory has always faced the charge that it is *normative* and, therefore, *un*scientific. Marxist theorists start from the premise that the capitalist system is necessarily 'bad' because it produces inequalities that cannot be eradicated by liberal democratic political institutions like 'one person, one vote', competitive elections held on a regular basis, and constitutional guarantees for individual freedoms. Avoidance of moral (good/bad) judgements is widely considered to be a hallmark of scientific analysis. The rejoinder to this argument is that analyses of society that claim to be value-free are simply unconscious of the value assumptions that determine how they interpret that society. Being unconscious of their value assumptions does not mean that these analyses travel without normative baggage. Indeed, their claim to scientific objectivity and moral neutrality lends implicit support to the dominant ways of thinking about society that they accept so uncritically. This debate is a complicated and long-standing one, and the interested reader will find that there is no shortage of writing on the subject of how values intrude on social analysis.[4]

The issue of normative premises in analysis arises again in the case of the third basis for distinguishing theories of public policy, that of the *methods* used to study it. A method is a procedure used to learn something about the subject under investigation. For example, students of political behaviour have for decades made extensive use of survey questionnaires whereby the responses of a more or less randomly selected sample of the population are generalized to the entire population. This method involves both a set of techniques, including sampling, questionnaire construction, and interviewing, as well as an assumption that the way to generate valid knowledge about political behaviour is through measurement of directly observable action (responses to a questionnaire are treated as actions). These methods are frequently employed in the study of policy formation, through interviewing the participants in the decision process. Another widely used method relies on historical data that are selected and interpreted within a particular theoretical framework. There is an unfortunate tendency to categorize this second method of analysis as 'qualitative' and to imply that it is scientifically less rigorous than the 'quantitative' approach described above.

The distinction between quantitative and qualitative methods is usually irrelevant and misleading. Both are *empirical*, that is, they rely on experience as the test of valid knowledge. Unlike a personal revelation or some other subjective mental state, experience is objectively verifiable and thus forms the basis for scientific analysis. Some subjects simply are not amenable to the application of quantitative methods, at least not without trivializing or distorting the research enterprise by shaping it to fit the sorts of data and questions these techniques can handle.

A method may be a model comprised of various assumptions. For example, one stream of Marxist theory shares with much of pluralist analysis a functionalist orientation. The behaviour of individuals, groups, or classes is interpreted in light of what the social system requires to maintain itself. Functionalist methodologies seek to explain behaviour by identifying the purposes it serves in relation to that social (or economic, or political) system. Probably the best-known functionalist model of politics is that developed by American political scientist David Easton. A simplified version of that model is portrayed in Figure 2.1.

A method may involve a small number of basic assumptions, sometimes called axioms, from which a number of ancillary propositions flow. We will see that this is true of *public choice* theory. It borrows from microeconomics the principle that individuals seek to maximize their self-interest and that, within the limits of the information at their disposal, their choices are rational. From this assumption that the behaviour of all players in the policy game—governments, bureaucrats, the media, interest groups, and voters—is rational and self-interested, public choice theory develops an explanation of policy.

Agreement that no single or even dominant theory of policy formation exists is not matched by agreement in identifying the main theoretical perspectives that contend with one another. In an influential article published in 1976, Richard Simeon grouped explanations of public policy under five headings: 'policy as a consequence of the *environment*, of the distribution of *power*, of prevailing *ideas*, of *institutional* frameworks, and of the *process* of decision-

FIGURE 2.1
David Easton's Simplified Model of the Political System

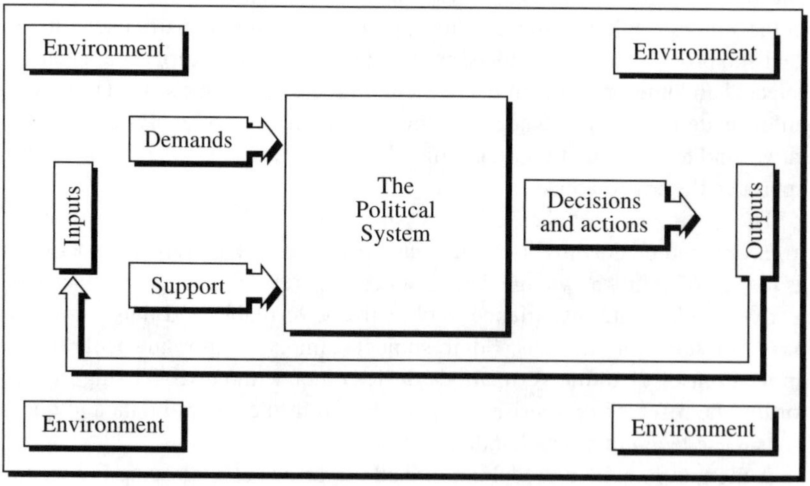

SOURCE: David Easton, *A Systems Analysis of Political Life* (New York: John Wiley and Sons, 1965), 32, Diagram 2.

making'.[5] Michael Atkinson and Marsha Chandler offer a leaner categorization of approaches, distinguishing between those that start from a Marxist view of the state (i.e., its relationship to class struggle) and those that place the state in the context of a competitive political marketplace in which class is only one of the lines of potential conflict. This second approach is described by them as pluralist.[6] Bruce Doern and Richard Phidd identify four models of the policy process, the rational, the incremental, the public choice, and the class analysis models. In addition, they offer their own approach, an eclectic framework that stresses the interaction of society's dominant ideas, the structure of government, and the private sector, including the élites who control these domains and the processes that characterize the policy process. Their theoretical perspective is fairly described as liberal-pluralist.[7] Finally, in one of the major textbooks on Canadian politics, Robert Jackson and Doreen Jackson distinguish between theories of decision-making (micro-level approaches) and theories of policy formation (macro-level approaches). The second group of theories seeks to identify the broader determinants of state action and includes environmental determinism, pluralism, public choice theory, and neo-Marxist analysis.[8]

In view of the diversity of ways in which some of the main Canadian writers on public policy have categorized theoretical approaches, one hesitates to develop yet another classification of the approaches. Classification for classification's sake is, after all, no virtue. The purpose should be to explain the different answers that theories give to the fundamental political questions of *why* the state behaves in particular ways and *who benefits*. The theoretical perspectives discussed in this chapter are pluralism, public choice, and Marxist political economy. Without wanting to get into a lengthy justification of why this way of carving up the world of theory was chosen over other possibilities, it has the virtue of using commonly used and widely understood labels for approaches that are arguably the main contemporary frameworks for understanding policy. Moreover, each of these perspectives coincides with a separate level of analysis as discussed earlier: individuals (public choice), groups (pluralism), and class (Marxism).

Three Perspectives on Policy

1. The Pluralist Model: Group Competition in the Political Marketplace

In the beginning there were individuals. These individuals, or at least the more perceptive ones, quickly realized that they stood a better chance of achieving their goals if they joined with others who had similar goals. Thus, groups were formed to influence the behaviour of governments. Political scientists looked upon the shifting sea of groups, all seeking to have their members' preferences translated into public policy, and called it *pluralism*. As time passed it became apparent that some groups possessed greater resources than others and that some demands tended to receive a more sympathetic hearing from government than others. Moreover, it became difficult to ignore evidence that many individuals were effectively excluded from the competition by virtue of not being organized into groups with representative spokespersons. Thus, while organization was theoretically open to all, it appeared that some parts of society, particularly the poor and less educated, were less likely than others to mobilize in a concerted effort to influence state action. The political marketplace was imperfect. In the words of E.E. Schattschneider, 'The flaw in the pluralist heaven is that the heavenly chorus sings with a strong upper-class accent. . . . The system is skewed, loaded and unbalanced in favour of a fraction of a minority.'[9] Pluralists' attention turned to explaining the imperfections in the political marketplace, especially the dominant position of business interests.

This is a short, and obviously very simplified, history of a model of politics that has dominated North American political science during much of this century. Applied to policy formation, it views state action as the outcome of a competition between organized groups that seek to protect or promote the interests of their members. Although versions of the pluralist model differ over how 'open' this competition is, they have a shared world-view that distinguishes them from Marxist theories of public policy. For Marxists, the foremost line of political conflict is that which divides economic classes. All other lines of conflict—*cleavages* in the jargon of political sociology—are subordinate to and shaped by class struggle. Pluralists concede that economic factors are important determinants of political conflict. But they view other lines of division, including ethnicity, language, religion, gender, region, and ideology, as having a significance that is not necessarily less than that of class. Moreover, these non-class divisions are not, in the pluralist model, merely class conflicts dressed up in ways that make them more difficult to recognize. As one of the main textbooks on Canadian politics puts it, 'From the [pluralist] perspective employed in this book, ethnicity, culture, religion, language, occupation, economic sector, region, level of income, gender and ideology are all important determinants of political phenomena, independent of the class structure.'[10]

The pluralist model of politics views policy-making in democratic societies as a competition between élites. Joseph Schumpeter was one of the first to attempt to reconcile the fact that political decision-making is concentrated in the hands of élites with the fundamental democratic premise that all just rule derives from the consent of the governed. In his book *Capitalism, Socialism and Democracy*,[11] he argued that the competition for political office is the key feature of democratic politics. Schumpeter likened this competition between élites for the votes of the general population to the operation of an economic market: voters (like consumers) chose between the policies (products) offered by competing parties (sellers). This reconciliation of élitist decision-making with democratic values proved to be enormously influential. It was reformulated by the American political scientist Robert Dahl in his definition of democracy as *polyarchy*, the rule of multiple minorities.[12] According to Dahl, minority rule takes place against the backdrop of a social consensus on democratic values that serves as a check on undemocratic behaviour by élites.

A number of implications for the theory of policy-making flowed from this work. First, the state was viewed as being essentially democratic. Though controlled by élites, governments were compelled to be at least minimally responsive to popular demands because of the possibility that they might be replaced by another élite coalition at the next election. Second, individuals and organized groups were the relevant units for policy analysis. Political conflict was seen in terms of shifting constellations of actors that varied from issue to issue. Opponents on one policy question might find themselves allies on another. Third, ideas were viewed as a major determinant of policy. The perceptions and beliefs of individuals were considered crucial to understanding their behaviour and, ultimately, policy outcomes. Major policy trends, such as the emergence of the welfare state, and cross-national differences in policy were explained in terms of national values, if not those of the general population, then those of political élites.[13]

The accusation that pluralism ignores the unequal basis of group competition has long been a straw man favoured by the approach's critics. Pluralists have put forward various explanations to account for the dominant position of business in the political marketplace. Robert Heilbroner has suggested that, in America at least, the dominant ideology compels non-business interests to 'accommodate their proposals for social change to the limits of adaptability of the prevailing business order'.[14] In his book *Politics and Markets*, Charles Lindblom attributes the 'privileged position of business' to a combination of superior financial resources and lobbying organization, greater access than other groups to government officials, and, most importantly, propagandistic activities that—directly through political advertising and indirectly through commercial advertising—reinforce the ideological dominance of business values.[15] A somewhat different perspective is offered by Theodore Lowi. He argues that the policy process 'is biased not so much in favour of the rich as in favour of the established and organized.'[16] While Lowi views political power as something that derives from organization *per se*, he, too, acknowledges that business interests occupy a privileged position within the policy-making system. According to Lowi, both the state and private business have a fundamental interest in stability. From the government's side, this means sensitivity towards the conditions necessary to ensure business performance.

Perhaps the most persuasive explanation of the unequal competition of interests to come out of the pluralist camp, an explanation that points out the hazards of pigeonholing theories, is that offered by Charles Lindblom in an article entitled 'The Market as Prison'.[17] Lindblom argues that policy-making in capitalist societies is imprisoned by the way a market economy works. A market economy operates on the basis of inducements. Short of replacing the market system with a centrally directed command economy, businesses cannot be ordered to produce or to invest. They must be persuaded: incentives and disincentives must be used to get them to behave in ways desired by policy-makers. When state action, or even anticipated state action, is perceived by business people to be harmful to their interests they react by cutting back on production, deferring or cancelling new investment, and perhaps shifting production to other countries. The reaction is automatic, triggered by a change in the environment in which business operates. And to the extent that it means unemployment and economic slowdown, the reaction is also punishing to the government. Lindblom writes, 'When a decline in prosperity and employment is brought about by decisions of corporate and other business executives, it is not they but government officials who consequently are retired from their offices.'[18] Thus the special sensitivity of public officials to business interests. Change is not impossible, but it is greatly constrained by the automatic punishment the market system imposes on governments that trespass beyond the line of business tolerance. None of this would be true were it not for the fact that in capitalist societies the market is a *chose donnée* in our thinking about policy. Interference with it might be desirable. Its elimination is unthinkable. The bars that imprison policy-makers are both structural (the reaction of business people) and ideological.

This explanation of business power is one that has long been familiar to Marxist theorists. What Lindblom calls the 'automatic punishing recoil' of the market to reforms perceived to threaten business interests has been called a 'capital strike' by others. But Lindblom's explanation is not a Marxist one. Though he assigns central importance to economic factors as determinants of policy, he continues to treat business as an interest, albeit the most powerful one, in society. The world-view that underpins Lindblom's theory does not see society in class terms or politics as class struggle. Though he arrives at conclusions quite similar to those of Marxist theorists, his reasoning is still within the pluralist world-view.

2. The Public Choice Model: Homo Economicus and Homo Politicus

In 1986 the American economist James Buchanan was awarded the Nobel Prize for economics. The selection jury for this prestigious award cited his work applying economic theory to political and constitutional issues as the basis for their choice. Buchanan is one of the founders of a theoretical approach that in Canada is usually referred to as *public choice* theory, in the United States as *political economy*, and in Europe as *political economics* or the economic theory of politics. His Nobel Prize was a highly visible indication of the growing importance of a theoretical model that, especially in North America, has acquired many converts in academe.

Public choice theory represents the colonization of traditional political science concerns by economics. Those working within this approach attempt to explain political behaviour, including the policy decisions of governments, in terms of a theory of individual choice developed in microeconomics. The central figure of microeconomic theory is, as veterans of introductory economics courses may be aware, *homo economicus*. Like his/her economics cousin, *homo politicus* also operates on the basis of rational self-interest, seeking to maximize satisfaction at the least cost within the limits imposed by the information available. What keeps competition in the political marketplace from degenerating into a no-holds-barred mêlée is the existence of rules—the constitution, laws—that constitute a web of incentives and constraints influencing an individual's choices. And as in the economic marketplace, the 'wrong' rules will distort the behaviour of individuals, resulting in outcomes that are inefficient from the standpoint of society as a whole.

We have seen already that the pluralist model views the state as the focus for a multilevelled competition between conflicting group interests. This competition may be *unequal*, and no serious analysis would deny that state organizations may sometimes defend and advance their own interests rather than simply mediating the competing demands of societal groups. But the pluralist world-view insists on the competitive nature of politics and on the 'group' or 'interest' as the basic unit of analysis for understanding the policy process. The public choice model shares the same competitive world-view, as shown by its use of the terms 'logrolling', 'bargaining', 'accommodation', and 'exchange'. In fact, public choice is a revised version of the pluralist model. This is evident in its characterization of the state. In the words of one of the main Canadian contributions to public choice theory, 'the role of the State in a modern representative democracy is centrally concerned with mediating interest group conflicts over distributive claims.'[19] Buchanan and Tullock acknowledge the similarity of pluralist and public choice approaches when they write that 'Throughout our analysis the word "group" could be substituted for the word "individual" without significantly affecting the results.'[20]

What is different about the public choice model is its strict insistence on the individual as the basic unit of analysis, a feature of this approach that Buchanan and Tullock describe as 'methodological individualism'.[21] The state is viewed in terms of the individual politicians and bureaucrats who occupy particular positions within it and who act on the basis of rational self-interest under conditions of imperfect knowledge. Politicians seek to be elected and, once elected, to maintain themselves in power (their motivations for wanting to be in office are beside the point). Bureaucrats seek promotion and/or more control over the environment within which their organization is situated. Expansion, increased budgets, new policy tasks, and capturing chief responsibility for a policy field are all means towards these goals. Based on the assumption that the rational self-interest postulate is at least more plausible than any other explanation of individual behaviour, the public choice model explains policy as the outcome of strategic behaviour within a system of overlapping games that connect the state to society.

It is important to keep in mind that none of the sets of participants in the decision-making process acts in a single-minded way. For example, the bureaucracy is divided into 'spender' organizations with large budgets, for whom financial restraint means placing limits on the goals that individual bureaucrats pursue, and 'savers' who operate under a very different system of incentives for behaviour. The incentive system of individual bureaucrats also varies according to the societal interests that 'consume' the services they provide, their regional focus, and their function. These divisions lead to competition and bargaining *within* the bureaucratic game. This is also true of the political game. Behind the façade of unity that typically characterizes the usual single-party government in Canada (coalition governments introduce another level of complexity), the fact that the re-election prospects of individual mem-

Figure 2.2
The Policy Process Viewed from the Public Choice Perspective:
Four Interrelated Games

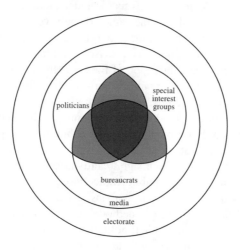

NOTES:
1. The darkest area of this figure is the heart of the decision-making process.
2. The lighter shaded areas show the interplay between each pair of policy participants.
3. The media interact with each set of policy participants, as well as being the channel through which the electorate perceives these participants and, to some degree, the channel through which the individual players learn about what is happening in their own and other games.
4. Voters are treated as non-participants in the decision-making process. They are important primarily because they choose the players in the political game.

SOURCE: M.J. Trebilcock et al., *The Choice of Governing Instrument* (Ottawa: Economic Council of Canada, 1982), Figure 2–1 at p. 7, and the explanation at pp. 6–7. Reproduced with permission of the Minister of Supply and Services Canada.

bers of the government are tied to different constituencies (regional, special interest, and ideological), and to the various parts of the state bureaucracy they oversee, ensures that they, too, are involved in this process of bargaining within the state.

The behaviour of those within the bureaucratic and political 'games' is influenced by the actual and anticipated behaviour of special interest groups, the media, and various segments of the electorate. Politics involves a continuous and multilevelled process of bargaining in which power is based on control over resources that can be used as the basis for profitable exchange.

Thus, as in the economy, power is a *transactional* property pervading the political marketplace. It is expressed in a number of ways that include the following:

- the votes of electors;
- the perceived capacity of the media to influence the views held by voters on particular issues and in relation to particular political parties or interests;
- the ability of special interest groups to mobilize supporters and allies for collective action, and to offer inducements or deploy what politicians believe to be credible threats;
- the control bureaucrats exercise over the flow of vital information and the delivery of programs;
- the capacity of governments to manage the public agenda and to confer benefits on voters or special interests whose support is up for grabs and to impose costs on those whose support is lost anyway. Where there is no avoiding the imposition of costs on possible supporters, this will be done in ways that soften or hide their impact.

It may sound as though the public choice model portrays policy formation as a wide-open mêlée—a sort of analytical version of Thomas Hobbes's state of nature.[22] This would be a wrong conclusion. Those who use this theoretical approach acknowledge that the constitution operates as a constraint on the behaviour of participants in the policy-making process. Indeed, constitutional rules assume major importance in the public choice model. If one accepts that individuals act on the basis of self-interest, and that it is unrealistic to assume otherwise, it follows that the way to change policy outcomes is to alter the incentives and constraints that influence individual decisions. In *The Choice of Governing Instrument*, Trebilcock and his colleagues argue that Canada's federal division of powers has sometimes caused governments to select inefficient means for achieving their policy goals. These means have been more costly, and have therefore imposed a greater burden on taxpayers, than others that under the constitution have not been available to that level of government.[23]

Is the public choice model as scientific as its proponents claim? Its logical rigour and formally stated assumptions give it an air of moral neutrality. But it certainly is not free of ideological preferences. Consider the following statement made by Nobel laureate James Buchanan in an article entitled 'Why Does Government Grow?'

> The nineteenth century record suggests clearly that an increasing governmental share is not a necessary and inevitable accompaniment to national economic development. The explosion in taxation and public spending that we live with is a twentieth century phenomenon, and the pattern that was changed before can be reversed.[24]

Without disputing the proposition that the size of the state can be reduced from its present dimensions, the parallel that Buchanan draws between the nineteenth and twentieth centuries is seriously misleading. It ignores the enormous changes that have taken place in the economies and social structures of capitalist societies. It ignores as well the dramatically different international economic order of these two centuries. These changes have been the major force behind the growth in the scope of state activities. Only by leaving historical developments out of the picture can one arrive at such a facile conclusion.

A fair assessment of the ideological disposition of public choice theory is provided by one of its Canadian scholars, Mark Sproule-Jones. He states that the 'public-choice approach is normative in cast, and is aimed at determining what kinds of institutional arrangements and constitutional arrangements work better for citizens.'[25] But what does Sproule-Jones mean by 'better'? It is clear from the work done within the framework of political economics that many of its supporters define 'better' as that which interferes least with individual choice and achieves a given policy outcome at the least cost. The first of these criteria, individual choice, is obviously a liberal value based on the belief that the rights and freedoms of the individual should be the foremost concern of government. The second criterion, economic efficiency, is probably one that people of all ideological stripes can agree on. Achieving one's goals at the least cost only assumes that one has limited resources (time, money, mental and physical energy, etc.) with which to pursue these goals. This seems a reasonable assumption.

A third criterion used by public choice theory is that of 'institutional fairness'. As Sproule-Jones puts it, 'If individuals perceive the institutional and constitutional arrangements as being fair to them as well as to others, then the policy outputs or policy changes can be evaluated as fair.'[26] As reasonable as this sounds, it still is grounded on liberal philosophy's belief in the primacy of the individual. Moreover, this proposition ignores the possibility that citizens' perceptions of what is fair may be conditioned by society's dominant ideology—and that this ideology may better reflect the objective interests of some groups than of others.

3. The Marxist Model: The State as a Structure of Capitalist Power

The Marxist theory of policy formation has four main elements. These are: (1) the *division of society into classes*, an individual's class position being determined by his or her relationship to the means of production; (2) the *pre-eminence of class* as the basis for political and economic conflict; (3) the *inequality of classes*, with society divided into dominant and subordinate classes; and (4) the *bias of the state* in favour of the dominant class(es), which in a capitalist society will be the capitalists or bourgeoisie.

This much of Marxist theory has remained unchanged from the writings of Karl Marx. Within contemporary Marxist theory, however, there are numerous divisions over some of these points, particularly over the relationship of the state to dominant and subordinate classes. The complexities of these debates need not concern us here.[27] Our chief interest is in identifying how Marxist explanations of policy formation differ from the other approaches examined in this chapter.

In terms of its world-view, the Marxist perspective sees the antagonistic relationship between classes as the central fact of politics in all societies. This premise has often been disputed by non-Marxists, who in North America at least are able to point to the absence of electorally strong working-class parties and to the widely shared sense of 'middle-classness' that attitudinal surveys show to exist in both Canadian and American society. Moreover, the declining size of the traditional blue-collar working class, the separation of ownership from effective control of the modern corporation (and therefore the declining importance of the individual capitalist), and the expansion of a middle class of relatively affluent professionals are developments that the critics of Marxist class analysis claim have actually weakened the political significance of class. Marxian insistence on the primacy of class is therefore dismissed by these critics as an expression of ideological preference rather than being a useful tool for understanding political behaviour.

While Marxists acknowledge that the subjective sense of belonging to a social class is weak in many capitalist societies and that social divisions have become more complicated as a result of changes in the economies of these societies, they are not prepared to jettison the concept of class. Instead, they argue that capitalism's proven capacity for coping with the challenges posed by periodic economic crises and by the political demands of subordinate classes is based on a couple of main factors. One of these is the role played by a society's dominant ideology. Marxists argue that this ideology includes beliefs about the limits of state interference with the economy. These beliefs have the effect of blunting fundamental criticism of the existing balance of economic and political power. They include beliefs about private property, the importance of profits, the possibility of upward socio-economic mobility, and, most importantly, the market as the basic organizing principle of the economy.

A government that trespasses beyond the limits set by these widely shared beliefs risks a serious decline in popular support. Even more importantly, it risks a damaging loss of *business confidence*. This constraint on state action is virtually identical to what Lindblom calls the 'automatic punishing recoil' of the market (see the earlier section on pluralist theory). It reinforces the ideological limits on public policy by ensuring that actions threatening business interest—in the eyes of those who make investment and other decisions affecting the level of economic activity—are punished.

Why should a government care about the business community's reaction, especially if the basis of its electoral strength lies with numerically large subordinate classes? Quite simply, because a crisis of business confidence would undermine its ability to finance state activities through taxation and borrowing. Moreover, an economic downturn is likely to result in reduced popular support for the government and its replacement by a party whose policies are viewed as more likely to generate business confidence and a growth in jobs and incomes. Theoretically, a government could always respond to the economic sanctions of the market by taking over businesses and placing restrictions on the transfer of capital out of the country. In practice, however, the economic ties that link capitalist societies mean that this sort of radical political agenda will be met with a negative reaction on the part of foreign investors, currency traders, and creditors. Thus, not only is domestic business confidence a brake on reformist policy, international business is as well.

Marxists argue that there is tension between the state's responsiveness to popular demands and its structural need and ideological disposition to support the general interests of capital. This tension ('contradiction' in Marxist terminology) surfaces at the level of public policy in two functionally different types of policies: legitimation and accumulation policies.[28] *Legitimation policies* are those that reduce interclass conflict by providing subordinate classes with benefits that reduce their dissatisfaction with the inequalities generated by the capitalist economy. Social welfare policies and labour legislation are examples of state actions that promote social harmony by legitimizing the existing capitalist system in the eyes of those classes that, it is argued, benefit least from its operation. These policies are indirectly supportive of the interests of capital because they maintain the social conditions necessary for profitable business activity. *Accumulation policies* are directly supportive of profit-oriented business activity. Examples would include grants and tax subsidies to business, tariff and non-tariff protection for industries, state expenditure on public works needed for business activity, and laws that control the cost of labour or that reduce the likelihood of work stoppages. Some Marxists have argued that the contradiction between state spending on the legitimation policies that comprise the welfare state and what the state must do to support capital accumulation has become sharper. The ascendance of neo-conservatism and pressures to cut back on social spending have been attributed to this heightened contradiction in the functions imposed on governments in capitalist societies.

Let us pause to take stock. The Marxist theory of policy formation argues that class divisions are the main basis for political conflict. The failure of many (or even most) people to think in terms of class demonstrates the strength of the dominant liberal ideology purveyed by the media, the schools, and the other agents of socialization. As well, the weakness of a subjective sense of class reflects the fact that many of the demands of subordinate classes for things like public education, health care, pensions, and income during unemployment have been met, thus attenuating the sources of class friction. This failure of people to think in terms of class does not, however, mean that class is irrelevant to an understanding of state action.

When Marxists argue that the state in capitalist societies serves the interests of the dominant economic class, this does not mean that every state action reflects the interests of the business/investment community. Nor does it suggest that those who control the means of production are always in agreement on what the state should and should not do. The overall pattern of public policy supports the *general* interests of capital. The reason for this is that policy-makers usually believe such policies to be in the public interest; also, failure to maintain some minimum level of business confidence leads to economic downturn, the consequences of which are reduced popular support for the government and losses in the state's ability to finance its activities. This second factor is an important structural constraint on policy-makers in capitalist societies.

A couple of features of this model need to be stressed. First of all, for the state to serve the general interests of capital, it is not necessary that policy-makers be drawn from the dominant class. In fact, some argue that the fewer the personal ties between the state and the dominant class the more effective will be the state in maintaining the interests of this class. This is because the reality of capitalist domination will to some extent be hidden by the appearance of government that is not in the hands of the members of any one class.[29] Second, policy-makers *are* receptive to the demands of subordinate classes. Their readiness to implement reforms that may in fact be opposed by powerful business interests does not result from any special vision on their part as to what concessions must be made to save the capitalist system from the shortsightedness of individual capitalists. Rather, governments are subject to popular pressures through elections and those who manage the state are unlikely to be concerned about the reactions of only one part of the business community. Governments therefore are willing to act in ways that offend parts of that community. This does not mean that state managers are more astute about what needs to be done to maintain the capitalist system than are the capitalists themselves. It does mean, however, that their concern for the overall level of economic activity—a factor that influences both the popular support of governments and the capacity of the state to finance its activities—frees policy-makers from the narrower interests of particular parts of the business community. Rational self-interest looks somewhat different from the standpoint of state managers than it does from the standpoint of individual capitalists. As Fred Block writes, 'Unlike the individual capitalists, the state managers do not have to operate on the basis of a narrow profit-maximizing rationality. They are capable of intervening in the economy on the basis of a more general rationality.'[30]

It would be a mistake to think that policy-makers consciously ask themselves, 'What do we need to do to preserve the capitalist system?' They do not need to consciously pose this question because their conception of the 'national interest' coincides with the general interest of capital. As Ralph Miliband explains, 'if the state acts in ways which are congruent with the interests and purposes of capital, it is not because it is driven out of dire compulsion to do so, but because it wants to do so.'[31] Ideology reinforces the structural mechanisms described earlier, to ensure that the interests of the business community are not treated like those of a mere special interest group. At the same time, this admission that the ideological dispositions of policy-makers matter is important. Ideology helps to explain differences between capitalist societies in the scope of state economic intervention and in the extent of the social reforms undertaken by governments in these societies.

The openness of governments to the demands of subordinate classes, demands that may be vigorously opposed by spokespersons for the business community, was mentioned earlier. A couple of qualifications need to be added. First, the limits of this openness are set by policy-makers' perceptions of how much reform the business community will tolerate before the combined response of individual corporations and investors results in a crippling downturn in the level of economic activity. Second, the concessions made to the demands of subordinate classes are likely to take forms that minimize the burden on the business community. There is strong evidence in support of this second point. As we will see in Chapter Six on social policy, most of the costs of financing social services—programs that are usually pointed to as demonstration of government's responsiveness to popular pressures—are borne by the middle classes. In a very real sense the welfare state involves the middle classes paying for services consumed by the middle and lower classes. Redistributive policies have not been at the expense of capitalist interests.

The Perspectives Compared

Each of the three theoretical perspectives examined in this chapter represents a different lens through which policy may be viewed. They vary in terms of the assumptions they make about the basis of political conflict, the level at which they analyse the policy process, and the methods they tend to use to explain state actions. It would be a mistake, however, to see these perspectives

as being mutually exclusive. Instead, they are more usefully viewed as emphasizing different aspects of the process through which policy is determined.
This was shown in the earlier example of the city council decision on whether
to develop or conserve a waterfront property. Very different explanations of
how an issue reaches the policy agenda, and what the influences are that determine the response of policy-makers, may appear reasonable. Does this mean
that the choice of theoretical perspective, like that in clothes, is a matter of
taste? And if no single perspective holds a monopoly on insight, is not the best
approach to understanding policy one that combines the separate theories?

The answer to both of these questions is a qualified no. It *is* reasonable to
view each of these theoretical perspectives as providing an incomplete explanation of policy formation. This does not require that they all be considered
equally useful. Each perspective has particular strengths on its 'home turf'.
The pluralist perspective emphasizes the competitive character of politics,
focusing on group interests and the behaviour and motivations of individuals.
These features of pluralism are confirmed by the reality of individuals differ-
ing over what the state should do, yet they combine with others of similar
views or interests to increase their political leverage. The home turf of the public choice perspective is the realm of individual decision-making. From the
standpoint of actual behaviour, it is undeniable that the individual ultimately
makes decisions and acts on them. Collective entities like 'groups', 'classes',
and the 'state' are not capable of deciding and acting except in some abstract
sense. Thus, the strength of the public choice approach is its treatment of individual choice. The Marxist perspective bases its analysis of policy on the
unequal competition between classes generated by the capitalist economy. Its
home turf involves the limits that the economic system places on the behaviour of the state and the relationship between the economy and political power.
The main points of similarity and difference between the perspectives are summarized in Table 2.1.

So how does one decide which theoretical perspective, or combination of
perspectives, is *scientifically* the most valid? Ideally, the test should be their
ability to provide a convincing explanation of the relationship of 'facts'. But
the facts are themselves disputed by different theories. For example, a pluralist is likely to view class either as a subjective phenomenon—and therefore to
measure it using attitudinal surveys—or as an objective condition that has
roughly the same meaning as social status, in which case income or occupational prestige may be used to distinguish between various gradations of class
(e.g., lower, middle, and upper). A Marxist will view the facts, in this case the
reality of classes, very differently. Individuals' beliefs about whether classes
exist and their self-perception of what class they belong to are considered
irrelevant. Nor will classes be considered to be the same as status groups.
Class is an objective condition determined by one's relationship to the mode
of production. For Marxists, the facts are that classes exist and the relationships between classes are the key to understanding politics. These are facts

Table 2.1
Three Theoretical Perspectives on Policy Formation

1. Level of analysis

Pluralist	Individuals, organized groups
Public Choice	Individuals
Marxist	Societal forces, classes

2. Major features of the perspective's world-view

Pluralist	a) Voluntaristic; policy outcomes are relatively 'open' due to the fact that individuals, alone and collectively, act on the basis of attitudes and perceptions that are changeable b) Politics is competitive, although the competition may not be an equal one
Public choice	a) Voluntaristic; the individual is the basic unit of social action b) Politics is competitive; power in the political marketplace is determined by control over resources that can be used as the basis of profitable exchange
Marxist	a) Deterministic; the antagonistic relationship between classes determines the course of history b) Politics is *not* competitive; patterns of domination/subordination derive from a society's mode of production

Table 2.1 continued

3. Chief constraints on policy-makers

Pluralist	Dominant ideology, balance of power between societal interests
Public choice	The possession by non-state actors of resources that can be used to reward or punish the behaviour of state actors; competition between political and bureaucratic actors *within* the state and *between* levels of government
Marxist	The capitalist economic system; this includes a major structural constraint, i.e., the refusal of the business community to invest and its capacity to move production to another jurisdiction, and a reinforcing ideological constraint, i.e., the widespread acceptance of values supportive of capitalism

4. How the state is viewed

Pluralist	a) Reactive, but with a margin of independence from societal interests: the state itself and its component parts have and pursue their own interests in addition to mediating societal ones b) Essentially democratic
Public choice	a) Active *and* reactive; in pursuing their own self-interest state actors are compelled to respond to non-state actors, including voters, special interest groups, and the media, whom they perceive as having the capacity to influence the attainment of their own goals b) Democratic but also heavily bureaucratic
Marxist	a) Reactive, but with a margin of independence from the narrower interests of individual capitalists; this independence enables the state to respond, within limits, to the demands of subordinate classes and to act in the *general* interest of capital b) Capitalist

regardless of whether a society's dominant ideology acknowledges the significance of class. For a public choice theorist, to speak of class is not only artificial but totally misleading. Individuals act on the basis of their perception of personal self-interest, not on the basis of class membership.

A large part of the reason why members of different theoretical 'camps' have so little success in communicating with one another is because they cannot even agree on the 'facts'. This communication gap is produced by differences in the world-views that underlie competing theoretical perspectives. Appeal to the 'facts' is unlikely to settle theoretical disputes when the data, let alone their interpretation, are contested. An appeal to 'common sense' runs up against the same problem. A theory is like a story: it gives an account of some part of reality. The story will strike us as being more or less convincing, and thus one can evaluate different theoretical 'stories' in terms of the plausibility of each one's interpretation of experience. This is not, however, a solution to the communication gap. It simply shifts the problem from the storytellers to their listeners. If a story's truth, like beauty, is in the eye of the beholder, then we are left with personal taste as the final judge of the validity of a particular theoretical story. And we are back to the proposition, dismissed earlier in this chapter, that theory is like opinion: a matter of personal preference.

There are some differences in interpretation and explanation that simply cannot be resolved and that must ultimately be ascribed to the personal and social characteristics of the beholders. For example, two people can look at Canadian society and one may see evidence of significant opportunities for upward socio-economic mobility while the other sees evidence of the barriers to mobility. These two people may agree on the *numbers*, yet they interpret them in very different ways.

Or consider the case of two people trying to explain the growth in social spending by the state in capitalist societies. One person points to a combination of the popular pressures generated by the growth of an urban-industrial society and the extension of voting rights to all adults, along with changing élite and popular views on the appropriate role of the state. The growth in social spending is explained as being a result of popular demands and changing social values. A second person agrees that there have been increasing popular demands for social services and that ideas regarding both the scope and areas of appropriate state activity have changed. But this other person explains the growth in social spending as being produced by class conflict under capitalism. Social spending by the state responds to the demands of the enfranchised subordinate classes that are produced by the twin processes of industrialization and urbanization. But it also responds to capital's need to preserve its ability to exploit the labour of subordinate classes. This is done by making public some of the social costs generated by the capitalist economy. Thus, social spending attenuates class frictions by meeting the demands of subordinate classes, while making sure that the burden of paying for social spending is not borne entirely (or even mainly) by the business community. Whereas the first explanation points to the power of groups and ideas as the main determinants of the increase in social spending by the state, the second points to class conflict. *The difference in their explanation of this policy trend is likely to reflect differences in the answer they give to the question of who benefits from state action.* Where the first person emphasizes the benefits experienced by those who are the immediate consumers of social services, the second emphasizes the indirect benefits that capital enjoys. This difference in explanation is not one that an appeal to either the 'facts' or 'common sense' is likely to resolve.

If all the differences in the way theoretical perspectives interpret and explain the reality of policy formation were of this sort, one would be justified in treating all theories as of equal worth. But in practical terms, agreement on some facts and their meanings obviously is possible; otherwise there would be no basis for communication whatsoever. This area of shared perception is where useful comparison of theories' explanatory power can be made. But even here, the dialogue of science is influenced by social factors that enable some theories to live on in the face of mounting evidence of their flaws. In the words of the German physicist Max Planck,

> ... a new scientific truth does not triumph by convincing its opponents and making them see the light, but rather because its opponents eventually die, and a new generation grows up that is familiar with it.[32]

Chapter Three

The Context of Policy-Making in Canada

Introduction

The path leading from an idea to its embodiment in public policy is sometimes short and direct. More often, however, it is long and sinuous, and marked by detours, roadblocks, and even dead ends. Sometimes the path is barely visible, obscured by the struggle of contending interests and ideas, by the inconsistencies or contradictions of government action (and inaction), or by fuzziness in how an issue is defined. Some students of public policy have argued that actions typically precede policies; that is, governments act and then develop the idea-justifications for their actions that we call public policies. But whether or not the idea comes first, the process of policy-making is usually complex and defies any one-size-fits-all explanation.

Attempts to understand the process of policy-making usually distinguish between what happens inside the state system—the 'black box' of Easton's systems model of politics—and the societal factors that influence the behaviour of policy-makers. As a rule, students of the policy process also distinguish between domestic and foreign policy-making, focusing on very different sets of actors and influences. As Doern and his colleagues put it, 'experts in international political economy and foreign policy [tend] to concentrate on international relations, integration, and conflict but to oversimplify domestic politics and policy institutions.'[1] Those who study domestic politics and policy-making, on the other hand, 'tend to treat international conditions simply as contextual factors and to ignore the influence of international agreements, regimes, and agencies.'[2]

These distinctions often do not hold up well under closer scrutiny. What Léon Dion called the *governmentalization of society*, and Alan Cairns calls the *embedded state*, undermines the usefulness of an analytical framework premised on the distinction between state and societal influences on policy. The phenomena of globalization and internationalization have increased the exposure of domestic institutions and interests to forces outside national borders, requiring that these forces be integrated into our understanding of how domestic policy-making works. A framework is needed to enable the student of public policy to identify those factors that affect policy, while avoiding the strait-jacket of a priori thinking about the relative importance of these factors and the relationships between them.

This is a tall order. It is not the intention here to try to develop such an integrated framework for the understanding of policy. Instead, we will examine several *contextual* influences on policy that constitute the background of policy-making. These influences may be distinguished from *proximate* influences, including the machinery of government, political parties, interest groups, and so on, whose impact on policy is more direct. These two sets of factors are listed in Table 3.1.

Contextual Influences on Policy-Making

1. Political Culture

Political culture consists of the dominant and relatively durable beliefs and values concerning political life that characterize a society. These are ideas with a taken-for-granted quality, such as the goodness of equality or respect for authority, and are shared by the vast majority of the population. A broad consensus on fundamental political values and beliefs is an important ingredient for political stability. Where this consensus is lacking or subject to stress, the peaceful resolution of political differences becomes more difficult and the job of governing becomes more problematic.

Table 3.1
Contextual and Proximate Influences on Policy-Making

Contextual	*Proximate*
political culture	Cabinet
the constitution	the legislature
characteristics of the economy and society	courts
globalization	media system
	public opinion
	political parties
	interest groups
	social movements

There is no agreement on the character of political culture in Canada. Indeed, disagreement begins over whether Canada has one, two, or several distinct political cultures. Those who argue that there is a *Canadian* political culture almost always describe that culture in comparison to the United States. In this vein, Canada is said to have a counter-revolutionary tradition, compared to the revolutionary tradition of the United States, to be more deferential towards authority, to be more collectivist and less individualistic (this becomes expressed, at the popular level, in claims that Canadians are more caring and compassionate than Americans), to be more tolerant of hierarchical social distinctions, and so on.[3]

Those who argue that Canada consists of two distinct political cultures associate these cultures with the two dominant language communities, French and English. One branch of this two-political-cultures approach emerges from the *fragment theory* of Louis Hartz, and has been applied to the Canadian case, most notably, by Kenneth McRae and Gad Horowitz.[4] It characterizes English-speaking Canada as a liberal society with Tory 'touches'—the importance of these Tory elements has long been a matter of dispute among Hartzians—and French-speaking Canada as a pre-liberal feudal society whose democratization and liberalization were retarded by its feudal past.

A third approach to Canadian political culture focuses on the distinctions between regions within English-speaking Canada. It accepts, of course, that French Canada has a distinctive political culture, which those who employ this approach associate with the region of Quebec. But it also insists that the different histories of regions in English Canada, including their different demographic and economic characteristics, have created distinct regional political cultures. The precise number of these is a matter for debate, some going so far as to argue that each of the 10 provinces deserves to be treated as a distinct political culture. More commonly, however, there are said to be four or five main regional political cultures. These include Ontario, Quebec, the West (or British Columbia and the Prairies), and eastern Canada (although Newfoundland is sometimes treated as a culturally distinct region).

From the standpoint of influencing public policy, all three approaches to political culture have been significant, although particularly the two-culture image of Canada. Indeed, the idea of Canada as a partnership between two founding peoples, English and French, has affected the process and substance of policy from Confederation to the present. Nationalist spokespersons for French Canada, and since the 1960s for Quebec, have always insisted that the differences between the two founding communities go beyond language and that the constitutional arrangements between French- and English-speaking Canada must allow the Francophone population to protect its distinctive traditions.

The two-culture image of Canada has long generated resentment in western Canada and, to a lesser degree, in the East. Telling the story of Canada as one of partnership between two founding cultures inevitably diminishes or even denies the importance of regional cultures outside of the Ontario-Quebec core. Westerners, in particular, have long complained that their interests and distinctive histories have been marginalized by the two-culture image of Canada, which, they say, is more correctly seen as the story of central Canada. The roots of western alienation have been nurtured not only by the West's economic and political grievances against Ottawa and central Canada, but also by this sense of being excluded from the image of Canada projected by federal policies and institutions and by central Canadian media and intellectual élites whose centres of gravity are Toronto and Montreal.[5]

There is no doubt that most Canadians in *all* regions and in *both* of the country's two major language communities share many fundamental values and beliefs about politics. The political culture they share is clearly a liberal-democratic one, whose core values include respect for individual freedom, equality of rights, limited government, and belief in the market economy. These abstract notions are no doubt understood somewhat differently in various parts of Canada, or between sociologically distinct segments of the population. For example, it may well be, as many argue, that the political tradition of French-speaking Quebec is more collectivist than those of the predominantly English-speaking provinces. And it is certainly true that patterns of political participation, political trust, sense of political efficacy, and regional versus national identities vary between the regions of Canada. But one finds the same sorts of variations in the United States, France, Britain, Italy, and elsewhere. Cultural differences linked to regional or group identification can coexist alongside a broad consensus on fundamental values and beliefs.

In the case of Canada, part of this broad consensus, or political tradition, has involved expectations for the state. Philip Resnick, among others, argues that Canada has a *statist* political tradition. This is a political tradition characterized by a relatively strong political executive and by a population that tends to be deferential towards those in power. The adoption of British parliamentary government, first in the colonial legislatures during the mid-nineteenth century and then through the British North America (BNA) Act, mainly reaffirmed the tradition of centralized executive authority that had existed before the elected legislature's approval was needed to pass laws. This reaffirmation of strong executive powers, Resnick argues, is apparent throughout the BNA Act:

> What our Founding Fathers were doing was consolidating an orderly move from direct colonial rule to House Rule. They had a particular kind of [political] order in mind, the parliamentary system as it had evolved in Britain, combining the interests of monarchs, lords and commoners. If by the latter part of the 19th century this system was increasingly responsive to the wishes of an electorate, restricted or enlarged, it was by no means a servant of the electorate.[6]

The institutions of government adopted through the Confederation agreement and, equally important, the expectations of the political élites who controlled the levers of state power reached forward to shape the future course of Canadian politics. Parliament was sovereign, but Parliament was not merely the people. It also included the Crown, the traditional seat of state authority whose powers came to be exercised by a Prime Minister and Cabinet with few serious checks from the legislature. 'Parliamentary sovereignty', Resnick claims, 'fostered attitudes in the population which were nominally participatory but maximally deferential towards those exercising political power. The mystique of British Crown and Constitution helped make illegitimate *all* forms of political activity not sanctioned or channeled through parliamentary institutions.'[7] This is an important point. Resnick is arguing that the more deferential political culture of Canada, as compared to the United States, did not simply happen. It was generated to some degree by parliamentary institutions that discouraged popular participation in politics, beyond the rituals of voting, and that enshrined a sort of top-down philosophy of governance.

Is Resnick right? The evidence suggests that he is. There have, of course, been influential currents of participatory politics in Canadian history, particularly coming out of western Canada. But these populist inclinations have had to struggle against a parliamentary tradition that concentrates political power in the hands of the Prime Minister (or premiers) and Cabinet. This style of governance is epitomized in the long tradition of élite deal-making that has characterized federal-provincial relations. But it also surfaces when this country's political leaders reject referenda or constituent assemblies on constitutional change as being 'un-Canadian' or foreign to our political tradition. Indeed, the statist political tradition fostered by British parliamentary government is apparent in a multitude of ways. 'Our governments', explains Resnick, '. . . become the organizers of our civic consciousness. National celebrations like Expo have to be staged; nationalist propaganda is transmitted across the airwaves, through the newspapers, along with our social security cheques.'[8] Many argue that the Canadian state's orchestration of culture has been a defensive response to the Americanizing pressures from mass media industries centred in the United States. To some degree this is certainly true. But this explanation of state-centred nationalism in Canada does not pay adequate attention to the possibility that the state's efforts may pre-empt those of groups in civil society and encourage a climate of dependence on governments to, in Resnick's words, 'organize our civic consciousness'.

The statist political tradition Resnick criticizes is also one that he and others on the left defend when it comes to state provision and financing of social services and various entitlements associated with the welfare state. In recent years this has become one of the chief battlegrounds in Canadian politics, as governments attempt to cut back on social spending without running afoul of core citizen beliefs concerning equality and the role of government. In this regard the actions of the Progressive Conservative governments in Alberta and Ontario and the Liberal government in New Brunswick illustrate well how pol-

icy-makers react to the constraints of political culture. These three governments have been the most vigorous in cutting government spending, including spending on social programs. But in selling these cuts to their respective
electorates, cuts that have been portrayed by critics as a betrayal of fundamental Canadian values, these governments have associated their actions with
other values that are likewise important to Canadians, including self-reliance,
limited government, and what are often labelled traditional family values.

2. The Constitution

As befits Canada's historical circumstances as a former colony of Great Britain
and a geographic and, in many ways, sociological extension of the United
States, the Canadian constitution represents a synthesis of principles developed from the experiences of these other countries. From Great Britain the
founders took parliamentary government and the host of conventions that
establish the relationships among the executive, legislative, and judicial
branches of the state. From the United States (but perhaps inevitably, given the
differences among the colonies that entered the Confederation agreement) the
founders took the federal form of government. Unlike American federalism,
the Canadian version included a number of provisions that appeared to and,
certainly in the minds of the founders, were intended to establish a centralized
form of federalism.[9] A combination of economic and social pressures, aided
by some 'imaginative' court decisions during the first several decades of this
country's history, produced a very different reality.

A constitution is the fundamental law of a political system. It is a set of
rules, either written down in documents like the British North America Act,
1867, and the Constitution Act, 1982,[10] or assuming the form of unwritten conventions. An example of such a convention is the principle that the leader of
the party commanding the greatest number of seats in the legislature is called
on to become the Prime Minister. A constitution regulates the relationship
among the various branches of government—the legislature, the executive, and
the courts (the constitutions of non-democratic states will occasionally include
the military, the monopoly political party, or the established religion as, effectively, a branch of the state). A constitution also regulates the relationship
between government and the governed. In a federal political system, one in
which the constitution establishes two levels of government, each possessing
exclusive authority to legislate regarding certain subjects, the constitution also
regulates the relationship between the national and regional state systems. An
essential feature of constitutional democracies is an independent judiciary
whose role is to interpret the constitution when its meaning is in dispute.

Canada's constitution includes both written documents and unwritten conventions.[11] The unwritten conventions of the Canadian constitution can be
divided into two categories, those regulating the relationship between parts of
the state system and those regulating federal-provincial relations. Canada
inherited from Great Britain a number of customary rules and traditional prac-

tices pertaining to the powers of and relations between parts of the state system. This British parliamentary inheritance is expressed in the preamble to the Constitution Act, 1867 (formerly known as the British North America Act), which states that the new country has adopted 'a Constitution similar in Principle to that of the United Kingdom'. Among the most important of these conventions of parliamentary government are the following:

1. *Those pertaining to the Prime Minister and Cabinet.* Examples of these conventions are that the leader of the political party with the most seats in the legislature becomes Prime Minister and has the right to appoint a Cabinet, and that a member of the Cabinet must resign from that position if he/she publicly dissents from government policy.

2. *Those pertaining to the relationship between the government and the legislature.* Most important of these is the principle of *responsible government*. This convention requires that a government must enjoy the support of a majority of members of the legislature in order to govern. If this support is lost, as on a vote of no confidence or a vote on spending legislation, the government is obligated to resign.

3. *Those pertaining to the relationship between the Crown, represented by the Governor-General in Canada, and the government.* Since the 1926 conflict between Governor-General Viscount Byng and Prime Minister Mackenzie King, it has become accepted that the Governor-General is required to accept the 'advice' given to him by the Prime Minister regarding the dissolution of Parliament and the calling of an election.

4. *Those pertaining to the relationship between the government and the bureaucracy.* Particularly important here are the requirements that the bureaucracy be non-partisan and that it serve the government of the day.

5. *Those pertaining to the internal operations of Parliament.* These include such matters as the rights of the opposition parties in the legislature and the privilege of parliamentary immunity enjoyed by all legislators.

Canada's British parliamentary inheritance provides no guide for the relationship between the federal and provincial governments. Here one must look to the written constitution and to the indigenously developed practices that have come to define the responsibilities and resources of each level of government and the procedures they follow in dealing with one another.

The fact of having two levels of government—each with bases of legislative authority and sources of revenue independent of the other—does not in itself complicate the policy-making process. Countries with unitary state systems may also be characterized by significant regional divisions that surface in policy-making in other forms (France, Great Britain, and Italy are good examples). In such cases, interregional conflict is expressed through national political institutions, such as the legislature, or through extra-governmental components of the political system, such as political parties and social movements. And even in federalized state systems the principal channel for the expression and mediation of regional interests may be national institutions. This is true of the United States, where members of Congress, especially senators and committee chairmen, are often more effective advocates of regional interests than most state governors.

The significance of federalism, particularly in a country where the regional states have significant lawmaking and taxing powers, is that it is more likely than a unitary state system to reinforce the regional divisions that probably were responsible for the adoption of federalism in the first place. Canadian political scientist Alan Cairns argues that Canada's decentralized version of federalism is 'a function not of societies but of the constitution, and more importantly of the governments that work the constitution.'[12] He writes:

> Governing élites view their task as the injection of provincial or federal meaning into society, giving it a degree of coherence and a pattern of interdependence more suited for government purposes than would emerge from the unhindered working of social and market forces . . . . each government transmits cues and pressures to the environment, thus tending to group the interests manipulated by its policies into webs of interdependence springing from the particular version of socio-economic integration it is pursuing. Provincial governments work toward the creation of limited versions of a politically created provincial society and economy, and the national government works toward the creation of a country-wide society and economy.[13]

Cairns is saying that it is rational for politicians and bureaucrats at each level of government to behave in ways that are likely to increase their control over the factors relevant to the future of the organizations to which they belong. These factors would include sources of revenue, the authority to regulate social and economic activity, and the support of citizens and organized interests.

Federal-provincial relations are regulated by both the written constitution and conventions that have developed over time. Canadian federalism is characterized by overlapping jurisdictions, shared revenue sources, and a high degree of administrative co-operation and executive interaction between the federal and provincial states. This is so despite a written constitution that includes a lengthy enumeration of the 'exclusive' legislative powers of each level of government. The founders' clear intention to assign the national government 'ample authority for the great task of nation-building entrusted to it',[14] leaving to the provincial governments what at the time appeared to be relatively unimportant powers over social, cultural, and local matters, was soon undermined by a combination of assertive provincial governments and decentralist constitutional rulings by the Judicial Committee of the Privy Council.[15]

Constitutional conventions are of vital importance for the financial dimension of federalism, for the process of intergovernmental relations, and for making and implementing foreign policy. The division of powers set down in the Canadian constitution and interpreted by the courts is complicated by the intricate network of financial and administrative agreements negotiated between Ottawa and the provinces. Some of the most important of these agreements are in the area of social policy, where the federal government annually transfers billions of dollars to the provinces in aid of provincially administered services. The process by which negotiations on such matters takes place is not established by constitutional law. Instead, it is bounded by certain conventional practices such as the annual meetings of the Prime Minister and the provincial premiers. In the case of foreign policy, consultation with provincial governments and in some cases provincial representation on the Canadian negotiating team are conventional practices. These practices are necessitated by the fact that although only the federal government has the authority to enter into agreements with other sovereign states, the subject-matter of such agreements may fall within provincial jurisdiction and therefore may require provincial concurrence to be implemented.[16]

Federal-provincial relations in Canada involve a continuous and multi-levelled process of consultation and bargaining among policy-makers representing Ottawa and the provinces. The term *executive federalism* is commonly used to describe this process. As Richard Simeon has argued, it often resembles the bargaining that occurs in international politics between sovereign governments.[17] It is a process from which legislatures are almost entirely excluded, except when called on to ratify an agreement reached between executives of the two levels of government.

Canada's constitution has two main effects on the policy-making process. The British parliamentary system concentrates power with Cabinet, the prism through which virtually all important policy decisions must pass and which generally is able to control the legislative agenda. Because the policy agenda is determined chiefly by Cabinet, those interests wishing to influence policy often focus their efforts on Cabinet and those parts of the state system that influence Cabinet's choices or implement its decisions.

The second main effect that Canada's constitution has on the policy process is to magnify the significance of regional divisions. The legislative powers the constitution assigns to the provinces have turned out to be very important ones. Combined with the relative weakness of national institutions for representing regional interests, this meant that the provincial governments early emerged as the main spokespersons for these regionally based interests. Consequently, regional conflicts are usually jurisdictional conflicts. The way policy issues are defined and conflict is played out tend to attach great importance to regional divisions because of the particular character of Canada's federal constitution.

A major reform of the Canadian constitution took place in 1982 when the Charter of Rights and Freedoms became law. The Charter is widely seen as a major step towards the democratization of the constitution and policy-making. Alan Cairns has described it as the basis for what he calls a 'citizens' constitution', as opposed to the old 'governments' constitution' of federalism. Of course, those older parts of the constitution are still with us, but Cairns's point is simply this: whereas during the pre-Charter era the Canadian constitution was primarily about the 'rights' of governments, since 1982 much of our constitutional discourse and activity focuses on the rights of individuals and groups—rights that may take precedence over the legislative powers of governments. This would appear to be a blow to the élitist style of policy-making that was nurtured under the 'governments' constitution' of federalism.

Cairns is right, but only to a point. What he calls the era of the citizens' constitution really only began with Ottawa's 1992 decision—a decision it took late and reluctantly—to hold a national referendum on the Charlottetown Accord. The Accord itself represented the product of a polyarchical policy-making style that broadened the range of consultation from first ministers to include the leaders of groups representing Aboriginal Canadians, women, labour, business, official-language minorities, ethnic and racial minorities, and so on. But, despite the unprecedented breadth of this consultation process, many believed that the constitution-making process remained highly élitist. They believed so for two reasons. First, greater consultation and the informal participation of non-state élites in the negotiations on constitutional reform did not mean that popular consent, expressed directly by the people, had been accepted as a *sine qua non* of the amendment process. Second, the form of politics that has emerged in Canada under the influence of the Charter of Rights and Freedoms, and which was so much in evidence between the demise of the Meech Lake Accord and the signing of the Charlottetown Accord, is still highly élitist. Cairns's assertion that the Charter has encouraged citizens to think of themselves as rights-bearers, and that this has generated a 'political culture increasingly sympathetic to constitutional participation by citizens, at least when their own status and rights are likely to be affected',[18] implies a new populism that, until the actual referendum campaign, was in fact stifled by the special interest politics the Charter had encouraged.

Ted Morton makes this point in explaining what he believes to be the true character of Charter politics. He notes the proliferation and heightened public profile of 'the new citizens interest groups that have sprung up around *their* sections of the *Charter*'.[19] Morton calls these groups the 'Court Party' because their preferred legal strategy is to rely on the courts and quasi-judicial human rights tribunals to achieve their goals. But these groups also favour media strategies that enable them to influence the terms and trajectory of political discourse. Indeed, there is a broad affinity of ideological outlook and educational and socio-economic backgrounds, and a complementarity of interests between the media and these rights-seeking groups. The 'rights talk' they generate and their apparent ability to speak on behalf of grassroots constituencies create the impression that Canadian politics has been democratized and made more participatory by the Charter. The impression is false. As Morton argues,

[The Charter] has shifted responsibility for a growing sphere of policy issues into a new arena where the costs of participation are prohibitive and debate is conducted in a foreign language—*Charterese*, a dialect of *legalese*. Politically [this] represents a horizontal transfer of power to a new élite, not a vertical transfer of power to the people.[20]

The same may be said of the more specialized case of constitutional reform. The apparent opening up of the policy-making process after the élitist debacle of the Meech Lake Accord represented a shift towards polyarchy, not an embrace of populist democracy. The message of the negotiations that produced the 1992 Charlottetown Accord was that consent has a group basis, a message consistent with Canada's deferential political culture. Groups purporting to represent various citizen identities encouraged by Charter politics staked out their right to a voice in the process of constitutional reform. Public opinion and citizens *qua* citizens still remained far from the policy-making process.

3. Social and Economic Characteristics

Protection for the French language in Canada has been on the policy agenda since before Confederation. It continues to be because over one-fifth of the Canadian population is Francophone and about 90 per cent of these French-speakers reside in Quebec. This is an obvious example of how the social characteristics of a country influence its politics, including the issues that get onto the policy agenda. But a word of caution: there is nothing automatic or inevitable about the sorts of social and economic issues that reach the policy agenda. The political cleavages and controversies within any given society are determined by a number of factors, including the structural features of the political system, political culture, and a society's history.

Issues do not just happen; they have to be defined. Likewise, interests and identities require learning and mobilization. This being said, it nevertheless is the case that the social and economic characteristics of a society make the emergence of certain issues more likely than others. Donald Smiley once wrote that Canadian politics has had three main axes: the relations between its French- and English-speaking communities, the Canada-United States relationship, and the regional dimension of Canadian political life. These correspond to three of the most prominent social and economic characteristics of Canada, namely, the existence and historically unequal circumstances of two major language communities, Canada's economic, cultural, and political ties to the United States, and the economic diversity and disparities between regions of Canada. French-English relations and language policy are discussed at length in Chapter Nine. I will focus here on Smiley's other two axes.

i. Living in the Shadow of a Giant

In the late nineteenth century Canada was a dependent society with close ties to the British economic system. During the twentieth century Canada shifted into the economic and cultural orbit of an ascendant power, the United States. This shift was partially due to transformations in the world economy, including the decline in Britain's economic stature and the relative increase in that of the United States. The transatlantic dependence based on the export of certain resource commodities and on the import of debt capital to finance the infrastructure of the resource-exporting economy was winding down. It was replaced by a continentalist dependence based on the export of natural resources to the United States and on the integration of Canadian industry into the American economy through ownership and imports of production technology. The shift was accompanied by transformations in the structure of economic and political power in Canada, notably the decline in the importance of financial and railway interests and an increase in that of the industrial subsidiaries—mainly American—that established themselves behind Canadian tariff walls. Thus, just at a time when Canada was shaking off the vestiges of its colonial status within the British Empire and establishing itself as a politically sovereign nation, this country's capacity for independent public policy was being undermined through Canada's integration into the economic empire of American capitalism.

Canada's economic ties to the United States take several forms. Among the most significant, in terms of their impact on public policy, are trade, investment, capital markets, and treaties.

Trade. Many developed economies are more dependent on trade than Canada's. None, however, is as dependent on trade with a single partner. Over 80 per cent of Canada's export trade is with the United States. About one-fifth of Canada's gross domestic product (GDP) is accounted for by sales to the United States. Matters look very different from the American side. Although Canada is still the United States' largest trading partner, American exports to Canada amount to only a small fraction of that country's national income. Trade dependence is, in this case, a one-way street.

The significance of this becomes apparent when the American economy goes into recession. A drop in demand for automobiles, softwood lumber, paper products, and other commodities that Canada exports to the United States translates into economic slowdown in Canada. Along with many products that originate in the United States, Canada 'imports' economic expansion and contraction because of the sheer magnitude of Canadian trade with the American economy. Fluctuations in the exchange rate between the Canadian and American dollars, or an increase in inflation in the United States (making American imports dearer), ripple through the Canadian economy, posing a serious dilemma for Canadian policy-makers. It amounts to this: when a significant portion of Canadian economic activity is tied to the behaviour of the American economy and, moreover, to the actions that American policy-makers take to influence their domestic economy, what margin of manoeuvre remains for Canada's economic policy-makers?

Investment. Much of the Canadian economy is owned by foreigners, and most of those foreigners are American. Roughly one-third of the 100 largest non-financial corporations in Canada are foreign-owned and several of the most important sectors of the Canadian economy, including the automobile industry, the petroleum and petrochemicals sector, and important segments of the food-processing industry, are dominated by American-based companies.

The roots of American investment in the Canadian economy go back to the National Policy of 1879. The high tariffs imposed on manufactured imports encouraged American companies to establish Canadian subsidiaries—branch plants, as they are often called—that would produce exclusively for the Canadian market, thus 'jumping' the tariff wall. Michael Bliss estimates that by 1913 about 450 subsidiaries, mainly American, had been established in Canada. The level of foreign investment peaked in the 1970s at about 37 per cent of total economic assets in Canada. Today the level stands at about one-quarter, about two-thirds of which are based in the United States.

The consequences of such high levels of foreign ownership, levels unmatched in any other advanced industrial democracy, have been debated since the 1950s. To some it is self-evident that Canadians have benefited from the billions of dollars that have been invested in their economy, mainly by Americans, while others think it equally self-evident that the costs have outweighed any putative benefits. What is beyond doubt, however, is that the high level of foreign ownership has increased the integration of the Canadian economy into the orbit of the United States and, moreover, rendered Canadian policy-makers more vulnerable to the foreign investment policies of the United States government.

This vulnerability was highlighted during the 1990s in the dispute over the Helms-Burton law. In pursuit of the US policy of not trading with Cuba, the American Congress passed legislation prohibiting the foreign-based subsidiaries of American companies from doing business with that country. The Canadian government and those of Western Europe protested that this represented a violation of international law. But for many countries their protest was little more than perfunctory indignation. For Canada, which has extensive trade ties to Cuba and is in fact the single largest foreign investor in the Cuban economy, the extraterritorial application of American law through US-owned subsidiaries in Canada represented a more serious matter.

For all of its history Canada has been a net importer of investment capital. However, since the 1980s the volume of Canadian foreign investment, chiefly in the United States, has increased enormously. By 1994 the stock of foreign direct investment in Canada stood at an estimated $148 billion, but the value of Canadian foreign investment was not far behind at $125 billion.[21] Canadian companies have participated in the globalization of investment capital. However, as Elizabeth Smythe observes,

> globalization, in Canada's case, has really meant ever closer economic integration with the United States in the 1980s and 1990s. In the light of the great disparities in the size of the two economies and their depen-

dence on trade, this trend has given the United States additional means of influencing Canadian policies in the event of investment disputes.[22]

Capital markets. Canadian companies, governments, and government agencies often borrow money. In the case of governments and government agencies, much of this money is loaned by foreign investors. In fact, roughly one-third of Ottawa's over $600 billion in indebtedness is owed to non-Canadians. Provincial governments and their agents, such as Ontario Hydro and Hydro-Québec, are also heavily indebted to foreign investors. Most of this debt is owed to Americans. This helps to explain the soothing noises that Canadian politicians, federal and provincial, regularly make when they visit the temple of Mammon—New York—and the fact that any pronouncement on Canada's creditworthiness by the oracles of international finance, Standard and Poors and Moody's, is considered front-page news in this country.

In recent years the possibility of Quebec separating from Canada has had a particularly unnerving effect on foreign moneylenders. During the 1995 Quebec referendum on sovereignty, the issue of foreign investors' reaction to a yes vote, and how this would affect the credit ratings of Canada and Quebec, figured prominently in the debate. The episode provided yet another illustration of how Canada's economic ties to the United States become felt as constraints on policy-makers.

Treaties. The ties of trade, investment, and borrowing that exist between Canada and the United States have been cemented by treaties. These treaties have a long history. In fact, the Americans' abrogation of the Reciprocity Treaty (1854–66) between the United States and Great Britain's North American colonies was an important catalyst for Confederation. Even before the Canada-United States Free Trade Agreement (FTA) came into effect in 1989, sectoral free trade existed between the two countries. The Defence Production Sharing Agreement of 1958 formalized sectoral free trade in defence-related products that had existed since World War II. More importantly, the Auto Pact of 1965 created free trade in automobiles and automotive parts. In addition to bilateral treaties, Canada and the United States were original members of the multilateral General Agreement on Tariffs and Trade (GATT), signed in 1947, which committed them to lowering trade barriers and to a code of conduct regarding imports and exports within the GATT community.

The FTA and NAFTA (North American Free Trade Agreement) have eliminated most of the barriers to the free movement of goods, sources, and capital in North America (although restrictions on the movement of people still exist, unlike in the European Union). Moreover, the World Trade Organization (WTO), which oversees implementation of GATT rules, joins the Canadian and American economies under the same multilateral trade umbrella. Multilateral trade commitments have often been seen as representing a potential counterweight to the inevitable dominance of the United States in bilateral Canadian-American trade relations. The constraints imposed on Canadian policy-makers by the WTO are much less restrictive than the obligations imposed by membership in the FTA and NAFTA. These free trade treaties reinforce Canada's economic dependence on the United States, guaranteeing access to the American market in exchange for restrictions on the ability of Canadian governments to favour domestic producers and investors over their American counterparts.

The ties that bind Canada to the orbit of the United States are not only economic. Militarily, the two countries have been joined by treaty obligations since the Ogdensburg Agreement (1940) and the Hyde Park Declaration (1941). The North Atlantic Treaty Organization (1949), the North American Air Defence Command (1958), and the Canada-United States Test and Evaluation Program (1983) deepened the military alliance between Canada and the United States.

Canadian nationalists and critics of American defence policy have often expressed the hope that Canada could free itself from its military alliance with the United States and develop the sort of non-aligned status that Sweden has long maintained. Prime Minister Pierre Trudeau took some tentative steps in this direction during the late 1960s and early 1970s, only to find that the political costs exceeded whatever nationalist satisfaction an autonomous defence posture might provide. The problem is simply this: Canada is not Sweden. Canada's geographic position and economic dependence on the United States rule out the possibility of military non-alignment. So while there is margin for independent manoeuvre in some matters, such as international peacekeeping, and even some room for minor criticism of American defence policies, there is no real possibility of Canada pursuing an autonomous line on the big issues of global security and the defence of North America.

Culture is another area in which the United States casts a long shadow across Canada. This influence operates at two levels. One involves what might be described as the global phenomenon of Americanization that operates through Hollywood films, pop music, mass fashion, CNN, and product advertising. This dimension of cultural globalization is often referred to as 'Westernization', on the grounds that it involves the worldwide diffusion of the mass-consumption individualistic culture of Western capitalist societies. But in fact it is more correctly characterized as Americanization, because the preponderance of symbols, ideas, and images and the particular English used to communicate the global culture have their roots in the American experience. Indigenous cultures throughout the world have been affected to varying degrees by American culture, Canada included. Indeed, in the Canadian case there were many fewer natural defences against the homogenizing tendencies of American culture than in, say, France where language and deeply rooted national traditions have offered somewhat more resistance to the culture of Walt Disney, Big Macs, and shopping malls.

A second level of American cultural influence of special significance for Canada involves the extraordinary penetration of American mass culture into Canadian, particularly English-Canadian, markets. Geographic proximity, a shared language, broadly similar cultural values, and the much greater size of the American market combine to explain Canada's vulnerability to cultural exports from the United States. American magazines dominate Canadian markets. American comedies and dramatic programming dominate Canadian television. American feature films open simultaneously in the United States and Canada, and the marketing campaigns used to promote them are identical. The national best-seller lists for fiction (less so for non-fiction) are dominated by many of the same American authors. In short, the Canadian market is a backyard for American cultural industries. Canadian governments have tried to put up various sorts of fences through policies that favour Canadian cultural producers, Canadian content requirements for television and radio, and direct involvement through the CBC and the National Film Board. But the numbers tell the story: by and large, Canadians prefer to consume the cultural products of the United States.

ii. Regionalism and Provincialism in Canadian Policy-Making

Provincial governments sometimes claim to speak on behalf of regionally distinct societies. This claim was forcefully expressed by Claude Morin, a constitutionalist and one-time member of the Parti Québécois government, in a book entitled *Quebec vs. Ottawa*.[23] Morin argued that the interests of Quebec society, by which he meant the Francophone majority of that province, can never be protected in a federal parliament in which Québécois will always be in the minority. Basing his argument on this simple proposition, he suggested that only the Quebec government was capable of protecting the interests of the provincial society because it was not compelled to make concessions to the interests of other regions. Spokespersons from other provinces generally have been less extreme in arguing their cases for provincial distinctiveness, but it none the less is true that every provincial government, regardless of partisan stripe, inherits a set of 'fairly durable and persisting interests'[24] that largely determine the demands they make on federalism. These interests, and what Alan Cairns has called the institutional self-interest of provincial state élites, are more important than culture in shaping the demands of the predominantly Anglophone provinces.

There are wide differences between the provinces in the types of economic activity that predominate. Provinces' economies also vary enormously in their trade relations with other provinces and their relationship to markets outside of Canada. Nevertheless, these interprovincial economic differences are no greater than those that exist between, say, New York and Nebraska or Ohio and Texas in the United States. How, then, does one explain the fact that in Canada the decentralizing pressures on the federal system appear to be far greater than those to which American federalism is subject?

Various explanations have been put forth, including a greater sense of national identity in American society.[25] A second line of explanation points to the existence in the United States of national political institutions, notably the

Senate, that are able to act as forums for the expression of regional demands. These national institutions play a role that in Canada is assumed primarily by provincial governments. A third explanation involves American Supreme Court decisions that have given an expansive interpretation to the federal government's power to regulate interstate commerce. In Canada the courts, at least until the 1970s, have historically imposed a more restrictive interpretation on Ottawa's trade and commerce and general legislative powers. While the significance of any of these factors should not be dismissed, the key to understanding Canada's decentralized federal system lies in the divisions between the central provinces—Canada's manufacturing and financial core—and the western and eastern peripheries and in the weakness of national political institutions in representing regional interests.

The uneven regional distribution of economic activity and power in Canada is confirmed by data on the interprovincial distribution of businesses by the size of firms and the location of head offices for the largest industrial corporations in Canada. Not surprisingly, one finds that the majority of large businesses are based in Ontario and Quebec. Thirty-five of the 100 largest industrial corporations in Canada are wholly owned subsidiaries of foreign corporations, and 21 of these are based in either Ontario or Quebec. Most of the multinationals that do not have their Canadian head offices in these two provinces are resource-based businesses. Corporate decision-making power is not evenly distributed across the country. It is still concentrated in central Canada, especially Ontario, although the last several years have seen a shift in the locus of corporate power towards Alberta and British Columbia. A bare handful of the largest companies are based in the Atlantic provinces (see Table 3.2).

The unequal distribution of economic activity across Canada would not by itself prove a source of decentralizing pressure on the federal system. These inequalities, however, combine with relatively weak structures for the expression of regional interests at the national level, and with a constitution that gives to provincial governments numerous levers for regulating their economies, to fragment the policy process along regional lines. Regionally oriented business interests have often viewed the provincial state as an ally in protecting and promoting their economic interests.

Decentralizing tendencies in Canadian federalism and policy-making have also resulted from the constitution and Quebec nationalism. Quebec nationalism is discussed in Chapter Nine. In the case of the constitution, the provinces possess important levers for regulating economic activity within their boundaries, they have wide-ranging taxing and borrowing powers, and they have jurisdiction over most areas of social policy. The constitution therefore provides significant jurisdictional opportunities for provincial intervention, though the provinces differ in their ability and willingness to take advantage of them.

The assertion of provincial powers under the constitution has a long tradi-

Table 3.2
Interprovincial Distribution of Corporate Head Offices
and Nationality of Ownership
for the 100 Largest Industrial Firms in Canada, 1991 and 1996

	Head Office		Foreign-Owned	
	1991	*1996*	*1991*	*1996*
Ontario	50	38	23	17
Quebec	21	22	5	6
Alberta	11	20	2	7
British Columbia	8	12	1	4
Manitoba	6	3	1	1
Saskatchewan	2	3	0	0
New Brunswick	1	1	0	0
Nova Scotia	1	1	1	0
Newfoundland and Prince Edward Island	0	0	0	0
Totals	100	100	33	35

SOURCE: Compiled from information provided in *The Financial Post 500*, 1992, 1997.

tion. During the first decades after Confederation the Ontario government of Oliver Mowat was a major force in resisting the centralist vision of federalism held by Ottawa under Sir John A. Macdonald.[26] Conflict between Ottawa's nation-building designs and the development goals of provincial governments led to the use of the federal government's powers of reservation and disallowance of provincial legislation on numerous occasions during this early period. Even when Canadian federalism was most centralized, as during the two world wars, and during the Great Depression when the provinces were financially at their weakest, the transfer of constitutional powers from the provincial to the federal level of government was resisted. The only occasion when the federal division of powers has been changed to the advantage of the national government was in 1941. An amendment to the British North America Act, agreed to by all the provinces, assigned legislative authority over unemployment insurance to Ottawa.[27]

While the scope of state intervention has increased at all levels of government during the postwar era, such growth has been greatest at the provincial level. This reflects both the escalating costs of provincially administered social programs and a restructuring of the financial relationship between the two levels of government. The extensive network of conditional grants erected in the 1950s and 1960s has been dismantled in favour of block transfers from Ottawa to the provinces (see the discussion in Chapter Six on social policy). Moreover, the relative taxing power of the two levels of government has shifted dramatically. In 1950 the federal government collected about two-thirds of all public revenues. Today, the provinces and municipalities collect over one-half of all tax revenues. None the less, some provincial governments remain heavily dependent on transfer payments from Ottawa. Newfoundland is the extreme case, with about 50 per cent of its total revenues coming from the federal government.

Not unexpectedly, growth in provincial state spending has been accompanied by an increase in the sheer size of provincial bureaucracies. From the standpoint of public policy-making this expansion in the size of the provincial state and in the scope of its powers is significant because of the natural tendency of regional governments, elected by regional electorates, to give expression to a narrower set of interests than are politically significant at the national level. Differences in culture, demographics, and economic structure between regions in Canada acquire a more comprehensive political importance than they would have in a unitary state. This is due to the fact that these differences are organized into politics around provincial governments that have extensive constitutional powers and that have developed large and complex state structures to rival those of the federal government.[28]

4. Globalization

The Harvard Institute for International Development estimates that as recently as 1980 only about one-quarter of the world's population, accounting for about half of global production, was linked by trade. Today, trade links close to 90 per cent of the world's population, whose economies account for all but a small share of the world's wealth.[29] The 'Canadian-made' mini-van that rolls off the assembly line at Windsor, Ontario, has an engine made in either the United States or Japan and component systems and various parts from Mexico, China, and elsewhere. The national identities of corporations have become increasingly indistinct as their activities fan out across the globe in search of the most favourable conditions for production. When the adverse publicity from a boycott of Walt Disney Corporation became more than that US-based entertainment giant cared to tolerate—a boycott prompted by what were alleged to be exploitative wages and working conditions at Disney's Haiti production facilities, where clothes and accessories were produced—company officials announced that they could close up shop and restart production elsewhere within 24 hours.

Unprecedented levels of world trade and internationalized production are characteristics of what is called globalization. They are not, however, the whole picture. Doern and his colleagues define globalization as 'primarily a technological and economic process driven by the revolution in telecommunications and computers, massive increases in the movement of capital around the world, greatly expanded capacities for flexible world-wide production sourcing by firms, especially multinational corporations, and growing ecological interdependence and environmental spillovers.'[30] Globalization is about economics, but it is also about technology and culture. It is a phenomenon that is indifferent, even hostile, to the idea of national boundaries, indigenous cultures, and tradition. Microsoft, Nike, Walt Disney, and CNN are among its cultural standard-bearers. Free trade is its religion.

The consequences of globalization are the subject of enormous controversy. The optimistic viewpoint is expressed by Harvard's Jeffrey Sachs: 'Global capitalism is surely the most promising institutional arrangement for worldwide prosperity that history has ever seen. Long cherished hopes for convergence between rich and poor regions of the world may at last be about to be realised.'[31] The optimists also point to what they see as the anti-hierarchical and democratizing character of the Internet, allowing for the instant exchange of information across the globe and access for anyone with a personal computer (PC) and modem. The information monopolies of the wealthy and the propagandistic activities of governments can be overcome through the levelling technology of globally linked computers.

There is, however, no shortage of pessimists. The French magazine *Le Monde diplomatique* provides this bleak assessment of globalization:

> Throughout the world it imposes 'the only policy possible', that of the search for maximum profits, invoking the imperatives of competition inherent in globalization. It does so in total indifference to the social ravages it provokes. From the Americas to Africa, passing through the continent of Europe, the implementation of neo-liberal policies has led to explosive growth in inequality and to the marginalization of millions upon millions of human beings, children being first among its victims, that capital does not require in order to reproduce itself.[32]

It is perhaps not surprising that the left-wing French intellectuals who write for *Le Monde* should be critical of globalization and its ideological handmaiden, liberalism. Doubts have been expressed, however, from many other corners as well. The American magazine *Newsweek* has criticized what it calls 'killer capitalism', a phenomenon it sees as being linked to globalization. Former United States Secretary of Labour, Robert Reich, argues that 'Globalization is creating, within our industrial democracies, a sort of underclass of the demoralized and impoverished.'[33]

As for the cultural consequences of globalization, critics level a number of charges. Global computer technology, they argue, is quickly reinforcing inequalities within societies—between the educated professional classes who tend to be most computer-literate and the rest of society—and between societies, the wealthy countries of the world being those where PC ownership and Internet use are highest. The global culture embodied in Walt Disney's corporate imagination, CNN's world-view, and Nike's fashion universalism is hostile to local traditions and cultures, and contributes to a denial of those aspects of the human condition that give life dignity and authentic meaning. The ability of national and subnational policy-makers to protect the distinct cultures of the societies they govern is undermined by the loss in national sovereignty that inevitably results from globalization. Finally—in fact, the list of criticisms is longer, but these are the main ones—the glorification of the market and individualism, which are the conceptual pillars of globalization, is blamed for the creation of a mean-spirited *sauve-qui-peut* attitude in societies and the erosion of the sense of community and mutual obligation, the institutional embodiment of which was the welfare state.

International influences on policy and policy-making in Canada are nothing new. Globalization multiplies and intensifies these influences, as well as adding to them novel dimensions generated by modern information and production technology. Doern and his colleagues identify several distinct ways in which policy-making has been affected by globalization.[34] They include the following.

Policy discourse has been internationalized. How policy issues are framed has changed, so that matters that previously were thought of as purely or chiefly domestic are now discussed in a context of influences and norms that are transnational. The issue of Native rights, for example, has been discussed in the context of United Nations declarations on human rights and the self-determination of peoples. Since the 1991 armed stand-off between the Canadian military and Mohawk warriors at Oka, Quebec, it has been fairly routine for Aboriginal groups in Canada to call for UN or some other international involvement in disputes with the Canadian or a provincial government. Moreover, Native leaders draw on an international discourse of human rights and Aboriginal rights that is kept in circulation through non-governmental organizations (NGOs), international bodies, conferences, and Web sites that contribute to the contextualization of such rights as matters that transcend domestic politics.

The number of such examples may be multiplied almost without limit. Activities like the trapping of animals for their fur or forestry methods in British Columbia are discussed in ways and in forums that make clear that their ramifications extend beyond Canada. Education policies and performance are discussed in terms of their meaning for Canada's (or a province's) international competitiveness. Trade considerations are ubiquitous, whether one is talking about reform of social policy, national unity, environmental regulation, culture, or whatever else might be on the agenda.

One of the key aspects of the internationalization of policy discourse involves the establishment of international norms and standards and their importation into domestic policy-making. This is obviously true in the case of trade and investment, where the rules set under the FTA and NAFTA and by the WTO became the benchmarks for assessing the actions of governments in

Canada. But it is also true of such matters as the status of women, poverty, and human rights, where the meetings and reports of international bodies and forums shape significantly the contours of policy discourse in Canada.

The internationalization of policy discourse challenges the concept of national sovereignty. But despite the erosion of the idea that domestic conditions are matters of national interest only, and of the notion that there is such a thing as purely domestic matters, the concept of national sovereignty is far from dead. Nor, as a practical matter, have governments lost all margin for independent policy-making, although this independence clearly is attenuated. What is certain, however, is that policy issues today are often framed in ways that are indifferent to national boundaries, and that the traditional integrity of policy fields has been breached and invaded by ideas and interests from outside the domestic sphere.

Interest groups and their strategies have been internationalized. Some interest groups, by their very nature, are international. Greenpeace, Amnesty International, Physicians for Nuclear Disarmament, and the World Wildlife Federation are examples of these. But many others, whose organization and finances are restricted to a single country, now seek alliances and support from outside their national borders. For example, Pal and Cooper note that three Canadian groups appeared before the UN Committee on Economic, Social, and Cultural Rights in 1995, complaining that Ottawa's decision to repeal the Canada Assistance Plan constituted a violation of the UN Covenant on Human Rights.[35] Attempting to embarrass the government at home by making noise abroad has become a fairly routine tactic in the arsenal of many interest groups, particularly environmental, Aboriginal, human rights, women's, and anti-poverty groups. Such tactics can prove effective not only because the national media in Canada are usually eager to report such stories, but also because the machinery of policy-making in Canada has acquired a greater openness towards the norms and decisions of international bodies. The Canadian and provincial human rights commissions take them seriously, as do various bureaucratic agencies such as the Human Rights Directorate in the Department of Canadian Heritage and the Justice and Health departments.

The traditional separation between foreign policy-making and domestic policy-making has been undermined. As the definition of foreign policy has changed, so, too, has the role of Canada's foreign affairs bureaucracy. Historically, foreign policy concerned itself chiefly with trade, national security, international peace, and what might be called humanitarian matters. Today, the definition of foreign policy encompasses these traditional concerns plus environmental ones, human rights issues, social policy, women's issues, telecommunications and culture, finance, and more. The Department of Foreign Affairs and International Trade (DFAIT) has seen its authority broadened by these developments, but also limited. In areas like agriculture, the environment, and telecommunications, DFAIT must share responsibility for policy-making with departments that have deeper technical expertise and already established relations to industry and interest groups. In some matters that have acquired foreign policy dimensions, like banking and social policy, DFAIT is not a player.[36]

The broadening of foreign policy also has implications for federalism. Doern and Kirton argue that because of provincial budget cuts, including the termination of international trade offices and missions by all provinces except Quebec, 'there has been a shift in foreign affairs capacity from the provincial to the federal level.'[37] We need to distinguish, however, between what they call 'foreign affairs capacity' and actual involvement in foreign policy-making. It may well be that the dismantling of provincial trade offices abroad has rendered the provinces more dependent on Ottawa for export-promotion and investment-attracting activities. This view probably overvalues, by taking at face value, the boastful and self-serving claims of trade/investment missions, such as the 'Team Canada' trips abroad, about the results of their activities. Some observers doubt that these government-sponsored missions and trade offices have much impact at all, and their elimination by the Ontario government, for example, certainly owed something to this belief. Moreover, even if the provinces, except Quebec, now rely more on Ottawa's formal machinery for trade negotiations and diplomacy, the broadening of foreign policy to include matters where provincial governments have a clear jurisdictional stake—the environment, social policy, telecommunications, and agriculture, for example—has also extended the range of foreign policy matters requiring provincial government input, co-operation, or even formal agreement for implementation. It may be premature, therefore, to conclude that the role of the provinces in foreign policy-making has declined.

The mixture of policy instruments used by governments has changed. During the last several years Canada has been on the receiving end of a number of direct and indirect hits targeted at long-standing policy instruments. For example, a 1997 WTO decision ruled that protectionist measures used to support Canadian-owned magazines violated the GATT rules on trade. GATT rules have also required Canada, and other GATT members, to reduce domestic and export subsidies to agricultural producers. Spending instruments and direct subsidies have been squeezed by pressure, much of it coming from foreign investors, to reduce budget deficits and public-sector debt. Liberalized trade has meant deregulation in some sectors, such as telecommunications and air travel, that traditionally have been closely regulated by the state. Canada's participation in international treaties and organizations, from the Group of Seven and the WTO to the United Nations Commission on Human Rights and international forums on the environment and the status of women, has increasingly affected policy-making in Canada by providing agreements and rules that serve as touchstones for domestic policy.

Doern and his colleagues caution that generalization about how the choice of policy instruments has been affected by globalization is made difficult by the fact that the traditional patterns of policy instruments varied widely between policy sectors (for example, industrial policy relied heavily on direct subsidies, export promotion, and direct state ownership, whereas environmental policy relied on regulation and monitoring). Nevertheless, they suggest that spending instruments have declined in importance at the same time as various forms of regulation and government exhortation have become more important. Pal demonstrates elsewhere that globalization, through its effects on policy networks, draws non-governmental organizations into the policy-making process in novel ways and in some cases transforms them into policy instruments.[38]

Chapter Four

Policy Implementation

It used to be believed that implementation was what happened after all the hard stuff was finished. Forging agreement on a policy, getting it embodied in a proposed law, and navigating that law through the various stages of the legislative process and past the sniping of opposition politicians, the media, and hostile interest groups were thought to be the tough parts of policy-making. After all of this was accomplished, lawmakers could heave a sigh of relief, knowing that their intentions would be translated into action by bureaucrats whose job was to do precisely that.

Some students of policy-making noticed that the translation of the politicians' decisions into administrative action was not as automatic as the academic neglect of implementation led one to believe. The wording of laws was often very general, and as time went on their subject-matter became increasingly technical, leaving it up to non-elected officials to determine how the law would be applied. These bureaucrats, like all human beings, had values that influenced how they implemented policies. Bureaucratic discretion and the impossibility of keeping values out of administrative process are problems as old as the modern study of public administration.[1] They are what we today would call implementation problems. But they are not the only or even the major source of distortion between what governments decide and what actually happens (or does not happen!).

Today, no one who knows anything about policy-making takes implementation for granted. To understand why this is so, consider the following three cases:

- *Regional economic development.* Since the 1960s, the federal government has pumped billions of dollars into the economies of the less prosperous eastern provinces. In 1965, the per capita income of the average Newfoundlander, excluding government transfer payments, was about 60 per cent of the Canadian average. Today it is a bit less. For the region as a whole, personal earned income levels are about what they were before the economic development pipeline opened.

- *Affordable housing*. In response to shortages of low-priced and moderately priced accommodation during the inflationary 1970s, many provincial governments slapped rent controls on landlords. Although the ostensible aim was to ensure a supply of reasonably priced housing for low-income earners, vacancy rates at the low end of the market declined in many areas and in some metropolitan regions the shortage of low-income housing became acute.

- *Control of toxic chemicals*. The Canadian Environmental Protection Act (1988) includes provisions for the regulation of toxic chemicals used in industry. Spokespersons for Environment Canada describe these provisions as 'cradle-to-grave' management of industrial toxins and consider them a major step forward in protecting the health and environment of Canadians. Rules were established giving any Canadian the right to request an investigation of the environmental effects of a particular substance and requiring the Department of the Environment to respond. But several years after CEPA's passage, only a few dozen of the perhaps 100,000 chemicals in commercial use in Canada had been placed on Environment Canada's Priority Substance List. The list includes those chemicals whose production, use, and disposal are closely monitored under CEPA. Many environmentalists argued that little had changed.

Policies often fail to accomplish the goals used to justify them. This failure may not be total and in many cases one might argue that failure is due to badly designed or ill-chosen programs rather than problems of implementation. But the study of policy implementation is not simply the study of failed policies. Policies do, after all, sometimes achieve their goals. Sometimes they produce results that, although desirable from someone's point of view, were not quite what policy-makers had in mind. Before we examine the dynamics of policy implementation, let us pin down what the term means and where it fits into the policy-making process.

What is Policy Implementation?

'To implement' means to complete, fulfil, or put into effect.[2] Implementation, therefore, is about doing, accomplishing a task, achieving a goal. *Policy implementation* is the process of transforming the goals associated with a policy into results. It follows the actual setting of goals and is necessary for their attainment. The rational model of policy-making places the implementation stage towards the end of the policy sequence. As Figure 4.1 shows, implementation is viewed as what happens between the adoption and evaluation of policy.

This appears to be very simple and straightforward. The reality, however, is a bit more complicated. To understand why, recall the formal distinction made in Chapter One between policies and programs. Policies, we said, are broad statements of goals that may assume two forms: general goals and operational goals. Programs are the measures taken to achieve those goals, to *implement* those policies. Implementation is what happens at the program stage and is chiefly the task of bureaucrats. But what if program administrators actually establish the operational goals of policy, as they often do? What happens then to our claim that implementation 'follows the actual setting of goals'? Or what about a policy where the means chosen are virtually indistinguishable from the ends? For example, a policy of deregulating a particular industry requires that various controls on firms in that industry be lifted. Here, the measures taken to implement the policy are identical to the policy itself. Or take the case of a policy that seeks to increase the representation of some targeted group(s) in the workforce of a public agency to some specified level by a particular date. Is there any useful distinction to be made between such a

FIGURE 4.1
Stages of the Policy-Making Process

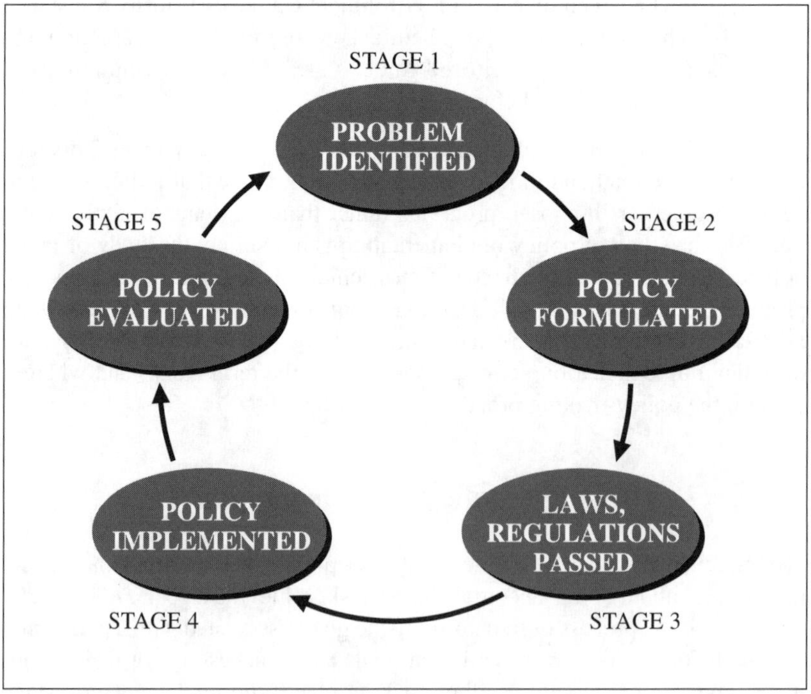

policy of affirmative action and the means selected to accomplish it? Although there is room for manoeuvre in the precise measures used to implement this goal, a policy of affirmative action means hiring more people who have certain characteristics and so is inseparable from the hiring process that implements affirmative action.

A definition of implementation as the process of transforming policy goals into results fails to capture the messy reality of policy-making. Although logic and democratic beliefs tell us that policy formation precedes and is separate from policy implementation, this neat linearity is not always characteristic of policy-making. Nevertheless, we may say that policy implementation involves such activities as the application of rules, interpretation of regulations, enforcement of laws, and delivery of services to the public. It is associated with a variety of officials who derive their authority and function from the law: bureaucrats, regulators, commissioners, inspectors, police officers, firemen, postal workers, hospital administrators, health care workers, and teachers, to mention a few.

Why Worry about Implementation?

For two main reasons implementation has long concerned those who study policy-making. One relates to democracy, the other to efficiency. The democratic concerns have a somewhat longer history than the efficiency ones, but both are prominent in contemporary work on policy implementation.

1. Democratic Dilemmas: The Politics/Administration Dichotomy

According to democratic theory, all just government rests on the consent of the people. For practical reasons the people do not rule themselves. Instead, they assign this function to elected representatives. Policy decisions—which must perforce involve choices and compromises between competing values and interests—should be made by the people's elected representatives. The reason for this is simple enough: if citizens do not like the policies of their government they can replace those who govern them at the next election. Competitive elections held every few years are the key to ensuring that government is responsive to the public will and accountable for its actions (or inaction) to the citizenry.

The role of the bureaucracy is to implement policies decided by the people's elected representatives, serving impartially whatever political party is in power. The bureaucracy is the machinery for translating political choices into action. It does not determine the *ends* of governance, but merely provides the *means* for accomplishing them.

The reality has always been rather different from the ideal. Indeed, the first modern writings on bureaucracy expressed concern over the discretionary powers of bureaucrats and their influence on policy.[3] Bureaucrats, it was believed, had a tendency to act in their own interests, which meant behaving in ways that might not be in the public's interest. Moreover, the reality of bureaucrats who had something to say about what got done and not simply how it got done confused the issue of democratic accountability and produced opportunities for arbitrary government. As power shifted from the elected politicians to the unelected bureaucrats, this would weaken popular control over government, and public authority would become increasingly arbitrary because it would no longer be firmly anchored in the democratic process.

The fear that bureaucrats could usurp powers that properly belong to elected officials is an old one. Its roots lie in the realization that unelected officials have considerable sources of power to affect policy and, moreover, that their values and interests might not be identical to those of their political masters (to say nothing of citizens). Implementation, according to this view, may subvert democracy. The likelihood of this happening increases as the discretionary powers of the bureaucracy grow.

2. Efficiency Dilemmas

Not only do we expect that the goals of policy will be accomplished, we also expect them to be achieved at a reasonable cost and without undue delay. In other words, we expect implementation to be efficient; at the same time, we expect to be disappointed. There is a long tradition of viewing public-sector bureaucracy as a form of organized inefficiency, suffering from seemingly incurable pathologies whose symptoms include waste, duplication, delay, and inflexibility. This tradition is kept alive by bureaucracy-bashing journalists and politicians, popular culture's stereotype of bureaucratic dithering and incompetence, and the regular criticisms of governments' own efficiency watchdogs, like the Auditor-General in Canada and the General Accounting Office of Congress in the United States.

The search for more efficient methods of implementation goes back to the late nineteenth century. Politics was largely about patronage, distributing the spoils of power once a candidate or party was elected to office. Administrative positions from deputy minister to customs clerk were among the spoils of power, distributed at the discretion of elected politicians. Administration by amateurs, by men and women (not many of the latter) appointed to public office because of party and individual connections rather than their expert qualifications to perform a job, became less and less acceptable as governance became increasingly complex and technical. The inefficiency generated by the patronage system of appointing and promoting those entrusted with the task of implementing policy became an issue in all the Anglo-American democracies, although their responses varied. In Great Britain, the tradition of administration by non-specialists continued in modified form. Technically trained specialists were increasingly hired, but generalists—often educated in the classics—continued to dominate the senior ranks of the public service. In the United States, the switch to a technical expertise-based system occurred earlier, although large elements of patronage appointment were retained and continue to characterize the American system. Canada opted for elements of both the American and British systems. National differences aside, the common thread has been the belief that policy implementation should be carried out by technically trained experts.

Replacing amateurs with specialists did not eliminate concern for the efficiency of implementation. Instead, concern shifted to other sources of bureaucratic inefficiency. Many of these came to be defined as problems of implementation. They include the following:

- uncertainty of goals;
- co-ordination;
- organizational culture;
- non-measurability of outputs;
- 'bureaupathic' behaviour;
- too much/too little authority in the wrong places.

Rationality and Its Illusions

In the rational model of policy-making, shown in Figure 4.2, implementation involves three hierarchical steps. First, an agent is chosen to carry out the policy. We may call this step *instrument choice*. The second step involves *communication*. Policy is communicated to the agent in the form of fairly precise instructions, leaving little doubt as to what is to be accomplished and how it should be done. Third, the agent carries out these instructions as directed by policy-makers. This is the *program delivery* stage of the policy process. These steps are shown schematically in Figure 4.2.

As Nakamura and Smallwood note,[4] this rational-hierarchical model rests on some rather fanciful assumptions about the real world of policy-making. These include the following:

- Policy formation and policy implementation are separate activities that occur sequentially.
- Policy-makers set goals and policy-implementers carry them out.
- Policy-makers are capable of formulating precise goals that are communicated to implementers in the form of unambiguous directives.
- Policy-implementers possess the technical skills and the will to carry out the instructions of policy-makers as expected of them.
- How policies are implemented is unaffected by the external environment of implementers—the organizations and groups they deal with, the political pressures on them, media scrutiny of their activities, and a host of factors over which they have no control.
- Implementation is *technical and non-political*.

To understand why these assumptions are necessarily false, we need to return to the three steps in the rational-hierarchical model: instrument choice, com-

FIGURE 4.2
The Rational-Hierarchical Model of Implementation

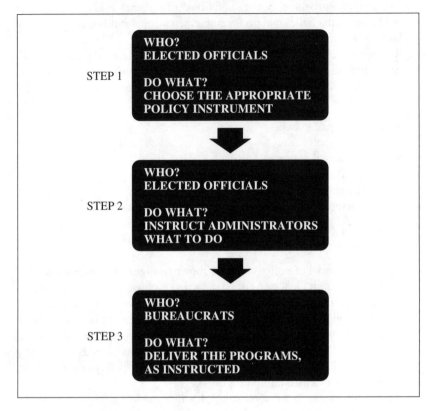

municication, and program delivery. At each of these steps the premises that underlie this model are undermined by some inconvenient realities. Let us examine them.

1. Instrument Choice

In deciding how best to accomplish a policy goal (or set of related goals), policy-makers consider a number of factors. Only some of these have to do with the cost-effectiveness or technical efficiency of the instrument chosen to implement a particular policy. Political considerations, past experience, bureaucratic preferences, and random factors like the personal values of key decision-makers may all play a role in the selection of the means to accomplish some policy goal(s). Indeed, simple efficiency considerations, such as how to maximize the achievement of value 'X' at least cost to taxpayers, are likely to be overshadowed by these rival concerns.

Does this mean that instrument choice is usually irrational? Not at all. What it means, in fact, is that there are often three sorts of rationality at play in deciding how to implement a policy. We may label these *technical* rationality, *political* rationality, and *bureaucratic* rationality.

Technical rationality. This is the classical-rational model of decision-making described earlier. In selecting the means to achieve given ends, it asks two main questions: 'What measures are most likely to achieve these goals?' and 'How can these goals be accomplished at least cost?' The key decision-makers here are technical experts: engineers, accountants, surveyors, economists, systems analysts, and so on. The decision-making process that leads to technically rational decisions is characterized by studies, interdepartmental committees, impact assessments, and perhaps commissions and task forces that solicit and distil expert opinion.

Although the two tests of technical rationality listed above may be applied to any policy decision, in practice these considerations seldom dictate instrument choice. This is particularly true in the following circumstances:

- when government is subject to many conflicting demands as to what should be done, necessitating compromises on both goals and how to attain them;
- when the goals and means of policy are not clearly distinct, so that non-technical considerations affecting the choice of goals necessarily influence the choice of means;
- when policy goals are vague, allowing administrators a large margin of discretion, and the interests with a stake in how these goals are implemented are well organized and politically active;
- when government already knows what interests it wants to listen to and what it wants to do, but is legally and/or politically required to go through the motions of respecting technical advice.

Technical rationality is most likely to determine the choice of policy instrument when policy goals are uncontroversial, intrabureaucratic rivalries are low, or the policy matter in question is relatively obscure, thus enabling experts to dominate the decision-making process.

Political rationality. A decision to locate a new government office in Windsor rather than Mississauga because of the perception that the governing party will benefit more—perhaps electing a new member or strengthening its support in a swing constituency it currently holds—is perfectly rational. It makes sense from the standpoint of the policy-makers taking the decision, if not from that of taxpayers footing the bill. We do not have to look very far for evidence that these sorts of considerations often determine the selection of policy instrument. Nor are politically motivated choices necessarily 'bad' ones.

Take the case of a government decision to award a major contract to a Montreal-based company rather than a Winnipeg-based one, even though the Winnipeg company's bid is technically superior (which actually happened in

1988, when the maintenance contract for the CF–18 fighter plane was awarded to Bombardier over Bristol Aerospace). If this choice is influenced by unity considerations—i.e., a desire to show Quebecers what they gain from their membership in Canada—or on simple distributive considerations like 'It's Quebec's turn for a piece of the public pie', who is to say that such a choice is bad? What represents a poor choice from an accountant's or engineer's per- spective may be a good one viewed in terms of that slippery concept, the 'national interest'. Or maybe not. But the point is that political considerations are often legitimate ones in instrument selection, and not simply when choos- ing goals.

Bureaucratic rationality. Why is it that bureaucrats rarely propose policy measures that do not involve government intervention of some sort? After all, it is not inconceivable that the best solution to a social or economic problem might be to lighten the hand of government, a solution that does not require a new program, budget, or staff. When the Canadian government decided to launch a program of privatizing some state-owned companies, thus downsiz- ing government, it set up a new administrative agency to oversee the project. More government to reduce government! In fairness, some bureaucratic agen- cies do not approach public policy based on the premise that a program or reg- ulatory approach is necessary to deal with a public policy problem. Financial watchdog agencies like the Office of the Auditor-General, the Treasury Board, and the Department of Finance are most likely to be sceptical about the effec- tiveness of new or existing programs. But as a general rule it is unwise to count on bureaucrats for non-bureaucratic solutions to public policy problems.

This is neither surprising nor nefarious. Bureaucrats, according to the pub- lic choice model discussed in Chapter Two, are motivated by a desire to hang on to what they have and, if possible, increase their budgets, staffs, program responsibilities, and prestige. Whether or not one accepts what public choice has to say about bureaucratic behaviour, there are other reasons for expecting bureaucrats to bring their own special rationality to policy problems, includ- ing the choice of policy instrument. This involves the *roles and rules* within which they operate. These include the following:

- shared professional norms;
- the imperatives of administrative co-ordination;
- the organizational 'culture' of a particular bureaucratic agency;
- unresolved political conflicts and imprecise directions to the imple- menting agency (the two often occur together).

We will elaborate on these factors in a later section on problems of imple- mentation.

2. Communication

In the rational model of policy-making, there is no slippage or distortion between the instructions of those who make policy and the actions of those who implement it. In other words, communication is not a problem. The reality, as anyone who has worked in a complex organization of any sort knows, is otherwise. Between the top and bottom of an organization much can happen to change or stymie the intentions of those who are at the beginning of the chain of communication. The same is true when communication between organizations is required to co-ordinate policy implementation.

There are several reasons why communication is a problem. First, lawmakers don't always know what they want, and consequently their instructions sometimes are imprecise or even conflicting. The goals established by policymakers are often extremely vague, relying on words whose meanings are ambiguous and open to interpretation. For example, the Bank of Canada Act includes the following statement of the Bank's goals:

> . . . to regulate credit and currency in the best interests of the nation, to control and protect the external value of the national monetary unit and to mitigate by its influence fluctuations in the general level of production, trade, prices and employment, so far as may be possible within the scope of monetary action, and generally to promote the economic and financial welfare of Canada.[5]

Politicians typically establish the *general* goals of an agency or program, leaving the *operational* goals to be determined by those entrusted with the implementation of policy. The distinction between general and operational goals is explained by James Q. Wilson:

> By goal I mean an image of a desired future state of affairs. If that image can be compared unambiguously to an actual state of affairs, it is an operational goal. If it cannot be so compared, and thus we cannot make verifiable statements about whether the goal has been attained, it is a general goal.[6]

A law that says 'Fifty per cent of television programming during the hours of 7:00 p.m. to 11:00 p.m. will be Canadian', and defines what constitutes Canadian programming, would set down operational goals for those who implement broadcasting policy. But the Broadcasting Act is not so precise, declaring instead that the Canadian Radio-television and Telecommunications Commission (CRTC) should regulate broadcasters so as to 'safeguard, enrich and strengthen the cultural, political, social and economic fabric of Canada'.[7] In other words, policy-makers have established very general goals, the operational ones being left up to those who implement the law.

This is usually the case, but such a lack of precision creates room for confusion, misunderstanding, and simple disagreement between politicians and administrators. Various formal and informal mechanisms exist to ensure that what elected officials intend is what administrators do, but they seldom eliminate ambiguity.

Communication problems are also created by differences in norms, perspectives, and jargon. Administrators do not all speak the same language. An agency staffed by accountants is likely to define the problems of social assistance programs differently from one comprised of social workers. Differences in professional norms and jargon can impede communication between agencies, sometimes creating confusion and misunderstanding and other times producing impenetrable barriers to co-operation because of widely divergent professional perspectives. A good example of this is provided by Leslie Pal in his study of Canada's unemployment insurance (UI) program. Pal shows that those who actually administered this program during its first few decades viewed it as essentially an insurance program that should be financed on an actuarially sound basis. Policy-makers associated with other agencies, like the Department of Labour, frequently proposed extensions and modifications of UI that would have compromised what Pal calls the 'actuarial ideology' of UI officials, generating conflict over the goals and implementation of the program.[8]

Communication problems are related to those of co-ordination within and between organizations. They also include problems of individual motivation, informal relations and networks within organizations, and what we might call the 'permeability' of organizations. By this we mean that the behaviour of those within organizations is often affected by exchanges between them and individuals/groups outside their organization. For example, some administrative agencies are in daily contact with the private-sector interests whose actions they regulate. In such circumstances it is quite normal, and not at all surprising, that a clientelistic relationship develops between regulators and regulated—a relationship characterized by close and formalized interaction, dependence of administrators on information provided by the regulated interests, and shared outlooks. These communications may explain more about the behaviour of program implementers than knowledge of the stated goals of the program or the formal lines of authority within the program's bureaucracy.

3. Delivery

At the third step of the rational-hierarchical model of implementation, administrators deliver the goods. They issue the cheques; inspect the premises, product, process, or files; decide who is eligible and who is not; process the applications; and so on. In short, they carry out the policy. But as in the case of the other two stages of the implementation process, things are not so simple. Program delivery is affected by a number of factors, one of the chief ones being the problem of co-ordination.

Program delivery typically requires the involvement of a large number of participants whose preferences have to be taken into account, and many decisions and agreements that must be reached before the 'output' is produced. Jeffrey Pressman and Aaron Wildavsky demonstrate that even an apparently straightforward program, where the goals are agreed upon and money has been allotted, can experience a long and troublesome delivery because of what they call the *complexity of joint action*.[9]

Virtually all programs depend on some level of joint action. In other words, the efforts of some number of people must be co-ordinated to accomplish program objectives. What is not often appreciated, Pressman and Wildavsky argue,

> . . . [is] the number of steps involved, the number of participants whose preferences have to be taken into account, the number of separate decisions that are part of what we think of as a simple one. Least of all do we appreciate the geometric growth of interdependencies over time where each negotiation involves a number of participants with decisions to make, whose implications ramify over time.[10]

They postulate that as the number of separate decisions that must be taken increases, the likelihood of successful implementation (whatever 'successful' might mean) decreases.

If nothing else, the complexities of joint action tend to produce delay. This is because the preferences of different organizations whose efforts must be co-ordinated, or even of different individuals within an agency, are unlikely to be identical. Nor is their level of interest in a program likely to be the same. What may be a burning priority for one agency may be a peripheral concern for another whose co-operation is necessary for program delivery. Moreover, the resources they are able or willing to devote to the program in question are unlikely to be equal.

Compromise is the first cousin of delay. 'Everyone wants coordination', note Pressman and Wildavsky, 'on his own terms.'[11] The reality, of course, is that co-ordination will carry a price in terms of the compromises that must be made to bridge the varying agendas, timeliness, and resources of those whose joint efforts are required at the program delivery stage. What results may seem more or less what policy-makers and societal stakeholders had in mind when the program was first launched. Or it may not. But what is certain is that the requirement of joint action introduces additional uncertainties into policy implementation, beyond those already discussed.

The Problems of Implementation

In the early summer of 1952, before the heat of the campaign, US President Harry S. Truman used to contemplate the problems of General Dwight D. Eisenhower if he were to win the forthcoming election. 'He'll sit here', Truman would remark (tapping his desk for emphasis), 'and he'll say, Do this! Do that! And nothing will happen. Poor Ike—it won't be a bit like the Army. He'll find it very frustrating.'[12]

We have touched on several features of implementation that may produce 'slippage' between what lawmakers decide and what ultimately happens. In this section we will elaborate on several of these and examine some additional problems of implementation. The focus here and throughout this chapter on the problematic characteristics of implementation should not be interpreted to mean that clear interactions never exist and that they are never translated into straightforward action. Instead, our goal is to demonstrate that what are often labelled implementation problems—and therefore mistakenly assumed to be problems of bureaucracy, *per se*—are often governance problems for which there are no administrative 'quick fixes'.[13]

1. Attitudes and Beliefs of Administrators

Administrators are not bloodless ciphers. They often have strongly held ideas about what they should be doing, how they should be doing it, and what is in the 'public interest'—or at least that segment of the public with which they deal. They may have served under a particular political party for years and grown comfortable with the policies implemented under its direction. What happens if their ideas are out of sync with what elected officials expect them to do?

This occasionally happens. But it happens much less often than one might suspect. While it is tempting to imagine that attitudes determine behaviour, psychologists have not found much evidence for this claim. Situational factors often appear to be more important. 'Our behaviour toward an object', observed James Q. Wilson, 'will be influenced not only by our evaluation of it but by the rewards and penalties associated with alternative courses of action.'[14] The tug of personal beliefs can be rather weak alongside these situational imperatives.

This is not to say that attitudes and beliefs are irrelevant. The influence of administrators' values on their behaviour appears to be greatest when the formal rules defining their roles and how their job should be done are weakly defined. In these circumstances the norms developed as a result of specialized training and membership in a professional group may be very significant determinants of behaviour. Likewise, the ideological predilections of administrators are allowed greater scope when roles and rules are weakly defined. Even so, empirical studies suggest that the political views of bureaucrats are more likely to correspond to the positions they occupy within the bureaucracy—the agency they are affiliated to and their role within it—than by their social background. An American study found that the social origins of senior-level bureaucrats explained only about 5 per cent of the variation in their opinions, while their agency affiliation—a situational factor—explained far more.[15]

There remains the possibility that the behaviour of those entrusted with the task of implementing policy will be influenced by what might be called the *bureaucratic personality*. The idea of the bureaucratic personality was developed by sociologist Robert K. Merton.[16] He argued that administrators acquire certain dispositions because of the nature of work in a bureaucratic organization. If they appear to be cautious, inflexible, rulebound, and conformist it is because these personality traits are reinforced by the reward/punishment systems of bureaucracies. Through a process of 'goal displacement', Merton argues, administrators will come to value means above ends. The bureaucratic personality is more preoccupied with behaving according to the rules than with achieving the goals that are supposed to be the organization's *raison d'être*.

2. Turf and Autonomy

Human beings are territorial animals. They are reluctant to give up that which they consider to be theirs, whether that is a bit of land, their office and status at work, or the affection or respect of those around them. They tend to be protective of their turf, and some are even rather imperialistic in craving that of others.

Bureaucrats are human beings, and exhibit these same territorial qualities. One of the most common assertions about bureaucrats and their agencies is that they are constantly struggling to capture larger budgets, bigger staff, and more prestige. Not only are they territorial, so the argument goes, they are driven by expansionist tendencies. This makes for a rather neat behaviourial generalization, satisfying both those who like their social science simple and others (sometimes the same people) who are ideologically disposed against bureaucracy and 'big government'. Unfortunately, the facts do not support this claim. Various studies have shown that agencies and their bureaucratic chiefs often resist the imposition of new tasks that would increase their resources, and in some cases they even part with a division or program without regret.[17] Does this mean that *homo bureaucratus* is less concerned with defending his or her turf than are other human beings?

Not at all. Philip Selznick argues that what organizations and those within them really seek is autonomy. What Selznick means by autonomy is a 'condition of independence sufficient to permit a group to work out and maintain a distinctive identity'.[18] In other words, bureaucrats do not crave turf *per se*, but the resources and conditions that enable them to protect what they see as their domain and their agency's mission (identity). This is a more sophisticated interpretation of the 'territorial behaviour' of bureaucratic agencies that allows us to make sense of those occasions—admittedly infrequent—when an agency accepts a budget cut or program loss without protest.

Concern with protecting turf and autonomy creates problems from the standpoint of co-ordinating the work of different agencies. Co-ordination, by its very nature, involves some loss of autonomy for the involved parties. When program implementation requires that the efforts of different agencies, and sometimes different levels of government, be co-ordinated, one may expect to observe some amount of what Merton called 'goal displacement'. The *policy* goals associated with the program may have to compete with the *organizational* goals of those involved in its implementation.

3. Interests

In a classic study of policy implementation, Philip Selznick argued that bureau-cratic agencies given a large margin of discretion in carrying out policy will be vulnerable to capture by interest groups. The agency's conception of its role and the way it administers the law are likely to be strongly influenced by pressures coming from the key external stakeholders affected by the agency's action. Selznick called this *co-optation*. Others who have focused on regulatory agen-cies observed a similar phenomenon: agencies originally established to serve the public interest end up as the compliant tools of the private interests they were supposed to regulate.[19] The lesson seemed clear: beware the influence of inter-est groups at the implementation stage of the policy process.

The problem of external stakeholders influencing the behaviour of an agency is greatest in the case of *client* agencies, such as the National Transportation Agency, which, among other things, approves the rates that may be charged and the routes served by the handful of airlines in Canada. The provincial energy boards that must approve the prices charged by local natural gas monopolies represent another example of client agencies. Without going so far as to say that agencies like these become 'captured' by the interests they regulate, it is reasonable to expect that the information provided by the regu-lated interests will have a significant impact on the decisions of the regulator. The ability of an agency independently to verify the information it thus receives, and its willingness to do so, will vary.

As Wilson notes, client relationships between bureaucratic agencies and societal interests are not limited to the business sector. The National Research Council, for example, is a grants agency whose clientele is mainly professors interested in research in the natural and applied sciences. The Canada Council and its provincial counterparts have clientelist relationships with groups in the arts community. It comes as no surprise to find that the views of these agen-cies generally reflect those of the clienteles who depend on the programs they administer.

Other agencies may also be significantly affected by external stakeholders. The policy community of which an agency is the focal point will often include a number of interest groups, representing a diverse and perhaps contradictory range of demands. This may help to liberate the agency from the clutches of any particular interests, or it may simply ensure that whatever the agency does will be criticized by somebody. What is certain is that the presence of highly organized external stakeholders is a factor that will affect the behaviour of agencies responsible for policy implementation.

4. Culture: Organizational and Political

'Every organization has a culture', argues Wilson, '. . . a persistent, patterned way of thinking about the central tasks of and human relationships within an organization.'[20] Philip Selznick called this the 'distinctive competence of an organization'.[21] An agency's culture—or cultures, because it is not unusual for more than one distinct culture to exist within an organization—is produced by a number of factors. These include the professional and ideological norms of its members, the techniques and practices commonly used in performing the organization's tasks, and the situational imperatives facing an organization. The vaguer the stated goals of a government organization, and therefore the more discretionary power it has, the greater will be the influence of organizational culture on how an agency's members define their roles and implement policy.

A good example of this may be seen in the case of provincial human rights commissions. Their mandate typically is quite vague. It involves hearing complaints of actions alleged to violate the province's human rights code and issuing orders for remedial action. Those who work for such agencies often have backgrounds in law, social work, and other social sciences. Their ideological dispositions, one may safely say, tend to be left of centre.

Given the background and leanings of those who staff them and the fairly wide latitude they enjoy in determining how they will carry out their vaguely defined tasks, it comes as no surprise when a human rights commission acts as an outspoken advocate for the rights of women, visible minorities, Aboriginal Canadians, and the handicapped. One would expect such an agency to be critical of government policies and social practices, and of institutions accused of being discriminatory. This is not to say that the culture of the agency, the dominant norms of those within it, determine agency behaviour in a predictable way. In this particular case, for example, the structural imperatives of a human rights commission—the legislation establishing it and its institutional role as a body to hear and adjudicate instances of alleged discrimination—create a web of expectations among those within it and in the eyes of external stakeholders like the media, rights-oriented interest groups, legislators, police forces, and so on. Thus, the norms shared by an agency's personnel, and often the predispositions of its chief administrator(s), can have a crucial impact on how policy is implemented.

Two concrete examples will illustrate this point. Les Pal describes how the orientation of the Department of Secretary of State (SOS) was strongly influenced by those who staffed key positions during the 1960s and 1970s. Many of those who held leadership positions, particularly in its Citizenship Branch, had been active in the Company of Young Canadians, a government-sponsored agency for social activism that was shut down only years after its creation because of what government interpreted as excessive radicalism. Company of Young Canadians 'alumni' carried into SOS a commitment to the activist agenda of the 1960s and a desire to transform the department into the vehicle for improving the status and political participation of disadvantaged groups. As Sandra Gwyn observes of a couple of these sixties radicals turned bureaucrats, '[they] turned the Citizenship [branch] into a flamboyant, free-spending *animateur sociale* (*sic*). Traditional, father-knows-best groups were upstaged. Instead, massive grants went out to militant native groups, tenants' associations and other putative aliens of the 1970s.'[22] In the words of one of these sixties radicals turned SOS administrator, the Citizenship Branch was 'the only part of government that seemed human'.[23]

The point is this: there was nothing inevitable about the social activism approach that characterized this agency during the late sixties and early seventies. The sense of mission that imbued SOS, in particular its Citizenship Branch, came largely from the administrators themselves. They carried into SOS a commitment to 'social action', what Pal describes as the deliberate mobilization of social sentiment in desired directions.[24] But desired by whom, and for what purposes? These matters were determined by the dominant culture of SOS's Citizenship Branch in those heady days.

A final example of how organizational culture affects policy implementation involves the Department of Finance, which is widely acknowledged to be the most influential agency within the federal bureaucracy, a status it has long enjoyed. As such, it attracts the 'best and the brightest', ambitious civil servants who recognize that Finance is where the action is. 'The department', writes Alan Freeman, 'has developed a corporate culture unparalleled in government. Staff members routinely work 12 hour days, seven days a week, to prepare a budget or develop [a policy like] the goods and services tax.'[25] A former high-ranking official in Finance compares the agency to a monastic order, committed to fiscal responsibility and debt reduction, and motivated by the belief that the Finance point of view is the one that should prevail in government policy-making.

How does this affect implementation? Finance administers virtually nothing, having been shorn of its program responsibilities in the 1960s when the Treasury Board became a separate agency. Nevertheless, Finance is able to influence policy implementation throughout government because of its key role in budget-making and its dominant status—rivalled only by the Bank of Canada—in economic policy-making. In the words of one federal economist, 'Finance wants to monopolize economic thinking in government. There is just no debate about alternatives.'[26] The organizational culture that nurtures this jealous hoarding of economic power apparently has resulted in struggles between Finance and other agencies, such as Statistics Canada, that have wanted to carry out economic analysis. Some Ottawa insiders argue that the 1992 decision to eliminate the Economic Council of Canada, Finance's chief rival in analysing economic trends and making policy recommendations, was influenced by Finance's desire to eliminate a competitor whose views were not always in tune with its own.[27] These claims suggest that Finance, like other agencies, is motivated by territorialism. But they also illustrate the impact that organizational culture can have on the behaviour of an agency.

5. Measuring Success

How do we know when a program works? How can we be sure that the results achieved by program administrators have been accomplished as efficiently as possible? What is the litmus test (or tests) of success in the public sector? These questions are crucial, because without some benchmarks for evaluating performance, policy implementation may be misdirected, counter-productive, or wasteful—or all of these at once!

Measuring success—in accomplishing goals and in doing so in an efficient manner—is no simple task. It is, however, easier in the private sector than in the public sector. The bottom lines that typically define organizational success in the private sector—profits, market share, share value, credit-rating, and the like—are much more elusive in the public sector. Nevertheless, one thing is clear: *when public and private organizations perform similar tasks, private ones generally perform them more efficiently*. There is an enormous amount of empirical research in support of this generalization.[28] Why does this difference exist? James Wilson identifies three main reasons:

1. *Situational ambiguity*. Public officials are less able than their private counterparts to define an efficient course of action. This is because they are often expected to achieve multiple goals with little or no guidance—or worse, in an environment of conflicting signals—about how to manage the trade-offs between these goals. For example, what is the goal of Canada Post? If you answered 'Delivering the mail as promptly and efficiently as possible', you were only partly right. Canada Post is also expected to operate in Canada's two official languages, serve customers in sparsely populated rural areas, carry out door-to-door delivery in residential districts built before the early 1980s, and implement employment equity policies. These are goals that do not burden Purolator or Federal Express.

2. *Incentives*. Public officials tend to be less motivated to identify an efficient course of action. This is not because they are lazier or less intelligent than their private-sector counterparts. Instead, the difference derives from the fact that private-sector managers will often profit personally from improving the efficiency of their organization, whereas these sorts of pay-offs are much less common and less considerable in the public sector.

3. *Authority*. Even if a public-sector agency is staffed by efficiency zealots whose greatest fulfilment comes from finding ways to do more with less, they will often lack the authority to carry out their schemes for improving efficiency. Their ability to hire and fire and determine compensation levels for employees is far less than that of their private-sector counterparts. Government agencies usually depend entirely on the budgets allocated to them by the legislature and do not have the freedom to impose user fees for their services or to raise money in ways not authorized by elected politicians. Measures like redesigning program delivery, closing or relocating regional offices, or altering the internal structure of the agency cannot be undertaken without the approval of other parts of government. And even when this approval is granted, the whole process is likely to take longer than in the private sector.

'Evaluation' is the term used for the measurement of an agency's performance. It is an important part of policy implementation. Evaluation is the stage that enables us to know how well we are accomplishing what we set out to do, and it is a function that has been institutionalized throughout government. Some agencies are specialized evaluation watchdogs with responsibility over a specific policy field (e.g., the Commissioner of Official Languages, who is responsible for monitoring the implementation of federal bilingualism policies) or an aspect of policy-making (e.g., the Auditor-General, who is responsible for ensuring that public money is spent as authorized and that taxpayers receive 'value for money'). Virtually all government departments, and many smaller agencies like the Canadian International Development Agency, have in-house program evaluation bureaus. Program evaluation is part of the budgetary process that requires all departments and agencies to justify their spending requests to the Treasury Board in terms of how their programs met the policy goals established by Cabinet. Evaluation before policy implementation is also legally required under the 1985 Canadian Environmental Protection Act, to determine whether a government project will have adverse environmental consequences. This is a form of evaluation known as impact assessment. Finally, evaluation of existing programs and assessment of proposed ones are frequently done by task forces, royal commissions, parliamentary committees, and other permanent or temporary government bodies.

Quantity does not, of course, mean quality. The fact that evaluation, pre- and post-implementation, is a permanent and pervasive feature of modern policy-making does not mean that governments have a much clearer idea of how well they are meeting their objectives than in the days before formal evaluation. One reason for this was identified by the federal Task Force on Program Review (1985). Its final report noted that most program evaluations are carried out by the implementers themselves, raising serious questions about the objectivity of such studies. Moreover, the possibility that program evaluation results will be disclosed under the Access to Information Act is another factor that, according to the Task Force, reduces the frankness of many evaluations.[29]

A second reason why evaluation may fail to produce accurate and useful measures of performance involves the nebulous character of many public policy goals. The objectives of government programs often involve such things as promoting Canadian culture, protecting the environment, improving the quality of life for some group or community, or promoting national unity. While it is possible to measure all of these things, it often requires considerable ingenuity and the final result is unlikely to convince everyone. Take, for example, an environmental program that establishes a wilderness park in an area of harvestable timber. The economic costs, as these are conventionally calculated, are easily determined. They involve the dollar value of the timber that could have been harvested and sold if the wilderness protection program had not been implemented. On the other hand, the benefits of this program are rather indeterminate. Economists only feel comfortable with values that can be expressed in terms of dollars. The best measure of satisfaction, they argue, is the price users would be willing to pay for a good or service. Thus, economists would probably measure the value of the benefits from wilderness protection by estimating what visitors to the park would be willing to pay if this 'good' were sold on a competitive market. If, as seems likely, the opportunity cost of not logging the area far exceeds the value of benefits derived by future users of the wilderness area, does that mean the program is inefficient?

Environmentalists would argue, of course, that such things as wilderness and species diversity have intrinsic value that cannot be reduced to dollars. Animal rights activists would make a similar case, arguing that conventional economics takes no account of the rights of non-human species except to calculate their consumption value for man. Many policy analysts—not necessarily environmentalists or animal rights activists—would object to the idea that different policies, intended to achieve different goals, can be rendered commensurable by expressing all impacts in dollar terms. This approach, they would argue, is biased in favour of programs that produce easily measurable benefits, and tends to undervalue policies whose measurement is more elusive.

A third factor that limits the usefulness of performance measurement involves politics. Who has an interest in hard numbers on how well programs are meeting their objectives and how efficiently they are being implemented? Who, on the other hand, has an interest in fuzziness, ambiguity, and soft data that 'prove' the worth of a program? The stakeholders with an interest in hard measures include taxpayers, various state agencies whose *raison d'être* is efficiency in government, such as the Office of the Comptroller General and the Auditor-General, and perhaps the clientele of the program in question. The stakeholders with an interest in soft measures include the departments and agencies that implement programs, the responsible Cabinet minister, and the government of the day, who probably have little if anything to gain but something more to lose from exposure of ineffective or wasteful programs, and perhaps the program's clientele, who may be comfortable with a program that is run inefficiently from the general taxpayer's point of view or that serves goals that are not exactly those lawmakers expected the agency to promote. The bottom line is this: program evaluation tends to take place on the periphery of the policy-making process, without powerful supportive constituencies among political and bureaucratic élites.

PART II

POLICY FIELDS

Chapter Five

Macroeconomic Policy

Introduction

Economics is often called the 'dismal science'. But dismal or not—and no doubt many survivors of introductory economics courses will agree that the description is appropriate—economics touches all of us in profound ways. Economics is about how wealth is generated and distributed. It deals with jobs, consumption, savings, investment, and all manner of transactions where services and goods are exchanged for money or for other services and goods. Most of us are or will be workers, consumers, savers (hard to believe, perhaps, for students who face the prospect of repaying thousands of dollars of debt after graduation!), and investors, and so the concerns and categories of economics matter to us in very personal ways. Likewise, what governments do— or neglect to do—to protect and promote economic activity matters to us all. The dismal character of economic science should never be allowed to blind us to this truth.

Probably all of the readers of this book have heard the terms 'budget deficit', 'Bank of Canada rate', 'money supply', 'trade surplus/deficit', and 'the business cycle'. Each of these refers to an aspect of the economy as a whole, or to government action intended to influence the overall state of the economy. They are part of the lexicon of macroeconomics and macroeconomic policy. Macroeconomics deals with the behaviour of the entire economy, and thus with large aggregate phenomena like employment, investment, inflation, growth, and trade. The distinction between macroeconomics and microeconomics is one of emphasis. Microeconomics focuses on components of the overall economy, such as markets, industries, firms, and consumers. Likewise, the distinction between macroeconomic policy and sectoral economic policy is not sharp and absolute, although there are important differences in terms of the policy instruments that governments employ. Macroeconomic policy is sometimes referred to as economic stabilization policy, a description that conveys the expectations that have developed for the state's role in maintaining acceptable levels of growth and employment.

Changing Paradigms in Macroeconomic Policy-Making

1. The Keynesian Consensus

Modern macroeconomics usually is dated from the publication of John Maynard Keynes's *General Theory of Employment, Interest and Money* (1936). Prior to Keynes the dominant view in economics was that supply created its own demand. This meant that in the absence of uncompetitive practices on the part of businesses, labour, or government, an economy would tend towards equilibrium (demand matches supply) and full employment. This view, known as classical economics, was associated with *laissez-faire* economic policies. It did not deny the existence of cyclical fluctuations in economic activity, but maintained that deviations from equilibrium were temporary and self-correcting. It therefore followed that government interference, no matter how well intentioned, would inevitably aggravate economic disruptions by interfering with the natural harmony of the price mechanism and markets.

Keynes argued that equilibrium might be reached at points other than full employment and focused on aggregate demand as the chief determinant of the level of economic activity. In calling into question the classical assumption of the inherent stability of a free market economy—arguing instead that the sum of consumer, business, and government demand might be insufficient to maintain full employment—Keynes supported government measures intended to increase the level of aggregate demand. The main tools of demand management that he suggested were measures to encourage private expenditure and government spending on public works.[1] 'Keynesianism' quickly came to be the general label for government policies intended to reduce the severity and duration of downturns in the business cycle.

The business cycle that concerned Keynes was that which economists call the intermediate cycle, determined by the rate of capital investment (we will have more to say about business cycles later in this section). Keynes argued that the level of capital investment, upon which growth and full employment depended, was determined by the marginal efficiency of capital. When the rate of return on new capital investment weakened, government could play a compensatory role either through investment in public works or through taxation policies that made private capital investment more attractive than it would otherwise have been (i.e., policies like investment tax credits and the removal or reduction of taxes on the purchase of new machinery or building materials, thus making new capital investment less costly). These stabilization measures came to be called *discretionary*, being government responses to observed and anticipated trends in economic activity. In addition, governments adopted *automatic stabilizers* that were intended to attenuate the fluctuations in the business cycle. Among the most significant of these were the income maintenance programs that comprised the planks of the emerging welfare state. To cite a Canadian example, it appears that the impetus behind the universal family allowance payment (introduced in 1945) was mainly the Keynesian economists in the federal bureaucracy who viewed this policy as a means of maintaining a high level of purchasing power in the economy.[2] Social policy could be harnessed for purposes of economic management, though it would be a distortion to attribute the emergence of the welfare state to the prior conversion of governments to Keynesian economic policies.

The theories and policies that came to be described as Keynesian dominated in the economics profession and among state élites in capitalist societies until roughly the early 1970s. Indeed, Milton Friedman, who would become associated with the monetarist 'alternative' to Keynesian policies, acknowledged this consensus when in 1965 he observed, 'We are all Keynesians now.'[3] The basis for this consensus was the apparent success of these policies. The annual rate of real economic growth for member countries of the Organization for Economic Co-operation and Development (OECD) averaged over 5 per cent between 1950 and 1970. Unemployment and inflation rates both averaged in the 2–3 per cent range. The trade-off between employment and inflation expressed in the Phillips Curve—developed by the British economist A.W. Phillips in the late 1950s—was widely accepted. Evidence from the real world at least did not contradict the idea that government action to stimulate growth and therefore employment would also result in upward pressure on prices due to the increased demand.

The fragmentation of the Keynesian consensus was largely, but not exclusively, due to evidence of the increasing unmanageability of capitalist economies. Between 1974 and 1983 the rate of annual growth in real GNP for OECD countries was 2.1 per cent, inflation averaged 9.7 per cent, and unemployment about 6 per cent.[4] The phenomenon of stagflation—low or no real economic growth accompanied by high levels of inflation—called into question the conventional wisdom regarding government's ability to manage the economy through taxation and public spending (i.e., fiscal policy). This economic disorder provided the impetus for the development of alternative theoretical models in macroeconomics, the most important of which have been monetarism and neoclassical economics. It is likely, however, that both the 'success' and subsequent 'failure' of Keynesian policies have been exaggerated. An important part of the explanation for both the general buoyancy of capitalist economies until the early 1970s and the comparatively unstable economic conditions that seem to have existed since then lies in changes in the conditions for economic growth, what we will call *structural changes*. These changes have not passed unnoticed by some economists, although both the mainstream of that profession and governments appear oblivious to them.

The Keynesian paradigm is interventionist. It provides a basis in economic theory for the *positive state*, a state dedicated to the maintenance of high levels of employment and economic growth. To stabilize economic activity, two conditions are necessary. First, the capacity to identify economic trends, particularly business investment and consumer expenditure, must exist before their consequences are experienced as either low growth and increased unemployment or excess demand and inflation. Second, if a shortage in effective demand is acknowledged to be the cause of economic recession and unemployment, governments must be willing to use demand policies (i.e., fiscal policies) to remedy market failure. Conversely, tax increases or the withdrawal of some deductions enjoyed by business can be used to cool off an overheated economy. Thus, the state is viewed as potentially part of the solution to the periodic failure of the market to produce adequate business investment and full employment. The main challengers to Keynesian economics, however, argue that the state is part of the problem.

2. The Monetarist and New Classical Challenges

It is widely accepted that the Keynesian consensus started to come unravelled in a major way around 1970. The causes of this were to be found in both the real world of economic phenomena and within the economics profession itself. As unemployment and inflation reached levels unprecedented in the postwar period and as economic growth slowed in several of the main capitalist economies, the effectiveness of the discretionary fiscal policies that comprised the key weapons in the Keynesian arsenal came increasingly to be questioned. The fragmentation of the Keynesian consensus provided the intellectual opportunity for challenges to the demand management model, and also created receptive conditions in some political systems for alternative economic policies. At the same time, the discipline of economics was developing in directions that stressed technique and the logical coherence of theory at the expense both of the reality of assumptions about economic behaviour and of policy relevance. The fact that this trend in the discipline has come under frequent criticism by some distinguished economists, including Nobel laureates Wassily Leontief and James Tobin, has not slowed its advance. Leontief's comments are typical: 'Page after page of professional economic journals are filled with mathematical formulas leading the reader from sets of more or less plausible, but entirely arbitrary, assumptions to precisely stated but irrelevant conclusions.'[5]

Of the two main challenges to Keynesianism, monetarism has certainly had the greatest influence on economic policy. Monetarist economic policies were adopted in both the United States and the United Kingdom at the end of the 1970s. Partly because of its association with the Thatcher government in the UK and with the anti-interventionist political views of its main economics advocate, Milton Friedman, the term 'monetarism' has acquired connotations of political conservatism. Before we consider whether this is a fair ideological characterization of the policy prescriptions that follow from the monetarist model, it is necessary to understand what monetarism says about the determinants of economic activity. This is not a simple matter. Monetarism is frequently misunderstood as the use of credit policy (i.e., interest rates) to influence the level of demand and, therefore, of economic growth and inflation. In fact, the major monetarist economists, such as Friedman and Karl Brunner, argue *against* the use of monetary policy to counter short-term fluctuations in economic activity.[6]

Monetarism has a fundamental principle from which all else follows. It is that the money supply (currency and deposits against which cheques can be written) and changes in the money supply determine the level of real economic activity. In Friedman's words, 'Erratic monetary growth almost always produces erratic economic growth.'[7] Based on historical studies of the American economy, Friedman concluded that periods of economic growth and inflation were associated with expansion of the money supply, while decreases in the stock of money were associated with economic recession and, occasionally, a fall in real prices. Friedman and other monetarists generally dismiss the influence of fiscal policy, taxation, and government spending on real economic activity, though they argue that these policies are important determinants of the size of government (too big) and its role in the economy (too interventionist). But they also argue against the deliberate manipulation of the money supply as a means of stabilizing the economy because the real effects of changes in the money supply are experienced only after a time lag. Friedman, using evidence from the American economy, estimates this lag at anywhere from six months to two years. Thus, by the time a government-induced increase in the money supply has its intended effect, the economic conditions that prompted the policy are likely to have changed. What was intended to be stabilizing may in fact have destabilizing consequences.

What, then, do monetarists propose as an appropriate macroeconomic policy? Monetarists argue that the money supply should be increased at a gradual and constant rate, perhaps 3–4 per cent annually. This policy prescription, referred to as the monetary rule, is based on the belief in the inherent stability of the private sector, a belief that has as a corollary the view that the main cause of adverse economic conditions is discretionary government policy. Monetarists advocate a predictable institutional framework for economic activity. The reasoning behind such a framework—what Brunner calls a 'policy regime'—is that it is expected to minimize the effort that private agents (consumers, businesses, and investors) must make in acquiring information about the probable consequences of their behaviour. If the future is predictable, this reduces the likelihood of the economy being shocked by misperceptions or the unexpected. Monetarists argue that misperceptions are the chief consequence of discretionary policy. An emphasis on the continuity of economic policy, as expressed in the monetary rule, is fundamentally at odds with the Keynesian argument that government policy should change as often as is required to compensate for significant fluctuations in the level of business investment and aggregate demand. It is, however, very similar to the emphasis on policy 'rules' advocated by the *new classical economics*.

The new classical economics is sometimes, and misleadingly, referred to as the 'rational expectations' school. It is distinguished by two main microeconomic assumptions that have important consequences for its analysis of the overall economy and, therefore, the policies it advocates. These assumptions are: (1) consumers, workers, firms, and businesses act from a position of perfect knowledge about the consequences of their behaviour and they attempt to maximize their utility (the rational expectations assumption); and (2) markets clear rapidly (the equilibrium assumption). The rational expectations assumption, while often derided as obviously unrealistic, is acknowledged by many leading neo-Keynesian and monetarist economists to be a useful hypothesis for model-building and possibly even the most accurate behavioural assumption for the long run.[8] The assumption that markets clear rapidly, and that therefore the economy is constantly in a moving equilibrium, is the main point of contention between the new classical economics and its critics.

Stated very simply the problem is this. If markets clear (that is, supply and demand quickly match) and the economy is in equilibrium, how is one to explain a persistently high unemployment rate of, say, 10 per cent? The new classical economics manages this by arguing that the 'natural rate' of unemployment has increased as a result of state benefits that are generous enough to cause many workers to choose to be unemployed (monetarists agree with this proposition that the level of 'voluntary' unemployment has increased significantly). A second part of this model's explanation of unemployment argues that workers may temporarily price themselves out of jobs by miscalculating the equilibrium wage. This argument is associated with Robert Lucas, one of the major figures in new classical economics. It stresses imperfect information and uncertainty as the basis of workers' misperceptions about the appropriate price for their labour. According to the new classical model these misperceptions will not persist, as workers quickly adjust their expectations to the new equilibrium wage. Discretionary economic policy is identified as one of the major sources of uncertainty in the economy and is opposed by new classical economists as destabilizing (exactly opposite to the role that Keynesians attribute to it).

If it sounds as though the new classical economics explains unemployment by explaining it away—by denying the existence (or persistence) of involuntary unemployment—that is indeed a correct conclusion. Asked whether he sincerely believed that the unemployment of the Great Depression could be explained as a problem of worker misperceptions, Robert Lucas responded:

If you look back at the 1929 to 1933 episode, there were a lot of decisions made that, after the fact, people wished they had not made; there were a lot of jobs people quit that they wished they had hung on to; there were job offers that people turned down because they thought the wage offer was crappy. Then three months later they wished they had grabbed [those jobs]. . . . People are making this kind of mistake all the time.[9]

The new classical economics denies the existence of persisting rigidities in wages and prices that in the Keynesian model constitute the basis for claims that the economy may be in persistent disequilibrium (demand and supply do not match) and that unemployment may be above the 'natural' rate.

3. Rules versus Discretion

From the standpoint of what they have to say about government's appropriate relationship to the economy, monetarist and new classical economists have much in common. Their emphasis is on predictable government behaviour. This requires the avoidance of discretionary policies intended to influence the level of investment and demand on the grounds that these policies are in fact destabilizing (because of the uncertainty they provoke) or ineffective. Neither monetarism nor the new classical economics advocates complete *laissez-faire* in macroeconomic policy. Instead, they argue for policy rules, like Friedman's monetary rule, which are intended 'to lower the burden of the information problem imposed by discretionary policy-making on agents.'[10] While not denying that cyclical fluctuations in economic activity occur, both monetarism and new classical economics maintain that the private sector is inherently stable and that economies tend towards full employment. They differ, however, to the extent that monetarists argue that it may take some time, even years, before prices and wages adjust to market-clearing levels. Finally, both schools have no difficulty with describing current levels of unemployment as near full employment. This is because of the significance they attribute to state benefits in increasing the level of voluntary unemployment.

The Keynesian position is very different. Economists like James Tobin, Franco Modegliani, and Alan Blinder attribute the prosperity and relative economic stability of the 1950s and 1960s to the use of active (discretionary) fiscal and monetary policies to compensate for fluctuations in the business cycle.[11] The economic disorder of the 1970s caused Keynesians to re-examine their theoretical understanding of the economy, but it did not undermine their faith in the capacity of government policy to stabilize economic activity through measures that influence the level of demand. It is hard to escape the conclusion that the difference between the Keynesian position that markets do not clear (except perhaps in the long run) and the belief of monetarists and new classical economists in the inherent stability of the private sector reflects a difference in political values as well. Asked about this connection, the Nobel laureate and prominent Keynesian James Tobin responded: 'Logically there need not be any. But there is a correlation. A neo-Keynesian seems to be more concerned about employment, jobs, and producing goods than people who have a great faith in market processes.'[12]

4. Three Business Cycles and a Political Cycle

The causes and even the existence of business cycles are matters of disagreement among economists. There can be no doubt, however, that both the language of macroeconomic policy (expansion/contraction, peak/trough, recession/recovery) and the behaviour of policy-makers reflect a belief in the periodic and more-or-less regular occurrence of fluctuations in the overall level of economic activity. The data from industrial capitalist countries tend to confirm the existence of cyclical variations in the degree to which both labour and capital are utilized, and thus in the rate of economic growth. Despite the evidence,[13] many contemporary textbooks in macroeconomics devote only passing mention to business cycles, and then in the context of stabilization policies that, logically, could be intended to compensate for random economic disturbances rather than cyclical variations. It should come as no surprise to find that neo-Keynesian economists like Paul Samuelson tend to take business cycles more seriously, because of their weaker belief in the inherent stability of the private sector, than do monetarist or new classical economists. The new classical economics, with its assumption of the economy being in a moving equilibrium, basically ignores the issue of business cycles. Monetarists like Friedman acknowledge the existence of cycles (which he attributes to fluctuations in the rate of growth of the money supply) but argue that government policies have actually aggravated the severity of economic fluctuations.[14]

The historical evidence suggests the existence of three distinct cyclical tendencies of different average durations. These are the short (3–4 years), intermediate (7–10 years), and long (40–60 years) cycles. The short and intermediate cycles are the least controversial in terms of their causes and therefore in terms of the sorts of government policies that would be appropriate to compensate for these fluctuations.

The shorter *inventory* cycle is linked to producers' responses to changes in the rate of consumer expenditure. The basic idea is that retailers eventually react to a decline in consumer spending—registered in excessive inventories—by cutting their orders for future stock. This tends to be an overreaction as the decline in orders reflects both retailers' adjustment to the new lower level of consumer spending *and* their efforts to reduce costly inventories. When the level of consumer expenditure recovers, at which point business inventories have been run down, the orders placed by businesses (and therefore the greater use of existing productive capacity in the economy) will increase at a faster rate than the increase in consumer spending. This overreaction results from the need to rebuild depleted inventories. If the level of consumer spending did not vary, the inventory cycle phenomenon would not occur. There is, however, very clear evidence of variation in consumer spending that is related in part to short-term trends in consumers' optimism or pessimism about the economy.

The short duration of the inventory cycle presents problems for policy-makers in their efforts to reduce the extent of these business swings. To be effective, policy measures must be timely (implemented at the beginning of a contraction or expansion to reduce its amplitude); they must be specific in their effects (aimed directly at the factors—particularly consumer spending on durable goods and producer inventories—that determine the short cycle); and they must be retractable (capable of being changed or eliminated when the economy enters another phase of the cycle). This would suggest that the most suitable as compensatory policies for dealing with the short cycle are measures like temporary reductions in the sales tax on durable consumer goods or special tax credits for business intended to reduce the costs of carrying inventories larger than warranted by a declining rate of consumer expenditure.

Reliable forecasts of trends in consumer expenditure and business inventories are necessary to ensure that the timing of compensatory policy is appropriate. Otherwise, what was intended as a stabilization measure will in fact contribute to the severity of a swing in the cycle.

The intermediate cycle has received the most attention from economists. It is related to investment in new productive capacity and to the periodic replacement of machinery and other durable goods. As Samuelson observes, 'it is the durable or capital-goods sectors which show by far the greatest cyclical fluctuations.'[15] The reason is that this sort of spending can be deferred during a period of weak economic activity, but it is subject to 'bunching' when times are good and businesses suddenly decide to invest in fixed capital (new plant, machinery, and equipment).

The causes of swings in the intermediate cycle are different from those that generate the short cycle. Consequently, different compensatory policies are appropriate. These may include government spending on public works, roads, harbours, buildings, and so on to take up the slack during periods of weak capital investment. A policy of public works spending was recommended by Keynes, but this is subject to a number of practical difficulties we will consider in our discussion of the political business cycle. Probably the most suitable policy is one that increases the marginal efficiency of capital (i.e., that increases the profitability of new capital investment). The reduction or elimination of sales taxes on the purchase of machinery and construction materials, tax changes to allow the more rapid amortization of the costs of new capital investment against corporate taxes, or investment tax credits are measures that would have the effect of reducing the cost of capital investment. If the problem is excessive investment generating inflationary pressures, the same policy instruments could be used in the opposite direction to make capital expenditures less attractive. In either case, if counter-cyclical policy measures are to be effective they must remain *discretionary*. For example, if a reduction in the sales tax on purchases of new machinery becomes 'permanent' as a result of the political influence of the business interests that benefit from it, the usefulness of this particular lever of economic management will be lost.

The most controversial of the three cycles is the long cycle. These are often referred to as Kondratieff long waves, after the Russian economist Nikolai Kondratieff. The idea that capitalist economies experience long phases of relative expansion and contraction was popularized among English-speaking economists by Joseph Schumpeter[16] and Alvin Hansen.[17] After several decades of general neglect, the theory of long waves of economic activity has recently become the subject of renewed interest. This is in part because of the failure of conventional economics to provide a satisfactory explanation for the weaker economic growth and higher levels of unemployment that have characterized most Western economies since about the early 1970s. The empirical evidence for the existence of the long cycle is not conclusive. Some maintain that sustained periods of growth are more correctly attributed to historical accidents like inventions and the 'discovery' and exploitation of new territories, rather than being caused by endogenous (i.e., internally generated) developments in industrial economies. If, however, the modern proponents of long waves are correct in their claim that industrial economies experience long periods of above-average growth followed by decades of below-average growth, and that these historical swings can be linked to recurring characteristics of economic development (that is, they are not random), the implications for economic policy are significant.

The theory that explains the long cycle has two main components. The first emphasizes the role of major technological innovations like the internal combustion engine in providing the impetus for a general increase in investment in new industries created by (and existing industries transformed by) the new technology. It appears, as Schumpeter argued, that major technological change has tended to occur in clusters and that the growth industries spawned by these innovations have led the general economic expansion that occurs during the upswing of the long cycle. As the new technologies spread throughout the economy in the form of new products and/or production processes and their innovative possibilities approach exhaustion (i.e., the technological revolution reaches maturity), the general level of investment also weakens. Thus, the peak of the long cycle is reached. This is followed by an extended period of lower levels of economic growth caused by the weakened inducement to invest.

The second part of the theoretical explanation for long waves of investment involves what the American Marxist economist David Gordon has called the 'social structure of accumulation',[18] or what might simply be described as the social climate of economic activity. The social climate characterizing a particular generation is influenced by the phase of the long cycle during which their attitudes towards work and business are formed and also has an independent effect on the trend of economic activity. Maurice Lamontagne puts it this way:

Generations reaching adulthood during hard times are more likely to respect the work ethic, to be more disciplined and to produce a harmonious social environment based on a broad consensus favouring economic growth. Generations reaching adulthood during prosperous times are more likely to be 'spoiled' by affluence, to be less motivated by the work ethic, to be more aggressive in the pursuit of their varied 'cultural' goals and to create an antagonistic social environment inimical to economic growth.[19]

Lamontagne is arguing that the downswing in the long cycle, in part brought on by the weakened social consensus in support of business values, gives rise towards the bottom of the cycle to a changed social climate that provides receptive ground for the next long phase of economic expansion.

The theory is logically tidy and certainly suggestive in view of the coincidence in time of weaker economic growth in most Western economies with the emergence of the so-called 'Me generation'. Moreover, the concept of social climate may help to explain what economists call labour market rigidities and 'stickiness' in wages during a period when the general level of unemployment is high and unemployment for young adults tends to be about twice the general level. Despite the logical plausibility of a relationship among generational experiences, social values, and the propensity to invest, the theory needs to be subjected to rigorous testing in several societies before it can be accepted as a real phenomenon. Assuming, however, that decades-long fluctuations in the propensity to invest do exist, and that they are linked to revolutionary 'bunches' of technological innovation and to the level of social consensus on the primacy of business values, the implications for economic policy are profound. Measures appropriate for countering swings in the short and intermediate cycle would not be suitable for dealing with the causes of the long cycle. In fact, short of replacing the market entirely with some sort of centrally planned economy, it is difficult to see how economic policy could be more than a palliative: an attempt to avoid a full-blown depression as the downswing of the long cycle approaches its trough.

If the heirs to Keynes are correct in their belief that the discretionary policies of governments can have a stabilizing effect on overall economic activity, it remains the case that the success of such policies depends on their timely application and on the selection of suitable policy instruments. Otherwise, what was intended as a stabilization measure may, in fact, have destabilizing consequences. For example, if businesses are cutting back on production and laying off workers because of excessive inventories, an across-the-board cut in personal income tax intended to stimulate consumer demand is probably the wrong measure to address what is a short-term source of instability. For political reasons, tax cuts of this sort are hard to reverse, at least in the short term. In this particular case they would probably result in inflationary pressures because a sledgehammer is used where a smaller tool (like reductions in the sales tax on selected consumer durables) would do the job. Errors in the selection and timing of discretionary economic policies may sometimes be due to inaccurate forecasting of economic trends and to wrong diagnoses of the causes of economic instability.

There is, however, evidence of another cause of failure in governments' attempts to manage their economies. This is often referred to as the *political business cycle*. It argues that governments will use economic policies, particularly spending and tax measures, to improve their chances of re-election. The Swiss political economist Bruno Frey has shown that governments in Britain and the United States have pursued expansionary policies leading up to elections where the outcome seemed uncertain.[20] It is well known that government decisions on where and when to spend money on public works are often influenced by their desire to secure re-election. Keynes's belief that governments should maintain a shelf of public works that could be dusted off to stimulate the intermediate investment cycle supposes that the signals policy-makers will respond to are economic ones. In the real world, of course, they will also be sensitive to political signals, particularly in the lead-up to elections.

Another explanation of the political business cycle is associated with the Polish economist Michael Kalecki. He maintains there is a fundamental contradiction between full employment and price stability, and that the only way governments can deal with the resultant 'cost-push' inflation when the economy is at full employment is to engineer deliberately an economic slowdown. Such a policy is likely to have adverse consequences for a government's public support. Consequently, it will be rejected or at least not implemented with the necessary vigour. The outcome, so Kalecki and contemporary economists such as Paul Samuelson argue, is an 'increasing bias toward rising prices rather than stable prices' and a situation in which 'larger and larger amounts of unemployment are needed today to have the same wage and price restraining effect as in the past.'[21]

The Goals of Macroeconomic Policy in Canada: A Case of Diminishing Expectations

The 'official' adoption of Keynesian stabilization policy in Canada generally dates from the federal government's 1945 White Paper on Employment and Income and the Liberal Party's election platform of that year. In the words of the White Paper:

> The Government will be prepared, in periods when unemployment threatens, to incur deficits and increases in the national debt resulting from its employment and income policy, whether that policy in the circumstances is best applied through increased expenditures or reduced taxation. In periods of buoyant employment and income, budget plans will call for surpluses.[22]

The White Paper, and the Liberal Party's election platform, explicitly committed the government to maintaining high and stable levels of employment.

Two aspects of this early commitment to macroeconomic stabilization are noteworthy for their differences from the more recently stated goals of government policy. First is the emphasis on employment and the general neglect of price stability as a goal of economic policy. This reflected the preoccupations of a generation for whom the Great Depression—when unemployment rates reached 20 per cent and prices actually declined—shaped their idea of what could go wrong with the capitalist economy. Inflation had averaged only 0.1 per cent, per annum, between 1927 and 1946, but unemployment had averaged 8.1 per cent. Second, the faith in fiscal policy, including budget deficits, as an instrument for achieving economic growth and full employment is in sharp contrast to much recent thinking on macroeconomic policy. In 1934 Keynes was confronted with the question, 'Can America spend its way into recovery?' His answer was unequivocal: 'Why, obviously! . . . We produce in order to sell. In other words, we produce in response to spending. It is impossible to suppose that we can stimulate production and employment by *refraining* from spending.'[23] Compare Keynes's answer to the following statement of Canadian Finance Minister Michael Wilson during the first Mulroney government in the mid-1980s:

> Ten years of stimulation and deficits have not solved our problems. They have stimulated only a mountain of debt—a mountain of debt which is now growing twice as fast as the economy. Even worse, not only did 10 years of attempting to solve our problems this way fail to produce the desired growth and jobs, but now, as a result, we have less and less flexibility to deal with pressing public priorities.[24]

A heightened concern with price stability and budget deficits distinguishes recent thinking on macroeconomic policy from that during the decades of the Keynesian consensus. It nevertheless is the case that the official goals of government policy have remained substantially unchanged. These were summarized in 1964 in the *Report of the Royal Commission on Banking and Finance*[25] as (1) rising productivity; (2) a high and stable level of employment; (3) price stability; and (4) a sound balance of payments. In its first annual review the Economic Council of Canada added a fifth goal to this list, that of an equitable distribution of income.[26] This does not, however, appear to have been an important goal of Canadian macroeconomic policy. Instead, the distributional aspects of taxation and spending policies are considered in our analysis of social policy (Chapter Six). The other four goals continue to be the main pillars of both the policy and rhetoric of governments, though their relative importance and the thinking about the appropriate means for achieving them have changed.

The most important change has been a retreat from the high employment objective that was a main pillar of Keynesian stabilization policy. Although parties continue to repeat the mantra of 'Jobs, jobs, jobs!', particularly around election time, when in power they have shown a much greater tolerance for unemployment than would have been considered appropriate a couple of decades ago. Issues like the deficit, accumulated public-sector debt, Canada's international competitiveness, and price stability have appeared to take priority over employment in recent years. The diminishing expectations held for government as a guarantor of employment are suggested by the Liberal Party's 1993 Red Book, in which the party's policy commitments were set out. It stated that,

> The role of government in the economy is twofold: to establish the overall framework, which includes monetary and fiscal policy, federal-provincial fiscal relations, and trade policy; and to work in partnership with provincial governments, business, labour, and non-governmental institutions to achieve national economic objectives.[27]

The role of government, says the Red Book, is to establish a framework for economic activity. This is a less active, and many would say a more realistic, role for government than the optimistic Keynesianism of the 1945 White Paper. This role was outlined even more clearly in the Liberal government's 1994 document, *A New Framework for Economic Policy*, in which government indebtedness was identified as the primary cause of economic malaise, including high unemployment.

The critics of this scaled-down economic role for government, including many within the NDP, labour activists, and generally those on the left, argue that it reflects the agenda of the Canadian corporate élite and international capital. The banks and Canada's chief monetary institution, the Bank of Canada, come in for particular vilification because high real interest rates serve the interests of investors at the expense of employment creation. Jim Stanford's argument is representative of this point of view: 'Monetary institutions . . . must be reformed to reflect a better balance of the needs of the whole macroeconomy, rather than (as at present) just the interests of the owners of financial wealth.'[28] Stanford and others on the left speak of the 'permanent recession' and the 'socialization of capital'.

To describe recent circumstances as a state of 'permanent recession' is rather a stretch. The facts are that Canada's net job-creation record has been one of the best among advanced industrialized democracies since the recession of 1981–3 and, moreover, the personal cost of being unemployed is lower today than prior to the welfare state reforms of the 1960s. In addition, the labour force participation rate, i.e., the proportion of people of working age who want jobs, is higher today than during the heyday of Keynesian economics. Keynesianism always implied a level of national economic autonomy that has become increasingly impossible in the global economy. Finally, those who hearken back to the golden years of 3–5 per cent unemployment appear to assume that government's economic management policies played a significant role in delivering such high employment levels, when in fact a cause-effect relationship between these phenomena has never been established. It may well be, then, that the diminished expectations held today for government's economic role constitute a realistic response to contemporary circumstances.

1. The Macroeconomic Record: Performance and Policy

Like most Western capitalist economies, Canada's has experienced higher levels of unemployment and price inflation, and a more erratic record of growth, since the early 1970s as compared to the previous two decades. At the same time the size of the federal government's debt (leaving aside that of the provinces) as a share of national income has about doubled in the last decade. It currently amounts to about a third of gross national expenditure. Whether or not this growth in government debt affects the economy's performance is a matter of dispute. It is, however, viewed as part of the problem by much of the public, the media, many politicians, and some (not all) economists, and for this reason we examine the deficit issue separately. Table 5.1 summarizes the trends in unemployment, economic growth and price stability, and productivity growth for the seven largest OECD economies over the period 1966–94.

While the Canadian trends are broadly similar to those for its major trading partner and for other Western economies, Canada's unemployment rate has been consistently higher than the OECD average and usually higher than that of the United States, despite the fact that Canada's record of economic growth has been slightly better than the OECD and American averages. The explanation for Canada's apparently higher 'normal' rate of unemployment is, as is true of so many economic questions, a contested issue. Some attribute it to greater 'rigidities' in Canada's labour markets, resulting from transfer payments to individuals and to provincial governments. These income transfers are argued to act as disincentives for individuals to move from economically depressed to more active regions of the country. While it certainly is true that Canadian governments 'invest' more in maintaining the viability of chronically depressed regions of the country than has been true of American governments, these rigidities are not greater than those that exist in many Western European countries.

For the student of public policy the relevant question is what, if any, influence did government policies have on the performance of the economy? Mancur Olson examined the relationship between rates of economic growth and levels of government spending (final consumption and transfers) in the developed Western economies and Japan for the period 1950–79. He concluded that, 'except for Japan, there is no clear relation between the extent of government spending and transfers and the rate of growth'[29] (see Figure 5.1).

There is a consensus among both mainstream and radical economists that the generally buoyant conditions of the 1950s and 1960s were propelled by internal forces within postwar Western economies rather than 'caused' by government policies. Economists W. Arthur Lewis (1954), C.P. Kindleberger (1967), and Nicholas Kaldor (1966) are associated with the idea that the existence of a large supply of labour available for employment in the expanding

Table 5.1
Trends in Economic Growth,
Unemployment, Inflation, and Productivity Growth
for the Seven Major OECD Economies, 1966–94

	Average 1966–73	Average 1974–9	Average 1980–4	Average 1985–90	Average 1991–4
(a) Growth in real GNP/GDP*					
United States	3.9	2.8	2.1	3.0	2.2
Japan	9.9	3.7	4.2	4.6	1.4
Germany	4.1	2.4	0.9	3.0	1.8
France	5.4	3.1	1.2	2.8	0.9
United Kingdom	3.2	1.4	0.8	3.2	0.9
Italy	5.4	2.7	1.1	2.9	0.7
Canada	5.5	3.2	1.5	3.3	1.4
Total average	5.4	2.8	1.7	3.3	1.4
(b) Unemployment rate					
United States	4.5	6.8	8.3	6.1	6.8
Japan	1.2	1.9	2.4	2.5	2.4
Germany	0.9	3.5	6.2	7.6	6.8†
France	2.2	4.5	7.8	9.9	11.1
United Kingdom	2.2	4.2	9.6	9.0	9.4
Italy	5.7	6.5	8.9	11.4	11.1
Canada	4.8	7.2	9.9	8.7	10.8
Total average	3.1	4.9	7.6	7.9	6.8
(c) Inflation rate					
United States	4.4	8.6	7.5	3.9	3.2
Japan	6.2	10.0	4.0	1.3	1.6
Germany	3.9	4.7	4.4	1.5	3.7†
France	5.1	10.7	11.1	3.5	2.4
United Kingdom	6.1	15.7	9.6	5.9	3.4
Italy	4.5	16.4	16.0	6.2	5.0
Canada	4.3	9.2	8.6	4.3	2.3
Total average	4.9	10.8	8.7	3.8	3.0

Continued

Table 5.1 continued

	Average 1966–73	Average 1974–9	Average 1980–4	Average 1985–90	Average 1991–4
			(d) Growth productivity		
United States	1.5	0.3	0.8	1.0	1.1
Japan	8.6	3.0	3.2	3.2	0.8
Germany	4.1	3.0	1.7	1.8	1.2†
France	4.8	3.0	1.7	2.0	1.5
United Kingdom	3.1	1.2	1.9	1.6	2.4
Italy	5.6	1.5	0.8	2.2	2.8
Canada	2.5	0.3	0.4	1.0	1.2
Total average	4.3	1.8	1.5	1.8	1.3

*GNP numbers are reported for the US, Japan, Germany; GDP numbers are reported for France, the UK, Italy, and Canada.

†West Germany only.

SOURCES: Department of Finance, *Economic Review* (Ottawa: Supply and Services, 1985), 174, table 9.1; Department of Finance, *Quarterly Economic Review* (June 1990), Reference Table 90; Department of Finance, *Economic Reference Tables* (Aug. 1995), Reference Table 79.

manufacturing sector of the economy was the principal factor that fuelled this economic growth. So long as the supply of labour remained abundant (as workers moved from the primary to other sectors of the economy) and, therefore, upward pressure on wages remained low, profitability in the expanding sectors of the economy continued to attract new capital investment. Andrea Boltho suggests that, besides a plentiful labour supply, cheap raw materials needed for industrial processes and business confidence promoted by the Keynesian and postwar reconstruction policies of governments also contributed to the buoyancy of this period.[30]

Marxist economists such as Ernest Mandel do not fundamentally disagree with this explanation of the extended postwar boom, although Mandel views business confidence as a consequence rather than a cause of the postwar expansion. Where the Marxists part company with mainstream economists is in

FIGURE 5.1
Economic Growth and Government Spending, Selected Countries, 1950–79

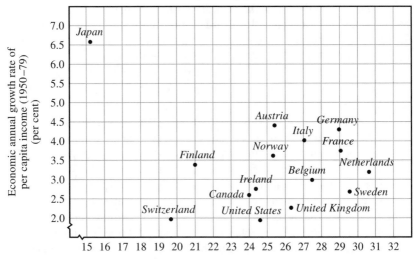

Average government expenditures and transfers
as percentage of GDP (1955, 1965, and 1975)

SOURCE: Mancur Olson, 'How Ideas Affect Societies: Is Britain the Wave of the Future?', in Institute of Economic Affairs, *Ideas, Interest and Consequences* (London: Institute of Economic Affairs, 1989), 39.

explaining why this expansion came to an end, and whether the much less propitious economic conditions of the 1970s and 1980s constitute a basic crisis in the capitalist system. There are four main explanations for the end of the full employment/steady growth/stable prices phase of the 1950s and 1960s.

1. *The labour market.* This explanation points to the end of abundant labour and to increasing wage demands, as well as to reduced flexibility in shifting workers between jobs and industries. This lost flexibility is greater in Western European economies than in North America. It is reinforced by legislation that makes layoffs and plant closures difficult, by state subsidies to declining industries, high levels of unionization, and rigidities in real wage rates.

2. *Unusual shocks.* Some argue that the general downturn that hit industrialized countries in the early 1970s was brought on by abnormal events that did not reflect fundamental flaws in these economies. The inflationary effects of American government spending on the Vietnam War and the OPEC price increases are commonly mentioned destabilizing events. In the words of a study commissioned by the OECD, 'our reading of recent history (1971–75) is

that the most important feature was an unusual bunching of unfortunate disturbances unlikely to be repeated on the same scale, the impact of which was compounded by some avoidable errors in economic policy.'[31]

3. *Contradictions of capitalism.* Marxist analyses maintain that what conventional economists typically regard as unusual events, and therefore as exogenous to the economy, were in fact the structural outcomes of relationships within the world capitalist system. Both the Vietnam War and the OPEC price shocks are interpreted 'as a part of the challenge to US domination in the world economy',[32] and not as temporary and accidental occurrences. Marxists view the 'crisis' of Western capitalism as the result of conflict in the world economic order. They emphasize what they argue to be the inherent contradiction between what the state must do to support business profitability and the concessions it must make to the working class to maintain popular support for a social order grounded on economic inequality. To put this in more concrete terms, as long as conditions allowed for a general expansion of Western economies the governments of these countries could afford to 'buy off the working class through reforms, among which full employment and social security policies played a key role.'[33] When these conditions no longer existed (and here Marxists accept the relevance of such factors as changes in the labour supply and the availability of cheap raw materials), governments resorted to measures intended to restore the rate of business profitability. (This is not an absolute rate, but depends on the rates of return on capital available elsewhere.) This assumed priority over full employment.

4. *The world economy in transition.* This explanation comes in a number of Marxist and non-Marxist varieties. We will focus on one non-Marxist version associated with economist Michael Beenstock. He argues that the economic slowdown in the Western economies has been caused by the transfer of manufacturing capacity from developed countries (DCs) to the less-developed countries (LDCs). Beenstock accepts the view that the growth in manufacturing fuelled the long postwar expansion. In response to such factors as the rise of the multinational corporation as the instrument for the transfer of technology from the DCs to the LDCs and the cheaper and more flexible labour force of the LDCs, industrialization took hold in these economies. The result was a shift in the world economy as the higher marginal return on capital in the LDCs attracted an increasing share of new investment in manufacturing. Beenstock shows that the LDCs' share of world trade in manufactured products increased from 4 per cent in 1960 to 9 per cent in 1980, and their share of world value-added in manufacturing grew from 9 to 14 per cent over the same period.[34] His conclusion that 'the economic upheavals that have taken place since about 1970 have been a consequence of a major realignment in the balance of world economic power'[35] might appear somewhat overstated in light of these figures. Combined with the increasing import penetration in the Western DCs of Japanese manufacturers, however, and with some of the internal developments mentioned in the previous three explanations of the economic downturn, the

shift of manufacturing production to the LDCs probably has contributed to the weaker economic performance of the developed countries. It certainly has contributed to increased political pressures on Western governments to protect domestic producers and jobs.

All of these explanations for the end of the stability and high growth generally experienced in Western economies during the 1950s and 1960s point to non-cyclical causes of weaker economic performance. However, in their response to these unfamiliar circumstances, governments initially continued to act as though the counter-cyclical policies that had become the standard repertoire of macroeconomic intervention could do the job. In several cases, including Canada, the US, and Great Britain, governments resorted to various temporary systems of wage and price controls. They did this in the belief that unusual interference with the price-setting mechanisms of the market (which economists such as John Kenneth Galbraith considered to be seriously flawed anyway), but particularly with wage increases, was necessary to bring inflation under control. By the middle of the 1970s many Western governments, including Canada's, had concluded that persistent inflation was the main economic problem and that the Keynesian repertoire of demand management techniques was not adequate to deal with it.

Disillusionment with Keynesianism did not result in a wholesale intellectual conversion to another philosophy of economic management associated with a different set of discretionary tools. Instead, confronted with the same disorienting circumstances that undermined the Keynesian consensus among academic economists, the reaction of policy-makers was an increased openness to new approaches for stabilizing the economy. When inflation came to be regarded by governments in several countries as the most debilitating problem confronting their economies, the emphasis in stabilization policy shifted from spending and taxation instruments to control over the money supply. Monetarism, which stressed a gradual expansion of the money supply, the announcement of long-term targets for monetary growth, and thus an increased policy role for the central bank, was embraced with varying degrees of enthusiasm in such countries as the United States, Great Britain, West Germany, and Canada.

In the Canadian case, the Bank of Canada's *Annual Report* for 1973 had expressed sympathy for the Friedmanite policy of steady and predetermined increases in the money supply.[36] It was not, however, until November of 1975 that the Bank began to announce targets for the annual growth of the money supply, accompanied by a policy of gradually reducing the rate of increase in the money stock. As we have seen, the argument in support of monetary targets and a policy of slow growth in the money supply is that such measures are most likely to succeed in restraining demand and thereby bringing inflation under control. Given that the annual rate of inflation did not drop below 7.5 per cent during the Bank of Canada's seven-year experiment with monetarism (1975–82), one might be tempted to conclude that there is little empirical evidence to support this claim. An evaluation of the effectiveness of monetarist policies is, however, complicated by at least a couple of factors.

First, with an open economy closely integrated by trade and financial markets with the United States, Canada's rate of inflation and overall level of economic activity were vulnerable to developments in the American economy. The high inflation of the period 1980–2 was to some extent 'imported' from the United States, particularly as a result of the policy of high interest rates pursued by the Federal Reserve Board (the monetary authority in that country). The Bank of Canada followed the Federal Reserve Board's lead for fear that failure to keep pace in interest rates would result in downward pressure on the Canadian dollar and therefore in inflationary pressure from an increase in the cost of goods imported into Canada.

Second, the Bank of Canada and some supporters of monetarism argue that the persistence of high levels of inflation after the adoption of a monetarist strategy is not proof that the theory is wrong. But it may indicate that monetarism was not applied properly. Speaking in 1980 before the House of Commons Standing Committee on Finance, Trade, and Economic Affairs, the governor of the Bank, Gerald Bouey, maintained that the Bank's policy of *gradually* reducing the growth in the money supply was at fault. A more radical policy of restraint, he argued, would have been more effective.

Studies on whether monetarist policies in such countries as the US, Great Britain, and Canada actually had an impact on inflation have reached mixed conclusions.[37] What is not in doubt, however, is that the shift to monetarism meant that price stability was the chief priority of macroeconomic policy, at the expense of employment. Statements of the Bank of Canda made this point time and again during the late 1970s and early 1980s. The intellectual guru of monetarism, Milton Friedman, has acknowledged that 'Experience and not theory has demonstrated that . . . monetary policy is not an effective instrument for achieving directly either full employment or economic growth.'[38] It is not intended to be a solution to the problem of weak economic growth and high levels of unemployment. It is fair to conclude, therefore, that monetarism represents not simply a change in policy instrument but also a reorientation in economic priorities away from traditional Keynesian concerns with full employment.

Since the abandonment in 1982 of targets for growth in the money supply, the Bank of Canada has made price stability its principal goal. Indeed, the current and previous governors of the Bank, Gordon Theissen and his predecessor, John Crow, have often stated that zero-inflation is the goal of Canadian monetary policy. In practice this means that the Bank has followed a policy of high real interest rates to dampen inflationary pressures. But the Bank of Canada, while quite independent from the government of the day, is subject to influences that restrict its margin for manoeuvre. In Gordon Theissen's words, the widely held view that the Bank of Canada controls the spectrum of interest rates in Canada . . . is a holdover from the days when financial markets here and elsewhere were subject to controls and restrictions of various sorts, and the pressures in markets tended to show up in limitations on the availability of funds rather than in interest rates. These days, markets are more open, more international, and, as a result, much more efficient. But it does mean that interest rates in Canada will move around in response to international events or domestic developments that alter market expectations.[39]

Theissen might have added that one international influence of particular significance is the United States Federal Reserve Board, whose policies are able to influence interest rates and economic activity internationally, but especially in Canada because of the high degree of trade and capital market integration between the two countries.

2. The Deficit and the Economy

Over the last several years Canadian governments have been less concerned with price stability because annual inflation rates have been at their lowest levels since 1971–2. Concern with inflation has been replaced by an increasing preoccupation with the size and persistence of government deficits and the amount of government spending—currently about 35 per cent of all federal spending—that goes towards servicing accumulated federal debt. A deficit is, quite simply, a shortfall between what a government raises from taxes and other sources of revenue during a given year and what it spends. Economists make a distinction between a deficit's *cyclical* and *structural* components. The cyclical deficit is that part of the shortfall caused by variations in expenditures and taxes related to the state of the economy. The structural deficit—or cyclically adjusted deficit, as it is often called—is the shortfall that would have occurred if the level of economic activity had been 'normal', i.e., if fluctuations in the business cycle were ironed out.

This distinction is a crucial one for two reasons. First, the cyclically adjusted deficit provides the correct measure of a government's *discretionary* fiscal policy. It eliminates the automatic increase in government spending that results when weaker than normal economic circumstances cause lower tax revenues and higher claims on public spending (through such statutory income maintenance programs as employment insurance and welfare). In other words, the fact that the size of a government's budget deficit has increased by 10 per cent from one year to the next does not necessarily mean that its fiscal policy has been counter-cyclical (i.e., spending to compensate for weakened demand). It could be that the entire increase in the deficit was due to automatic changes in government revenue and spending that are linked to the state of the economy. Or the increase could have resulted from a rise in the interest rates that governments, like other borrowers, must pay on the new debts they assumed during that year. The cyclically adjusted deficit often is much smaller than the overall deficit.

The deficit has become the symbol of economic mismanagement for conservative critics of government, some of whom argue that government budgets should always balance. This suggestion is both unrealistic and potentially harmful for the economy. To illustrate this, consider the consequences of a constitutional requirement that the government's annual revenues and expenditures balance. Fluctuations in the level of economic activity are unavailable. This means that the income the state receives from individuals and corporations will vary with the health of the economy, as will its expenditures on statutory income maintenance programs. If the budget must balance, this means that the level of taxation and/or the level of benefits paid to individuals must constantly be readjusted. The political and administrative impracticability of this is clear enough. But in addition, an automatic increase in taxation or cut in state benefits to offset the deficit resulting from weak economic circumstances would aggravate the severity of an economic downturn. Thus, in addition to the Keynesian argument that the deficit can be used as an instrument of macroeconomic stabilization, another benefit from unbalanced budgets is that they allow for greater stability in taxation rates and social programs.

How large is the deficit in Canada and what are its causes? Figure 5.2 shows a widening gap between Ottawa's expenditures and revenues during the early to mid-1980s. This was fuelled largely by weak government revenues during the 1981–3 recession and by the fact that the additional debt acquired during those years was taken on at exceptionally high rates of interest. Growth in tax revenues and cuts to spending have narrowed the deficit gap considerably. As a percentage of GDP, the federal deficit fell from 7 per cent in 1984 to about half of 1 per cent in 1997. But at the same time the size of the federal government's accumulated debt has climbed vertiginously to about $600 billion (provincial and municipal debt adds close to $300 billion to the total). Total public-sector debt in Canada is just about equal to the country's annual GDP. Among OECD countries, only Belgium, Italy, and Greece have greater debt-to-GDP ratios than Canada. Today, about one-third of every dollar spent by the Canadian government goes towards paying interest on its accumulated debt.

The burden of accumulated federal debt of over $600 billion has been the target of four main criticisms. (1) Debt represents a transfer of the burden of paying for current consumption onto the shoulders of future generations, and therefore involves intergenerational inequities. (2) Given a limit on available savings, government borrowing may displace other potentially productive uses for investors' money. In fact, because a significant share of the money that Canadian governments and their agents borrow is raised outside the country— about one-quarter of Ottawa's debt is owed to foreigners—this investment displacement effect is less than it would be in a closed economy. A new problem results, however, that of foreign indebtedness and the vulnerability to the preferences of non-Canadian agents that this involves. (3) If a large share of what government spends must go towards paying the interest on its debts, a non-discretionary expenditure item, this reduces government's ability to finance new activities and maintain current ones. (4) Debt has a psychological dimension. If investors *perceive* the government's debt to be excessive,[40] this may contribute to a reduced willingness to invest.

The rhetoric of deficit management favoured by Canadian governments has conveyed the impression that the legacy of debt has resulted from excessively generous social programs and government waste. A different perspective is provided by David Wolfe. He argues that the real cause of the deficit problem lies with public revenues, not public spending:

> Paradoxically, the countries that have run the largest deficits, and the ones in which deficits have emerged as the most significant political issue, are the ones where centrist or right-wing governments have predominated in much of the postwar period. Because of the political con-

FIGURE 5.2
The Federal Deficit, 1980–96

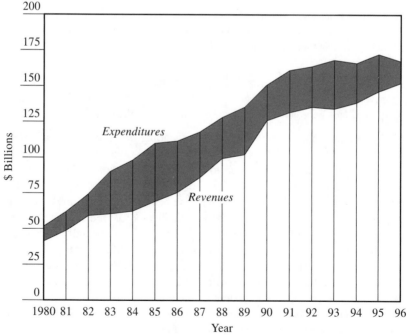

SOURCES: Canada, *Public Accounts* (Ottawa: Supply and Services, 1980–91; Statistics Canada, *Canadian Economic Observer: Historical Statistical Supplement* 1995/96, cat. no. 11–210–XPB.

FIGURE 5.3
Public Sector Debt as a Percentage
of GDP, Canada and OECD Average, 1980–96

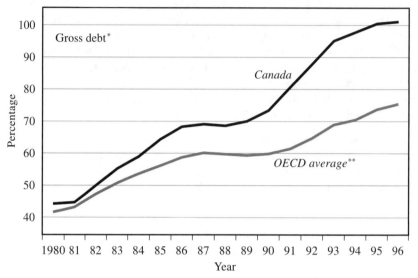

*General government debt, *National Accounts* definitions; 1996 data are OECD projections.
** Weighted average of 17 countries (1987 GDP weights and exchange rates).
SOURCE: OECD, National Accounts; Secretariat estimates.

straints imposed upon them by their own electoral constituencies, these governments have been less able than left-wing ones to implement the tax policies necessary to finance existing levels of expenditure.[41]

Wolfe notes that no major new social spending programs have been instituted in Canada since 1975. The cost of those programs already in place has increased, he argues, mainly due to weak economic conditions during the recessions of 1981–3 and 1989–92 and the high levels of unemployment that have persisted even when the economy has been in a growth phase. But the key factor, according to Wolfe, is that politically centrist federal governments have been unwilling to increase the level of taxation—especially of business and the wealthy—to keep pace with expenditure growth. Their unwillingness to do so has been reinforced by the concern of Canadian policy-makers that the level of taxation stay in line with the level in the United States. Finally, Wolfe argues that political and bureaucratic pressures for the use of tax expenditures to pursue policy goals—resulting in losses to the revenue budget—have increased the size of Ottawa's structural deficit.[42]

In fact, however, taxation levels did increase significantly under the Progressive Conservative government after its 1984 election. Indeed, some very unpopular taxes, notably the GST, were imposed by the Tories. This may seem to refute Wolfe's claim that centre-right parties are unwilling to raise taxes to deal with public-sector deficits. The reality is that the Conservatives' ideological dislike of higher taxes was tempered by an important maxim of deficit management: politically, it is easier to raise taxes than to cut spending. This is a truth that all parties, whatever their ideological bent, quickly realize when they inherit a deficit problem.

The External Dimension of Macroeconomic Policy

We occasionally hear news stories to the effect that 'The Bank of Canada today made large purchases of Canadian dollars in order to defend the dollar's value', or that 'In response to recent increases in American interest rates the Canadian prime rate has moved upwards.' Several important features of macro-economic policy are conveyed in these statements. At the most general level, they suggest that Canada's economy is a very open one, influenced by events beyond our borders. The reference to defending the dollar implies that the international valuation of a country's currency (particularly the rate of exchange between its currency and those of its major trading partners) is a matter of some policy importance. At a more specific level, a major policy-making role for the central bank (the Bank of Canada) is indicated, and the dependence of the Canadian economy on developments in the United States is highlighted.

If an economy were closed—if it were entirely self-sufficient in what it sells and buys and in financing the expenditure requirements of both the private and public sectors—management of the overall economy would focus exclusively on internal factors. Of course, no modern economy is closed, all of them being open to external influence in varying degrees. In comparison to other developed capitalist economies, Canada falls towards the middle of the spectrum with both exports and imports accounting for about a quarter of the value of gross domestic product. The Canadian economy, however, is exceptional in the extent to which its openness is directed towards a single trading partner. Close to one-fifth of Canada's GDP is accounted for by exports to the United States.

The transactions an economy has with other economies are expressed in a country's balance of payments. This is an account of all the income flows entering (credits) and leaving (debits) the economy. The balance of payments is closely, but not perfectly, related to the value of a nation's currency (i.e., the exchange rate). This can be understood from a simplified illustration. If a Canadian corporation purchases a shipment of radios from a Japanese corporation, the Japanese exporter will naturally expect to be paid in yen, its national currency. Likewise, a Canadian exporter of coal to a Japanese electrical utility will expect to be paid in Canadian dollars. If the sum of all transactions in this bilateral trade relationship is not in balance, say that Canadian businesses and individuals buy $1 billion more from Japan than our economy sells to the Japanese, this shortfall must be covered through buying yen. This introduces two complications. First, Canadians who need yen for their vacations in Tokyo, or businesses that require yen to pay for the Japanese merchandise they are importing, exchange their dollars for yen at banks. Thus, the problem of trade imbalances is not experienced individually by people or corporations. Rather, it is felt at the level of the national financial system in terms of reserves of foreign currencies in demand. Second, persistently greater Canadian demand for the yen than Japanese demand for the dollar will result in an increase in the value of the yen *vis-à-vis* the dollar. This means that the cost of goods imported from Japan will increase, while it will cost fewer yen to buy the same volume of Canadian goods.

With imports becoming dearer and exports cheaper, it may appear that a change in the value of a nation's currency in relation to that of one or more of its trading partners is a matter of unimportance. This is not so. First of all, if an economy experiences a chronic deficit in its balance of payments, its government probably will come under pressure to devalue the national currency to bring in line the value of what it buys from and sells to the outside world. Second, a decline in the value of a nation's currency relative to that of its main trading partners may produce inflationary pressures if the foreign goods and services that now cost more to buy are ones whose consumption is not easily or quickly reduced (they are, in the economist's jargon, relatively demand-inelastic). Since 1971 the capitalist world has been on what economists call a 'managed floating' exchange-rate system. The relative value of national currencies is allowed to float in response to supply and demand. But the state, through the central bank, may interfere with the market for the national currency, for example, by buying the currency when demand for it is weak and imports are becoming increasingly expensive. Because of their effects on domestic price levels and employment, the foreign exchange rate and balance of payments are matters of public policy in all capitalist societies.

These general observations on the relationship between trade and macroeconomic policy are uncontroversial. In the Canadian case, however, controversy surrounds the particular matters of the profile of our trade with other economies and the concentration of that trade with the United States. The earlier example of Japanese radios and Canadian coal implied that trade involves transactions in commodities. In fact, however, a significant portion of trade takes the form of such foreign ownership-related transactions as dividends paid to the foreign shareholders of corporations in Canada and income transfers from Canadian subsidiaries to their foreign parent corporations, both direct transfers and those made through various other payments such as licensing fees for the use of technology owned outside of Canada. In the terminology of the national accounts, these are *service transactions*. In addition to the items just mentioned, service transactions also include tourism and interest paid to the foreign holders of Canadian debt. Trade in commodities is referred to as *merchandise transactions*. Together these comprise what is referred to as the *current account*. Although the annual value of Canadian merchandise exports usually exceeds the value of imported commodities, Canada has registered a deficit in service transactions every year since 1950. This deficit has contributed to an overall balance-of-payments deficit on the current account during 29 of the 34 years between 1961 and 1995.[43] The significance of chronic balance-of-payments deficits for public policy is explained by Molot and Williams:

> Ideally, governments would like to ensure that the value of what is brought into the country is less than, or only as much as, the value of what is sent out. Otherwise, the resulting international indebtedness will force policy makers to divert energy and capital into a search for the means to repay the deficit.[44]

The two major negative contributors to Canada's balance of trade are payments associated with foreign ownership of economic assets in Canada and, more importantly, interest paid to the foreign holders of Canadian debt. Short of placing serious restrictions on foreign ownership and/or imposing currency controls to stem the flow of profits leaving the country—measures that, aside from being political non-starters, would violate Canada's treaty obligations under the Canada-US FTA, NAFTA, and the WTO—nothing much can be done about the first drain on the balance of payments. As for the outflow of money to the foreign holders of Canadian debt, reneging on those obligations clearly is not an option. The one-third of public-sector debt held by non-Canadians represents a significant drain of money out of the Canadian economy, through the interest payments on this debt. But it also increases the influence of external investors and credit-rating agencies whose judgements affect the level of interest that governments must pay to attract buyers of their debt. The only way out of this circle of debt and dependence would seem to be to borrow less abroad. Easier said than done!

Walls, Doors, and Plans: Economic Policy in an International Context

The influence of external economic and political circumstances on the performance of the Canadian economy has been significant from the time of the initial European settlement of this country. Indeed, the Canadian economy began as a colonial extension of the French and, after 1760, the British commercial empires. The subsequent record of Canada's economic history has been punctuated with such political developments as annexationist (to the US) sentiments in the 1840s, the National Policy of 1879, the national election of 1911 (fought largely on the issue of free trade with the US), the foreign ownership debate of the 1960s and early 1970s, the 'Third Option' policy of the 1970s (the aim of which was to diversify Canada's external trade), the Canada-US Free Trade Agreement (1989), the North American Free Trade Agreement (1993), and Canada's participation in the General Agreement on Trade and Tariffs, leading to the creation of the World Trade Organization in 1995. At issue in each case was the appropriate stance for Canadian economic policy in relation to challenges from the outside world. Tariffs on imports and subsidies for domestic producers are main features of *protectionist* economic policies. This is one of three general stances that governments may adopt towards the international economic system of which they are a part. The other two are *free trade* and *economic planning*. A fourth, which we will not discuss because it has not been relevant in the modern economic history of Canada, is *territorial expansionism* motivated by economic factors.[45] In reality, none of these stances is found in a pure form. They are most appropriately described as policy orientations, given that a nation's economic policy invariably has elements of more than one stance.

Protectionist measures have a long history in Canada. The first 'made-in-Canada' tariff (as opposed to tariffs set by the British Colonial Office) was set in 1858.[46] The National Policy of 1879 elevated tariff protection to a major component of Ottawa's economic development strategy. Whether the Conservative government of John A. Macdonald was acting principally on some vision of the country's economic future or on more crass considerations of popular support and business pressures is an open question (though most studies by economists and historians point to the political power of business interests as a major factor, especially in determining the tariff rates applied to particular commodities).[47] What is not in dispute is that the 1879 tariffs, and those since, have been intended as measures to protect domestic producers. They have never been primarily devices for raising public revenue. The average rate of the 1879 tariffs was 28 per cent, with the highest of these placed on such manufactured items as agricultural implements, railway equipment, iron, and clothing.[48] Tariff walls remained high until World War II. Since then they have declined significantly, and under the FTA tariffs between Canada and the United States have been virtually eliminated.

Tariffs are only one of the walls that governments may use to protect their domestic industries. Non-tariff barriers such as voluntary export restraints negotiated between countries, import quotas, technical and administrative barriers to the free entry of imports, marketing boards, and subsidies to domestic producers have proliferated in the world trading system at the same time as the general level of tariff protection has fallen. The numerous forms and Byzantine complexity of non-tariff barriers, as well as disagreements between governments over what is and is not a restrictive trade policy, have presented greater problems for trade negotiators than tariffs.

As the historical recurrence of proposals for some form of free trade between Canada and the United States suggests, some interests in Canada have supported 'doors' rather than 'walls' as the appropriate policy stance towards the outside world (or at least towards that part of the world of greatest economic importance to Canada). The free trade position is one supported by most economists. They argue that the maximization of a nation's wealth is best achieved by pursuing its *comparative advantage* in the world trading system. This means that an economy will export those goods and services whose costs are determined by factors of production with which it is abundantly endowed relative to other economies, and will import those products that rely on factors of production with which it is poorly endowed. Canadian exports are more skewed towards non-manufactured goods than is true of other advanced capitalist economies. On the other hand, our imports are overwhelmingly skewed towards manufactured products that require a relatively higher level of skilled labour and technical knowledge. This suggests that Canada's comparative advantage lies in its natural resource industries.

The policy implications of the theory of comparative advantage are potentially disturbing. First, the theory suggests that the current profile of Canada's international trade, with its attendant problems, is rational from the standpoint of maximizing the nation's wealth. Second, if the Canadian economy has a relative cost advantage in natural resource factors this might be taken as an argument for 'mega-project' industrial strategies that would see government channel investment into such multibillion-dollar projects as northern pipelines, freshwater exports, hydroelectric exports, and offshore oil. The case for mega-projects rests on the expectation that the construction phase of such projects will generate activity in other sectors of the economy and that a substantial export market will exist for the resource being developed. The downside is that such a strategy increases the vulnerability of an economy to fluctuations in international markets for the targeted resources. This was clearly demonstrated by the precipitous drop in the world price of oil and gas during the 1980s. This drop resulted in cancellation of plans for a gas pipeline from the Canadian Arctic to American markets, plans for a number of synthetic oil projects in Alberta, and uncertainty over the future of the Hibernia oil reserves off the coast of Newfoundland (the Hibernia project has continued thanks to enormous subsidies from Ottawa to the petroleum industry).

When the advocates of freer trade between Canada and the United States made their case during the 1980s, they did not rely on arguments of comparative advantage. Instead, they argued that free access to the American market would eliminate the inefficiencies of firms producing behind tariff walls for the domestic market, and so would improve the competitive performance of Canadian industry. Free-traders claimed that, due to the small size of the Canadian market, protectionism prevented the development of internationally competitive industries and resulted in a transfer of income from Canadian consumers to the businesses (many of them foreign-owned) protected by tariffs and non-tariff barriers. In addition to their economic arguments, the advocates of free trade put forward a political one. Pointing to mounting protectionist sentiment in the US Congress, which erupted in a number of sectoral trade disputes between the two countries during the 1980s, they argued that a free trade agreement with the United States would provide political security against the escalation of trade hostilities that would harm Canada more than the United States.

The case for free trade rested on a combination of the economic benefits it promises with its claim to be hard-headed political realism. Its opponents made three main counter-claims.[49] First, they argued that the economic adjustment costs—businesses closing and workers unemployed—were likely to be greater than free-traders estimated. A second argument against free trade focused on the longer-term economic costs of such an agreement. It was argued that free trade would result in a permanent shift of production facilities to the United States, in possible downward pressure on wages in Canada, and in a loss of research and development activity currently carried out in this country. The third objection against free trade was that it would undermine Canada's political sovereignty. According to this view, greater economic integration would ultimately lead to greater pressure on Canadian governments to bring their policies in line with those of the United States. This claim is not easily proved or disproved. It resonates, however, with some very old fears about Canada's national identity and our ability to maintain it in the face of Americanizing pressures.

Four years after the FTA came into effect, the Progressive Conservative government signed a treaty with the United States and Mexico that created the North American Free Trade Agreement (NAFTA). As in the case of the FTA, NAFTA generated enormous controversy in Canada and was even more controversial in the United States, a fact that generally was not appreciated in Canada. The fears associated with NAFTA were rather different. Because this free trade partnership involved two wealthy developed countries and one poor developing economy, the chief concern was that investment and jobs would flee the relatively high-wage economies of Canada and the United States for the paradise of the *maquiladoras*. 'That giant sucking sound' was how American billionaire Ross Perot described this expected flood of dollars and jobs. Lax environmental regulations and rudimentary labour laws, added to lower taxation of business, were additional factors expected to lure capital from Canada and the United States to Mexico. To make matters worse, said the critics, ordinary Mexicans would not even benefit from this surge of investment and economic activity. Instead, NAFTA would put them at the mercy of rapacious capitalists, paying them low wages while pouring filth into Mexico's air and rivers. Defenders of NAFTA argued that the trade deal would make Mexicans richer and thereby enable them to buy more goods from Canada and the United States. Moreover, they said, the growth of a middle class in Mexico would put increasing pressure on that country's authorities to protect the environment and improve working conditions. In response to fears about NAFTA's possible consequences for the environment in Mexico and the very real gap between labour standards in that country and those in Canada and the United States, side agreements on these matters were negotiated. These side agreements are generally acknowledged to be toothless.

How has Canada fared under the FTA and NAFTA? It depends on who you ask. On the whole, those who supported free trade before these deals were signed continue to stand by it, while those who opposed it argue that their worst fears have come true. The bottom line is that any fair-minded assessment of the economic, social, and political effects of the FTA and NAFTA must take into account a multitude of other influences. These include interest rates, business cycles, international economic developments, government's preoccupation with deficit and debt management, and federal-provincial relations, to mention some of the more important ones. There are no easy answers about who wins and who loses under free trade.

But several things are clear. First, even supporters of free trade have been disappointed over the continuation—even escalation!—of trade skirmishes between Canada and the United States. These have involved a wide range of goods, from softwood to salmon. The dispute settlement mechanisms established under the FTA have not taken the politics out of cross-border trade wars. American policy continues to be as protectionist as it was before the FTA, testimony to the ability of interest groups to work the fragmented American system of policy-making to their advantage.

Second, naysayers' claims that the FTA was responsible for the job losses experienced during the recession that followed the agreement were exaggerated. The timing of the deal was unfortunate for free trade boosters, coinciding as it did with the beginning of recession in the United States that, as inevitably happens, pulled the Canadian economy into recession, too. High interest rates in 1989–90 and the rising value of the Canadian dollar, making Canadian exports more expensive in the United States, almost certainly overshadowed whatever impact free trade had on employment and investment in Canada. Moreover, the migration of manufacturing jobs from Canada to lower-wage locations in the American South, Mexico, and elsewhere was happening before the FTA. Although some argue that the pace of this outflow was increased by the FTA and will accelerate even further under NAFTA, such claims are difficult to prove.

Fears that the FTA and NAFTA would undermine Canadian social programs, culture, and political sovereignty are difficult to substantiate. Social programs have been under enormous pressure in recent years, but for reasons that have little to do with these free trade agreements—at least not in a direct sense. Rather, these agreements are more properly viewed as the political products of the same broader forces of economic globalization that have, in Keith Banting's words, 'placed enormous pressure on the welfare state, creating contradictory pressures for the expansion of the redistributive role of the state, and for its contraction and redesign.'[50] There is a sense among decision-making élites and the more educated and affluent strata of Canadian society that globalization is an inevitability to which governments must adapt through policies aimed at reducing the role of government and increasing the competitiveness of Canadian business. The general population appears not to share this enthusiasm and is more likely than the élites to see in freer trade a threat to their incomes and job security.[51] While the ideology of free trade has less secure roots among average citizens than in the corridors of power and privilege, ordinary Canadians do respond to claims that their governments spend and tax too much and that public-sector deficits and debt are serious problems. The cuts to social spending that began gradually under the Conservatives in the 1980s and that have accelerated under the Liberals in the 1990s—to say nothing of those implemented by provincial governments—owe more to domestic political forces than to the free trade bogeyman.

In regard to cultural sovereignty—a value that has never set racing the pulses of ordinary Canadians—the FTA and NAFTA are far less significant than Hollywood, the Internet, world Disney culture, and *the preferences of ordinary Canadians*. Canada's protectionist cultural policies were never a response to popular demand, although nationalist élites have always tried to portray them in this light. When the WTO decides, as it did in the summer of 1997, that the Canadian government's long-standing policy of favouring Canadian-owned magazines violates that organization's trade rules, it would seem ridiculous to point an accusing finger at the FTA.

Dissenters from the dogma of free trade, including many in the NDP, labour leaders, social activists, cultural nationalists, and left-wing academics, are not unanimous in the alternative they propose. No one, however, seriously suggests protectionism as an option. The word has virtually disappeared from the lexicon of Canadian economics. Canada's heavy dependence on international trade and its participation in global trade liberalization through the GATT and, more recently, the WTO rule out protectionism as a viable framework for economic policy. Instead of protectionism the opponents of free trade tend to support an industrial strategy or planning option. This is not inconsistent with limited free trade for particular industrial sectors, as has existed under the Auto Pact since 1965. The planning option places its main faith, however, in the capacity of the state to co-ordinate the development of the economy.

The obstacles to planning are very serious ones. They include the following:

1. *Co-ordination between governments*. The federal division of powers and the possession by provincial governments of important levers for influencing economic activity mean that either the provinces would have to give up some of the powers they currently have (an improbability, to say the least) or the mechanisms for co-ordinating federal-provincial economic activity would have to be strengthened. This second possibility seems only slightly less remote than the first.

2. *The electoral cycle*. It is axiomatic that all governments in liberal democracies are influenced to greater or lesser degrees by short-term factors of electoral expediency and manoeuvring for political support, at the expense of long-term economic strategies.

3. *Social structures*. Canadian society is characterized by an almost complete absence of umbrella institutions representing labour organizations and businesses. In countries like Germany and Sweden, these institutions have operated to generate social consensus on the objectives of economic policy,

and therefore to overcome the 'short-termism' of electoral politics.

4. *Inertia of the past*. Past policies and government inaction have contributed to a level of integration between the Canadian and United States economies that is unparalleled. From a practical standpoint this means that planning, which implies both a relatively high degree of state intervention in the economy and that the goals of economic policy be determined by Canadian interests, is likely to encounter vigorous opposition from those American and domestic economic interests that have developed around continentalist trade linkages.

5. *Existing free trade obligations*. Canada is currently a member of the FTA, NAFTA, and the WTO. The Canadian government has signed a free trade agreement with Chile and bilateral negotiations on freer trade between Canada and the European Union have been ongoing for a number of years. In short, a web of treaty commitments and trade institutions exists to lock Canadian governments into the free trade orbit. These commitments are not easily cast aside or changed. Indeed, it is hard to imagine the circumstances necessary for the Canadian government to invoke the termination clause of the FTA or to demand major reforms to the FTA or NAFTA that its partners are not willing to concede.

In view of these obstacles, is planning really an alternative stance for macroeconomic policy in Canada? At a minimum, planning would require significant institutional changes in the way policy is made, including the creation of state structures capable of representing and accommodating regional and functional (particularly business and labour) interests. But institutional change not grounded on receptive attitudinal and social conditions is useless. As Hugh Thorburn observes, 'But even before this [institutional change] comes the leap of faith—the decision and collective will to set up the machinery around which a consensus can be built on a basis of rational planning for agreed-upon objectives. If we cannot agree to do that, then we cannot do anything.'[52] Little in Canada's contemporary history suggests that such a 'collective will' is on the horizon. The fractious character of federal-provincial relations is by itself sufficient to cast serious doubt on the viability of economic planning. Moreover, élite decision-makers in both the public and private sectors tend to support a smaller, rather than larger, role for government.[53] Given the forces ranged against it, the state planning option is clearly a non-starter.

Chapter Six

Social Policy

Introduction

Many of the most expensive functions carried out by the state in advanced capitalist societies are associated with social policy. These functions include public education, health-care services, publicly subsidized housing, and the provision of various forms of income support to such segments of the population as the unemployed, the aged, and the disabled. Together they comprise that dimension of state activity conventionally labelled the *welfare state*. The welfare state is generally understood to encompass state interference with the operation of market forces in order to protect or promote the material well-being of individuals, families, or groups on grounds of fairness, compassion, or justice.

Few people are opposed to fairness, compassion, and justice. Nevertheless, the term 'welfare state' carries negative connotations in our society. There are two main reasons for this. First, ours is an individualistic culture that values self-reliance and tends to reject the notion that society has an obligation to support those who are capable of working. While Canadians tend to be less individualistic than Americans, they are less collectivist than, say, Swedes, Danes, or Belgians. Second, while the welfare state is associated with compassion for society's least privileged elements and with the redistribution of wealth from those who can afford to pay to those in need, in the eyes of many it is also associated with inefficiency, disincentives to work, and even fraud. For these reasons few Canadian politicians dare to utter the words 'welfare state', unless they have something bad to say about it. Even the friends of the welfare state tend to speak in codewords like 'social justice', 'the caring society', and 'Putting People First',[1] avoiding the words 'welfare state' because of the unfavourable baggage the term carries in our society.

Despite the negative connotations evoked by the term 'welfare state', it is worth retaining as a shorthand label for that area of state intervention that involves social policy. There can be no doubt that the state's role in the provision of social services and the share of national income devoted to welfare-state policies have increased enormously during this century. Social programs account for just over 40 per cent of federal spending, but closer to 60 per cent of all program expenditure. Expressed as a percentage of GNP, welfare-state spending currently ranges from a high of about 33 per cent in Sweden to a low of about 12 per cent in Japan. Canada ranks slightly below the OECD average, although international comparisons are complicated by various sorts of social benefits that do not appear on the state's expenditure books.

Too much should not be read into international comparisons such as these. Part of the greater level of social spending in Western European countries can be attributed to their older populations. One way of controlling for the effects of differences in the age profiles of societies is to count only social spending on the working age share of the population. For all but a few countries the majority of this spending takes the form of expenditures on forms of unemployment insurance. As Figure 6.1 shows, levels of spending on those who are of working age vary enormously, from a high of about 13 per cent in the Netherlands and Finland to a low of about 1 per cent in Japan. Canada is just slightly below the average at about 7 per cent.

Although the sheer growth in social spending is beyond dispute, there is considerable disagreement over the causes and significance of welfare-state expansion. The conventional view maintains that the welfare state has emerged as a result of the socio-economic pressures and political demands produced by industrialization and urbanization. Developments in the economy and in the way society is organized are accompanied by the political mobilization of the general population. This political mobilization takes such forms as the extension of universal voting rights, unionization, the emergence of mass political parties, and the proliferation of interest groups. Thus, industrialization and urbanization confront policy-makers with a new set of problems and popular expectations, and the extension of mass democracy increases the responsiveness of governments to popular demands. How governments respond will vary, however, according to the particular structures of association (churches, labour organizations, co-operative societies, and so on) and cultural values that characterize each society. Although the timing and extent of welfare-state reforms are influenced by the particular characteristics of each society, the pressures for their introduction can be attributed to socio-economic changes and to the political democratization experienced in all advanced capitalist societies.

An alternative interpretation of the welfare state argues that the social reforms introduced to a greater or lesser degree in all capitalist societies represent attempts to defuse social tension and thus to protect the interests of capital. The American Marxist James O'Connor describes this as the state performing its *legitimization function*.[2] Welfare spending is used to promote social

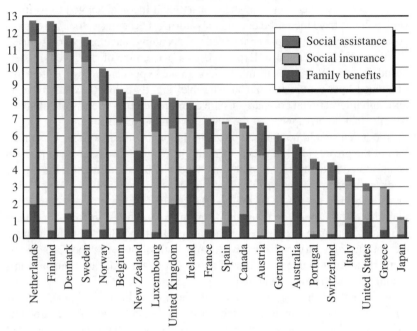

FIGURE 6.1
Working-Age Transfers by Type,
as Percentage of GDP, 1992

SOURCE: OECD, *OECD Economic Studies No. 27, 1996/II*, 153.

harmony and to legitimize the existing economic system in the eyes of those who benefit least from its operation. It is perfectly reasonable to accept O'Connor's claim that the welfare state has the effect of smoothing over the social frictions generated by the capitalist system of production, without having to accept the suggestion that those who manage the state consciously set out to protect the interests of the capitalist class.

Policy-makers, whatever their ideological bent, must occasionally balance popular demands against the preferences of the business/investment community in circumstances where the reconciliation of these competing interests is difficult, to say the least. The historical record shows that they have often come down on the side of popular demands, instituting social policies that have been vigorously opposed by powerful elements of the business community. But history also shows that they have done so within the limits of business confidence (limits that vary among societies) and in ways that minimize the cost burden shouldered by business. In other words, the welfare state is neither purely the result of democratic pressures nor purely a contrivance for anaesthetizing class conflict and protecting the interests of capital. Instead, it is produced by the tension between the state's democratic character and the limits imposed on policy-makers by the capitalist system.

The Canadian Welfare State in Comparative Perspective

The defenders of welfare-state spending usually base their case on society's obligation to alleviate the financial hardship suffered by its least privileged members and on the desirability of narrowing the inequalities in wealth generated by the market economy. It is therefore worth considering both the extent of economic hardship in Canada and the distribution of income. These data provide the background for any evaluation of the need for, and success of, social expenditures. One way of looking at this background is to compare Canada to other advanced capitalist societies. The problem with this approach is that an unemployed single mother in Halifax is unlikely to be impressed by news that she is better off than her counterpart in Louisville, Kentucky. For someone experiencing economic hardship the relevant measure of his or her condition is that of others within the same society. This does not mean that international comparisons are beside the point. What it does mean, however, is that these comparisons cannot be the sole basis for assessing the extent of the social needs to which welfare spending responds.

It has become popular to portray Canada as a society whose standard of living has been overtaken and even surpassed by that of many other countries over the past two decades. But if a measure of real purchasing power—what economists call 'purchasing power parities' (PPPs)—is used rather than nominal income, one finds that few countries surpass Canada in their standard of living. For decades only the United States had a higher average real purchasing power than Canada. In recent years Canada has slipped a bit in the rankings, but still is among the handful of wealthiest countries (see Figure 6.2). Of course, 'averages' may conceal inequalities in the extent to which a relatively high standard of living is shared by different segments of the population. Various studies of the distribution of income in Canada compared to that in other developed capitalist societies all point to the same conclusion: Canada falls somewhere in the middle. The distribution of income is more equal than in the United States or France, but less equal than in Japan, Sweden, or Norway.

The well-being of a society obviously cannot be reduced to the purchasing power of its 'average' member and the distribution of income. Without becoming sidetracked into a long discussion of the material and psychological components of personal well-being, we must at least acknowledge that measures of the quality of life (QOL) need to be included in any attempt to compare the levels of welfare in different societies. The QOL cannot be measured directly. Instead, it is necessary to infer QOL from one or more factors that, arguably, reflect some dimension of life experience.

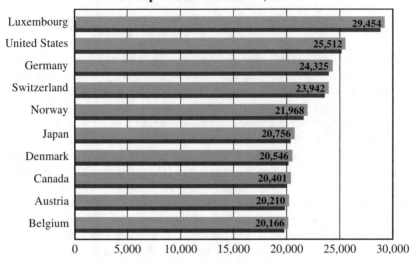

FIGURE 6.2
Per Capita Purchasing Power Parities
for Top 10 OECD Countries, 1994

SOURCE: OECD, *OECD Economic Surveys, Canada 1996* (Paris: OECD, 1996).

This gets us onto very controversial terrain. For several consecutive years the United Nations Development Program has ranked Canada first in the world on its 'human development index'—a composite measure that includes real purchasing power, life expectancy, adult literacy, and mean years of schooling.[3] Canadians have grown used to hearing that the UN rates their country the best place to live in the world. Canada does less well in the UN's ranking of countries when gender equality and inequalities in the distribution of income are added to the picture, but it still places in the top 10. One can take issue with the validity of the UN's human development index, but it would take a churlish disposition or the blindness of an ideological malcontent to deny that Canada is a pretty good place to live—for most people.

In terms of the state's response to social needs, governments in Canada together spend less on welfare than do many Western European countries. This is not meant to imply that the 'right' level of welfare expenditure is higher than the Canadian level. Comparisons like this do not take into account demographic differences, nor do they tell us anything about how efficiently the money is spent. Moreover, 'right' in this context is a matter of ideological preference. Some people are willing to tolerate large inequalities in wealth if the alternative is extensive state interference with individual choice through high levels of taxation and public spending.

Leaving aside the question of what the 'right' level of social spending might be, one can at least say that Canadian governments have been slower than their Western European counterparts in assembling the structure of the welfare state and that the contemporary Canadian welfare state is less developed than that found in many other capitalist societies. Canada's slower implementation of major social reforms probably owes less to a lower level of need in Canada than it does to political factors. These would include a comparatively weak labour movement, the absence of an electorally strong left-wing party on the national stage, the ability of the dominant political parties to structure the nation's political agenda around non-class divisions like language and region, and even the effects of Canada's federal constitution.

The Extent of Social Need in Canada

Social policy is essentially a response to inequality. Indeed, the cornerstone of the welfare state is payments made to individuals and families in financial need. Their need may be temporary, related to fluctuations in the economy, to declining demand for their particular skills, or to a stage in an individual's life cycle (e.g., maternity leave, retirement). Or their need may be chronic, as in the case of those who because of sickness, injury, or some other condition are unemployable, or those whose employment incomes are insufficient to maintain what the state has determined to be a socially acceptable standard of living. These payments are usually assumed to be *redistributive*—transferring money from those who can afford to pay to those who are in need. The distribution of income, however, has changed relatively little despite the implementation of major social security programs. In 1951 the top 20 per cent of income-earners in Canada accounted for 42.8 per cent of total money income, and the bottom 20 per cent of income-earners accounted for 4.4 per cent. In 1995 the top quintile accounted for 40.2 per cent of money income and the lowest quintile for 6.4 per cent.[4] When social security benefits are excluded from the picture, the inequality gap is much wider.

The distribution of income is, of course, only part of the story in any assessment of social well-being. The other part involves the extent of poverty. The distribution of wealth in a society may be very unequal. But if the material condition of society's least privileged members is high enough that they are able to afford a lifestyle that includes life's necessities and allows them to maintain their personal dignity, it would seem capricious to speak of poverty. This condition of universal (if unequal) affluence was the vision that American President Lyndon Johnson expressed in the 1960s in the slogan 'the Great Society' and that Pierre Trudeau promised when he spoke of 'the Just Society'. The reality, of course, is that poverty has not been erased from the social landscape in United States, Canada, or any other capitalist society.

It is true that what is meant by the term 'poverty' suggests something different in these advanced capitalist countries from what would be considered poverty in Congo or Mexico. Poverty is a relative concept. This is reflected in the fact that poverty is defined by organizations like Statistics Canada, the National Council of Welfare, and the Canadian Council on Social Development (CCSD) in terms of the share of household income spent on food, shelter, and clothing.[5] There is nothing sacred about a poverty line set in this way. Indeed, among those who study poverty there has been considerable controversy in recent years over the methodology used to measure this condition.[6] These debates are not merely academic, for the simple reason that statistics on poverty are routinely reported by the media and are used by individuals and groups in debating social conditions and social policy. The low-income cut-off lines (LICOs) set by Statistics Canada become referred to as 'poverty lines' by many journalists, academics, politicians, and interest groups, and those who fall below them are said to live in poverty. Poverty is, we all agree, an undesirable condition. To say that over four million Canadians live below the low-income cut-off line established by Statistics Canada lacks the political punch of saying that this same number of Canadians live in poverty. Here is what Statistics Canada says about the nature and appropriate interpretation of its low-income cut-offs:

> . . . *the cut-offs are not poverty lines and should not be so interpreted.* The setting of poverty lines necessarily involves a value judgement as to the level of minimum income below which an individual or family would generally be regarded as 'poor'. No such judgement has been attempted in constructing the low-income cut-offs. Rather these cut-offs were designed in response to the need to qualify the numbers and characteristics of individuals and families falling into the lowest level of income category—defined in relative terms, taking into account current overall levels of living. . . . As a result, while many individuals or families falling below the cut-offs would be considered in 'poverty' by almost any Canadian standard, others would be deemed by most to be in quite comfortable circumstances.[7]

Keeping in mind the controversy associated with the measurement of poverty, we will use the Statistics Canada measure of low income in analysing social need in Canada. Currently the low-income cut-off line—Stats Can does not call it the poverty line—is 56.2 per cent or more of gross household income spent on food, shelter, and clothing. This is about 20 percentage points above the national average of household income spent on life's essentials.

Three main facts emerge from an analysis of statistics on poverty in Canada. First, a large number of Canadians fall below the poverty line. As of 1995, about 5.1 million people, or 17.4 per cent of the population, fell below Statistics Canada's low-income level. This is, admittedly, an improvement over poverty levels of a couple of decades ago. In 1969 the poverty rate was 23.1 per cent, or 4,851,000 people. Second, poverty is not distributed equally. The likelihood of being poor is greater for families led by women, elderly single women, single people aged 25 or less, and families living in

Newfoundland. The National Council of Welfare uses the term the 'feminization of poverty' to make the point that women account for a larger share of the poor in most age and family status categories than men. While the general trend has been towards a decrease in the poverty rate, in the case of single-parent families led by women the poverty rate actually increased from about 53 per cent of these families in 1981 to close to 60 per cent today. Third, for those individuals and families without employment or other private source of income, the level of social assistance benefits they are eligible to receive leaves them considerably below the poverty line. Because of provincial differences in eligibility requirements and in benefit levels for provincially administered welfare and social services, the extent of this shortfall varies among provinces. Table 6.1 shows the welfare income paid to a family of two adults and two children in 1995, compared to the poverty line, for each province. Even if the value of the Child Tax Benefit, the GST rebate, and such in-kind transfers as subsidized housing are added to these welfare levels, they still remain below the poverty line in most provinces.

Three Pillars of Social Policy

1. The Income Security System

The income security system includes those programs intended to protect or supplement the incomes of individuals and families. Some of these involve direct money transfers to those who meet specified criteria of eligibility. Old

Table 6.1
Welfare Income as Percentage of Poverty Line, 1996

	Single Employable	Disabled Person	Couple, Two Children
Newfoundland	19%	61%	53%
Prince Edward Island	40	67	64
Nova Scotia	43	62	58
New Brunswick	24	47	48
Quebec	39	53	51
Ontario	42	73	57
Manitoba	39	51	56
Saskatchewan	42	62	62
Alberta	31	42	55
British Columbia	39	60	56

SOURCE: National Council of Welfare, *Welfare Incomes 1996* (Ottawa: Health and Welfare, Winter 1997–8), Table 6.

Age Security (OAS) payments, the Guaranteed Income Supplement (GIS), employment insurance (EI) benefits, and social assistance are examples of these. Others involve benefits received through the tax system, such as Registered Retirement Savings Plan (RRSP) deductions and marital, child, and age exemptions. Spending on social policy, of which income security programs constitute the major share, accounts for over 60 per cent of all program spending by Ottawa. After payments on the public debt, this has been the most rapidly growing area of federal spending. A number of factors suggest that the demands on the income security system will continue to grow in the future.

Among these factors is Canada's aging population. This translates into increased demand on the OAS and CPP/QPP systems, not to mention the added pressures on the health-care system because of the fact that the elderly are society's heaviest consumers of health services.

Changes to the family have also increased the pressure on the income security system. Since the 1968 reform of Canada's Divorce Act, single-parent families have increased steadily. Over four-fifths of these families are headed by women. Female-led single-parent families experience a high rate of poverty: about five times higher than that for male single-parent families. To put this a bit differently, even though single-parent mothers with children comprised only 3 per cent of Canadian households in 1994, they accounted for about one-third of the approximately one million families falling below Stats Canada's LICO. This high rate of poverty among single-parent families headed by women indicates a major failing of the existing income security system. There is no reason to expect the percentage of single-parent families to decline in the future.

A third factor that has increased demands on the social safety net involves economic change. While Canada's job creation record has been quite good compared to most other advanced capitalist economies, many of these new jobs have been in low-paying service occupations—'McJobs' as they are sometimes called. Moreover, much of the growth in service-sector employment involves part-time jobs, and therefore part-time pay as well as no benefits. An increasing number of Canadians have fallen into the category of the working poor, people who are employed for some or even all of the year, but whose incomes leave them at or below social assistance levels.

In response to the challenge posed by the increasing costs of social programs, an old debate has resurfaced. It pits those who support universal eligibility for social benefits against those who argue for selective eligibility based on some sort of income test. Those on the political left view social benefits as entitlements that go with citizenship. They oppose selectivity on the grounds that means-tested benefits carry a social stigma that is repugnant in a society that values equality. Those on the right are more likely to support selectively paid social benefits on the grounds that this is a more efficient way to target benefits where they are most needed. The most important universal income security program is OAS. Although there is no means test to determine eligibility, OAS payments are treated as income for tax purposes. Thus, lower-income recipients retain a larger share of those benefits than do higher-income recipients. What is a universal program in terms of eligibility, therefore, is actually geared to income in its application.

Programs directed at elderly Canadians are an important part of the income security system. Federal spending on these programs came to about $20 billion in 1996, which does not include the separately financed CPP. In addition, several of the provinces have income supplement programs for the elderly that, like the federal Guaranteed Income Supplement, are income-tested and thus are targeted at those with little or no private income. Housing subsidies, subsidized drugs, and various tax credits represent other ways in which provincial governments provide benefits to the elderly.

Aside from the inevitability of rising program costs associated with an aging population, two other main policy issues are raised by the existing retirement income security system. One relates to equity. Thomas Courchene demonstrates that elderly Canadians with significant private income gain most from the current system of benefits.[8] This is because the value of the deductions for occupational pension plans and RRSPs under the tax system increases with one's income. '[T]he main result', argues the National Council of Welfare, 'is to enhance the tax advantages of the rich.'[9] Consequently, even though the universally paid OAS benefits are progressive because they count as taxable income, this progressivity is offset by the regressive impact of benefits received by the elderly through the tax system.

Another issue associated with income security for the elderly involves the Canada and Quebec Pension Plans. The CPP faces a funding crisis. The benefits paid to pensioners under the plan are supposed to be financed by contributions and the plan's investment income. But in 1985 the benefits paid by the CPP exceeded contributions to the fund for the first time. A Department of Finance study published that same year indicated that if the contribution rate, which is split evenly between employees and their employers, remained unchanged the CPP would be bankrupt by the year 2004.[10] Estimates indicate that if university graduates just now entering the labour force are to collect the level of benefits currently received by CPP recipients, the contribution rate will have to increase about 100 per cent by the time these graduates reach retirement age (from about 6 per cent of earnings in 1997 to about 12 per cent by the year 2040).

The funding issue raises a question of intergenerational equity. Future generations of workers are going to have to devote a considerably larger share of their income to the CPP than earlier generations who received benefits under the plan. This means that earlier generations of workers have effectively deferred paying taxes that must now and in the future be borne by workers to ensure that the CPP remains self-financing and that current benefit levels can be maintained.

The persistence of high levels of unemployment in Canada has focused

Table 6.2
Public Pension Programs

Program	Nature	Benefit*	Financing	Expenditure (1995, $ billion)
Old Age Security	Demogrant payable to those over 65 subject to residency requirement	Maximum annual pension is $4,737; clawback of 15 per cent on income greater than $53,215; fully indexed to consumer price index (CPI); taxable.	General tax revenues	15.478
Spouse's Allowance	Income-tested; payable from age 60 to 65 to widows, widowers, and spouses of OAS pensioners.	Maximum annual allowance to spouse is $8,404; to widows and widowers $9,278.	General tax revenues	0.429
Guaranteed Income Supplement	Income-tested benefit; recipient must be over age 65 and eligible for OAS pension.	Maximum annual pension is $5,630 for singles, $7,334 for married couples; reduced by 50 per cent of recipient's income in excess of OAS benefits; fully indexed to consumer price index; not taxable.	General tax revenues	4.604

Continued

Table 6.2 continued

Program	Nature	Benefit*	Financing	Expenditure (1995, $ billion)
Canada Pension Plan	Earnings-related designed to replace 25 per cent of average lifetime earnings, up to the average industrial wage; also pays death and disability benefits.	Maximum annual pension is $8,725; after retirement, indexed to consumer price index; taxable.	Equal employer/ employee contributions, presently set at 2.8 per cent of covered earnings.	21.400**

*All amounts pertain to 1 January 1996. The provinces of Alberta, British Columbia, Nova Scotia, Manitoba, Ontario, and Saskatchewan provide income-tested supplements, thereby raising the guaranteed annual income of those aged 65 in excess of OAS/GIS benefits.

**Includes Quebec Pension Plan.

SOURCE: OECD, *OECD Economic Surveys, Canada 1996*, 117.

attention on the costs and economic effects of those components of the income security system associated with being out of work. The most important of these are employment insurance and the provincially administered welfare programs to which Ottawa contributes through the Canada Health and Social Transfer program (formerly the Canada Assistance Plan or CAP). Federal spending on EI and welfare came to about $20 billion in 1996. These programs are an important source of income for millions of Canadians and their dependants. This may be appreciated from the fact that in recent years about one in four members of the Canadian labour force collected unemployment benefits at some point, and close to three million Canadians annually receive welfare payments.

Employment insurance is funded through the contributions of employees and employers, as well as by money from the federal government. It provides most claimants with benefits equal to 55 per cent of their income prior to becoming unemployed for a period up to 45 consecutive weeks. The main policy issues relate to the way benefits are distributed and the effects of this program on the labour force (and therefore on economic performance). Unlike social assistance, EI is not targeted at the poor. But EI does have a couple of redistributive effects, as it redistributes income between regions and between sectors of the economy. Provinces with the highest rates of unemployment derive the greatest benefits from EI, receiving transfers in excess of their contributions to the program. Moreover, the period of employment prior to collecting EI also tends to be shorter in these high-unemployment provinces. EI is a normal part of annual income for a large part of the labour force, particularly in the Atlantic provinces. Most economists argue that EI benefits, which are paid to individuals, have the same economic effect as equalization payments from Ottawa to the less affluent provinces. Both provide disincentives for the movement of people from areas with weak economies to more economically vibrant parts of the country (see Figure 6.4).

Some sectors of the economy, including fishing, forestry, tourism, and the construction trades, are characterized by seasonal unemployment. As it happens, some of the high-unemployment provinces—including British Columbia, Newfoundland, and New Brunswick—are also provinces in which seasonal industries account for a large share of provincial economic activity. In a very real sense EI subsidizes these industries because of the fact that the contribution rate is the same for employees and employers in all sectors of the economy, but the risk of becoming unemployed varies greatly between sectors (see Figure 6.3). The existence of EI makes it less costly for individuals to remain in industries characterized by erratic employment or seasonal lay-offs.

This raises a question of how social policy may affect economic performance. Both the Royal Commission on the Economic Union and Development Prospects for Canada (Macdonald Commission, 1985) and the Royal Commission of Inquiry on Unemployment Insurance (Forget Commission,

FIGURE 6.3
Net Transfers under Employment Insurance
(Dollars of Benefits per Dollar of Contributions),
by Industry, 1995

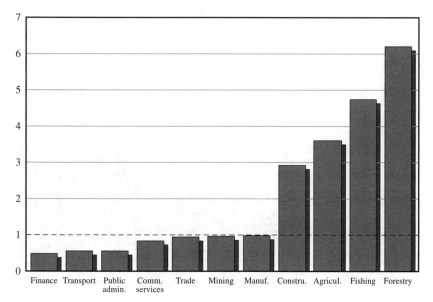

1986) recommended that what was then called unemployment insurance (UI) should be reformed to eliminate disincentives to work and to labour mobility. While their diagnoses of the effects of UI on economic performance were the same, their prescriptions for change were different. The Macdonald Commission recommended raising eligibility requirements, lowering the level of benefits, and gearing employer/employee contributions to the risk of lay-off in an industry. These cost-saving measures were accompanied by the commission's recommendation that a 'Transitional Adjustment Assistance Plan' be created that would essentially subsidize the incomes of those moving between sectors and regions of the economy.[11] The *Report* of the Forget Commission took a different line on reforming the UI system. It recommended that claimants be automatically entitled to the full 50 weeks of benefits, but that their level of benefits be based on their earnings during the entire year prior to their claim. This is referred to as *annualization*. The commission recommended that this change be accompanied by a form of guaranteed annual income designed to supplement the earnings of low-income households.[12]

In 1994 the Liberal government released a discussion paper entitled *Agenda for Jobs and Growth: Improving Social Security in Canada*. The 'Green Book', as it was dubbed, argued that the existing unemployment insurance sys-

FIGURE 6.4
Net Transfers under Employment Insurance
(Dollars of Benefits per Dollar of Contributions),
by Province, 1995

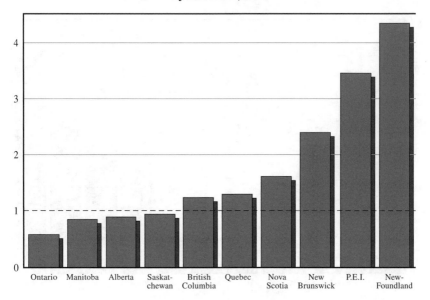

SOURCE: OECD, *OECD Economic Surveys, Canada 1996*, 76

tem was an important cause of unemployment, creating rigidity in Canadian labour markets and slowing adjustment to economic change. This view was repeated several months later in the government's 1995 budget when Minister of Finance Paul Martin Jr stated that 'a key job for unemployment insurance in the future must be to help Canadians stay off unemployment insurance.'[13] When reforms to the system were finally brought in about one year later, they involved a combination of tightening and redirected spending. On the tightening side, benefits were lowered, especially for repeat claimants, eligibility was made more difficult, and premiums were reduced to encourage businesses to take on new workers. The redirected spending involved job training programs intended to improve the employability of those receiving employment insurance benefits.

Social assistance—or welfare, as it is commonly referred to—used to be funded on a 50/50 basis by Ottawa and the provinces. However, beginning in 1990 the federal government 'capped' its contribution to Ontario, British Columbia, and Alberta, then in 1995 the previous cost-sharing formula was replaced by the Canada Health and Social Transfer, which is not tied to provincial spending levels. Unlike EI, welfare eligibility is determined by a means test. Both eligibility requirements and the level of welfare benefits are determined provincially and, as we saw earlier in the chapter, benefits vary significantly between provinces (see Table 6.1).

The total cost of social assistance has roughly quadrupled in real terms since the CAP was launched in 1966. This growth can be attributed to a couple of factors. First, because Ottawa covered half the cost of assistance and of the various social services that fell under the plan, there was less pressure on the

Table 6.3

Evolution of the Unemployment Insurance System since 1971

1971	The 1971 Unemployment Insurance Act is passed. Coverage is extended to virtually all employees, the replacement rate is increased to 67 per cent; benefit durations are increased and made a function of local and national unemployment rates.
1977	The minimum weeks of work needed to claim UI (the entrance requirement) is increased from 8 weeks to 10–14 weeks, depending on the local unemployment rate.
1979	The replacement rate is lowered to 60 per cent. New entrants to the labour market and repeat claimants are required to have extra weeks of work to qualify for benefits.
1990	Entrance requirements are increased to 10–20 weeks, depending on the local unemployment rate. Benefit durations are reduced.
1993	The replacement rate is lowered to 57 per cent. Those who quit their jobs are made ineligible for UI.
1994	The minimum entrance requirement is raised to 12 weeks. Benefit durations are reduced, so that a claimant in a low unemployment region can receive a maximum of 36 weeks of benefits. The replacement rate is lowered to 55 per cent, except for low-income claimants with dependants, for whom the replacement rate is raised to 60 per cent.
1996	Repeat users face a lower replacement rate, and those with high incomes will have part of their benefits clawed back by the income tax system. Claimants with relatively few hours in their qualifying periods receive lower benefits. Low-income claimants with children receive an additional supplement. Maximum duration of benefits capped at 45 weeks.

NOTE: 'Unemployment insurance' was renamed 'Employment insurance' in 1995.

SOURCE: OECD, *OECD Economic Surveys, Canada 1996*, 78.

provincial governments that actually administered welfare programs to control the growth in spending than they would have been felt if they had had to bear the full cost of financing these programs. Second, and more important, is the fact that demand for welfare has increased. Like EI, expenditure on welfare is related to the level of unemployment. Figure 6.5 shows that the number of welfare recipients rises and falls lockstep with changes in the unemployment rate. Or at least this was true until the early 1990s. Since then, the number of persons receiving social assistance has been greater than the number of people receiving EI, a troubling fact that reflects an increase in the number of 'employable unemployed'. Indeed, the employable unemployed currently account for between about one-third and three-quarters of provincial welfare rolls.

We have already seen that benefit levels paid under social assistance are not adequate to enable recipients to maintain a standard of living above Statistics Canada's 'poverty line'. The large increase in the number of 'employables' receiving welfare has focused attention on a rather different aspect of this program: whether social assistance is designed in a way that discourages the employable unemployed from seeking work. Leaving aside the question of the appropriate balance between society's obligation to the individual and the individual's personal responsibility for his or her material well-being, it appears

FIGURE 6.5
Unemployment and Social Assistance Caseloads
as Percentage of Working-Age Population, 1981–95

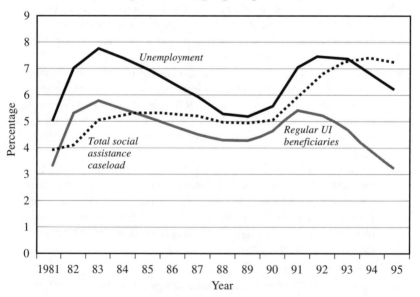

SOURCE: OECD, *OECD Economic Surveys, Canada 1996*, 81.

that the current welfare system may discourage some of those who are compelled to seek social assistance from re-entering the labour force. The reason for this is that the marginal taxation rate implicit in going off welfare to take a low-paying job is extremely high. In other words, if a person on welfare accepts a low-paying job that, nevertheless, pays enough to disqualify that person from receiving social assistance benefits, the effective rate of taxation on the income earned over that which would have been received on welfare is extremely high. Concretely, this means that the transition from welfare to work may actually, and perversely, result in no improvement in one's standard of living. This is sometimes called the 'poverty trap': for many whose employment prospects are limited to low-paying jobs it makes economic sense to stay on welfare. But as we noted earlier, welfare levels are not compatible with what most Canadians would consider a decent standard of living.

The poverty trap is unlikely to grow less serious. Most of the new jobs created by the Canadian economy are in low-paying occupations in the service sector—fast-food restaurant jobs and the like. Although the general level of poverty in Canada has declined over time, the number of working poor has increased. In 1976, 46 per cent of families with incomes below the poverty line had some employment income. In 1994 the figure was 60 per cent, and over one-third of these families included someone who was employed for the entire year. For a single mother faced with the choice of either remaining on welfare or accepting a job at the provincial minimum wage, it may not make economic sense to enter the labour force. All provinces allow welfare recipients to earn a certain amount without any reduction in their welfare benefits. And some provinces allow earnings exemptions for such work-related expenses as child care. Measures like these are intended to reduce the disincentives to work that have plagued the welfare system.

But do they work? The idea behind letting welfare recipients keep all or part of their earnings is, of course, to eliminate financial disincentives to work and, ultimately, to wean people from welfare dependence. A number of studies suggest, however, that instead of reducing the number of people on welfare and thus lowering total welfare costs, greater work incentives may actually contribute to an increase in the welfare rolls. According to these studies, the attraction of being able to collect welfare benefits and retain earned income has the effect of pulling more people into the welfare system while doing little to discourage those already on welfare from leaving the system.[14] Economist Doug Allen goes so far as to argue that an increase in allowable earnings, combined with other measures that have the effect of raising the incomes of welfare recipients, 'would lead to increases in the number of participants on welfare, single parents, births to unwed women, and divorces, along with lower labour force participation rates among low-income individuals.'[15] It is still possible to advocate such measures on the grounds that they may help alleviate poverty, but it does not follow from this that welfare rolls will shrink and costs will be cut.

2. The Health-Care System

The health-care system illustrates as well as any area of social policy the way in which government's response to popular demands is contained within the ideological limits of capitalist society. Starting in Saskatchewan during the late 1940s, health services have become 'democratized'. The private fee-for-service system has been replaced by one where most services are paid by the state. Universal access, where a person's ability to consume medical services is not dependent on income, has emerged as a major principle of health policy. The five principles specifically mentioned in the Canada Health Act include portability (residents of one province are entitled to coverage in other provinces), comprehensiveness (all important health needs should be included), universality, public-funding, and public administration.

This reform has been gradual, beginning with hospital services and extending to physicians' services only in the 1960s and early 1970s. Moreover, the principle of universal access has seen setbacks. During the late 1970s and early 1980s most provinces allowed doctors to charge their patients a fee on top of the amount covered under the provincial fee schedule.

Most doctors continue to operate as independent business people with relative freedom to determine whom they will accept as patients, where they will practise, and the sort (and therefore cost) of care they prescribe. In recent years, however, the public and universal character of the health-care system has been chipped away at by provincial governments that have 'de-listed' many services that previously were publicly paid and by the willingness of some provincial governments to allow private clinics to operate in certain areas of specialized treatment.

Health care is one of the hottest of hot-button issues in Canada. We all rely on the system at some point in our lives, and the possibility that adequate care might not be available when we need it is enough to set off alarm bells for most people. Moreover, the vast majority of Canadians are convinced that their health-care system is superior to the 'private' American model, a belief nurtured by those politicians, journalists, academics, and health-care professionals who portray user fees and other deviations from a strictly public and universal health-care model as being 'American' and 'bad'.

In fact, however, the Canadian system has never been a purely public one, nor is the American system of providing health care purely private. They are both mixed systems in terms of how they are financed and delivered. Indeed, virtually all health-care systems in the world's capitalist democracies involve a mixture of public and private elements, Norway coming closest to a purely public model and the United States having the smallest public component. But even in the United States about 40 cents of every dollar spent on health care comes from the public purse. Canada falls between these extremes (see Table 6.4).

Although Canada's health-care system is predominantly public, it is not and

Table 6.4
The Public Share in Total Expenditure on Health,
Selected Countries, 1991

Country	%
Australia	67.8
Austria	67.1
Belgium	88.9
Canada	72.2
Denmark	81.5
Finland	80.9
France	73.9
Germany	71.8
Iceland	87.0
Ireland	75.8
Italy	77.5
Japan	72.0
Luxembourg	91.4*
Netherlands	73.1
New Zealand	78.9
Norway	96.6
Portugal	61.7*
Spain	82.2
Sweden	78.0
Switzerland	68.3
UK	83.3
US	43.9

*1990 values

SOURCE: Organization for Economic Co-operation and Development, *OECD Health Systems: Facts and Trends, 1960–1991*, vol. 1 (Paris: OECD, 1993), 252.

never has been a system of 'socialized' medicine. Nevertheless, there are significant limits on doctors' freedom, such as provincial caps on physician billings to the publicly paid system. But the fact that patients no longer pay directly for most medical services has not changed the for-profit orientation that characterizes much of the health-care system. According to health economists, the self-interest of non-salaried doctors lies in maximizing the number of patients they see, in specializing in areas where the fees are higher, in protecting their monopoly on health care, and in prescribing expensive medication and procedures for their patients.

The for-profit orientation of the health-care system is reinforced by the ideological values that characterize the medical profession. Numerous studies have demonstrated what one knows intuitively from listening to spokespersons for the medical profession: professional autonomy is the foremost value for most doctors. Anything that interferes with their ability to conduct their practice as a private business is considered repugnant.[16] There are, of course, reasonable grounds for leaving decisions on how much and what sort of treatment patients receive in the hands of those who have received long and specialized medical training. The point is that 'professional autonomy' may also be used to defend the occupational privileges—including the income status—of the medical profession.

A second dimension of health care that has remained largely unchanged, despite the democratization of access to health services, is the overwhelming emphasis on curative as opposed to preventive care. There is a broad consensus that the causes of many illnesses lie in the environment, are attributable to conditions in the workplace, or are the result of personal lifestyles. In other words, it is well established that having more doctors does not necessarily mean better health.[17] And yet health policy continues to be oriented towards the cure rather than the prevention of disease. Part of the explanation lies in the system of incentives within which the medical profession works. These incentives mainly reward the treatment of illness rather than its prevention. It would be unfair, however, to place the major responsibility for the curative orientation of the health-care system on the medical profession. The reason health policy is geared towards curing people who are already sick lies deeper than this. To shift the emphasis to prevention would, in fact, require that fundamental characteristics of our industrialized mass consumption society be called into question and reformed.

Such problems as toxic contaminants, stressful levels of noise and traffic congestion, chemicals added to food directly to preserve and 'enhance' it and indirectly through modern farming techniques to grow it more efficiently, and harmful lifestyle habits are acknowledged to be major contributors to heart disease, cancer, and the other 'diseases of affluence'. To deal with the causes of preventable diseases (as opposed to treating their symptoms), the very structure and value system of urban-industrial civilization would have to be reformed. Government advertising campaigns against smoking and programs to encourage individuals to stay fit (such as Ottawa's 'Participaction' program), and banning leaded gasoline or well-known carcinogens do in fact focus on prevention. But the most effective reforms would involve changes in cultural values and lifestyles, changes that do not require expensive government programs and phalanxes of health-care professionals but that are not easily achieved.

Leaving aside the efficiency of the health-care system and whether resources would be better deployed in preventing rather than treating illness, two main issues have dominated recent debate over health policy: cost and access. The cost issue has come to the fore as a result of two factors: an aging population and Ottawa's determination to transfer more of the burden of paying for health care onto the provincial governments. Viewed from an international perspective, the level of public spending on health in Canada is higher than the average for industrial democracies (see Figure 6.6). What is more relevant from the standpoint of policy-makers in Canada is the share of public resources that go towards health services. That share levelled off in the late 1970s but has shown signs of growth in some provinces during recent years. As the Canadian population continues to age there are good reasons to expect that this pressure on costs will increase.

Another factor that contributes to increasing health-care costs is technology. 'Our technological ingenuity in inventing things to do to people, in the cause of health care', says Dr H.E. Emson, 'has long since outstripped our communal ability to pay for them.'[18] An American study published in 1984 concluded that 'the introduction of new technologies has caused an annual percentage increase, in real costs, of between one and three per cent of total health

FIGURE 6.6
Health Spending ($000)
per Person in Purchasing Power Parities, 1995

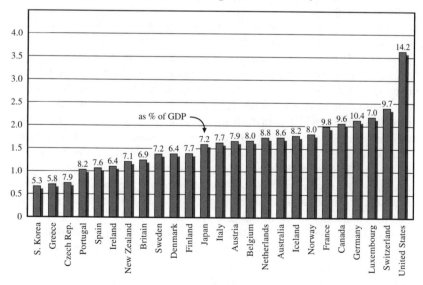

SOURCE: *The Economist*, 14 June 1997, 112, from OECD.

expenditures per year over the last decade.'[19] This was also the conclusion of the Canadian Medical Association Task Force on the Allocation of Health Care Resources (1984),[20] and has since been confirmed by other studies. Increasing costs due to technology might be tolerable if the expensive machines and procedures responsible for these increases could be shown to contribute to a significant improvement in people's health. It appears, however, that sophisticated medical technology such as that used for treating coronary and cancer patients has contributed to the life span of the ill and to the over-all costs of the health-care system without reducing the incidence of disease in society. This certainly is not an argument against spending money on pro-longing life. But the effect of curative medical technology should not be con-fused with the effects of earlier (and cost-saving) innovations in immunization against disease and in antibiotics.

Spending more on health care does not ensure better health, as the American case so amply demonstrates. Despite spending a considerably greater share of national income on health than any other industrial democ-racy, the United States has life expectancy levels and an infant mortality rate that are inferior to some countries that spend half as much on health. Canadians have no reason to feel smug on this count. Although our popula-tion is younger than that of Japan and most Western European countries, we devote a greater share of our economic resources to health care than they do, without having superior health performance to show for our investment. 'The message', writes demographer David Foot, 'is inescapable: Canada is spend-ing more on health care than most other advanced countries and not getting better health in return.'[21]

Most scenarios for the future point to an increase in the level of spending on health services, primarily due to the greater demand created by an aging population. If the demographic changes that form the basis for such scenarios are highly probable, then provincial governments are faced with some hard choices regarding reform of the health-care system. This is particularly true of the distribution of health spending between expensive hospital and chronic-care facilities, for which demand is greatest among the elderly, and other com-ponents of health spending such as physicians' incomes. The most effective method of keeping costs under control is to transfer some existing health-care resources to services delivered in the home, through local clinics, and by nurses and paramedical professionals. Alternatives are to devote a greater share of public expenditure to the health sector, limit the supply of doctors, or rede-fine the boundaries of the health-care system.

A second dimension of the cost issue involves the relative contributions of the federal and provincial governments. Until 1977, when the Established Programs Fiscal Arrangements Act (EPF) was passed, Ottawa basically matched provincial spending for health services on a dollar-for-dollar basis. EPF eliminated the 50/50 cost-sharing formula and replaced it with a block transfer of cash and tax points (i.e., the value of Ottawa transferring to the provinces a part of its taxation of income). The value of these transfers would increase at the rate of growth in GNP rather than, as previously, according to the level of provincial spending on health. A large part of the federal government's motivation in proposing this change had to do with fiscal restraint. As Prime Minister Trudeau put it at the time, 'the Provinces will have a greater incentive to implement what are admittedly difficult measures designed to restrain spending in these fields to reasonable levels.'[22] Throughout the 1980s and continuing in the 1990s Ottawa cut back on its contribution under the EPF formula. The National Council of Welfare projects that if this trend continues, Ottawa's cash payments to the provinces under EPF, which came to about $10 billion in 1992–3 and had fallen to about $8 billion in 1996–7, will disappear entirely by the early twenty-first century.[23] Given that health care is an area of provincial jurisdiction under the constitution, Ottawa's involvement being through the back door of its spending power, it is not clear how the federal government would enforce national standards in medicare if it were no longer paying some of the bills.

As was also true of social assistance, Canada's modern-day health-care system was built on a foundation of shared-cost programs under which Ottawa paid 50 per cent of the costs. Those days are long gone. The decisive moment in Ottawa's retreat from this method of paying for social policy occurred in 1995 when Finance Minister Paul Martin announced a 'new vision of Confederation'. The shared-cost programs that paid for welfare and social services under the Canada Assistance Plan and EPF funding for health and post-secondary education were replaced by a single block transfer to the provinces called the Canada Health and Social Transfer (CHST).

In explaining the advantages of the CHST, the 1995 budget documents stated that it would 'end the intrusiveness of previous cost sharing arrangements'.[24] More specifically, the transition to block funding under the CHST was argued to have the following beneficial effects:

- Provinces will no longer be subject to rules stipulating which expenditures are eligible for cost-sharing.
- Provinces will be free to pursue their own innovative approaches to social security reform.
- The expense of administering cost-sharing will be eliminated.
- Federal expenditures will no longer be driven by provincial decisions on how, and to whom, to provide social assistance and social services.

Provinces would not, however, be free to do whatever they please under the new fiscal arrangements. The Liberal budget mentioned health care and social assistance as two areas where national standards would be maintained. In the case of social assistance this amounted only to an interdiction on minimum residency requirements. In regard to health care, the Liberals insisted that provinces would have to respect the principles of the Canada Health Act.

The Liberals' determination to rein in federal transfers to the provinces has not been matched by a corresponding rhetoric of decentralization. On the contrary, the Liberal government has refused to concede an inch on the issue of national standards, particularly in regard to the health-care system. Their message to the provinces has been this: We will give you fewer and fewer dollars with which to pay for your health-care services, but we will continue to set conditions on how those services must operate. The Liberals' resolve has been put to the test by the Conservative government of Alberta, which has allowed the establishment of private clinics where patients, for a price, can jump the queue they would otherwise face in the publicly funded system. At the end of the day, however, all Ottawa can do is withhold some of the health-care dollars it would otherwise transfer to Alberta or any other transgressing province. This may be a penalty without much sting. As economist Paul Boothe observes, 'The amount of money coming from Ottawa compared to the total health budget is trivial.'[25]

The erosion of national standards in health care is far from being an isolated Alberta phenomenon. Faced with pressure from a number of provinces there is good reason to expect that Ottawa will eventually decide that *national* standards do not mean *identical* standards across provinces.

3. Redistribution: Class and Regional Dimensions

It is widely assumed that the welfare state involves some significant redistribution of income from those who can afford to pay to those who are in need. This redistributive function is often assumed to take place through the tax system, particularly through progressive personal income taxation. On the expenditure side, income security programs are believed to comprise a social safety net that provides greater benefits to the poor than to those who are well off. In fact, however, those who study the distributive effects of taxation and public spending are not in agreement on whether the growth of the state has been accompanied by a significant narrowing of income inequalities. The majority opinion tends to side with the conclusion of economist Irwin Gillespie: 'In Canada, at least, a larger state has not led to a more egalitarian state.'[26]

By itself, the tax system *does not* redistribute income from the wealthy to the poor. The reason for this is that only some forms of taxation are *progressive* (i.e., the rate of taxation increases with one's income). Some taxes, notably sales and property taxes, the health insurance premiums that still exist in Alberta, and the GST (except for the least well-off) are *regressive*. They weigh more heavily on those with lower incomes because the amount of the tax one pays does not depend on one's level of income. When income transfers from the state to individuals and families are left out of the picture, the overall distributional impact of taxation is regressive. Lower-income groups pay a much larger share of their income in taxes than do high-income groups.

Separate studies by Gillespie, Maslove, Dodge, Gray, and the National Council of Welfare all find that the highest effective rate of taxation is experienced by the lowest income-earners.[27]

One should not conclude from this evidence of regressivity in the burden of taxation that the state is a sort of perverse Robin Hood: taking from the poor instead of the rich. Any proper assessment of the distributional impact of government policies must include the income benefits from public spending. There is no doubt that the total effect of the money transfers received under income security programs and public spending on education, housing, health care, transportation, and a host of other programs favours the poor.[28]

Combining the distributional consequences of taxation with those of public expenditure provides one with the necessary basis for conclusions about whether government policies in fact promote greater equality of income. Basing his research on 1969 income data, Gillespie concluded that the total *fiscal incidence* (i.e., distributional impact) of taxation and spending by all levels of government in Canada was favourable to the poor.[29] This redistribution was due to public expenditures, not to the tax system. There is evidence, however, that the taxation side of the public finance equation has become more favourable towards the poor since Gillespie's earlier studies. Using data on of total tax incidence between 1951 and 1988, Gillespie, Vermaeten, and Vermaeten[30] arrive at the following conclusions:

- the average tax rate for persons increased from 27 to 37 per cent.
- tax rates for the poorest 10 per cent of families have fallen since 1969, from about 37 per cent to 31 per cent.
- tax rates for the richest 2 per cent of Canadians have fallen slightly since 1951, from 46 to 42 per cent.
- the greatest burden of increased taxation has been borne by the middle class, tax rates for families in the 31–98 percentile groups increasing from about 22–3 per cent in 1951 to 36–7 per cent in 1988.

The most controversial reform to the tax system in recent years was the introduction of the Goods and Services Tax on 1 January 1991. It replaced the previous federal sales tax that had been levied on manufacturers. Sales taxes are by their very nature regressive, so Ottawa's claim that the GST was intended to be a fairer tax was greeted with scepticism by many. In fact, two aspects to the GST made this claim at least somewhat plausible. First, unlike the older federal sales tax, the GST is applied to services as well as goods. Higher income-earners spend more on services than lower income-earners, and so will carry more of the burden of this tax. Second, Ottawa introduced a refundable sales tax credit designed to compensate for the regressive effects of the GST. The tax credit reduces the regressive impact of the GST, but it is not eliminated. Nevertheless, Gillespie and his colleagues argue that the declining share of total tax revenue accounted for by sales taxes, combined with tax credits for lower income-earners, have decreased the regressive impact of federal and provincial sales taxes.[31]

Another way of looking at the distributional effects of public policy is to consider the relative importance of different sources of public revenue. What one finds is that since the early 1950s, when revenues from personal and corporate taxation were roughly in balance, the share of public revenue accounted for by taxation of personal income has increased while the importance of corporate income taxation has fallen dramatically. Personal income tax revenues today account for close to 40 per cent of total government revenue, compared to well under 10 per cent in the case of corporate taxes (see Figure 6.7). Federal and provincial payroll taxes have become increasingly important as a source of government revenue, growing from about 5 per cent of total revenue in 1951 to 14 per cent in 1988. The burden of this increase has fallen mainly on middle income-earners.

The conclusion is inescapable. The welfare state has been financed mainly by the users of public education, public health services, and income security programs. The idea that business has been squeezed to finance politically popular social programs is a gross misrepresentation of the facts.

FIGURE 6.7
Relative Importance of Various Taxes in Canada, 1951, 1969, 1988

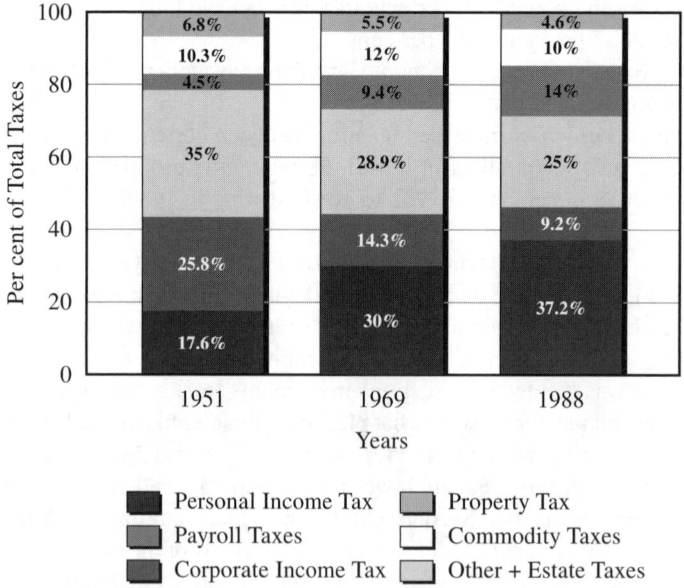

SOURCE: W. Irwin Gillespie, Arndt Vermaeten, and Frank Vermaeten, 'Who Paid the Taxes in Canada, 1951–1988?', *Canadian Public Policy* 21, 3 (Sept. 1995): 319.

No discussion of redistribution in Canada can ignore the ways the federal government has attempted to affect regional inequalities in income. These have taken three main forms: (1) equalization payments from Ottawa to the less affluent provinces, intended to ensure 'that provincial governments have sufficient revenues to provide reasonably comparable levels of public service at reasonably comparable levels of taxation';[33] (2) income transfers from Ottawa to individuals that, as we saw in the earlier discussion of EI, are a major source of income in communities where employment opportunities tend to be seasonal; and (3) industrial assistance programs that subsidize businesses in economically depressed regions.

Economists have tended to be critical of these regionally redistributive programs on the grounds that they reduce the incentives for people to move to more prosperous regions of the country where jobs are more plentiful. The overall efficiency of the economy, they argue, suffers as a result of programs intended to subsidize incomes and public services in economically weak regions. The usual rebuttal to this economic efficiency argument is that the price of these programs is worth paying to achieve the goals of fairness—no Canadian should be seriously disadvantaged from the standpoint of educational opportunities, health care, and other public services as a result of where they live—and national unity. Moreover, some economists contend that equal-

FIGURE 6.8
Index of Family Income before Transfers,
by Highest and Lowest Quintiles in Constant (1995) Dollars,
1980–95

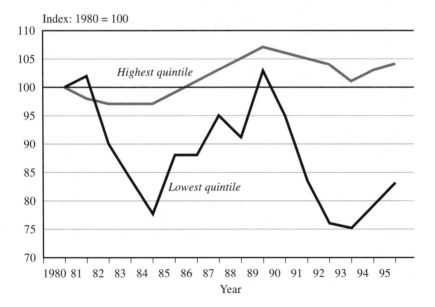

ization can actually *promote* efficiency. Robin Boadway and Frank Flatters
make this case by arguing that without equalization payments there might be
an excessive movement of people from the poorer to the richer provinces,
based on their desire to receive a higher level of services (which are, after all,
real economic benefits) than is available in the poorer provinces. They argue
that the migration resulting from such considerations, as opposed to movement
based on market factors, may be costly to the overall economy.[33]

Leaving aside the economic arguments for and against programs that transfer resources from more affluent to less affluent parts of the country, it has long
been recognized that the constitution assigns to the provinces responsibility
for expensive social programs. However, the capacity to raise revenues to
finance these primary responsibilities varies widely among the provinces.

FIGURE 6.9
Index of Family Income after Tax,
by Highest and Lowest Quintiles in Constant (1995) Dollars,
1980–95

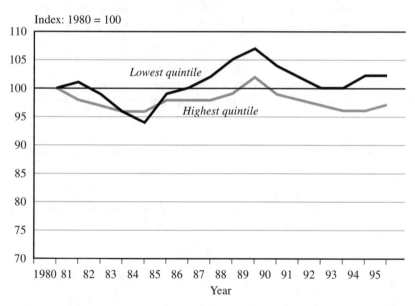

NOTE: The value of 100 on the index for Figures 6.8 and 6.9 represents the share of
family income that the highest and lowest quintiles accounted for in 1980. Thus,
when a quintile's line moves above 100 this represents an increase in its share of
total family income. Falling below the 100 line represents a decline in a quintile's
income share.

SOURCE: Figures 6.8 and 6.9: Statistics Canada, *Income after Tax, Distributions by
Size in Canada*, cat. no. 13–210–XPB, 21.

Equalization is intended to address the inequality in provincial fiscal capacity, and to do so in a way that does not interfere with the constitutional right of provincial governments to determine their policy priorities. It is clear that the approximately $10 billion per year that Ottawa devotes to equalization— money that comes without strings attached as to how recipient provinces must spend it—does help to equalize provinces' financial capacities to offer 'reasonably comparable' levels of social services. And while Ottawa's transfers to the provinces under the CHST are declining, equalization payments have actually increased in recent years. Because the most affluent provinces do not qualify for equalization payments, this means that they are bearing the brunt of federal cutbacks (see Table 6.5).

Erosion of the Welfare State?

Have the egalitarian gains—limited but none the less real—of the postwar welfare state been undermined by recent policies intended to rein in public spending and the deficit? The conventional wisdom is that they have indeed been undermined, and that Canadian society is becoming increasingly polar-

Table 6.5
Major Transfers to Provinces and Territories, 1994–5 and 1996–7
(estimated entitlements in millions of dollars)

	1994–5	*1996–7*	*Change*
Newfoundland	1,484	1,512	+28
Prince Edward Island	316	323	+7
Nova Scotia	1,932	1,949	+17
New Brunswick	1,610	1,632	+22
Quebec	11,446	11,096	–350
Ontario	10,530	9,653	–877
Manitoba	2,039	2,032	–7
Saskatchewan	1,411	1,450	+39
Alberta	2,525	2,313	–212
British Columbia	3,573	3,291	–282
Northwest Territories	74	68	–6
Yukon Territory	34	32	–2
Total	36,974*	35,351**	–1,623

*Made up of equalization, EPF, and CAP.
**Canada Health and Social Transfer and equalization.

SOURCE: Department of Finance, *Budget 1995: Key Actions and Impacts* (Feb. 1995).

ized between the well-off and the poor. But the facts do not provide unambiguous support for this claim. Consider the following:

- the percentage of Canadians below Statistics Canada's low-income cut-off lines has fluctuated between about 14 and 18 per cent since 1980, and was higher during the recession of the early 1980s than it has been at any point in the 1990s.
- the poverty rate for families has fluctuated between about 11 and 15 per cent since 1980, and is about the same in the late 1990s as it was in 1980.
- the poverty rate for elderly Canadians has been cut in half since 1980.
- the poverty rate for children under 18 has fluctuated between about 14 and 21 per cent, but has tended to be a bit higher in the 1990s than during the 1980s (in part due to the increasing percentage of children living in single-parent families).
- family incomes have remained unchanged since 1980, and are about 20 per cent higher than they were in 1970.

The acid test of whether the welfare state continues to cushion lower-income groups from the inequalities generated by the economy, or whether recent policy changes has left these groups more exposed to fluctuations in economic activity, must be the actual distribution of income. As Table 6.6 shows, the distribution of family income has fluctuated very little since the early 1970s, when all the chief components of the Canadian welfare state were already in place. Although it is widely believed that the distribution of family income has become more unequal since the rise of neo-conservatism in the 1980s, the data do not support this claim. Figure 6.8 does indeed show a dra-

Table 6.6
Income Distribution for Families by Quintiles,
1971–95

	Lowest	Second	Middle	Fourth	Highest
1971	5.6	12.6	18.0	23.7	40.0
1975	6.2	13.0	18.2	23.9	38.8
1981	6.4	12.9	18.3	24.1	38.4
1986	6.3	12.3	17.9	24.1	39.4
1990	6.4	12.4	17.9	24.0	39.3
1995	6.4	12.0	17.4	23.9	40.2

SOURCES: Keith Banting, 'The Welfare State and Inequality in the 1980s', *Canadian Review of Sociology and Anthropology* 24, 3 (Aug. 1987): 331; Statistics Canada, *Income after Tax, Distributions by Size in Canada*, 1995, cat. no. 13–210 annual.

matically widening gap between the highest and lowest family income cohorts, *before government transfers and taxes are taken into account.* But Figure 6.9 tells a very different story. After taxes and transfers the relative income shares of the richest and the poorest did not change much between 1980 and 1995.

Chapter Seven

Family Policy

Depending on one's point of view, developments over the past few decades have represented either a renaissance of the family or its decline into the dark ages. Those who subscribe to the renaissance view see little to lament in the demographic shift away from the so-called traditional family characterized by a male breadwinner, a stay-at-home financially dependent wife, and children whose legal rights and social status were such that they were little more than the property of their parents. Moreover, they celebrate the new diversity in family forms—which includes same-sex couples, single-parent families, and cohabiting partners with or without children—as more in tune with the values of pluralism, tolerance, and individual choice than the 'Leave it to Beaver','Father Knows Best' family of the 1950s. The idealized portraits of life in the nuclear family that dominated television's early decades have been replaced by the unflattering caricatures of 'The Simpsons' and 'Married, With Children', occasionally disturbing portrayals as in 'Twin Peaks', and alternative configurations such as unwed motherhood in 'Murphy Brown', male-female role reversals in 'Who's the Boss?', and man-as-nurturer households in 'Full House'. In a society where close to half of all new marriages will end in divorce and single parenthood has become common, and in which most women with young children work outside the home, traditional notions of family and public policies based on these notions are no longer appropriate to the times. The clock cannot be turned back, say those who celebrate the demise of the traditional family, nor should we wish to do so.

Not everyone shares this view. Indeed, recent years have seen the emergence of a powerful backlash in response to what is perceived to be the moral decay of modern society and a resurgence of what are often labelled 'traditional values'. This backlash exists at several different levels and assumes various forms. At the top end intellectually, it includes the cerebral and carefully argued positions of such people as Daniel Patrick Moynihan, who talks about contemporary efforts to accommodate increasing levels and types of deviance into a conception of acceptable behaviour, and Barbara Dafoe Whitehead's highly controversial analysis of the social, psychological, and economic costs associated with single parenthood. Lower down the scale it finds expression in the social conservatism of a Dan Quayle, Pat Buchanan, or Ralph Reed in the United States, where intense controversy over family and family values has existed for years. In Canada, conservative social commentators such as David Frum, Ted Byfield, and Barbara Amiel provide the intellectual weapons for those who lament the decline of the traditional family. The Reform Party and some provincial organizations of the Progressive Conservative Party, particularly in Ontario and Alberta, as well as such groups as Right to Life and REAL Women, provide the chief political vehicles for the expression of this resurgence of traditional family values.

Issues concerning the family force us to confront some of our most deeply cherished and least questioned beliefs. Mention of the family triggers an emotional response that, for many people, is much more intense than that elicited by the other communal groupings to which they belong. Moreover, people whose eyes might glaze over at the mention of tax policy will often become attentive when the same policy matter is discussed as family policy.

Part of the reason for this is quite simply that we are more likely to pay attention to things when their connection to our own lives is made obvious. But there is more at work here. We are all products of families—'intact', 'broken', 'traditional', 'nuclear', 'same-sex', 'nurturing units', 'dysfunctional', or however else we choose to characterize our own family—and we are more likely to have ideas about what constitutes a good family than, say, a good foreign policy. In addition, family policy has in common with such issues as abortion, capital punishment, and assisted suicide the fact that most people consider these to be morality issues. These are hot-button issues whose emotionally charged character derives from the realization that fundamental questions about the meaning of human existence and how we should live our lives are at stake. In confronting our beliefs about the family, we are, unavoidably, confronting the most fundamental questions about ourselves and the society in which we live.

What Is Family Policy?

Family policy is seldom referred to by this name. Nevertheless, as *The Economist* puts it, 'Governments act in ways that, intentionally or otherwise, affect the family: in this sense every country has a "family policy".'[1] Margrit Eichler makes the same point:

Family policies are not a clear set of policies since they include all those that affect families. This includes social welfare legislation, policies concerning social services (such as day care), income tax regulations, provisions in civil and criminal codes that determine who is responsible for certain types of dependants, family law, regulations concerning most social benefits, custody decisions, and many other social tools. These and other policies together constitute what we tend to call 'family policy', although not all of them are always considered.[2]

In some societies family policy assumes obvious forms, such as the one-child-per-family limit in China. More commonly, however, family policy involves a more subtle combination of measures based on some conception of what constitutes a family, and that seeks to accomplish certain goals relating to families. These goals may be cultural, social, or economic. For example, laws that do not recognize same-sex couples as families for purposes of social benefits, inheritance rights, adoption rights, and so on embody certain cultural values about the legitimacy of heterosexual relations and the cultural illegitimacy and moral inferiority, in matters relating to the family, of same-sex relationships. A law that makes divorce extremely difficult, as existed in Canada before 1968, is likely to be based on traditional religious values regarding the sacred character of marriage. A family studies curriculum that teaches children that all family configurations are morally equivalent conveys, and is intended to convey, a cultural message. Treating people in common-law relationships the same as married persons sends one cultural message, and laws that treat these relationships differently send another.

The cultural goals that public authorities, whether secular or religious, associate with families overlap with the social expectations held for the family. These expectations often have a taken-for-granted character that depends on cultural norms rather than laws and regulations. For example, it is generally expected that parents or guardians are primarily responsible for ensuring that their children are adequately fed, clothed, and sheltered. In other words, the costs and responsibility for child-rearing are expected to be private matters, borne mainly by parents. The benefits that flow from this care, when it is done well, are experienced by both the individuals who receive it and society as a whole. Likewise, the costs of a childhood of deprivation are not entirely private. Society will bear some of the burden of whatever dependencies and behavioural dysfunctions can be traced to an individual's family circumstances.

Families are expected to perform many of the tasks that shape the character, habits, and abilities of those who, in their turn, will become adult members of society. The possibility that they might fail in this awesome responsibility, and that society may be the poorer for their failure, has long been recognized. Plato was convinced that the family was an essentially selfish institution whose narrow interests were often at odds with the collective interests of society. The solution, he argued, was for the state to take over the traditional functions of the family, including the determination of who should be allowed to procreate and the upbringing of children. In this way society would be guaranteed virtuous citizens whose first thoughts would be for the good and glory of their country.

While most of us would reject Plato's proposals for the family, there is a logic in his reasoning that many would find persuasive. For example, most Canadians believe that health care is a public matter that should be paid for and provided chiefly by the state. Under such a system, should parents-to-be and families be allowed to behave in ways that produce or nurture children who suffer from preventable diseases or conditions that impose costs on all of us? The issue arose in a highly dramatic fashion in 1996 when a Winnipeg mother of two children, who had a serious record of substance abuse and was on social assistance, became pregnant and refused to attend a substance abuse program that was demanded by the local Children's Aid authorities. In the United States judges have required certain women—substance abusers or women with records of child abuse—to have contraceptive devices implanted in their arms to prevent further pregnancy. Less dramatically, the idea that prospective parents should be required to take some sort of course on parenting is often heard and considered to be reasonable by many. Plato would have agreed, although he would have viewed this as a rather pathetic half-measure.

Family policy may also be designed to achieve economic goals. For example, the Swedish tax system provides no tax benefits for married couples or deductions for dependent children. This goes back to the 1970s when Sweden was experiencing an acute shortage of labour. The government reformed the tax system to encourage more married women to enter the labour force (in addition, state-subsidized day care, generous maternity leave, and flexible work hours all reduced the cost of having children and remaining in the labour force). The 1945 introduction of family allowances in Canada could not have been sold politically had it not been for the Department of Finance's belief that these payments would be part of a Keynesian fiscal strategy aimed at propping up household purchasing power. Those who advocate a national program of subsidized day care routinely use economic arguments (among others). Margrit Eichler is typical: 'It would . . . make good economic sense to provide child care for all children who need it. This would generate jobs for the childcare workers and enable mothers to work for pay.[3]

Despite the fundamental importance of the family and the number of policies that seek to influence its character or behaviour, or compensate for what may be perceived as its shortcomings, governments in Canada have not created the sort of institutions one might expect to be associated with weighty policy matters. Unlike most Western European countries, where Ministries of the Family have existed since after World War II, Canada relies on an unco-ordinated hodge-podge of policies implemented at various levels of government by an assortment of agencies, some governmental and others, like Children's

Aid Societies, that are funded by government but operate independently. Such an approach is not necessarily a bad thing. The absence of an institutional 'home' for family policy does, however, help to conceal the fact that such a thing as family policy actually exists. Not only does it exist—though often treated as some minor backwater within the field of social policy—family policy has become in recent years an increasingly important and controversial subject.

Canada's Families: Yesterday and Today

When the law that created family allowance payments—the 'baby bonus' as it was called for years—was passed in 1945, the typical Canadian family consisted of a married couple with two children. About one-quarter of families had three or more children. By 1993, when these payments were abolished (they were replaced by a geared-to-income tax credit), it had become much more problematic to speak of the 'typical' Canadian family. Married couples still predominated. However, many of these couples were the result of remarriages, the rate of divorce having skyrocketed after the 1968 reforms to the Divorce Act. Over a tenth of all couples were living in common-law relationships, a category that was not recognized by Canadian law in 1945. Single-parent families, usually headed by women, were comparatively few and were typically caused by abandonment or the premature death of a husband. By 1994, there were roughly one million single-parent families, comprising about 13 per cent of all families. Families tend to be smaller than in the past, and whereas the vast majority of women with young children did not work outside the home in 1945, a clear majority do today.

The Canadian family has undergone enormous changes over the last two generations. The implications of these changes for Canadian society are the subject of heated debate. Some attribute what they perceive as the moral decay of contemporary society to the demise of the traditional family. Others applaud the new family configurations as being potentially liberating for women. Virtually everyone agrees that the increased number of single-parent families is a major factor in explaining why the level of poverty (a hotly disputed concept, as explained in Chapter Six) has remained static over the last few decades. But this agreement does not provide the basis for a consensus on what governments should be doing in relationship to the family.

In the best-selling book, *Boom, Bust, and Echo*, demographer David Foot attributes much of the controversy surrounding Canadian families to changes that have taken place, and continue to unfold, in the characteristics of Canadian families. Let us examine some of these changes.

1. Number of Families

The vast majority of Canadians continue to live in families. Following the Statistics Canada definition of 'family' used for census purposes, i.e., a currently married or common-law couple with or without never-married children living in the same household, or a single parent with never-married children in the same household, we find that about 80 per cent of all Canadians live in families. Although an even greater share of the population lived in families a generation ago—about 87 per cent in 1971—the family remains by far the most typical home situation in Canadian society. Far more significant than the rather marginal decline in the percentage of Canadians living in families are the changes that have occurred in the size and marital characteristics of these families.

2. The Shrinking Family

The large family has become a social anomaly. As recently as 1971 about 14 per cent of all families comprised six or more persons. Today only about 2 per cent fall into this category. Over half of all husband-wife families have either one or two children, compared to about 40 per cent of such couples in the 1960s. Childless couples have also become more common. Over a third of all families do not have children living at home, an increase of several percentage points from the level in the 1960s. This increase is due to a combination of Canada's aging population, the fact that both marriage and childbirth typically occur later today than in the past, and deliberate choice.

3. Traditional and Non-Traditional Families

The traditional family in which the parents of most readers of this book were raised consisted of a married man and woman with children. The man was the family's breadwinner and the woman stayed home with the children. This family configuration has not disappeared—indeed, some demographers suggest that it is making something of a comeback—but it is much less prominent than it was a couple of generations ago. Childless families, one-parent families, common-law couples with children, and step-families are all more common today than in the past.

Hard numbers on children living in non-traditional families before the 1970s are virtually impossible to acquire. Before the explosion in the number of divorces, remarriages, and common-law relationships brought on by changes to the law and in social mores since the 1960s, census-takers and demographers seldom concerned themselves with this group. This is no longer the case. As of 1994, about 83 per cent of Canadian children lived in two-parent families. The remaining 17 per cent lived in single-parent families, the vast majority of which were headed by women. It is estimated that close to a half-million of Canada's 7.8 million families are step-families, i.e., families in which one of the parents is not the biological parent of all the children. And while common-law couples are less likely than their married counterparts to have children, slightly more than 40 per cent of all common-law couples have children living with them, a figure that represents more than 300,000 families.

4. Fractured Families

In 1951, the ratio of marriages to divorces was 24 to 1. Today the ratio is closer to 3 to 1. The percentage of the population that has been through a divorce has increased by over 400 per cent since the early 1970s. This means, of course, that an increasing number of children spend at least part of their years at home in single-parent families or step-families. The economic consequences of this phenomenon are clear: children raised in intact families are much less likely to experience poverty than those in fragmented families. The social and psychological consequences of being raised in single-parent or step-families are, on the other hand, the subject of enormous disagreement.

There has also been a sharp increase in the number of common-law households, which today account for about 11 per cent of all couples. There is, however, considerable regional variation in the popularity of common-law relationships. They are almost three times more popular in Quebec (19 per cent of all couples, as of 1991) than in PEI (6.9 per cent). Common-law couples, as noted above, are less likely than married ones to have children living in the household (about 40 per cent versus 60 per cent).

5. Working Mothers and Children

Another striking change in Canadian families involves the enormous increase in the percentage of mothers who work outside the home. Before World War II, fewer than one of 10 married women worked outside the home. Today, six out of 10 are part of the labour force. Only about one-quarter of couples with children today conform to the traditional model of male breadwinner and stay-at-home mother. In most couples with children both parents are employed, including a majority of couples where there are children younger than seven years of age. Figure 7.1 provides a snapshot of some of the labour force characteristics of families.

The increase in the number of working mothers has generated an unprecedented need for alternatives to the traditional mother-at-home child care. Most of this need continues to be met by employing sitters. The National Child Care Survey estimated that, in 1988, about 70 per cent of non-parental child care was being provided by other family members or sitters. Only slightly more than 10 per cent of care was being provided through licensed day-care centres or before- and after-school programs.[4] Despite calls from women's groups and others for a nationally subsidized day-care system, the priority that Ottawa and provincial governments have attached to deficit reduction in recent years has prevented the adoption of such a program.

6. Family Incomes: Increasing Polarization?

Family incomes are considerably greater today than they were a generation ago. Measured in 1994 dollars, the average family income climbed from $40,516 in 1971 to $52,858 in 1994. Most of that growth, however, took place

FIGURE 7.1
Labour Force Participation of Couples with
Children and Single Mothers with Children, 1971 and 1995

A. Participation rate for married women with children under 6 years.

B. Participation rate for single mothers with children under 6 years.

C. Participation rate for couples with children under 7 years, 1993.

SOURCE: The Vanier Institute of the Family, *Canada's Families—They Count*
(Neapean, Ont.: Vanier Institute of the Family, 1996).

in the 1970s. Family incomes have been more or less stagnant since the early 1980s and, by some measures, have actually been falling over the last decade. If instead of averaging all family incomes we look at the median family income, i.e., the income level below which are grouped 50 per cent of families and above which are grouped the other 50 per cent of families, we find that the median family income for 1994 was only $46,908, down from $49,091 in 1990. Median income probably provides a fairer picture of what is hap-

pening with family incomes. This is because average family incomes are
pulled up by the very high incomes of a comparatively small group of families at the top of the income scale.

In recent years it has become popular to claim that a growing percentage
of Canadian families fall below the 'poverty line' and that more and more children are raised in poverty. The National Council of Welfare estimated that in
1996 one in five children under the age of 18 years lived below the poverty
line.[5] The likelihood of a child being poor is five times greater in a female lone-
parent family than in a two-parent family. Figure 7.2 shows the percentage of
families, for each of four different family types, falling below the low-income
cut-off line set by Statistics Canada.

Are Some Types of Families Better Than Others?

Pop psychologist John Bradshaw maintains that 97 per cent of families are
what he calls 'dysfunctional'. In other words, almost all families are broken

FIGURE 7.2
Low Income by Family Type, 1980–95

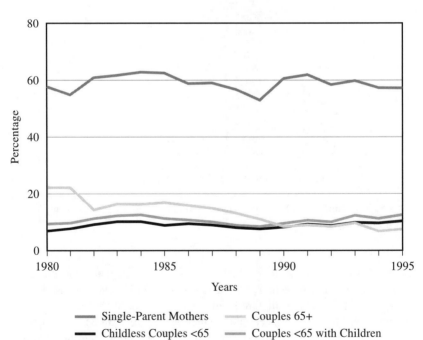

SOURCE: National Council of Welfare, *Poverty Profile 1995* (Ottawa: Supply and
Services Canada, 1997), 16.

and need to be fixed! This certainly makes for an attention-grabbing message, but is not very helpful as a practical guide to the sort of family arrangements that work best from the standpoint of family members and society as a whole. Emotional serenity and robust psychological health for everyone would certainly be nice, as would families in which everyone loves unconditionally and is supportive. But in the real world policy-makers need to aim for more modest targets—love still cannot be legislated, although support payments can—such as reducing the social costs of forms of deviancy that may be more common among those who experience certain family circumstances.

Is it really possible to determine whether some family configurations are 'best'? Or is this the short path to an intolerant and reactionary judgemental-ism that ends up condemning square pegs simply because they don't fit into holes that someone decides should be round? The fact of the matter is that, since the 1960s, an enormous amount of study has been devoted to this question, starting with Daniel Patrick Moynihan's controversial report on the pathology of inner-city Black families in the United States. And while some experts and advocates argue that family configuration either does not matter or would not matter if the right social and economic policies were in place, the preponderance of the evidence suggests that they are wrong.

The research on family structure and its consequences is vast and nuanced. Nevertheless, it is possible with a bit of crimping to squeeze this literature into two main camps. One argues that there is nothing inherently better in a particular family configuration than in another and that most or all of the negative consequences attributed to certain family types, such as single-mother families, are spurious. In other words, these consequences are caused by such factors as low income rather than the family configuration *per se*. The other camp argues that the heterosexual two-parent family is superior to alternative family structures in virtually all respects: economically, socially, and culturally. Unlike writers on the family of a couple of generations ago, those who subscribe to this second view today base their argument on social scientific evidence rather than biblical injunctions and moral precepts. So do experts in the first camp.

Neither camp, however, is free of moral criteria, although these are not always acknowledged, in part because moral arguments today are viewed with suspicion in debates on public policy. And yet moral concerns are always just below the surface of debates that purport to be purely scientific, whether one is talking about the effects of deficit reduction, free trade, environmental regulation, or most other policy matters. In examining the two broad camps in the literature on family structure and public policy we will, therefore, consider both the scientific and moral arguments of these opposing groups of experts.

1. 'It Takes a Village': The Collectivist Model for Family Policy

Many families are able to take care of themselves. They can feed and clothe their children, nurture their self-esteem, teach them values and skills that will enable them to deal competently with life's challenges: in short, these families are able to give their children a future, and in doing so they benefit us all. But many families are unable, or in some cases unwilling, to provide their children with the material circumstances and nurturing that contribute to the development of an autonomous and socially well-adjusted person, one capable of knowing right from wrong, of holding a job, and of forming healthy relationships to others. In other words, these families cannot or will not give their children a future, and we all experience the negative consequences of this failure.

This is where the 'village' comes in. In her bestselling book, *It Takes a Village, and Other Lessons Children Teach Us*,[6] Hillary Rodham Clinton uses the village of traditional societies as a model and metaphor for the role that community organizations and, chiefly, the state must play to help families in need and to provide disadvantaged children with a future. The village Clinton describes 'can no longer be defined as a place on a map, or a list of people or organizations, but its essence remains the same: it is the network of values and relationships that support and affect our lives.'[7] It is not enough, she argues, indeed, it is downright harmful, to base family policy on the premise that only parents (or guardians) are responsible for raising their children. The entire village has a responsibility toward *its* children, a responsibility that in most cases will be borne chiefly by parents but that is none the less a collective responsibility.

This means a greater public investment in health care, education, and income assistance for needy families, as well as measures to improve the safety of neighbourhoods and to provide jobs for all who want them. This approach is familiar enough. It is echoed by Canadian writer and social activist June Callwood, who says the following about child poverty:

> The obvious key to ending child poverty is a collaborative model which brings a community together on behalf of all its children, and puts money where its mouth is. It must involve a holistic approach which includes adequate income, quality licensed child care, job training and education upgrades for youth and adults, affordable and decent housing, access to community supports, and at the end of the day, a real job.[8]

Callwood, like Clinton, believes that much of what is wrong with the contemporary family can be fixed through the village assuming its proper responsibility for the well-being of children and other vulnerable members of society. But aside from the low incomes of many families, what aspects of the family are broken and how did this happen? Here Clinton offers an analysis not very different from that provided by those, such as David Popenoe, James Q. Wilson, and Barbara Dafoe Whitehead, who usually are characterized as 'conservatives' in the debate on family policy. She points to the generally harmful consequences for children of marital breakdown, the inability of many parents to spend adequate time with their children, the negative influence of the mass media, and the problems often associated with teenage pregnancy.

Without falling into a syrupy nostalgia for 'the good old days', which Clinton dismisses as being largely a fabrication of marketing people and those with a conservative ideological agenda, she clearly believes that families and children confront more difficult challenges today than they did a generation or two ago. The way to deal with these challenges, she argues, is not to emphasize a return to a supposedly lost world of 'family values'. Rather, the solution lies in using the village—government agencies, experts, community groups, churches, etc.—to provide families with the support that is often missing in today's world. Clinton's approach may be best understood from some of her more concrete suggestions for policy reform. The following are three examples.

Infant health. Clinton recognizes that some mothers have lifestyles, during pregnancy and/or after childbirth, that place their children at greater risk of developing health problems. The village needs to step in. Support and advice from family and friends may not be available or of adequate quality and, in Clinton's words, 'are no substitute for formal systems that have as their primary mission good health for all women and babies.'[9] She cites those European countries where a mother's eligibility for state-paid monetary benefits is tied to her agreement to allow home visits by health specialists or to participate in other forms of parent education.

Parenting skills and a child's cognitive development. Clinton emphasizes the importance of early talking, reading, and parent-child interaction for the child's acquisition of verbal and analytical skills. Summarizing the conclusions of research by Betty Hart and Todd Risley, she observes that 'The biggest difference among the various households . . . was in the sheer amount of talking that occurred. The more money and education parents had, the more they talked to their children, and the more effectively from the point of view of vocabulary development.'[10] While insisting that the amount and quality of parent-child interaction are the determining factors, Clinton acknowledges that working-class and lower-income families are much less likely than more privileged families to offer a milieu that provides a child with the benefits of early language exposure.

So what, if anything, is to be done? Presumably talking, much less what Clinton would consider quality talking, cannot be legislated. Nevertheless, says Clinton, 'The village can encourage this all important activity.'[11] She points to a government-funded program administered by the American Library Association that attempts to help parents improve their reading skills and emphasizes the importance for children's cognitive development of reading to them at an early age.

Marriage breakdown. Clinton recognizes that the explosion in the divorce rate since the 1960s has had negative social consequences. 'More than anyone else,' she writes, 'children bear the brunt of such massive social transitions . . . studies demonstrate convincingly that while many adults claim to have benefited from divorce and single parenthood, most children have not.'[12]

What can the village do? Clinton suggests that when children are involved there perhaps should be a mandatory 'cooling off' period before a legal divorce is allowed, during which education and counselling for parents can be provided. She leans towards some form of obligatory counselling when she cites approvingly court rulings that require divorcing parents to attend classes on the potential consequences of divorce for children.

The collectivist approach to family policy that Clinton advocates enjoys wide popularity among social workers, sociologists, child psychologists, counsellors of various sorts, and other experts on the family. It is, quite obviously, an approach that requires the professional skills of these people who are, in Clinton's view, integral parts of the village. Despite her insistence on the 'personal' character of the village, the network of supportive relationships she envisages obliterates the distinction between those relationships that are truly personal and intimate and those that take place with strangers—however well-meaning those strangers might be. In the words of Jean Bethke Elshtain, 'Clinton's village [is] a juggernaut of parents, or whatever is left of parents, neighbours, or whatever is left of neighbours, judges, lawyers, the police, all educators everywhere, politicians (the "non-regressive" ones), the media (good and very bad), doctors, psychiatrists, child welfare bureaus, "civil society", the food industry, the clothing industry. This is a boundary-less village.'[13] The key to being part of the village is that a person or organization attempts to help families and children. By calling this sprawling network a village, Clinton seeks to give her approach to family policy a human face and thus disarm those who detect in it a justification for meddlesome bureaucracy and the extension of public authority.

Richard Weissbourd's *The Vulnerable Child* echoes Clinton's philosophy. He says, 'Important as family and friendships are to children, across the political spectrum there is a growing consensus that both children and parents depend on wider nets of social ties, on communities.'[14] The disintegration of communities under the pressures of modern life has placed children at greater risk, Weissbourd argues. Like Clinton, he places his hope in the new village, the role of which is to create 'environments that ease the task of parenting and that provide stimulation and support to children at every stage of development.'[15]

It is hard to disagree with such sentiments. But the hard question remains, what should be done? At this point one's analysis of the problem—or, more accurately, cluster of problems—of the family is crucial in determining the sorts of policies most likely to help families and in determining one's view of what sort of help is actually needed. Clinton parts company from many of her political soulmates when she argues that 'every society requires a critical mass of families that fit the traditional ideal, both to meet the needs of most children and to serve as a model for other adults who are raising children in difficult settings.'[16] And her acknowledgement of the economic and emotional damage children often suffer as a result of divorce likewise distances her from those who deny that family configuration, *per se*, is a key factor in accounting for the undeniable differences in the school performance, social behaviour, and adult lives of those from single-parent and step-families compared to those from traditional nuclear families.

What Clinton does not do, however, and this is crucial in distinguishing the collectivist from the personal responsibility approach to the family, is emphasize traditional families as the key to family policy. The dilemma for those who advocate a collectivist approach—as Clinton does, as Weissbourd does, as most family policy specialists do—is to avoid stigmatizing those who find themselves in non-traditional families. And, indeed, non-traditional families can and often do work! But the data on families show very clearly that they are more prone to various forms of hardship than are traditional families. To go from this awareness to policies that privilege traditional families and/or reduce the ease of divorce when children are involved is a leap too far for the collectivist camp. Such policies, they believe, inevitably stigmatize non-traditional families.

In what is probably the standard Canadian textbook on family policy,[17] sociologist Margrit Eichler takes a step beyond Clinton's village-based model of family policy, developing a more radically collectivist approach to the family. She contrasts what she calls the *individual responsibility model* of the family, upon which current policy is based, with the *social responsibility model* that she advocates. Some of the key differences between these models are summarized in Table 7.1. Eichler argues that the assumptions underlying family policy in Canada have evolved from a patriarchal ideology before the 1970s, to an individualist ideology in recent decades. The main principles of the patriarchal model, and examples of policies based on these principles, are shown in Table 7.2.

Changing social values and pressure from the women's movement resulted in a steady erosion of the patriarchal model during the 1960s and 1970s. It was replaced by the individual responsibility model of the family, whose capstone would be the guarantee of gender equality in the Charter of Rights and Freedoms. This transition represents undeniable progress in the direction of gender equality within families, and has also eliminated the legally privileged status of married over common-law couples. However, Eichler notes that in the real world men and women are not similarly situated when it comes to the raising of children; nor, generally, are the economic opportunities available to women equal to those of men. Consequently, she argues, the individual responsibility model of the family does not abolish sexism in family policy. Indeed, the formal equality that the Charter and Canadian laws now guarantee may serve to hide the gender inequalities that policy allows to persist. For example, the average income of a female single parent is only about 60 per cent of that of a male single parent, and female-led single-parent families are several times more likely to depend on social assistance than are male-led single-parent families. This is what critics of the individual responsibility model of the family would characterize as equal in law, unequal in life.

Table 7.1
The Individual Responsibility and Social
Responsibility Models of the Family

	Individual Responsibility	Social Responsibility
1. Gender assumptions	Equal status and rights of men and women.	Committed to eliminating as far as possible the real-world inequalities between men and women.
2. Family definition	Families may be created by legal marriage or co-habitation. The law does not distinguish between these types of families, nor between the children produced within or outside of marriage.	Same as under the individual responsibility model.
3. Economic obligations	Married or common-law partners are equally responsible for each other's economic well-being and for that of their dependant children.	All dependancy relations are recognized in law, whether or not they are between family members. Adult members of a functioning interdependent unit are responsible for each other's economic well-being.
4. Parental rights and responsibility to provide care	Fathers and mothers are equally responsible.	Mothers and fathers are both responsible. Parents retain responsibilities, though not necessarily rights, towards dependent children with whom they do not live.
5. Appropriate role of public authority	The state's role *vis-à-vis* the family and children should be supplementary and temporary. It is assumed that parents will be responsible for the economic welfare and care of family members, and that public authorities enter the picture only when these forms of support are not provided by a family member.	The care and support of dependent children is a responsibility that the public authority shares with parents. The cost of caring for dependent adults is a public responsibility.

Continued

Table 7.1 Continued

	Individual Responsibility	Social Responsibility
6. Sexuality of family units	Same-sex couples are recognized as family units for certain purposes.	No distinction is made between same-sex and opposite-sex couples.

SOURCE: Adapted from Margrit Eichler, *Family Shifts: Families, Policies, and Gender Equality* (Toronto: Oxford University Press, 1997), 14–17.

In place of the individual responsibility model of the family, Eichler advocates a social responsibility model that would extend enormously government's responsibility for the well-being of families. She identifies six main policy goals associated with this model:

- minimizing social stratification based on sex;
- collective support for all dependants;
- collective support for all those who provide care for dependants;
- social recognition for all those who provide care and support for dependants, regardless of whether they are related;
- facilitating self-support and autonomy for all those who, given adequate means, can take care of themselves;
- social and legal recognition for same-sex families.[18]

Eichler provides several examples of policies that would be required to promote these goals. They include:

- a nationally financed day-care program;
- longer and financially more generous parental leave provisions;
- a federally organized child support assurance system (essentially a guaranteed minimum income for custodial parents and their children) to insulate children from the loss of income that often accompanies the separation and divorce of parents;
- far greater child benefits provided through the tax system for low-income families;
- refundable tax credits for caregivers, most of whom are women (this would be a publicly paid form of income for domestic work in families where there are dependent children or adults).

The philosophy behind Eichler's approach to the family and her recommendations for policy reform are straightforward: 'to the degree that it is

Table 7.2
The Patriarchal Family: Principles and Policies

Principles	*Policies*
1. Legal marriage was the basis for families.	Common-law unions were not accorded the same rights as married couples. Children born out of wedlock did not have the same rights as the offspring of married couples.
2. The husband/father was considered the head of the family and the primary breadwinner.	The law failed to protect women who were discriminated against by employers. The law treated the wife and children as economic dependants of the husband/father.
3. The economic contribution of a husband to a family was assumed to be superior to that of his wife.	Property acquired by a husband during the course of a marriage, and held in his name only, was considered to be his alone. In the event of a divorce his wife had no legal claim on this property.
4. The wife/mother was expected to be the primary caregiver for the children and other dependent members of the household.	No state-subsidized day care existed, nor were there tax deductions for child-care expenses.
5. The economic welfare of family members was not a public responsibility.	Aside from family allowance payments, which were always rather small, there were no public maternity benefits until the 1970s when the Unemployment Insurance Commission began to pay them to women who took time away from their jobs for childbirth.
6. Families were considered to be heterosexual, by definition.	Until the 1970s, and even the 1980s, it was common to treat homosexuality as a psychological illness. Same-sex couples were not recognized as legal families, nor were the members of such couples eligible for any of the social benefits to which members of opposite-sex couples were entitled.

socially useful, give it social support.'[19] This is, however, a deceptively simple formula. What counts as 'socially useful'? Eichler uses three tests: gender equality, social fairness (between classes), and economic efficiency. Gender equality and social fairness are good in themselves, she argues, but there are often economic efficiency reasons for doing the right thing. For example, Eichler makes the following argument about the economic efficiency of a national day-care system:

> There is a substantial literature that suggests child-care monies are better expended by establishing and supporting public day-care centres than by transferring the monies directly to the parents. It would also make good economic sense to provide child care for all children who need it. This would generate jobs for the child-care workers and enable mothers to work for pay, while allowing children to profit both from the social setting of day care and the home setting of individualized attention.[20]

As is usually the case when an argument for government spending is based on the claim that such spending will in fact generate income by producing jobs (in this case, for day-care workers) and enabling more women to enter the labour force, no attention is paid to the fact that the taxation needed to pay for such measures involves a diversion of purchasing and investment dollars that would have gone towards other uses. One can argue that the uses proposed by Eichler are economically more productive than alternative uses of these dollars, but this is not obvious.

In answer to the questions of what family configuration is best, Eichler would say that none is inherently superior to the others. She certainly does not agree that legal marriages between men and women constitute the best circumstances in which dependent children can be raised. Based on her review of the scientific literature she concludes that no empirical evidence indicates that legal marriages provide better emotional and material support than common-law unions. Eichler goes on to say that, 'In general, some families (of whatever type) function better than others. Some legal marriages involve emotional, physical, and sexual abuse, as do some common-law unions and some same-sex unions.'[21] At another point she observes that 'there is now solid research evidence that children's well-being is *not* related to the amount of continued contact between fathers and children.'[22]

These claims fly in the face of an enormous amount of social scientific research that Eichler alludes to only in passing, completely ignoring many of the most often cited studies on family structures and their consequences for children. These studies form the basis for what I will call the personal responsibility model of the family. Let us examine this model.

2. 'It Takes a Family'[23] (Preferably an Intact One)

David Popenoe is one of the best known critics of the decline of traditional families and a vigorous advocate of the nuclear family. He frames the question this way: 'What family structure, under the conditions of industrial, liberal-democratic nations, is best able to produce offspring who grow up to be both autonomous and socially responsible, while also meeting the adult needs for intimacy and personal attachments that become ever more compelling in an increasingly impersonal world?' His answer is the nuclear family. Before some readers become ballistic with indignation, it is important to understand that Popenoe's definition of the nuclear family is not necessarily the male-breadwinner, stay-at-home-wife family. 'I refer instead', he writes, 'to the nuclear family in more general terms—consisting of a male and female living together, apart from other relatives, who share responsibility for their children and for each other.'[24]

This definition of the nuclear family will not cool the rage of some readers, many of whom spent at least some part of their childhood in families that did not conform to this model. As Barbara Dafoe Whitehead observes, 'it is nearly impossible to discuss changes in family structure without provoking angry protest.'[25] This is more than unfortunate, because the available evidence shows quite clearly that *family structure has an independent effect on the material, emotional, and even physical well-being of children.* By 'independent effect' I mean that these consequences are not simply the result of income or other differences between intact and other families (although these differences certainly increase the magnitude of the well-being gap between different family configurations).

The impact of family breakup and unwed motherhood on the material well-being of women and children is easiest to establish, and is also the least controversial component of the literature on the effects of family structure. Most single-parent mothers, and therefore their children, have low incomes. The vast majority of children living below the poverty line are in single-parent families. As of 1995, over 80 per cent of single-parent families led by women under the age of 25 fell below the poverty line. The rate was just under 60 per cent for single mothers between the ages of 25 and 44.

Separation and divorce usually end with the mother receiving custody of the children, and in a drop in the income of this single-parent family. 'Divorce', says Barbara Dafoe Whitehead, 'almost always brings a decline in the standard of living for the mother and children.'[26] The problem of poverty is to a large degree a problem of single parenthood, which in turn is caused by the increase in divorce and in the number of births outside of marriage (about one-quarter of all annual births in Canada). About one-third of all welfare recipients in Canada are single mothers. Evidence from the United States shows that single-mother families experience a form of welfare dependency. Not only do they stay on welfare longer than other recipients (not in itself surprising, given the demands of raising children), but their dependency on welfare tends to be passed on to the next generation. Sara McLanahan and Gary Sandefur observe that 'Evidence on intergenerational poverty indicates that, indeed, offspring from [single-mother] families are far more likely to be poor and to form mother-only families than are offspring who live with two parents most of their pre-adult life.'[27] This is true of both Whites and Blacks.

The issue of child poverty is, in fact, largely a function of changing family structure. David Eggebeen and Daniel Lichter estimate that over half the increase in child poverty in the United States during the 1980s was attributable to changes in family structure (i.e., the increase in single-parent families). Given what we know about the economic consequences of single parenthood in Canada—children in single-mother families are about five times more likely to fall below the poverty line than those in intact families—it is probable that Eggebeen and Lichter's conclusion is valid for Canada as well. To the degree that poverty begets poverty, the problem of low incomes in single-parent families threatens to become a new class division, separating those whose material circumstances in childhood provide them with the possibility of leading a middle-class life (vacations, participation in sports or other cultural/recreational activities, post-secondary education, etc.) from those whose circumstances make this life much more difficult to attain. Investment in education provides an important example of this difference. As Dafoe Whitehead observes, 'The parents in intact families are far more likely to contribute to children's college costs than are those in disrupted families.'[28] Research by Judith Wallerstein, director of the California Children of Divorce Study, supports this not very surprising conclusion.[29] Moreover, it is well known that a significant share of first-time home purchases involve help from relatives, usually parents. As in the case of post-secondary education, children from single-parent families (and, according to some research, even those from step-families) are less likely to be the recipients of such help. In ways like these the class divide between those from intact and fragmented families is likely to be reinforced over time.

Those who take a collectivist approach to family policy respond to these findings by calling for increased public support for single parents and all those who are raising children on low incomes. But the consequences of family breakup and single parenthood are not simply economic. A survey of over 60,000 children in the United States found that at every income level except the highest (households with income of more than $50,000/year in 1988), children living with single mothers were considerably worse off than those living in two-parent families.[30] This finding applied to both boys and girls, and across racial groups. James Q. Wilson summarizes the study's findings as follows: 'Children living with never-married mothers were more likely to have been expelled or suspended from school, to display emotional problems, and to engage in anti-social behavior.'[31]

This conclusion has been corroborated by numerous studies. Relying on longitudinal studies that now span two decades, Sara McLanahan and Gary Sandefur arrive at some dismal findings. In *Uncertain Childhood, Uncertain Future*, they conclude that even after controlling for race, income, and parents' education, being raised in a single-mother family decreases a child's chances of finishing high school, increases a girl's chances of becoming a teenage mother, and increases a boy's chances of becoming a jobless adult.[32] All of these risks increase substantially in the case of families headed by teenage mothers. Nicolas Zill and Charlotte Schoenborn report that children from single-parent families are two to three times as likely as those from intact families to have emotional and behavioural problems, and this difference persists after controlling for family income.[33] Studies by Zill and others show that family breakup has a strong impact on school achievement—again, even after controlling for the effects of family income, race, and religion.[34]

Sociologist Amitai Etzioni, one of the leading communitarian intellectuals in the English-speaking world, offers an explanation for the impact of family disruption on children's academic performance:

> The sequence of divorce followed by a succession of boy or girlfriends, a second marriage, and frequently another divorce and another turnover of partners often means a repeatedly disrupted educational coalition. Each change in participants involves a change in the educational agenda for the child. Each new partner cannot be expected to pick up the previous one's educational post and program. . . . As a result, changes in parenting partners mean, at best, a deep disruption in a child's education, though of course several disruptions cut deeper into the effectiveness of the educational coalition than just one.[35]

These are circumstances that greater income support for single-parent families will not alter.

Since Daniel Patrick Moynihan's 1964 report on the crisis of fatherless, low-income black families in the United States, it has been widely recognized that the absence of fathers in single-parent families has negative consequences for children that go beyond the economic ones. In Moynihan's words, a community without fathers 'asks for and gets chaos'.[36] And yet Margrit Eichler claims that 'there is now solid evidence that children's well-being is *not* related to the amount of continued contact between fathers and children.'[37] Who is right?

The preponderance of the evidence comes down on the side of Moynihan and those who argue that fatherlessness tends to have negative consequences for both children and society. *The Economist* summarizes these consequences:

> For boys, the absence of men can induce what sociologist Elijah Anderson calls 'hypermasculinity', characterised by casual, even predatory, sex and violence. Fatherless girls, like their brothers, tend to do less well in school and have greater difficulty in making the transition to adulthood; they are much more likely than girls who grew up with a father to be young and unmarried when they first get pregnant.'[38]

It is well known that fatherless boys are much more likely to engage in antisocial behaviour than those who grow up with fathers. In the words of one study, 'The relationship is so strong that controlling for family configuration erases the relationship between race and crime and between low income and crime. This conclusion shows up time and again in the literature.'[39] Studies by

Judith Wallerstein, Sara McLanahan, Urie Bronfenbrenner, and Nicolas Zill, among others, confirm that fatherlessness carries personal and social costs.

Family breakup is often followed by remarriage or cohabitation with another partner. Consequently, the number of step-families—or what today are sometimes called 'blended families'—has increased dramatically over the last couple of decades. Indeed, they have been celebrated by the Hollywood dream factory for years, going back to the 'Brady Bunch' television series of the 1970s. Research suggests, however, that the reality of these increasingly common family structures is often less positive than the saccharine portrayals of television and film. 'In general', says Barbara Dafoe Whitehead, 'remarriage neither reproduces nor restores the intact family structure, even when it brings more income and a second adult into the household. Quite the contrary.'[40]

David Popenoe cites the findings of the National Child Development Study in Great Britain, which tracked the development of 17,000 children born in 1958. He notes that 'the chances of stepchildren suffering social deprivations before reaching 21 are even greater than those left living after divorce with a lone parent.'[41] Sara McLanahan's research shows that children in step-families report lower educational aspirations held for them by their parents and less parental involvement in schoolwork.[42] It appears, however, that the effects on girls and boys are not the same. Research from the United States suggests that boys often respond positively when their mothers remarry, being less likely to drop out of school than boys in single-mother families. In the case of girls, those who have close ties to their mothers often perceive the stepfather as a rival and an intruder, and are *more* likely than girls in single-mother families to drop out of school.[43]

One of the most disturbing issues to emerge from recent studies of step-families is that the risk of children being physically abused, including sexual abuse, is much greater in such families than in intact families. Canadian researchers Martin Daly and Margo Wilson estimate the risk as being 40 times greater for children in step-families. Stepfathers are not the only culprits. Daly and Wilson report that much of the abuse is committed by neighbours, a stepfather's male friends, or some other non-relative. However, they also conclude that stepfathers are far more likely to abuse their stepchildren than their biological children.[44] The risk of girls being sexually abused by their stepfathers is much greater than for those who live with their biological father. As Judith Wallerstein explains, 'The presence of a stepfather can raise the difficult issue of a thinner incest barrier.'[45]

Finally, there is the issue of parental time for children. Stanford economist Victor Fuchs observes that the main source of social investment in children is private, coming chiefly from their parents. Family breakup is often a major factor contributing to a reduction in the time that parents spend with their children. The involvement of fathers with their children typically declines dramatically. But even the custodial mother's investment of time often declines as she tries to balance the raising of children with the need to work outside the home. The problem of time may be more acute in the case of single-parent families, but it also exists in intact families. One researcher estimates that the amount of time parents spend with their children has declined by about one-third over the last 30 years.[46] The perceived need for both parents to work outside the home is a chief reason for this decline.

There exists a long-standing and acrimonious debate over whether the investment of time that children require is best provided by parents, or whether it can be provided as well in institutional settings. Less controversial is the importance of time for a child's intellectual and emotional development. David Popenoe writes:

> The significance of time in childrearing is highlighted by empirical findings on the promotion of 'prosocial behavior' in children. The development of prosocial behavior—which includes helping, sharing, and concern for others—has been shown to stem from early attachment experiences, from the modelling by children of their parents' prosocial behavior, and from good nurturing, especially the way children are disciplined. At heart, prosocial behavior is based on strong feelings of empathy for other people. The type of discipline that best promotes the development of empathy in children is that which involves reasoning with the child. . . . Discipline with reasoning and explanation is time intensive. . . . Today, when the time devoted to parent-child interaction in decreasing, especially in the father-absent family, it is likely that the teaching of empathy correspondingly suffers.[47]

Those who reject the conclusion that seems to flow inescapably from studies like the ones reviewed in the preceding pages—namely, that intact families tend to be superior for children and for society to single-parent or other alternative family configurations—often respond by pointing to the undeniable fact that many intact families do a lousy job of raising children. Moreover, intact families certainly are not free from such pathologies as incest, physical and emotional abuse, child neglect, alcoholism and other forms of addiction, and so on. Confronted with the news that a child from a broken family is more likely than one from an intact family to have difficulty maintaining a stable relationship with a partner during adulthood, many will respond that it simply is not possible that a childhood spent in a home where parents show no love for one another, but stay together, is somehow less damaging for a child than divorce.

Nevertheless, the literature on the consequences of family structure for children's development shows that intact families work better, even intact families that are far from being models of domestic bliss. Sara McLanahan identifies three advantages that intact families usually have over other family structures:

- *Economic.* The children of intact families are less likely to experience poverty. Inasmuch as the two-income family seems to have become increasingly necessary to sustain a middle-class lifestyle, this particular advantage of intact families has grown in importance.
- *Authority structure.* Intact families are more likely than fragmented ones to provide children with a stable structure of authority.
- *Household personnel.* The composition of an intact family is more likely to be stable than that of a fragmented one. In the latter case family breakup is often followed by the introduction of new adults into the household with the potential to undermine children's sense of security and affect their relationship to their parents.[48]

In Canada the issue of the family has been defined primarily in economic terms. Organizations like the National Council of Welfare and the Vanier Institute of the Family locate the roots of family problems chiefly in low incomes and lack of public resources targeted at those families, particularly single-mother ones, most in need. While the economic dimension is certainly important, it is not the whole story. Policies built on the premise that more public dollars will solve the problems that afflict disrupted families more than intact ones ignore the independent effects of family structure. Acknowledging these effects can be personally difficult for some and ideologically inconvenient for others. Serious policy reform must, however, take them into account.

The literature reviewed above forms the basis for what I call the *personal responsibility model* of the family, in contrast to Eichler's *social responsibility model*. By 'personal responsibility' I mean that this model emphasizes the primary obligation of parents for the welfare of their children and for one another, and that policy should be built on the assumption that parents should be the main source of social investment in children. I hesitate to call it the individual responsibility model of the family—a category Eichler uses—because it does not rest on an individualistic philosophy. On the contrary, it sees in rampant individualism and the ethic of personal fulfilment one of the sources of the problem of modern families. As Dafoe Whitehead argues, 'Increasingly, political principles of individual rights and choice shape our understanding of family commitment and solidarity. Family relationships are viewed not as permanent or binding but as voluntary and easily terminable.'[49] The family is a communal institution that stands as a bulwark against the sort of corrosive individualism that many, on the right and the left, argue is characteristic of our age.

Policy Options for the Family

Generally speaking, family policy in Canada may be characterized as a rather unco-ordinated mix of policies, based on assumptions that are not always clearly recognized or even consistent, and delivered by agencies of all three levels of government and also by privately run organizations such as provincial Children's Aid Societies, Big Brothers/Big Sisters, and family planning clinics. Some provinces have attempted to develop a more systematic approach to family issues, as in New Brunswick through that province's Ministry of State for Family and Community Services. For the most part, however, family policy continues to be homeless. Responsibility for matters affecting families is divided between agencies responsible for health, social services, public housing, education, income support, and law enforcement. The courts also play a major role in family policy, particularly concerning matters relating to divorce, child custody, and both parental and children's rights.[50]

Unless one believes that central planning and a one-stop-shopping approach to policy delivery are by definition superior to looser, less co-ordinated approaches to policy-making and implementation, the fact that responsibility for matters affecting families is shared by all levels of government and a plethora of agencies is not in itself a problem. The real problem is the failure of governments to develop a clear vision of the family and of the appropriate balance between family autonomy and societal responsibility. Instead, one finds all sorts of assumptions and definitions of the family jockeying for public recognition. Should a gay or lesbian couple be recognized in law as a family in matters concerning spousal benefits? Some private companies already treat same-sex couples on a par with heterosexual ones when it comes to pension rights and so on. In the summer of 1997 the NDP government of British Columbia extended equal rights to same-sex couples. The controversy generated in Ontario in 1995, when the NDP government proposed a similar redefinition of families, demonstrated that many Canadians maintain more traditional notions about what constitutes a family. These notions are expressed in the Reform Party's official position on the family: '[A] family should be defined as individuals related by blood, marriage or adoption. Marriage is the union of a man and a woman as recognized by the state and this definition will be used in the provision of spousal benefits.'[51] This definition includes common-law unions.

Precisely because the issue of what constitutes a family is so controversial, politicians have tended to avoid hard choices that would offend vocal interests. The fate of same-sex benefits legislation in Ontario under the NDP government of the early 1990s illustrates this. Although the NDP had promised to introduce such a law, its commitment wavered in the face of considerable public hostility and the intention of some NDP legislators to vote against it. When the government decided to hold a free vote on the issue—government members were not required to support the bill—the NDP as much as conceded defeat. Since then, however, the battle has shifted to the courts. In *Egan v. Canada* the Supreme Court of Canada rejected a homosexual male's argument that he should be entitled to the same spousal rights as a partner in a heterosexual couple.[52] The federal Liberal government is on record as supporting legal reform to allow what was denied in the *Egan* decision. (At this writing no such reform has been introduced.)

The same-sex issue certainly pushes a hot button for most people, and it is an important one in terms of rights and the values we wish to see reflected in our society. But it is far less important in terms of social costs than, for example, the consequences of family breakup, teenage motherhood, child poverty, and many other matters that concern the family. We will examine three policy proposals that address these more pressing issues: public day care, reform of divorce rules, and guaranteed child support.

1. Day Care versus Home Care

'If you want to open the floodgates of guilt and dissension,' writes Hillary Rodham Clinton, 'start talking about child care. It is an issue that brings out all of our conflicted feelings about what parenthood should be and about who should care for children when parents are working or otherwise unable to.'[53] Few people would disagree, or at least few parents who have had to confront the dilemma Clinton describes. While a clear majority of parents with young children work outside the home—including about 6 of 10 women—public opinion surveys show that an even greater percentage of women would rather stay home with their children than put them in day care. Moreover, most Canadians believe that the family has suffered as a result of both parents working. Danielle Crittenden refers to this angst as 'the Mother of all problems'.[54]

The issue of publicly subsidized day care has been one of the chief nodal points in debates on family policy since the 1971 Report of the Royal Commission on the Status of Women. At the present time about 1 in 5 preschoolers whose mothers work outside the home is in a provincially licensed day-care facility. Most parents rely on other child-care arrangements, particularly family members and sitters. The federal and Quebec tax codes permit a deduction from taxable income for child-care expenses. They do not, however, permit a similar deduction for parents who take care of their own children.

The arguments for and against an expanded system of publicly financed, state-regulated day care can be grouped into three categories: economic, fairness, and child development.

Economic

As mentioned earlier in this chapter, the advocates of publicly financed day care argue that such an investment would yield economic returns in the form of more jobs for child-care workers and greater opportunities for parents, especially mothers, to participate in the labour force, thus earning income and paying taxes. There are two problems with this argument. First, it ignores the fact that creating such a system is not costless and that the taxes needed to pay for increased spending on day care represent a diversion of income from taxpayers in general to the users of the public day-care system. It is not self-evident that this use of spending is more efficient from the standpoint of creating jobs and generating economic activity than the spending/investment choices of tax-payers, if this money was left to them to spend. Second, the argument suffers from the supply-creates-its-own-demand fallacy. Simply because a public day-care system similar to those that operate in several European countries would create greater opportunities for parents to participate in the labour force does not guarantee that the number of jobs available will expand to absorb the increased supply of workers. Supply does not create its own demand. If, on the other hand, there were acute labour market shortages, as existed in Sweden in the 1970s, policies like day care that are designed to increase the supply of available workers would make economic sense.

Fairness

One of the principal arguments for publicly subsidized day care is that it pro-vides women, who are far more likely than men to bear the chief responsibil-ity for child-rearing, with the possibility to continue working even when they have preschool children, thus narrowing the earnings and career-advancement opportunity gaps between men and women. But in addition to this gender fair-ness argument, there is a class-based case to be made for publicly financed day care. Affluent parents can afford the cost of private care for their children. The less well-off would be the primary beneficiaries of public day care, although a universal system without user fees for higher-income parents would also pro-vide benefits to the affluent.

The tax code permits a parent to deduct up to $5,000 per child from his or her taxable income for child-care expenses. A similar tax benefit is not avail-able to parents who choose to stay home with their children. Some argue that this is unfair in that it provides tax relief to parents who work outside the home and pay someone to look after their children, but not to those who stay home with their children. In May 1996 Liberal MP Paul Szabo presented a motion to amend the tax code to extend this tax relief to parents who stay home with their children. His motion accomplished the remarkable feat of achieving agreement between the Reform Party and the Bloc Québécois, both of which supported it.[55] Finance Minister Paul Martin Jr rejected the proposal, saying that while he was sympathetic with the objectives of the suggested reform, the federal government could not afford the cost of implementing it.

The problem with the reasoning that underlies Szabo's proposal is that it ignores the fact that parents who choose to stay home with their children already experience all of the financial benefit of their investment in caring for their children. So if, for the sake of argument, one argues that the imputed cost of caring for a preschool child is $5,000 per year, that money stayed in the pocket of the parent who stayed home, rather than flowing into the pocket of someone else. An identical criticism is made by economists of proposals to create a publicly financed homemaker's income that would recognize the undeniable value of work done in the home. These proposals overlook the fact that households already reap 100 per cent of the imputed value of the domestic labour provided by one or more family members.

Child Development

'Imagine a country', writes Hillary Rodham Clinton, 'in which nearly all children between the ages of three and five attend preschool in sparkling classrooms, with teachers recruited and trained as child care professionals. Imagine a country that conceives of child care as a program to "welcome" children into the larger community and "awaken" their potential for learning and growing.'[56] That country, she says, is France, where the long-standing system of *écoles maternelles* provides a model for what she believes preschool care can and should be.[57] Clinton describes these preschools as 'modern and inviting', with interiors that are 'bright and colorful' and spaces designed for all the child's physical and affective needs. She argues that the care provided in such settings contributes positively to the emotional, social, and intellectual development of children. '[T]he most important thing for a child', she says, 'is the quality of care he receives, not necessarily the setting he receives it in.'[58]

Arguments about the putative advantages and disadvantages of day care versus home care for the child's social, emotional, and cognitive development are never far away when the issue of day care is debated. Some parents do a good job, others do not. Likewise, some day-care facilities conform to this glowing description of France's *écoles maternelles* and others are better described as warehouses for kids. No expert would disagree that the quality of the care experience is more important than the setting. But this just begs the question: What level of public resources would need to be invested in a universal day-care system in order to provide children with a developmental experience equivalent to that which caring, reasonably competent parents can provide in their home? And even if Canadian society was willing to invest in a system like France's (which is not, by the way, as uniformly positive as Clinton asserts), is the developmental experience the same as in a caring home setting? The research on this question is inconclusive.

What is beyond doubt, however, is the fact that the child-care facilities that the affluent rely on tend to be of a better quality and more developmentally appropriate to the age and cognitive needs of the child than those relied on by the poor. And so the issue of day care's consequences for children's development has an important class dimension. Just another reason, say advocates of universal publicly financed day care, for a greater social investment in preschool care and education in order to close a developmental gap between affluent and poor children that the existing system reinforces.

2. Divorce

As we have seen, much of the problem of family poverty, including child poverty, is attributable to family breakup. More controversially, the children of divorced parents appear to be at greater risk of developing emotional and behavioural problems, doing poorly at school, running afoul of the law in the case of boys, becoming teenage mothers in the case of girls, and suffering from emotional problems as adults. These elevated risks exist even after controlling for such factors as family income and parents' education. The obvious answer to many of the problems that beset families and children would seem, therefore, to be a reduction in the number of divorces. This probably is not a realistic option. Some would go further and argue that it is not a desirable option, but in making this case one should be aware that the happiness of parents and the welfare of their children are not always identical in these matters. As David Popenoe writes, 'The central problem is the so-called individualistic divorce when children are involved—typically one partner departs in order to achieve self-fulfillment, leaving the children in the lurch.'[59]

So what, if anything, can be done to reduce the frequency of divorce? A number of proposals have been put forward in recent years. They include the following:

- *A two-tier system of divorce.* Under such a system, marriages with no minor children involved would continue to be easy to dissolve. However, if a couple has minor children the law could require a longer waiting period before legal divorce is permitted and/or mandatory marriage counselling.
- *Covenant marriages.* A variation on the above principle was adopted in Louisiana in 1997. The state passed a law creating an optional form of marriage called 'covenant marriages' that are harder to enter into and harder to leave than the usual sort. A couple entering a covenant marriage must participate in premarital counselling and may only divorce if one of a handful of comparatively rigorous conditions is met. These conditions include abandonment, two years' separation, adultery, physical or sexual abuse, and the sentencing of one of the partners to a lengthy jail term (or death).
- *The 'children first' principle.* Mary Ann Glendon has proposed that, in those cases where the terms of a divorce settlement are contested in court, judges should first determine the best possible division of assets and income from the children's point of view. Only then would the judge turn to other contested issues.
- *Value change.* As Popenoe observes, 'the problem is at heart cultural, not political or economic. Married couples must increasingly come to believe that they live in a society where marriage and marital permanence are valued, and where divorce is to be undertaken only as a very last resort.'[60] Barbara Dafoe Whitehead has suggested that the government and the public health community could portray divorce as a public health problem, as has been done in the case of smoking. It would not take much trouble or imagination to show that the economic costs associated with high levels of divorce are enormous.

- *Stigma*. The analogy to smoking raises the issue of social stigma. Anti-smoking campaigns in Canada and the United States have attempted to stigmatize smokers, portraying this lifestyle habit as unhealthy, filthy, selfish, unsexy, and generally undesirable from both personal and social points of view. Could, or should, social stigma be enlisted in the cause of reducing divorce? Probably not. But stigmatization can be and is used in some jurisdictions—Massachusetts, for example—to publicly shame parents who fail to meet their legal child-support obligations.
- *Mass media*. The role played by television, film, popular music, and the mass media generally in generating social acceptance of divorce and non-marital childbirth is difficult to establish conclusively, as is also true of the media's impact on other forms of social behaviour. What is beyond dispute, however, is that most of the media's images and messages concerning the family convey little sense of the negative consequences that tend to be associated with family breakup and single parenthood. It is difficult to see what could be done to change this, short of some unacceptable form of censorship.

3. Guaranteed Income for Families with Children

It certainly is true that many of the problems that beset families have their roots in inadequate family incomes. In response to this hard reality, Ottawa and the provincial governments agreed to a revised system of Child Tax Benefits that would target income support primarily at poorer families. This agreement was announced in the 1997 federal budget and was implemented through the Canada Child Tax Benefit in July 1997.[61]

Critics argue that these tax benefits do not go far enough. The problem of low family income is one to which single-mother families are especially vulnerable. To address the more acute need of this group, some have proposed a child-support assurance system that essentially would guarantee a minimum level of child support to single parent families. The non-resident parent would be expected to pay child support, but in cases where he (usually he) fails to meet this obligation or where the amount paid is less than the guaranteed minimum payment that would be established under this system, taxpayers would cover the difference.

There are several obstacles in the way of a guaranteed income for families with children. The first involves costs. As Woolley, Madill, and Vermaeten observe in their examination of child benefits, 'It is not clear that there is political will on the part of the government or sufficient pressure from the public to find additional funding for child benefits through increased taxes.'[62] They note that more public money for single-parent or other low-income families with children would very likely be at the expense of single men and women receiving income assistance. Moreover, beefing up support for poorer families with children could threaten existing social programs. Indeed, by increasing the Child Tax Benefit the federal government appears to expect that provincial governments will be able to lower their social payments to some categories of recipients and shift some spending away from cash transfers to in-kind benefits and services like drug and dental care and child care, or provincial family allowances.[63] Finally, no guaranteed income program for families with children can work without the co-operation of provincial governments. There is little reason for optimism on this score.

Chapter Eight

Aboriginal Policy

Labour Day traditionally marks the end of the summer camping season and the closure of many provincial parks across Ontario. Camp Ipperwash, located on the eastern shore of Lake Huron, is one of these parks. But in the spring of 1996 Camp Ipperwash did not reopen. This was because in September 1995 a group of Aboriginal Canadians broke through the park gate and claimed the park, arguing that it was sacred land where their ancestors had been buried. A confrontation between the Native occupiers of the park and the Ontario Provincial Police ensued, during which shots were fired and a Native man was killed. The main highway in the area was blockaded for a time by Aboriginal protesters and tension ran high as the spectre of another Oka crisis seemed to hang over the community. As the weeks and months passed the situation stabilized. Property values in the communities adjoining Ipperwash plummeted; non-Aboriginal residents organized through a group called On Fire to oppose what they believed to be unfair concessions to Natives; an investigation into the shooting of the Native man was concluded and charges of criminal negligence causing death were laid against an OPP officer, who was found guilty in May of 1997. Through all this the Native occupiers of Camp Ipperwash remained in control of the land.

Circumstances like those that unfolded at Ipperwash are no longer uncommon. The Oka crisis of 1990, where a Quebec police officer was killed and an armed stand-off between Mohawk warriors and the Canadian military dragged on for over two months, was the most spectacular of such confrontations in recent years. Moreover, there can be little doubt that Oka—and the sympathy blockades of roads, bridges, and railway lines in various parts of Canada triggered by the confrontation—opened a new and more violent frontier in relations between Aboriginal Canadians and the non-Native population. Since Oka there have been numerous episodes of violent conflict in Native–non-Native relations. Words have matched deeds, as the rhetoric used by many Native leaders has acquired a much harder and occasionally bellicose edge than was heard before Oka.

Without apportioning blame for the events at Oka or Ipperwash, or for any of the other confrontations of recent years, it is clear that violence of this order and frequency points to a major failure of public policy. An approach to Canada's Native communities developed more than a century ago is today considered to be unacceptably paternalistic. There is, however, no agreement on what should replace it. At one extreme are those who maintain that Aboriginal communities should be recognized as sovereign nations within Canada, empowered to pass laws that supersede those of the Canadian Parliament and constitution. At the other extreme are those who insist that the entire edifice of laws and programs set up over the years to handle Aboriginal Canadians as a group apart from the rest of the Canadian population should be eliminated and the law should treat Native Canadians identically to other citizens. Between these two positions are a broad range of proposed reforms whose common feature involves some form of limited self-government for Aboriginal communities.

As is also true of language policy and multiculturalism, an analysis of the multiple problems that needed to be addressed in the field of Aboriginal politics forces one to ask fundamental questions about rights and identities within this country. It also raises questions of justice and cost, and of the trade-offs that may be necessary during a period when many politicians are deeply sceptical of spending solutions to social problems. This chapter seeks to provide the reader with the information necessary to arrive at his or her own conclusions about what reforms to Aboriginal policy are best for Native Canadians and all of Canada. It does so by examining the following matters:

- Aboriginal status;
- the size and characteristics of the Aboriginal population;
- the reserve system;
- the legal status of Native claims to sovereignty and landownership;
- the principles underlying Aboriginal policy.

Who Is an Indian?

It has become unfashionable in some circles to use the word 'Indian' when speaking of the descendants of those who occupied North America before the arrival of Europeans. 'Amerindian' is an alternative that has long been used by anthropologists and population geographers. 'Aboriginal peoples', 'Native peoples', and, more recently, 'precontact peoples' and 'First Nations' are also part of the lexicon. However, there are extremely practical reasons for not banning the word 'Indian' from a discussion of government policies towards Aboriginal peoples. Under Canada's Indian Act, which has been on the statute books since 1876, a person who qualifies as an Indian under the law has certain entitlements that do not apply to non-Indians. Moreover, those Indian bands that live on land referred to in law as Indian reserves are subject to special legal provisions concerning such matters as individual landownership and transfer, a prohibition against mortgages on reserve land, and numerous restrictions on permissible economic activities. Until the Indian Act and the legal status of Indian are abolished, any analysis of Aboriginal policies cannot avoid using these terms.

In law, an Indian or 'status Indian' is anyone who has been registered or is entitled to be registered under the Indian Act, including those who belong to communities covered by treaties. The defining characteristics are both biological and social. The Indian Act of 1876 stipulated that an Indian was any male person of Indian blood who belonged to a band recognized by the federal government, and any child of such a person or a woman married to such a person. An Indian woman who married a non-Indian lost her legal status as an Indian and the entitlements associated with that status.

This changed in 1985. In response to pressure from Aboriginal women, Canada's obligations under the United Nations International Covenant on Civil and Political Rights, and, most importantly, the sexual equality provisions of the Charter of Rights and Freedoms (sections 15 and 28), the federal government eliminated this obviously discriminatory section of the Indian Act. Since then female Indians, women who marry male Indians, and the children of such women enjoy the same rights under the Act as male persons. Women who lost their Indian status under the pre-1985 provisions of the Indian Act were permitted by this amendment to apply for reinstatement of their band membership and re-registration as status Indians.

The fact that non-Native women married to Native men and, since 1985, non-Native men who marry Native women acquire the right to Indian status indicates that lineage is not the only criterion determining who is an Indian under the law. Indeed, the courts have long recognized that a person's 'associations, habits, modes of life, and surroundings' may weigh more heavily in the balance than the extent of one's Native ancestry in determining legal status as an Indian.[1] Writing in 1971, Cumming and Mickenberg observed that 'The questions of how much Indian blood a person must have, and of how closely an individual must be associated with a native community before he will be considered a "native person", have not been answered.'[2] This remains true today.

Canadian law also recognizes the Métis and Inuit as two other categories of Aboriginal peoples of Canada. Although the Constitution Act, 1867, speaks only of 'Indians, and Lands reserved for Indians' (s. 91, 24), a 1939 decision of the Supreme Court of Canada pronounced the Inuit to be Indians within the meaning of the constitution.[3] They are excluded, however, from the provisions of the Indian Act. Métis, the mixed-blood descendants of unions between Indian women and Scots or French-speaking settlers in the Red River region of Manitoba, may also be considered Indians under the law if they are the descendants of Métis who were part of Indian communities that came under treaty. Descendants of Métis who received scrip (certificates that could be used to purchase land) or lands from the federal government are excluded from the provisions of the Indian Act. Nevertheless, Métis are considered to be 'Indians' within the meaning of the constitution, and so Ottawa has the authority to pass laws concerning the members of this group. The Inuit and Métis are grouped with the Indian people of Canada by s. 35 of the Constitution Act, 1982, which recognizes and affirms the 'existing aboriginal and treaty rights of the aboriginal peoples of Canada'.

Canada's Aboriginal Population

In recent years the actual size of Canada's Aboriginal population has become a matter of some controversy. It is variously estimated at between 1 and 2 million people, or 3.7 to roughly 8 per cent of the population. Professional demographers are inclined to accept the lower figures, while Aboriginal spokespersons and some politicians maintain that the higher figures are the true ones. The numbers matter for two reasons. First, certain entitlements accompany Indian status under Canadian law, and so the determination of who is an Indian in the eyes of the law has practical and financial consequences. Second, the political weight and even moral authority of a minority's demands may be related to its size. This is especially true when the material stakes are high and some segments of the population stand to lose in proportion to the minority's gains. In such circumstances demography can become a political battleground.

Despite the widely divergent estimates offered for the size of the Aboriginal population, it is possible to arrive at a reasonably accurate assessment based on clear criteria. The 1991 census, conducted by Statistics Canada, provides the following numbers:

- 1,002,675 people, representing 3.7 per cent of the Canadian population, gave as their ethnic origins North American Indian, Métis, Inuit, or a combination of one of these with some other ethnic origin.
- 626,000 people, or about 2.3 per cent of the national population, reported identifying with an Aboriginal group.
- 553,316 persons, or about 2 per cent of the Canadian population, are status Indians, i.e., those to whom the Indian Act applies (this number had increased to 610,874 in the 1996 census).
- 305,247 persons, representing about 1 per cent of the population, live on reserves or in other Aboriginal settlements.

The regional distribution of Canada's Indian population is shown in Figure 8.1.

FIGURE 8.1
Registered Indian Population by Region, 1977, 1987, 1995

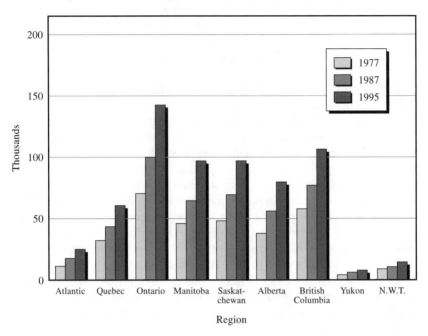

SOURCE: Department of Indian Affairs and Northern Development, *Basic Departmental Data 1996* (Ottawa: Supply and Services Canada, Jan. 1997), 8.

When the 1981 census was taken, the number of status Indians was estimated to be 335,475 or 1.4 per cent of the national population. It appears, therefore, that this segment of the Aboriginal population grew by an astounding 60 per cent during the decade of the 1980s, a jump that cannot be fully explained by natural increase. Two additional factors contributed to this growth. One involved a 1985 amendment to the Indian Act that restored the right to Indian status for those women and their children who had lost status as a result of marrying non-Indians. The other factor was surely the attraction of increasing benefits, including potential land claims settlements, paid by the federal government to those qualifying for Indian status. Whatever the causes of this dramatic growth in recent years, the Aboriginal share of Canada's population, including those who fall under the Indian Act and those who do not, is much smaller than the share claiming Italian, German, Chinese, or Ukrainian ethnic origins.

Language is believed by many to be one of the key elements of a culture—perhaps *the* key element—and a reasonable barometer of the real viability of a cultural community. According to the 1991 census, 190,170 Canadians, or considerably less than 1 per cent of the population, claimed an Aboriginal language as their mother tongue. This was down from 359,640 people at the time of the 1971 census. Those who claim a Native language as their mother tongue are outnumbered by about a 2.5 to 1 ratio by native speakers of Italian (511,000), Chinese (500,000), and German (466,000).

The Reserve System

Indian reserves have been called by some Canada's own system of apartheid. On the face of it the description seems a fair one. Average life expectancy and incomes of those who live on reserves are significantly lower than the Canadian norms. Rates of suicide, alcoholism, violent death, unemployment, crowded housing conditions, and infant mortality are all higher than the Canadian average, in some cases dramatically higher. Moreover, although being of Aboriginal descent is not a necessary condition for residence on a reserve, the reserve system was created to provide a sort of fixed homeland for Indians and the vast majority of those residing on reserves today are, in fact, status Indians. This combination of enormous disparity between life on reserves compared to that in the mainstream of society and the racial basis for the physical segregation of Indians does sound a lot like apartheid. Euro-Canadians who have seen firsthand the squalor and obvious destitution that characterize many of this country's reserves often wonder how such a system has been allowed to survive in a country that prides itself on being a compassionate democracy.

But when the Liberal government's 1969 White Paper proposed the abolition of reserves along with all the other legal structures that have treated Indians differently from other Canadians, the leadership of Canada's Native communities responded with a vehement 'No'. This, despite the fact that everyone acknowledged the reserves involved a sort of paternalistic control by Ottawa over the lives of those living on reserve. This paternalistic, racially based system, whose origins in Canada appear to go back to New France, continues today, as does Native resistance to its abolition. If this system is truly a form of apartheid, as many of its critics have charged, why then is it not rejected outright by the very people who are its 'victims'?

The answer is complex. To understand how a racially based system of segregation manages to survive in a liberal democratic society one must examine the origins and operation of Indian reserves in Canada. One must also consider the goals of today's Aboriginal leaders, who in important ways are opposed to dismantling the reserve system.

The Indian Act of 1876 defines reserves in the following way:

> The term 'reserve' means any tract or tracts of land set apart by treaty or otherwise for the use or benefit of or granted to a particular band of Indians, of which the legal title is in the Crown, but which is unsurrendered, and includes all the trees, wood, timber, soil, stone, minerals, metals, or other valuables thereon or therein.

At the heart of this definition and central to the quandary of the reserve system is the guardianship relationship established between the federal government and Indians living on reserves. The legal ownership of reserve land belongs to the Crown, but the land and all the resources appertaining to it must be managed for the 'use or benefit' of the particular band of Indians residing there. In practice this means that virtually no legal or commercial transaction of consequence may be undertaken by Indians living on a reserve without the permission of the federal government. This is what critics are referring to when they speak of the Indian Act's paternalism. For example:

- Band members may not sell any part of the reserve.
- The federal government retains the ultimate authority to grant timber-cutting licences and to establish their terms.
- Reserve land may not be used as security for loans.

Today there are 2,323 Indian reserves in Canada, about 70 per cent of them in British Columbia. Together they comprise about 10,000 square miles, an area roughly half the size of Nova Scotia. Most reserves are uninhabited. Reserve populations vary from 2 to about 12,000, and most inhabited reserves have populations of fewer than 1,000 people. Just over 300,000 Indians live on reserves, or about 60 per cent of all status Indians. Although there are reserves in all regions of the country, most reserves and the vast majority of those living on them are located in rural and remote areas. This has important social and economic consequences. Job opportunities are fewer, those residing on reserves are generally required to leave home in order to acquire post-secondary education, and physical isolation impedes the integration of reserve populations into the rest of society. This last effect is not considered to be a bad thing by many in the Indian community. As Harvey McCue explains,

> To many Indians, reserves represent the last visible evidence that they were the original people of this country. The reserve nurtures a community of 'Indianness' and reinforces spiritual unity among Indians. Despite the manifest poverty, ill health, poor housing and lack of services, the life-style on reserves, traditional values, kinship affiliations and the land itself all contribute to an Indian's identity and psychological well-being. The relative isolation of most reserves enables Indians to socialize their children to values important to their culture: reticence and noninterference, consensus decision making and nonverbal communication. Reserves, since they are set apart both physically and legally, help Indians to maintain an ethnic identity within Canada.[4]

Sovereignty, Landownership, and the Law

It has always been our belief that when God created this whole world he gave pieces of land to all races of people throughout this world, the

Chinese people, Germans and you name them, including Indians. So at one time our land was this whole continent right from the tip of South America to the North Pole. . . . It has always been our belief that God gave us the land . . . and we say that no one can take our title away except He who gave it to us to begin with.[5]

Disputes over land—who owns it, who has the right to live on it, to benefit from it, to make laws that apply to those within the boundaries of a particular territory—are among the most intractable of disputes. Only recently have more than a small minority of non-Aboriginal Canadians come to realize that the crux of Native demands involves land. Phrases like 'self-government for Canada's Aboriginal peoples' have inoffensive and even positive associations for many Canadians until they are linked to exclusive Native ownership of land and political sovereignty in territory that the majority of Canadians assume to be part of Canada. The words of James Gosnell, quoted above, have been repeated by many Native leaders, from Louis Riel to Phil Fontaine, the Grand Chief of the Assembly of First Nations (AFN). Their message is simple: the land belonged to us, much of it was never lawfully surrendered by us, and much of what was surrendered under the terms of treaties was little more than a swindle of major proportions. Ownership and control over lands to which Aboriginal peoples claim a historic right are argued to be necessary for the survival of Aboriginal culture. In analyses of what are said to be the chief differences between Aboriginal and European-based cultures, nothing is invoked more often than how these respective cultures view the land and their relationship to it. Clearly, the land was crucial to the traditional lifestyles of Native peoples. For this reason such matters as Native hunting and fishing rights were recognized in the treaties entered into between Natives and Euro-Canadians. Somewhat more controversial, however, are claims to control mineral or other resources that are important to the lifestyles and economic activities imported into North America by Europeans, but that have little or no relationship to traditional Aboriginal cultures. This is an issue that Canadian courts have addressed in recent years.

The question of who owns the land and the related issue of whether Native communities should be considered sovereign are enormously important. At present literally the entire province of British Columbia is subject to land claims. 'We can claim downtown Vancouver', says an AFN representative. 'It is ours. There is nothing in anybody's laws saying that it is no longer belonging to Musqueam or Squamish or Capilano or Wet'suwet'en. . . . Yes, there's a whole province under claim because there's a whole province that hasn't been paid for, hasn't been negotiated.'[6]

Landownership is one thing. Sovereignty is another. The fact that a person or group of persons owns a particular parcel of land, regardless of its size and other characteristics, does not exempt them from the obligation to obey the law of the sovereign country within which their land is located. But many leaders within Canada's Native communities deny the sovereignty of the Canadian state over them and their land. The comment of Ovide Mercredi, at the time the Grand Chief of the AFN, is fairly typical: 'We will not allow some other society to decide what we can do and determine the limits of our authority.'[7] Native assertions of sovereignty are sometimes more belligerent than this. Bargaining rhetoric and bottom lines are not always the same, of course. It needs to be said that while virtually all spokespersons for Native groups express support for the principles of Aboriginal self-government and Native rights, most advocate some form of self-determination that would be realized within the context of the Canadian state. The nature of such an arrangement, however, is the subject of much dispute.

The issues of sovereignty and landownership are obviously intertwined. There is no question that a sovereign people owns the land over which their sovereignty extends. Sovereignty, by its very nature, is a concept with territorial implications, including the exclusive right to make laws and dispose of property within certain boundaries. The first question that must be addressed, therefore, is whether Aboriginal communities are sovereign nations.

1. The Legal Case

It is usual for those who make the case for Aboriginal sovereignty to begin with the Royal Proclamation of 1763 and end with the Supreme Court of Canada's decision in *Calder et al. v. Attorney-General of British Columbia* (1973). The Royal Proclamation dealt with the North American territories formally surrendered by France to England under the terms of the Treaty of Paris. It included detailed provisions regarding relations between the British and the Aboriginal inhabitants of these territories (see Appendix). These provisions, says Donald Purich,

> . . . [suggest] that all lands that had not been surrendered by the Indians to the Crown belonged to the Indians. It reserved all unsettled land for the use of the Indians as their hunting grounds. It provided that lands required for settlement had to be bought from the Indians and could only be bought by the Crown at a public meeting. The Royal Proclamation set the stage for the land surrender treaties signed by the Indians with the Crown in Ontario and on the prairies.[8]

Native leaders generally view the Royal Proclamation as an affirmation of their existing right to the lands they occupied. George Erasmus, a former Grand Chief of the Assembly of First Nations, argues that 'by virtue of that Proclamation, it can be said that First Nations became protected states of the British, while being recognized as sovereign nations competent to maintain the relations of peace and war and capable of governing themselves under this protection.'[9] Regarding the treaties that were subsequently entered into between Aboriginal communities and the British and then Canadian authorities, Erasmus writes, 'First Nations did not perceive the treaties as being a surrender of authority.'[10]

In fact, however, it is not entirely clear that the Royal Proclamation of 1763—which was formally incorporated into the Canadian constitution through s. 25 of the Charter of Rights and Freedoms—recognizes Native sovereignty. What is clear, however, is that the Proclamation speaks of the 'Sovereignty, Protection, and Dominion' of the Crown in relation to the Native inhabitants who 'live under our protection'. That the Royal Proclamation recognizes Aboriginal rights is indisputable. It is quite a stretch, however, to maintain that the Proclamation recognizes Native sovereignty.

In the case of *St Catherine's Milling and Lumber Company v. The Queen*, decided by the Judicial Committee of the Privy Council in 1888, the Proclamation was interpreted as establishing for Indians 'a personal and usufructuary right, dependent on the good will of the sovereign'. In other words, the Proclamation neither established nor recognized Indian sovereignty over their traditional lands, but quite clearly refers to the sovereignty of the British Crown over these lands. While one might wish on various grounds to question the legitimacy of this assertion of British sovereignty, the point is simply that there is no explicit recognition of Indian sovereignty, despite what George Erasmus and other Aboriginal leaders claim.

But perhaps there is an implicit recognition of Aboriginal sovereignty. This seems to be the argument of those who characterize the Proclamation as a nation-to-nation agreement, a characterization that seems to receive some support from the Proclamation's use of the words 'the several Nations or Tribes of Indians', and also from the fact that the Proclamation states clearly that certain lands are reserved for the use of Indians and may not be purchased by private individuals or organizations, but only by the Crown. This restriction on the alienation of what the Proclamation refers to as 'Lands of the Indians' might be interpreted as an acknowledgement of Native sovereignty. At the very least it seems to establish an Indian right to compensation for land transferred by them to the Crown.

Lawyers, politicians, and academics will quibble about the correct interpretation to be placed upon the Royal Proclamation of 1763. In what is perhaps the standard treatise on Aboriginal rights, Cumming and Mickenberg's *Native Rights in Canada*, the authors conclude that 'On both legal and logical grounds, it seems apparent that [with some exceptions] Indian title should be viewed as having all the incidents of a fee simple estate.'[11] In other words, they own the land outright. However, in *Our Home or Native Land?*, Melvin Smith, a British Columbian constitutional expert, states that 'to my knowledge no court in Canada has found that aboriginal title includes fee simple ownership.'[12] At issue is more than who has the right to benefit from and dispose of lands in what circumstances. The question of what sort of title Aboriginals have to the land they claim by historic right of occupancy is often linked to the larger issue of their status *vis-à-vis* the Canadian state. This is apparent both in the statements of Aboriginal leaders and in certain court cases, two of which—the *Calder* and *Delgamuukw* decisions—will be discussed below.

The legal case for Aboriginal sovereignty, which today is often expressed in the form of demands that the inherent right of self-government for Natives be recognized in the constitution, and for Native landownership draw significant inspiration from a case that was not even decided by a court with jurisdiction over Canadian affairs. The 1832 decision of the United States Supreme Court in *Worcester v. Georgia* is often cited by advocates for native sovereignty. Although this case has no official standing in Canadian jurisprudence it nevertheless has been influential in a number of important Canadian decisions on Native rights.[13]

Writing for the majority in *Worcester v. Georgia*, Chief Justice John Marshall distinguished between the *right of discovery and possession* that European powers could enforce against one another in the New World and the *right of historical occupancy* enjoyed by the Aboriginal populations who already inhabited land 'discovered' and claimed by Europeans. The right of discovery and possession, said Marshall,

> ... gave to the nation making the discovery, as its inevitable consequence, the sole right of acquiring the soil and of making settlements on it. It was an exclusive principle, which shut out the right of competition among those who had agreed to it; not one which could annul the previous rights of those who had not agreed to it. It regulated the right given by discovery among the European discoverers; but could not affect the right of those already in possession, either as aboriginal occupants, or as occupants by virtue of a discovery made before the memory of man. It gave exclusive right to purchase, but did not found that right on a denial of the right of the possessor to sell.[14]

Marshall's pronouncement on the prior right of occupancy enjoyed by Native populations—a right that the discovery claims of European powers could not legally impair—is generally construed as an argument supportive of Native land claims and even sovereignty. But the Chief Justice also had this to say:

> In the establishment of [relations between Whites and Natives] the rights of the original inhabitants were, in no instance, entirely disregarded; but were, necessarily, to a considerable extent, impaired. They were admitted to be the rightful occupants of the soil, with a legal as well as a just claim to retain possession of it, and to use it according to their own discretion; *but their rights to complete sovereignty, as independent nations, were necessarily diminished, and their power to dispose of the soil, at their own will, to whomsoever they pleased, was denied by the original fundamental principle, that discovery gave exclusive title to those who made it.*[15]

This part of *Worcester v. Georgia* is problematical for those who purport to find a legal basis for Native claims to unrestricted landownership and sovereignty in that judicial decision.

The legal principles that emerge from this much-cited ruling may be summarized as follows:

- Natives enjoy a right of occupancy and land use that predates the arrival of Europeans.
- Legal title to New World territory claimed by a European power belongs to the discovering nation.
- Native rights of occupancy and land use are not unrestricted, but rather are limited by the fact that discovery and possession gave the European authorities legal title to and sovereignty over these lands.

Marshall went on to say that the alienation of Indian land could be only to the state or Crown, and that Indian title to lands they claimed by historic right of occupancy and use could be extinguished by either conquest or legal purchase. The Chief Justice made specific reference to the Royal Proclamation of 1763, which, as we have seen, sets down precisely these conditions for the alienation of Indian lands.

The nature of Natives' interest in lands they occupied and used, and which had never been alienated by either military conquest or surrendered under the terms of a treaty, was elaborated further in *St Catherine's Milling and Lumber Company v. the Queen* (1888). Based on the Royal Proclamation of 1763 and the practice of colonial and Canadian administrators, this ruling of the Judicial Committee of the Privy Council (JCPC) determined that Indians had only a 'personal and usufructuary right, dependent on the goodwill of the Sovereign'. The JCPC characterized the Crown's interest in the land under dispute as 'proprietary' and the Native interest as a 'mere burden' on this legal title.[16]

The land title issue was revisited in a 1973 decision of the Canadian Supreme Court. In *Calder et al. v. Attorney-General of British Columbia*, the majority ruled against the Nishga claim to have unfettered legal title to land that they had occupied before the arrival of Europeans. In fact, the case was dismissed on procedural grounds. The court did, however, express itself on the matter of Aboriginal title, one judge denying that it existed, three others recognizing original Aboriginal title that, they argued, had been extinguished, and three others arguing that Aboriginal title continued to exist. So while six of the seven judges recognized the concept of Aboriginal title, the majority determined that it did not exist in the case of the Nishga claim.

Because the *Calder* decision is so often cited as the legal basis for a right of Aboriginal landownership, it is worth quoting from the two sets of arguments given in this case. '[W]hatever property right may have existed', said Mr Justice Judson, 'it had been extinguished by properly constituted authorities in the exercise of their sovereign powers.' In case there was any doubt regarding his meaning, he went on to say that,

> [Crown] Proclamations and Ordinances reveal a unity of intention to exercise, and the legislative exercising of, absolute sovereignty over all

the lands of British Columbia and such exercise of sovereignty is inconsistent with any conflicting interests, including one as to 'aboriginal
title'.[17]

Why, then, is *Calder* generally viewed as a victory for the advocates of
Aboriginal title? In a word, the answer is politics. Since the *Calder* ruling successive governments in Ottawa and Victoria have preferred to emphasize the
arguments of the three judges who maintained that Aboriginal title still existed.
In the words of Mr Justice Emmett Hall,

> This aboriginal title does not depend on treaty, executive order or leg-
> islative enactment but flows from the fact that the owners of the interest
> have from time immemorial occupied the areas in question and have
> established a pre-existing right of possession. In the absence of an
> [explicit] indication that the sovereign intends to extinguish that right the
> aboriginal title continues.[18]

In view of the fact that no treaty or other legal instrument specifically extinguished the Nishga's title in the land they claimed, it continued to be theirs.
The practical ramifications of such a legal opinion, expressed by a minority
on the Court, were potentially enormous given that virtually none of British
Columbia was covered by treaties between the Crown and Native communities.

It is simply incorrect to suggest, as many have, that the Supreme Court's
Calder ruling confirmed the existence of Aboriginal title in Canadian law.
Only three of the seven judges deciding the case took this position. At the time
of the decision, however, only a few years after the political disaster of the
1969 White Paper on Indian Policy, Ottawa was heading in the direction of a
more conciliatory policy on Native land claims. Consequently, the federal government chose to rely on the arguments of the dissenters as a framework for
future negotiations, rather than those of the technical majority in the *Calder*
case.

The issue of Aboriginal title has been addressed in a number of cases since
Calder. In *Hamlet of Baker Lake et al. v. Minister of Indian Affairs* (1980), the
Federal Court of Canada appeared to accept the spirit and reasoning of the
minority in *Calder*, arguing that 'The law of Canada recognizes the existence
of an aboriginal title independent of the Royal Proclamation of 1763 or any
other prerogative Act or legislation. It arises at common law.'[19] While acknowledging, as has every other court decision on the issue, that the Crown exer-
cises sovereign authority over Native lands, the *Baker Lake* ruling repeated the
view, expressed by the minority in *Calder*, that Aboriginal title continued to
exist until explicitly extinguished by legislation passed by Parliament.

A decade later, in *Regina v. Sparrow* (1990), the Supreme Court of Canada
again addressed the issue of Aboriginal rights, including property rights. This
decision continued the line of reasoning found in the *Calder* dissent and the

Baker Lake ruling, holding that Aboriginal rights are pre-existing rights that are not created by government legislation and continue to exist until such time as they are explicitly extinguished. 'Historical policy on the part of the Crown', said the Court, 'can neither extinguish the existing aboriginal right without clear intention nor, in itself, delineate that right. The nature of government regulations cannot be determinative of the content and scope of an existing aboriginal right. Government policy can, however, regulate the exercise of that right but such regulation must be in keeping with s. 35(1) [of the Charter of Rights and Freedoms].'[20]

The specific issue in *Sparrow* was whether the right to fish was an inherent Aboriginal right. Buried in the Supreme Court's ruling was a warning that common law notions of property are not always appropriate in cases involving Aboriginal rights. 'Courts must be careful to avoid the application of traditional common law concepts of property as they develop their understanding of the "*sui generis*" nature of aboriginal rights.'[21] What does this mean? It could, one might argue, be interpreted as an argument against an unrestricted right of use and sale of a resource like fish or timber, if that use were to be inconsistent with the traditional practices and values of a Native community.

Calder, *Baker Lake*, and *Sparrow* were, in a sense, preliminaries to the main event that took place in 1993. In *Delgamuukw v. Attorney-General of British Columbia* the issue of Aboriginal title was addressed head on. A group of Gitksan and Wet'suwet'en chiefs argued that they owned an area in British Columbia roughly the size of the province of Nova Scotia. In their Statement of Claim they asked the court to make three specific findings:

- The Gitksan and Wet'suwet'en owned the territory in question.
- They had the right to establish their own laws for this territory, and these laws would supersede those of the province.
- They were entitled to compensation for all the resources exploited and removed from the territory since 1858.

The stakes could hardly have been greater, nor the issues of Aboriginal title and the inherent right to self-government more squarely put.

On the first question of whether the Gitksan and Wet'suwet'en owned the land they claimed by historic right of occupancy, British Columbia's Court of Appeals said 'no'. Only existing reserves within the disputed territory were deemed to be owned by the Native plaintiffs. On the second question of whether the plaintiffs had an inherent right to self-government, the court also said 'no'. Finally, on the third question of whether the Native plaintiffs should be compensated for resource exploitation, BC's Court of Appeals answered 'no'. An appeal to the Supreme Court of Canada was filed by the Gitksan and Wet'suwet'en but was dropped in June 1994 when the plaintiffs decided to pursue a negotiated settlement with the province. The appeal was later resuscitated and produced what may prove to be Canada's most important court ruling on Aboriginal land title.

In a unanimous decision, the Supreme Court ruled that the Gitksan and Wet'suwet'en are the owners of the land to which they claim a historic right of occupancy and use. Where Aboriginal title to land has not been extinguished by the terms of a treaty—and this would include most of the territory of British Columbia as well as parts of Atlantic Canada—Aboriginal communities able to prove that they historically occupied and used the land continue to have property rights. Does this mean that a non-Aboriginal family living in the Okanagan Valley on a piece of land they thought they owned are in fact illegal squatters? Will a flurry of eviction notices hit residents of Vancouver? Does a forestry company like MacMillan Bloedel now have to renegotiate leases it signed with the BC government that cover land rightfully owned by its original occupants?

In fact, the decision generated more questions than answers. What is clear from the *Delgamuukw* decision, however, is that the Supreme Court's interpretation of Aboriginal title means that at the very least Aboriginal communities like the Gitksan and Wet'suwet'en have a right to compensation for land that is determined to be theirs by historical right. The ruling strengthens the hand of Aboriginal groups, who previously went into negotiations with governments armed with a rather nebulous concept of Aboriginal title but who now can say that they have a constitutionally protected right of ownership that can only be extinguished through the terms of a treaty with the Crown. Landownership issues aside, the Supreme Court's 1997 decision did not establish a constitutional right to self-government for Aboriginal communities.

There remains the possibility, however, that what Canadian law does not recognize *is* recognized in international law. Those who make this argument point to various United Nations declarations and covenants to which Canada is a signatory, such as the 1960 Declaration on the Granting of Independence to Colonial Countries and Peoples. The Declaration states:

1. The subjection of peoples to alien subjugation, domination and exploitation constitutes a denial of fundamental human rights, is contrary to the Charter of the UN and is an impediment to the promotion of world peace and cooperation.
2. All peoples have the right to self-determination; by virtue of that right they freely determine their political status and freely pursue their economic, social and cultural development.

What constitutes a 'people' is left undefined by the UN Declaration. Moreover, the Declaration clearly refers to colonized peoples, and it is at least arguable that it was not meant to apply to indigenous populations in liberal democratic societies like Canada. Finally, the Declaration itself pulls back from the abyss of international disorder and partition that would surely follow from its unqualified application throughout the world. It states:

6. Any attempt aimed at the partial or total disruption of the national unity

and the territorial integrity of a country is incompatible with the purposes and principles of the Charter of the United Nations.

What the UN giveth, so too it taketh away!

A rather different argument from international law is to maintain that the treaties and other agreements between Aboriginal peoples and the Crown are tantamount to international treaties. If this is so, then it would seem to follow that these Aboriginal peoples have been recognized as sovereign nations that were capable of entering into agreements with other nations on a basis of legal equality. But as Cumming and Mickenberg say in what is generally a sympathetic treatment of Native rights, historically and legally there is little basis for interpreting treaties as international treaties. They note that the Supreme Court of Canada has expressly rejected this view of treaties.[22] In addition, they suggest that 'the Government did not consider the Indians to be independent nations at the time the treaties were made . . . and both the Government representatives and the Indian negotiators indicate that they considered the Indian peoples to be subjects of the Queen.'[23]

Despite the courts' lack of sympathy for the interpretation of Indian treaties as international agreements, Native spokespersons and some governments have insisted that treaties be viewed in this light. Speaking of those Native people who agreed to treaties with European powers, George Erasmus and Joe Sanders state, 'The way [our people] dealt with the Europeans is ample proof of their capacity to enter into relations with foreign powers.'[24] On the same subject they write:

Our people understood what the non-native people were after when they came amongst our people and wanted to treaty with them, because they had done that many times amongst themselves. They recognized that a nation-to-nation agreement, defining the specific terms of peaceful coexistence, was being arranged.[25]

Not only are treaties agreements between sovereign nations, according to this view, they are emphatically not real estate transactions comparable to, say, the United States' purchase of Alaska from Russia. This point is crucial, because the position taken by the courts and most governments in Canada has been that any Aboriginal right to ownership of the land covered by the terms of a treaty is extinguished by such an agreement. The nation-to-nation view of treaties denies that any extinguishment occurred, on the grounds that this was not how treaties were understood by the Natives who agreed to them. That non-Natives understood these agreements differently does not, Native leaders argue, mean that their view, rather than that of Aboriginal people, should be considered the correct one.

On a number of occasions courts have interpreted Indian treaties as contractual agreements. They certainly resemble contracts in that they typically include a rather detailed enumeration of mutually binding obligations. '[T]hey

constitute mutually binding arrangements which have hardened into commitments that neither side can evade unilaterally.'[26] The courts have, however, recognized that Indian treaties constitute a rather unique sort of contractual agreement. This may be seen in the courts' tendency to interpret any ambiguous
terms of treaties in favour of Aboriginal rights. As the British Columbia
Supreme Court said in *Regina v. Cooper* (1969), 'The document embodying
this larcenous arrangement must have been drawn by or on behalf of the
Hudson's Bay Company and so any ambiguity must be construed in favour of
the exploited Chiefs.'[27] The Supreme Court of Canada repeated and expanded
on this rule of treaty interpretation in a 1983 decision. The Court declared that
'Indian treaties must be construed, not according to the technical meaning of
their words, but in a sense in which they would naturally be understood by the
Indians.'[28]

However treaties were viewed by the Aboriginal people who agreed to
them, there is little doubt as to how the colonial and, after them, Canadian
authorities interpreted these agreements. As Cumming and Mickenberg write:

> The language of real property law as used in the treaties and the reports
> of the Government negotiators indicate that the purpose of the treaties
> was to extinguish Indian title in order that lands could be opened to
> white settlement. The treaties, therefore, can be best understood, from
> both a legal and historical point of view, when considered as agreements
> of a very special nature in which the Indians gave up their rights in the
> land in exchange for certain promises made by the Government.[29]

The issue of whether Aboriginal property rights are extinguished by the
terms of treaties is highly controversial. As a matter of law—leaving aside
whatever moral or justice issues may arise—Indian treaties were intended by
the governments negotiating them to put an end to Aboriginal title to land in
exchange for specific promises. This certainly is how the courts have interpreted treaties. Moreover, it is probable that the promises made by governments to Natives through treaties and, for that matter, through the Indian Act
did not constitute inalienable rights as we understand these today. To understand this, one must keep in mind the fact that assimilation of the Aboriginal
population was an underlying assumption of Indian policy from early times.
As well, colonial and Canadian authorities certainly anticipated that the
European population of Canada would expand and increasingly occupy lands
traditionally occupied by Aboriginal communities. Finally, the Indian Act of
1876 offered Indians the possibility of enfranchisement, whereby they would
lose their Indian status and acquire in exchange the same citizenship and legal
rights as non-Aboriginal Canadians. Taken together, it is clear that what today
are often characterized as Native rights under treaty law 'were seen more as
transitory means of protection rather than as inalienable rights as we would
perceive such today.'[30]

In summary, the legal case for Aboriginal sovereignty and landownership is less than compelling. Where treaties exist, the courts have taken the view that any Native claim to own land outright has been extinguished in exchange for various entitlements. In the case of territory not covered by treaties, such as British Columbia and the northern reaches of Canada, the courts have not been sympathetic to the argument that the land belongs outright to the descendants of the Aboriginal peoples who occupied it before European settlement.

There is, however, another argument used to support Native land claims, even where treaties exist. As Donald Purich observes, 'In Canadian law, contracts can be set aside if it can be proved that one of the parties to a contract was of unsound mind, was pressured to sign the contract, was being unfairly taken advantage of, *or was clearly unaware of the consequences of the contract he was signing.*'[31] Although it is undoubtedly the case that the Native leaders who agreed to treaties did not always understand these agreements in the same way as the colonial or Canadian negotiators, the courts have never set aside a treaty on these grounds. The courts have, however, taken the position that 'treaties and statutes relating to Indians should be liberally construed and uncertainties resolved in favour of the Indians' (*Sioui*, 1990). In such instances, oral testimony and historical evidence relating to the circumstances of a treaty's negotiation may be considered by the court.

Negotiating Aboriginal Claims

Since 1973 federal policy has distinguished between specific and comprehensive Native claims. *Specific claims* involve the alleged non-fulfilment of the terms of a treaty or the misappropriation of money or misuse of land under the Indian Act. Specific claims relate to land or money, and do not involve such issues as hunting, fishing, and trapping rights, which are routinely covered by Indian treaties. Included under the category of specific claims is an important subgroup of claims known as *treaty land entitlements*. They involve alleged discrepancies between the amount of land promised to Natives under a treaty and the amount of territory actually covered by a reserve. *Comprehensive claims* are based on Aboriginal title to land not covered by the terms of a treaty.

This distinction and the terminology of 'claims' are often rejected by Aboriginal leaders, who object to the suggestion that they are claiming something that no longer belongs to them. Moreover, because claims negotiations usually have been linked by federal authorities to the extinguishment of Aboriginal rights—a concept rejected outright by many Aboriginal leaders—the language of claims is viewed with disfavour from the Native side.

1. Specific Claims

There currently are about 400 unresolved specific claims. They deal with matters ranging from alleged government failures to respect ammunition or livestock allotments for band members under treaties to claims that reserve land has been improperly alienated from a reserve. This last group of claims is the most common one. In the event that the Specific Claims Commission within the Department of Indian and Northern Affairs determines that a claim has validity, a cash settlement is paid as compensation for the loss. Some examples[32] of resolved specific claims include the following:

- Penticton band, British Columbia. Compensation for lands cut off from reserves in 1920. Settled in 1982 for $14,217,118 and 12,243 acres of land.
- Six Nations, Ontario. Faulty expropriation of lands for railway purposes. Settled in 1984 for $1,000,000.
- Blackfoot, Alberta. Failure to fulfil treaty livestock entitlement. Settled in 1984 for $1,675,000.
- Kitigan Zibi Anishinabeg band, Quebec. Illegal alienation of 200 acres of reserve land in 1868. Settled in 1988 for $2,686,187.
- Nanaimo band, British Columbia. Just under three acres of land used for railway right of way since 1883 were determined to have been improperly acquired. Settled in 1994 for $1,835,000.

The total cost of the 159 specific claim and land treaty entitlements settled by the end of the 1995–6 fiscal year, including the value of approximately 300,000 acres of Crown land transferred to the bands as reparation, came to well over $1 billion.[33] Some argue that the cost of settling specific claims is small in comparison to the losses experienced by Aboriginal people. Those who have been the victims of theft or malfeasance, even if it occurred 100 years ago—the normal time limitations on bringing a claim before the courts do not apply to specific claims—deserve to be compensated for their losses. A deal is, after all, a deal, and its terms must be respected. Others maintain that it is neither reasonable nor just to expect current Canadians to pay the bill for non-compliance with certain provisions of Indian treaties. Melvin Smith makes this case:

How is it that when it comes to invoking treaties, the native people demand every jot and tittle of compliance—even to the extent of pressing hundred year old grievances. On the other hand, governments for their part have extended benefits to all Canadians, especially natives, far and beyond anything ever contemplated by the terms of any treaty: medicare, welfare, economic assistance, higher education, housing, pensions, tax exemptions, etc. Surely it is not unreasonable for governments to say that they have more than 'paid in full' any and all obligations arising under these old treaties and, from here on, treaty Indians will be dealt with on the same basis as ordinary Canadians.[34]

Pierre Trudeau took a similar position at the time the now infamous 1969 White Paper was introduced. 'It's inconceivable', he said, 'that in a given society one section of the society have a treaty with the other section of society. . . .

things that in the past were covered by the treaties like so much twine or so much gun powder and which haven't been paid must be paid. But I don't think that we should encourage the Indians to feel that their treaties should last forever within Canada. . . . They should become Canadians as all other Canadians'. Compare this to Ovide Mercredi's statement that 'We will not allow some other society to decide what we can do and determine the limits of our authority.' The philosophical chasm could hardly be wider.

Trudeau's remarks cut to the crux of the Native claims dilemma. The case for Native land claims ultimately rests on a particular vision of Canadian society, one that views Aboriginal peoples as separate from the rest of Canadian society. It is based on a philosophy of group rights and even group autonomy that sees the separateness of Native communities from the rest of Canada and a distinct status for Native Canadians (sometimes described as 'Citizens Plus', the title of an Aboriginal response to the 1969 White Paper) as desirable in themselves and certainly necessary for the survival of Native cultures. It is a vision that is irreconcilably opposed to the universalistic one-Canada vision expressed by Trudeau and Smith.

2. Comprehensive Claims

Nunavut, meaning 'our land' in Inuktitut, is the name of the eastern Arctic region that extends from 60 degrees north to the North Pole and from Great Bear Lake in the west to Baffin Bay and the Davis Strait in the east. It is a territory about twice the size of Ontario, with a population that would about fill the Molson Centre, home of the Montreal Canadiens. Under the terms of a 1993 agreement the territory will have its own elected legislature whose powers are broadly similar to those of provincial legislatures. The government of Nunavut will receive about $580 million (in 1989 dollars) paid out over 14 years, full landownership over about 350,000 square kilometres, exclusive hunting and fishing rights, a share of resource royalties, and participation in all decision-making involving land, water, and environmental management. In short, the Nunavut comprehensive claim settlement provides for self-government, financial compensation, and an ongoing voice for the Inuit who comprise the vast majority of its population, in exchange for extinguishment of any other Aboriginal claims and interests in the territory covered by the agreement. Under the terms of s. 25 of the Constitution Act, 1982, the Nunavut settlement has the status of constitutional law.

The background to Nunavut and other comprehensive claims lies in the decades of the 1960s and 1970s. As Murray Angus explains, this period was marked by increasing pressure for exploitation of the mineral resources known to lie buried under the land and seas of Canada's North. The federal government looked favourably on mega-projects, such as a proposed Mackenzie Valley natural gas pipeline, particularly after the escalation of world petroleum prices triggered by the 1973 Arab oil embargo. Development on the scale of a pipeline that would carry gas from the Arctic Sea to the markets of the American Middle West clearly had implications for Aboriginal communities and traditional activities. The push for northern resource development was met by a reaction in the form of increased political mobilization on the part of northern Natives, whose claims were assisted by the anti-development efforts of environmentalists.

The 1977 Report of the Mackenzie Valley Pipeline Enquiry, generally known as the Berger Inquiry after its commissioner, Mr Justice Thomas E. Berger, was a foremost case of this political reaction. The Berger Inquiry was established in 1974, during a period of escalating world petroleum prices and widespread fears of rapidly diminishing recoverable reserves of oil and gas. After three years of study and hearings, including extensive hearings in the North, the commission produced a two-volume report that recommended against the construction of gas pipelines across the Yukon and Northwest Territories. In arriving at the decision that pipeline development should be put on hold, Berger examined everything from its possible affects on the flora and fauna of the region to the cultural, social, and economic impacts of development. Moreover, he concluded that no pipeline construction should take place before Native land claims in the affected regions were settled and the structure of Native self-government was established.

Berger, who earlier had served as counsel to the Nishga in their land claims case, looked at northern resource development from the standpoint of those for whom the North was their homeland. An alternative perspective, and one that the federal government and the petroleum industry probably expected to assume greater weight in Berger's eyes than was ultimately the case, was to assess frontier development against the economic and consumer needs of southern Canada. This second perspective was rejected by Berger. He said:

> The establishment of an economy based on mining or, more particularly, on the oil and gas industry could deprive the people who live on the frontier of their rights to their lands, and it could offer them employment for reasons that have nothing to do with their real needs. Because the oil and gas industry does not depend upon them, the native people cannot depend upon it. And if they can no longer rely upon the land for their living, they will cease to have any essential relation to any form of economic activity. The native people's assertion of their claims must, in this historical perspective, be seen as an attempt to negotiate an alternative course of economic development.[35]

Noting the failure of Aboriginal policy in southern Canada to bring Native people into the mainstream of society, Berger argued that a new model was required to protect the Native communities of the North from experiencing the same dependency and social pathologies as their southern counterparts. The model he proposed rejected the practice of cash for land, whereby future

Aboriginal claims to their land are extinguished by compensation. Instead, Berger called for the entrenchment of Native rights through structures of Native self-determination. The ideas and recommendations of the Berger Report would eventually find expression in the 1993 Nunavut agreement, although that massive comprehensive claim settlement does include an extinguishment clause.

A second factor that has influenced the land claims process was the *Calder* decision in 1973, after which Ottawa and some provincial governments have taken the stand that Native land rights can only be extinguished through a land claims agreement. The nature of Aboriginal title is ambiguous at best, as even some supporters of Aboriginal ownership acknowledge.[36] Nevertheless, since 1973 successive federal governments have conceded that, at a minimum, the *Calder* ruling imposes on Ottawa an obligation to compensate Aboriginal groups for the 'loss and relinquishment' of 'traditional interest in land'.[37]

A third factor has been élite opinion in Canada's non-Native population. Since the demise of the 1969 White Paper and its liberal vision of full Native integration into Canadian society—not the same as assimilation, which is used to mean cultural genocide by critics—'progressive' thinking on Aboriginal issues has been supportive of demands for Aboriginal control and even outright ownership of traditional lands, Native self-government, and even some form of political sovereignty for Aboriginal communities. In the main, opinion leaders in Canada support the continued integrity of Native communities within the larger Canadian society, but on much better terms than have existed in the past. Acknowledgement of Aboriginal title to non-treaty land, financial compensation for contemporary uses of that land such as resource extraction, and a Native role in management of these lands are all part of these better terms. Progressive opinion accepts the designation of Aboriginal peoples as First Nations, a label that carries a whole conceptual framework and set of political claims relating to self-determination and ethnicity-based nationalism: precisely the sorts of ideas and claims pioneered successfully by Quebec nationalists in the 1960s.

It was not always this way. Until the discrediting and abandonment by Ottawa of the 1969 White Paper, the vision of liberal integration put forward by Pierre Trudeau was considered to be progressive. Indeed, it was widely acknowledged that the system of reserves and the fiduciary relationship of the federal government to its Aboriginal wards were, at best, patronizing sources of shame and, at worst, Canada's particular version of apartheid. Integration of Aboriginal people into the wider Canadian society on the basis of equal and identical rights was the progressive view among non-Aboriginal Canadians. In retrospect, the Trudeau government seriously misjudged the intensity of Aboriginal opposition to the integrationist reforms it proposed. Within a few years the compass of élite thinking swung around to a collectivist pole, so that opposition to the 1969 White Paper became a litmus test of one's progressive-mindedness.

The huge scale of comprehensive claims, in both dollars and territory, is reason enough for the attention devoted to them in recent years. As a Bank of Montreal executive put it, 'The fact is that by the end of the decade, aboriginal people are going to own or control a third of the Canadian land mass and be the recipient of $5 or $6 billion.'[38] But the other reason why comprehensive claims are so controversial is that they inevitably raise issues of Aboriginal self-government and the relationship of Native communities to the Canadian political system.

This dimension of Native land claims was acknowledged by the 1986 federal task force report, *Living Treaties: Lasting Agreements*. The report recommended that comprehensive claims agreements 'should encourage aboriginal communities to become not only economically self-sufficient but also to establish political and social institutions that will allow them to become self-governing.' It called for an end to the extinguishment of Aboriginal rights as a condition for land claims agreements, rejecting what had to that point been Ottawa's policy of treating such agreements as final cash-for-land deals. Instead, the report proposed that comprehensive claims agreements be viewed as 'living', 'flexible' documents that would facilitate the development of 'self-sufficient aboriginal communities'.[39]

Notwithstanding the enthusiasm of Native leaders for such an open-ended approach to the land claims process, all 10 comprehensive claims agreements signed by Ottawa between 1975 and 1993, including the massive Nunavut agreement, contained an extinguishment clause. However, it is important to realize that what is extinguished by such clauses are 'All native claims, rights, title and interests, whatever they may be, in and to the Territory.'[40] Whatever rights, benefits, and entitlements the Aboriginal people covered by such an agreement may have, either by virtue of their Indian status under the law or owing to their Canadian citizenship, are not diminished by the extinguishment of their Aboriginal property rights. Comprehensive claims settlements do not 'cut the cord' between Ottawa and Native communities, leading some critics to question the claims of self-sufficiency for Native people that are often made for such agreements.

The Principles Underlying Aboriginal Policy

Although some of the major components of present-day Aboriginal policy have been in place since before Confederation, the principles underlying federal policy have undergone important transformations. These transformations began during the 1960s, embodied in the Trudeau government's controversial and ill-fated 1969 White Paper. Since the abandonment of the White Paper successive federal governments have been groping towards a new set of principles on which to base Aboriginal policy. The most recent formulations appear to involve a new form of communal integrity based on a collectivist ethos and Ottawa's willingness to recognize a Native right to self-government.

1. Dependency and Assimilation

The prevailing view until at least the middle of the twentieth century was that Indians would gradually abandon their language, customs, and lifestyles and be absorbed into Euro-Canadian society. Compare, for example, the words of Sir John A. Macdonald in 1880 to those of Minister of Indian Affairs Walter Harris in 1950:

> [Our policy is] to wean [Indians] by slow degrees, from their nomadic habits, which have become almost an instinct, and by slow degrees absorb them on the land. Meantime they must be fairly protected. (1880)

> The ultimate goal of our Indian policy is the integration of the Indians into the general life and economy of the country. It is recognized, however, that during a temporary transition period . . . special treatment and legislation are necessary. (1950)

Assimilation progressed slowly, however, despite various prohibitions and inducements intended to eradicate 'backward' practices and reward bands that behaved in what were considered to be suitable ways. The 1884 ban (repeated and made clearer in 1895) on the potlatch ceremony and Tamanamous religious dances exemplify the sanctions used to stamp out Native traditions. The Indian Advancement Act of the same year, whereby much more extensive powers could be delegated to a band 'declared by Order of the Governor in Council to be considered fit to have this Act applied to them', was an example of the carrot approach to encouraging compliant Native leadership and advancing the goal of assimilation.

Revisions in 1951 to the Indian Act did not change its paternalistic character and assimilationist logic. The major change in Aboriginal policy during the postwar years was the extension of voting rights to Natives in 1960. But although their political status was thereby brought closer to that of non-Native Canadians, their legal and social status, and their civil rights, remained quite distinct. Moreover, instead of disappearing from the scene as the early architects of Canada's Indian policy doubtless hoped and expected, Native reserves continued to exist as islands of shame within an affluent and democratic society. The 1968 election of a Liberal government under Pierre Trudeau, dedicated to building what Trudeau called the 'Just Society', created the moment for the first major change in the direction of Aboriginal policy since the passage in 1876 of the Indian Act.

2. The 1969 White Paper: Integration and Equality

The conventional wisdom is that the 1969 White Paper simply continued along the assimilationist path of previous federal policies, but with a vengeance. The White Paper proposed nothing short of the total dismantling of the Indian Affairs bureaucracy, an end to the reserve system, the abolition of different status for Indians under the law (for example, their exemption from taxation in certain circumstances), and the transfer of responsibility for the education, health care, and social needs of Indian citizens to the provinces, in line with provincial responsibility for all other citizens. The White Paper proposed that most of these reforms be accomplished within five years but recognized that some changes, such as the transfer of reserve land owned by the Crown in trust for Natives, would probably take more time.

The White Paper was met by a chorus of condemnation from Aboriginal leaders. Chief Harold Cardinal of the National Indian Brotherhood (now the Assembly of First Nations) wrote:

> Now, at a time when our fellow Canadians consider the promise of the Just Society, once more the Indians of Canada are betrayed by a pro-gramme which offers nothing better than cultural genocide. . . . [The White Paper] is a thinly disguised programme of extermination through assimilation. For the Indian to survive, says the government in effect, he must become a good little brown white man.[41]

'Betrayed', 'cultural genocide', 'extermination', 'assimilation': words like these measured the depth of opposition that the Trudeau government's rec-ommendations provoked. Since then, the widely accepted verdict on the White Paper is that it proposed to replace paternalism—a bad thing—with assimila-tion—another bad thing.

The reforms proposed in that document, however, need to be understood in the context of both the times and the political and social thinking of Pierre Trudeau. Moreover, the entirety of the White Paper's analysis and recom-mendations needs to be examined, not just those bits that critics find conve-nient to pounce on. What emerges is a vision for Canada's Native population that is more accurately characterized as *integrationist*, not assimilationist. Those who would argue that the distinction is merely one of semantics do not understand the background against which the White Paper was formulated.

That background involved an elevated awareness of social inequality and discrimination during the 1960s. The Black civil rights movement in the United States and the student activism that arose during those years took aim at the exclusion of minority groups from the rights and opportunities available to the majority. The remedy social activists and civil libertarians proposed was integration, whereby barriers to the full economic, social, and political partic-ipation of historically disadvantaged minorities would be abolished. Integration was, in fact, the banner under which the civil rights movement marched in the 1950s and 1960s. It was not believed to be synonymous with assimilation, much less the 'cultural genocide' and 'extermination' that some critics have since equated with the liberal integrationist vision. While it is true that many leaders of the Black movement in the United States eventually came to reject the integrationist approach (characterized by one prominent leader as 'The movement of all things black toward all things white'), the approach was not intended by its advocates to lay waste to minority ethnic cultures. This certainly was not the expectation of either Trudeau or the 1969 White Paper for Native Canadians.

The White Paper called for 'positive recognition by everyone of the unique contribution of Indian culture to Canadian society'. This goal would be promoted through the Department of Secretary of State, which was carving out a role for itself as the key federal agency for promoting the interests and identities of disadvantaged groups.[42] The White Paper suggested that some of the effort to promote Aboriginal cultures would have to be done by the provinces because of their responsibility for education. In the context of the time it is entirely reasonable to expect that Ottawa was prepared to help finance the cost of these provincial programs, as it did in so many other areas during the 1960s and 1970s.

The White Paper made clear that an end to 'a policy of treating Indian people as a race apart' did not mean that this profoundly disadvantaged segment of Canadian society would suddenly be cut loose from government support systems and expected to fend for itself. 'Equality before the law and in programs and services', the White Paper declared, 'does not necessarily result in equality in social and economic conditions.' Ottawa proposed that programs targeted specially at Native Canadians would be delivered through such federal ministries as Manpower and Regional Economic Expansion. The latter was expected to be particularly important in providing assistance to isolated Native communities within the context of the federal government's policy of alleviating regional disparities in economic well-being. In line with the Trudeau government's commitment to social justice the White Paper acknowledged that 'those who are furthest behind must be helped the most.' But at the same time the new approach proposed for Indian policy was based on another idea central to Pierre Trudeau's political thinking, namely, that 'Separate but equal services do not provide truly equal treatment.' When the United States Supreme Court said exactly this in the 1954 decision that marked the beginning of the end of legal racial segregation in that country, it was hailed as a great step forward for human equality and freedom. If Ottawa expected a similar reaction to its restatement of this liberal principle it surely was disappointed.

While much in the White Paper proved to be controversial, nothing galvanized Aboriginal opposition more than its proposals concerning treaty obligations and Native land claims. The White Paper acknowledged that the lawful obligations of the Canadian government must be respected. However, it went on to argue that a 'plain reading of the words used in the treaties reveals the limited and minimal promises which were included in them' and that they should not be expected to define in perpetuity the relationship between Natives and the government of Canada. Here is what the White Paper said on the subject of treaties:

The significance of treaties in meeting the economic, educational, health and welfare needs of the Indian people has always been limited and will continue to decline. The services that have been provided go far beyond what could have been foreseen by those who signed the treaties. The Government and the Indian people must reach a common understanding of the future role of treaties. Some provisions will be found to have been discharged; others will have continuing importance. Many of the provisions and practices of another century may be considered irrelevant in the light of a rapidly changing society, and still others may be ended by mutual agreement. Finally, once Indian lands are securely within Indian control, the anomaly of treaties between groups within society and the government of that society will require that these treaties be reviewed to see how they can be equitably ended.[43]

Alarm bells went off in the Native community. The Trudeau government was proposing nothing less than the gradual phasing out of Indian treaties and an end to whatever special rights Aboriginals had under these agreements. This was, of course, entirely consistent with the philosophical and practical thrust of the White Paper, which was to integrate the Native population into Canadian society on the basis of equal treatment. Obligations regarding 'twine', 'ammunition', and annuities that made sense a century ago had become, the government believed, irrelevant relics in the modern world. Moreover, because reserve land would be transferred into the hands of Indians—thus ending a system as old as the Royal Proclamation of 1763, whereby Indian land was owned and controlled by the Crown for the use and benefit of Aboriginal people—and educational, health, and social services would be provided to Natives through the same provincial channels used by other citizens, treaties would no longer have practical importance. Moreover, the very concept of a treaty between one part of society and the government of all the people was morally and philosophically repugnant to Trudeau and the vision laid out in the White Paper.

Here we arrive at the crux of the controversy over the White Paper. It is about competing and irreconcilable visions of the appropriate relationship of Aboriginal Canadians to the rest of Canadian society. The vision held by Native leaders like George Erasmus, co-chair of the Royal Commission on Aboriginal Peoples, and Ovide Mercredi, former Grand Chief of the Assembly of First Nations, sees Natives as standing apart from Canadian society as self-governing nations that should continue to have some relationship to the federal government. The nature of that relationship primarily involves the fulfilment of Ottawa's treaty obligations towards Native people. The integrationist vision of equal and identical status for Native and non-Native Canadians has been rejected outright from Harold Cardinal's broadside against the 1969 White Paper to the 1996 Report of the Royal Commission on Aboriginal Peoples, on the grounds that it is a recipe for what Native leaders see as cultural genocide. The survival of Native communities and cultures depends on the recognition of the distinct status and rights due to them as the original occupants and owners of the land that is today known as Canada.

The White Paper vision, which flowed directly from Pierre Trudeau's political philosophy, rejects outright the notion that a just solution to the problems that beset Canada's Native peoples must rest on a recognition of their sovereignty and distinct status. Critics of the White Paper and Trudeau argue that this rejection is due to Trudeau being a liberal individualist. In fact, however, there is a powerful collectivist strand woven through Trudeau's brand of liberalism. As Trudeau has written, 'It is not the concept of the *nation* that is retrograde; it is the idea that the nation must necessarily be sovereign.'[44] His political philosophy accommodated the existence of national communities within society and even some forms of constitutional recognition for these communities. He rejected, however, the concept of the nation-state, the argument that nations have a right to self-determination, and any form of government that rests on the primordial importance of the nation or of any other collectivity that is defined in racial, ethnic, or cultural terms.

Trudeau did not deny the importance of collective identities and group recognition in politics. His government, after all, passed the Official Languages Act, introduced Canada's policy of official multiculturalism, and proposed a Charter of Rights and Freedoms that includes guarantees for members of official-language minorities and Aboriginal Canadians. He was well aware that an individual's dignity may be undermined by social practices and government policies that deny recognition to the group that is crucial to one's identity and self-image.

However, recognizing that equality and dignity have collective dimensions, Trudeau was always firm in maintaining that 'only the individual is the possessor of rights'[45] and in rejecting any concept of human dignity, such as that associated with nationalism, that locates the primary sources of dignity in one's association with a collectivity that is more narrowly drawn than society. Dignity and equality are states that can only be achieved by man in society, he would argue, but they do not require one's communal identity to be central to personal fulfilment. On the contrary, elevating communal identity to the top rung in politics, and all that this may entail such as constitutional recognition of a community's distinct status and rights and guaranteeing these rights to the community as such, rather than to individuals, actually undermines dignity and equality, according to Trudeau.

The liberal-integrationist vision of the 1969 White Paper, and the philosophical premises on which it was based, survives as a minority point of view among Canada's political and cultural élites. Indeed, it is ironic that the sort of principles espoused by Pierre Trudeau in rejecting the system of segregation upon which Canadian Aboriginal policy was based are today most likely to be expressed by members of the Reform Party of Canada—hardly Trudeau's soulmates in any other respect!

3. The Royal Commission on Aboriginal Peoples: Separate Is Equal

A very different vision is set forth in the 1996 *Report of the Royal Commission on Aboriginal Peoples*. The long-awaited report of the most expensive royal commission in Canadian history started from the premise that Aboriginal Canadians constitute First Nations whose sovereignty should be respected by the government of Canada. In practical terms this would involve providing Native communities with a sufficiently large land base and either control over or a guaranteed stake in resource development and revenues generated from such development on Native land. The *Report* called for the creation of an Aboriginal third order of government whose existence would be based on the acknowledgement by Ottawa and the provinces that the inherent right to self-government is a treaty right guaranteed by the constitution of Canada. A form of dual citizenship for Native Canadians, who would be both Canadian citizens and citizens of First Nations communities, was proposed. The philosophical premises and policy proposals of the royal commission could hardly have been further from those of the 1969 White Paper. Its proposals included the following:

- The government should issue a new royal proclamation admitting the wrongs done to Aboriginal peoples and promising a new relationship between Aboriginals and governments in Canada.
- The inherent right of Native self-government should be recognized by all governments as a treaty right affirmed by the constitution.
- An independent lands and treaties tribunal should be established to determine land claims and ensure that the terms and financial arrangements of treaties are fair.
- The Canadian Human Rights Commission should be given responsibility to investigate any complaints relating to the relocation of Aboriginal communities and to recommend appropriate redress.
- Natives should hold dual citizenship, as Canadians and as citizens of their First Nations communities.
- An Aboriginal parliament, to be known as the House of First Peoples, should be established with an advisory role concerning all legislation that affects Aboriginal Canadians.
- The Department of Indian and Northern Affairs should be replaced by a new bureaucracy that would involve an Aboriginal relations department and an Indian and Inuit services department.
- The government should negotiate with Métis representatives on self-government and the allocation to the Métis people of an adequate land base.
- Aboriginal representatives should be participants in all future talks on constitutional reform, with a veto over any changes that affect Aboriginal rights.

- An additional $30 billion over 15 years should be spent on Aboriginal programs (on top of the estimated $13–$14 billion spent by Ottawa and the provinces on Aboriginal programs in 1996).

Running through the 440 recommendations of the royal commission is a simple and fundamental premise: the original sovereignty of Native peoples and their ownership of the land must be acknowledged, and their continuing right to a land base and self-government must be embedded in the constitution. Moreover, the survival and development of Aboriginal cultures can only be achieved through policies that recognize Aboriginal people as distinct communities with special rights and powers. The problem with federal policies for over a century is not that they have treated Indians differently from other Canadians. It is that these policies have not provided the Native population with either the decision-making autonomy or financial resources to take control over their lives and escape the cycle of dependency that the Indian Act's paternalism established.

A year before the commission's final report was issued, Indian Affairs Minister Ron Irwin stated that the over $50 million the commission was expected to cost would have been better spent building houses for Natives in the North. So it came as no great surprise that the federal government was rather cool towards the commission's sweeping vision for reform. Ottawa stressed that the dollars needed to implement the recommendations simply were not available, implicitly rejecting the commission's claim that the cost of sticking with the status quo would be even more expensive. And despite the sympathy expressed by some government spokespersons for the aims of the commission, it was clear that Ottawa's conception of self-government for Natives did not involve the creation of a third order of government.

Indeed, only weeks before the *Report* was issued the government had released a draft bill proposing extensive revisions to the Indian Act. The affront to the commission was clear. Ottawa's proposed reforms were not only far more modest than the grand design it was known the commission would produce, but they also included some changes that were entirely out of step with the philosophy of the commission. The most important of these were the proposals involving the legal obligations of Indian bands and the status of reserve land. Bands would, for the first time, be able to hold land in their own right, could sue and be sued, and would be able to borrow money using reserve land as security.

Ovide Mercredi lost no time in denouncing the particular set of proposals as an attempt to impose on Aboriginals the 'whiteman's system of private property'. One of the fundamental tenets of Native culture, he insisted, is the collective ownership of the land. Mercredi argued that an approach to land that treats it as just another commodity or possession, to be bought and sold as an individual chooses, is alien to the way Natives view their relationship to the land. Even if Mercredi was right in his characterization of Aboriginal traditions relating to the land, it was clear that at least some high-profile Native leaders, including Blaine Favel, the head of the Federation of Saskatchewan Indian Nations, supported Ottawa's proposal.

By issuing its proposed reforms to the Indian Act Ottawa sent a clear signal that grand schemes of the sort favoured by the Royal Commission on Aboriginal Peoples simply were not in the cards. The reason was not simply money, although the cost excuse provided a convenient public justification for not accepting the commission's recommendations. An additional reason was the nature of Native self-government envisaged by the commission, which went considerably beyond the federal government's notion of what it should mean for Native communities to be self-governing. Few concepts in public policy debates are as slippery as self-government, but one of the clearest statements of what it should involve was made by George Erasmus to a national conference on the subject in 1990:

> The kind of powers that would probably be acceptable to us are those that provinces already have in their areas of sovereignty. Canada lends itself very easily to what indigenous people want. We already have a division of sovereignty. We already have a situation where the federal government has clear powers, s. 91 powers, and provinces have clear powers, s. 92 powers, many in which they are absolutely paramount and sovereign. Not another government anywhere in the world can interfere with their legislation. That model lends itself very nicely to what First Nations always told the people in this country. You already have federal powers, and provincial powers. Let's look at First Nations powers. And we will have three major forms of government. Three different types of sovereignty. Two coming from the Crown, one coming from the indigenous people, all together creating one state.[46]

Erasmus does not address here the controversial question of how the Charter of Rights and Freedoms would apply to an Aboriginal third order of government—would it apply in its entirety and in the same way as it does to Ottawa and the provinces?—or other contentious matters such as the applicability of the Criminal Code to self-governing Native communities. But while some detail may be lacking, the vision of self-government that Erasmus sets forth is one shared by many Aboriginal leaders.

For its part, however, Ottawa prefers something more modest than self-governing Native communities with province-like powers. An example of the sort of self-government model that a federal government would be likely to approve is seen in the Sechelt Indian Band Self-Government Act, 1986, which transferred outright ownership of reserve land to this British Columbia band, relieved it of most provisions of the Indian Act, and assigned the band council a list of powers similar to those exercised by municipal governments across Canada. Since the Sechelt agreement Ottawa has shown a willingness to concede more ambitious models of self-government, such as those adopted for

Nunavut and the Yukon. The legislative powers assigned to the Legislative
Assembly of Nunavut and to several Aboriginal communities in the Yukon are
similar to those assigned to provincial legislatures by the constitution. But
what Ottawa has not been willing to concede, at least at this writing, is a one-
size-fits-all model of Aboriginal self-government, preferring instead to negotiate particular agreements on an individual-case basis.

Aboriginal Rights and Quebec Sovereignty

If Quebecers vote to separate from Canada, what becomes of those Aboriginal
Canadians who would find themselves living in an independent Quebec? It is
clearly established in law that the federal government owes what is called a
fiduciary responsibility to the country's Aboriginal population. A fiduciary
relationship is one of trust between two parties, one of whom is required to
protect the interests of the other. Moreover, the constitution states very clearly
that 'Indians and Indian lands' fall under the exclusive jurisdiction of the federal government, an authority that Ottawa inherited from the British colonial
authorities. For their part, Aboriginal communities across Quebec have made
clear that they want no part of an independent Quebec. In a separate Aboriginal
referendum held a few weeks before the 1995 Quebec referendum, over 90 per
cent of those who voted said no to independence for Quebec. Several Native
spokespersons have supported the idea of severing off those parts of Quebec
where Aboriginal communities live, in order to retain a relationship to Canada.
Some have even spoken of the possibility of violent resistance against the
authority of a sovereign Quebec state.

There are two main scenarios for Quebec separation. One involves a unilateral declaration of independence by the Quebec government, most probably after winning a provincial referendum on sovereignty for Quebec. The
other scenario would see Ottawa agree to negotiate the terms of independence
with the government of Quebec, again presumably after a separatist referendum victory. These two scenarios give rise to rather different consequences for
the Aboriginal peoples of Quebec.

Under the first scenario, the status of Native Canadians living in Quebec
and their relationship to the Canadian government after a unilateral declaration of independence by Quebec become highly problematic. As Kent McNeil
writes in a study done for the Royal Commission on Aboriginal Peoples,

> The government of Canada has a constitutional responsibility for
> Aboriginal peoples and cannot renounce that responsibility unilaterally.
> If Aboriginal peoples do not accept Quebec independence, the govern-
> ment of Canada has a constitutional obligation to ensure that their inter-
> ests are protected in [the] face of a UDI [unilateral declaration of inde-
> pendence].[47]

Does this mean that Ottawa has a legal obligation to act if Aboriginal communities in an independent Quebec request the support of the Canadian government to resist the authority of the Quebec state? McNeil suggests that it does, and that if Ottawa either neglected or refused to take 'adequate actions', then Aboriginal peoples in Quebec would have grounds to go before Canadian courts to seek a judicial ruling compelling the Canadian government to fulfil its fiduciary responsibilities towards them. The prospect of Canadian courts ordering Ottawa to take actions that could range from a declaration refusing to recognize the independence of Quebec to sending in the troops may appear rather far-fetched. Even more far-fetched is the likelihood that such an order would have any impact on the behaviour of an independent Quebec government. This is not to say that Ottawa would not respond sympathetically to Native calls for support, but merely that it is naïve to imagine that the Canadian court system would play much of a role in the resolution of the triangular relations between the Canadian state, an independent Quebec state, and Quebec-based Aboriginal communities.

The second scenario—Ottawa agreeing to negotiate the terms of independence and association with a sovereign Quebec—gives rise to rather different issues. The Canadian government's fiduciary responsibility towards Aboriginal peoples, in Quebec and elsewhere, clearly requires that Ottawa take serious account of Aboriginal interests in any such negotiations. It is doubtful, however, that Ottawa has any constitutional obligation beyond this. In a study for the Royal Commission on Aboriginal Peoples, Renée Dupuis argues that the constitution 'provides specifically for the participation of Aboriginal peoples in constitutional issues affecting them directly',[48] and notes that participation of Aboriginal leaders in the constitutional talks that led up to the 1992 Charlottetown Accord. The first claim is dubious—the Constitution Act, 1982, required that a constitutional conference on Aboriginal issues be convened within a year, which it duly was, but it is a stretch to argue that the constitution imposes an ongoing obligation on Ottawa to bring Aboriginal representatives into any talks on constitutional change. And while it is true that several Aboriginal leaders participated in the Charlottetown Accord negotiations, they were excluded from the final stages of the talks between the first ministers. Nor is it very convincing to argue that the experience of 1992 has hardened into a constitutional convention. Perhaps the most reasonable conclusion to be drawn about Aboriginal participation in any negotiations on Quebec Independence is that provided by Dupuis herself: 'governments have no legal obligation to ensure that Aboriginal peoples participate directly in bilateral negotiations between the governments of Canada and Quebec preceding any constitutional process leading eventually to sovereignty. Instead, considerations of legitimacy or political advisability would come into play.'[49]

Whatever circumstances might attend Quebec's separation from Canada, it is difficult to imagine that Aboriginal issues would be among the most pressing concerns of the governments of Canada and Quebec. A whole range of matters, including division of the federal debt, the future of federally owned property in Quebec, the terms of trade between Quebec and Canada, currency and the co-ordination of monetary policy, the demands of Quebec partitionists, transportation between the Atlantic provinces and Canada west of Quebec, and the necessity of reforming federal political institutions, to mention only several, would no doubt overshadow the Aboriginal agenda. Indeed, depending on the degree of resentment generated by Quebec independence among Canadians in the rest of the country, it is not inconceivable that Aboriginal demands and rights, as well as multiculturalism, could suffer at the hands of a popular backlash against any measures perceived as contributing to the further fragmentation of Canadian society.

On the other hand, it is quite possible that neither the Canadian government nor an independent Quebec government would be allowed to ignore the voice of Aboriginal communities in Quebec. There is a long history of mutually antagonistic relations between the Quebec authorities, particularly Quebec's provincial police force, the Sûreté du Québec, and many Aboriginal groups. Moreover, the Mohawks of Quebec have shown themselves to be willing to use aggressive means in defence of their land and their claim to be an independent nation. If there is violence in the aftermath of Quebec independence, most observers expect that it will be triggered by Native resistance to the authority of an independent Quebec state. Should this happen, what would be the response of the Canadian government? It is hard to imagine that it would extend to military intervention, even if this sort of protection was requested by Aboriginal communities. It is not difficult to imagine, however, international involvement in the form of UN observers, reports, condemnations, and so on. With the eyes of the world upon them, it is doubtful that either the Canadian or Quebec government could ignore the demands of Native communities in Quebec.

Appendix: Excerpts from the Royal Proclamation of 1763

And whereas it is just and reasonable, and essential to our Interest, and the security of our Colonies, that the several Nations or Tribes of Indians with whom We are connected, and who live under our protection, should not be molested or disturbed in the Possession of such Parts of Our Dominions and Territories as, not having been ceded to or purchased by Us, are reserved to them or any of them, as their Hunting Grounds — We do therefore, with the Advice of our Privy Council, declare it to be our Royal Will and Pleasure, that no Governor or Commander in Chief in any of our Colonies of Quebec, East

Florida, or West Florida, do presume, upon any Pretence whatever, to grant Warrants of Survey, or pass any Patents for Lands beyond the Bounds of their respective Governments, as described in their Commissions; as also that no Governor or Commander in Chief in any of our other Colonies or Plantations in America do presume for the present, and until our further Pleasure be Known, to grant Warrants of Survey, or pass Patents for any Lands beyond the Heads or Sources of any of the Rivers which fall into the Atlantic Ocean from the West and North West, or upon any Lands whatever, which, not having been ceded to or purchased by Us as aforesaid, are reserved to the said Indians, or any of them.

And We do further declare it to be Our Royal Will and Pleasure, for the present as aforesaid, to reserve under our Sovereignty, Protection, and Dominion, for the use of the said Indians, all the Lands and Territories not included within the Limits of Our Said Three New Governments, or within the Limits of the Territory granted to the Hudson's Bay Company, as also all the Lands and Territories lying to the Westward of the Sources of the Rivers which fall into the Sea from the West and North West as aforesaid;

And We do hereby strictly forbid, on Pain of our Displeasure, all our loving Subjects from making any Purchases or Settlements whatever, or taking Possession of any of the Lands above reserved, without our especial leave and Licence for the Purpose first obtained.

And, We do further strictly enjoin and require all Persons whatever who have either wilfully or inadvertently seated themselves upon any Lands within the Countries above described, or upon any other Lands which, not having been ceded to or purchased by Us, are still reserved to the said Indians as aforesaid, forthwith to remove themselves from such Settlements.

And Whereas Great Frauds and Abuses have been committed in purchasing Lands of the Indians, to the Great Prejudice of our Interests, and to the Great Dissatisfaction of the said Indians; In order, therefore, to prevent such Irregularities for the future, and to the End that the Indians may be convinced of our Justice and determined Resolution to remove all reasonable Cause of Discontent, We do, with the Advice of our Privy Council strictly enjoin and require, that no private Person do presume to make any Purchase from the said Indians of any Lands reserved to the said Indians, within those parts of our Colonies where, We have thought proper to allow Settlement; but that, if at any Time any of the said Indians should be inclined to dispose of the said Lands, the same shall be Purchased only for Us, in our Name, at some public Meeting or Assembly of the said Indians, to be held for the Purpose by the Governor or Commander in Chief of our Colony respectively within which they shall lie; and in case they shall lie within the limits of any Proprietary Government, they shall be purchased only for the Use and in the name of such Proprietaries, conformable to such Directions and Instructions as We or they shall think proper to give for the Purpose. . . .

Chapter Nine

Cultural Policy: Language and Ethnicity

Introduction

The word 'culture' evokes responses ranging from indifference to intense emotion. For some the term is a vague label associated with museums, art galleries, and classical music. For others culture has a more general significance, referring to the widely shared values, beliefs, practices, and institutions of an entire community: features that define a community by distinguishing it from those that do not share those values, beliefs, and practices. This second meaning of the term conforms closely to the technical definition of culture used in anthropology and sociology.[1] It includes such highly visible characteristics as language, religious practices, methods of work, family structure, and typical dwelling places, as well as attitudes and ways of perceiving the world that are by their very nature not directly observable, although presumably they influence the behaviour of those who hold them. In no political system do all individuals share equally in the same cultural heritage. These differences between groups often form the basis for important political conflicts, as between Catholics and Protestants in Northern Ireland, Serbs and Croats in what used to be Yugoslavia, and French and English in Canada. Cultural differences between religious, ethnic, or language groups may give rise to political conflicts when they are associated with inequalities in the economic status and political power of these groups.

This chapter examines two of the major themes of Canadian cultural policy: language and multiculturalism. Since the Royal Commission on Bilingualism and Biculturalism issued the final volume of its report in 1970,[2] these themes have often been linked in the official rhetoric of federal cultural policy. 'Multiculturalism within a bilingual framework' expresses the attempt of successive federal governments to manage the long-standing tensions in relations between French and English Canada in a way that also satisfies the demands of other ethnolinguistic groups for a share in the Canadian symbolic order. In terms of dollars devoted to these policy goals and the measures taken to achieve them, there is no question that the emphasis has been on the 'bilingual framework' rather than on 'multiculturalism'.

Language Policy

1. From the Plains of Abraham to the Quiet Revolution

The military victory of Wolfe over Montcalm in 1759, and the subsequent transfer of *la Nouvelle France* to Britain as part of the terms of the Treaty of Paris, established the basis for language politics in what eventually would become Canada. Anglophones assumed the positions of political authority in what became British North America, and they quickly displaced the Francophone *commerçants* in the trading economy of the colony. But the vast majority of the population was French. Only after the American War of Independence (1776) was there a significant influx of Anglophones—the defeated Loyalists. Indeed, the linguistic balance in British North America remained on the side of the French until well into the nineteenth century. This changed as a result of the wave of immigration from the British Isles that began around 1815. By Confederation those of French background comprised about a third of Canada's population, but Francophones made up roughly three-quarters of the population of Quebec. The identification of French Canada with Quebec was reinforced by the unilingual English development of the western provinces. Early guarantees for the French language in Manitoba were abrogated by an 1890 provincial statute that made English the sole official language and by another measure that eliminated public funding for the Catholic, and largely Francophone, school system.

By the turn of the century three main pillars of language politics were in place. First, Francophones comprised a large share of the country's population, a share that was remarkably stable in view of the almost total lack of French-speaking immigration after 1759 and the massive emigration of French Quebecers to the New England states during the latter half of the nineteenth century. Second, they were concentrated mainly in Quebec, the other provinces proving unreceptive and sometimes even hostile to the principle of equal status for the French language. Third, Francophones were largely excluded from Canada's economic élite. Even within Quebec the levers of economic power were controlled by Anglophones. This third factor would eventually prove crucial when, after 1960, the pressure of social and economic transformations in Quebec combined with the fall of the conservative Duplessis government to open the way for a more assertive approach in that province's language policy.

Before the changes ushered in by Quebec's Quiet Revolution, the protection of the French language had depended mainly on the constitutional division of powers. Under the BNA Act the provinces were assigned control over such culturally sensitive policy areas as education and social services, and the Duplessis government of Quebec had been a vigorous defender of provincial autonomy in these matters. This approach was a defensive one that sought to preserve the traditional values of French Canada and was unconcerned with the domination of the provincial economy by Anglophone capital.[3] At the national level, the *lingua franca* of the state was clearly English. Francophones were concentrated in lower-level administrative support categories of the public service. Even within the cabinet, where language had been an important basis for membership from before Confederation, Francophones were excluded from the key economic portfolios. Until Jean Chrétien became Minister of Industry, Trade and Commerce and later Minister of Finance in the 1970s, no Francophone had ever held these positions. As the challenge of Quebec nationalism emerged onto the political scene in the 1960s, Ottawa lacked anything that could be called a language policy. The constitutional guarantee of the coequal status of the French and English languages (s. 133 of the BNA Act) and the political importance of Francophone support for any party serious about forming a national government had not produced an effectively bilingual state.

2. Challenge and Response: Language Policies in Conflict

The origins of present-day language policy in Canada lie in developments in Quebec during the 1960s. The 'Quiet Revolution' is the term generally used to describe a number of institutional reforms that occurred in Quebec during this decade, including the creation of several important state enterprises and the transfer of authority over the province's educational system from the Church to the state. But more importantly, the term expresses the change that took place in the dominant ideology of Quebec society. The traditional ideology had stressed the *preservation* of the distinctive cultural values and social characteristics of French-speaking Quebec, including the French language, the Catholic religion, and the centrality of rural life to the ideal of French Canada.

With the death of Maurice Duplessis in 1959 and the election of the Quebec Liberal Party in 1960, the political obstacles to change were largely removed and the outdated character of this conservative ideology was exposed. It was replaced by an emphasis on *rattrapage*—catching up with the level of social and economic development elsewhere. The provincial state, traditionally viewed as a second-class institution in a province in which most social services were controlled by the Church and government was associated with crass patronage, became the focus of nationalist energies. The fact that it was the *provincial* state to which the new nationalism of the Quiet Revolution turned— the state in which French-speaking Quebecers were unquestionably in the majority—reinforced the identification of French Canada with the territory of Quebec. The provincial Liberals' 1963 campaign slogan, *maîtres chez nous,* gave popular political expression to what had become the dominant view of French Canada as being coextensive with Quebec.

The ideology of *rattrapage* and the identification of French Canada with Quebec had important consequences for language policy in that province. As the instrument for economic and social development, the Quebec state assumed functions previously administered by Church authorities and also expanded the scope of its economic activities. In doing so it provided career opportunities for the growing number of educated Francophones graduating from the province's universities. Access to high-paying managerial and technical jobs in the private sector, however, remained blocked by Anglophone domination of the Quebec economy. The relative exclusion of Francophones from positions of authority above that of foreman and the concentration of Francophone businesses in the *petites et moyennes entreprises* sector of the economy had long been known.[4] This situation ran directly counter to the expectations of the Quiet Revolution and became an important political issue when the capacity of the public sector to absorb the increasing ranks of highly educated Francophones became strained.

Demographic trends comprised an additional factor that shaped provincial language policy in Quebec. Immigrants to the province overwhelmingly adopted the English language. This fact, combined with the dramatic reduction in the birth rate among Francophones, seemed to lend credibility to a scenario where Francophones might become a minority in Montreal and even, though much later, within Quebec. These trends, along with evidence that Francophones were excluded from much of the province's economic structure, formed the basis for the policy recommendations of the Quebec Royal Commission of Inquiry on the Position of the French Language and on Language Rights in Quebec (the Gendron Commission, 1972). The commission recommended that the provincial government take legislative action to promote the use of French in business and in the schools. These recommendations were translated into law under the Quebec Liberal government that introduced the Official Language Act[5] and in the Charte de la langue française[6]—or Bill 101, as it is more commonly known outside Quebec—passed under the Parti Québécois government in 1977. Without going into the detailed provisions of this legislation, three principal features of Quebec language policy since the passage of Bill 101 can be identified.

1. French is established as the sole official language in Quebec, and therefore the exclusive official language for proceedings of the provincial legislature and the courts and the main language for public administration in the province. In a 1979 decision the Supreme Court of Canada ruled that this section of Bill 101 violated s. 133 of the BNA Act, which guarantees the coequal status of the French and English languages at the federal level and in the province of Quebec.[7]

2. Through the requirement that businesses with 50 or more employees receive a 'francisation' certificate as a condition of doing business in the province, the

Quebec government seeks to increase the use of French as a working language of business in the province. The language charter does not establish linguistic quotas for corporations. Instead, it leaves the conditions of certification a matter for individual negotiations between a firm and the Office de la langue française. Despite some initial resistance from the Anglophone business community, symbolized by the move of Sun Life's head office from Montreal to Toronto, this section of Bill 101 has generally been accepted by employers. More controversial have been the provisions requiring that public signs and advertisements be in French only. A 1988 Supreme Court decision held that this violated the freedom of expression guaranteed in the Charter of Rights and Freedoms.[8]

3. The provisions of Bill 101 that originally provoked the most controversy were those restricting access to English-language schools in Quebec. Under this law, children could enrol in an English school if one of the following conditions was met: their parents had been educated in English in Quebec; they had a sibling already going to an English school; their parents were educated in English outside of Quebec but were living in the province when the law was passed (1977); they were already enrolled in an English school when the law came into effect. The intent was obviously to reverse the overwhelming preference of immigrants for the English language, a preference that demographers predicted would eventually change the linguistic balance in the province, and even more dramatically in Montreal, which attracted the vast majority of immigrants. In one of the first Supreme Court decisions on the Charter of Rights and Freedoms, the Court held that the requirement that at least one of a child's parents must have been educated in English in Quebec violated section 23 of the Charter, a section that clearly had been drafted with Bill 101 in mind. The practical importance of this ruling is small, given the low level of migration to Quebec from other Canadian provinces. More significant is the fact that the Supreme Court was unwilling to accept the Quebec government's argument that the demographic threat to the position of the French language justified this restriction on language rights under the 'reasonable limits' section of the Charter.

Despite some setbacks in the courts, the main features of Quebec's language policy have remained substantially unchanged since the passage of Bill 101. The only significant reform occurred after the Supreme Court's 1988 ruling that the ban on languages other than French for commercial signs violated the Charter's guarantee of freedom of expression. Within weeks the Quebec legislature passed Bill 178, which invoked the 'notwithstanding clause' of the Charter in order to reaffirm the prohibition on languages other than French for commercial signs *outside* a business. Bill 178 does allow, however, the use of other languages on signs *inside* a business, but French signs must be predominant. Judged according to its two main objectives—increasing the use of the French language in the Quebec economy and stemming the decline in the Francophone share of the provincial population—this policy must be judged a success.[9]

Language policy in Quebec has been shaped by the idea that French Canada is coextensive with the boundaries of that province. The Office de la langue française and the law it administers build on an approach to language promotion that can be traced back to the early 1960s. The Liberal government of Jean Lesage set out to increase Francophone participation in the economy through such provincial institutions as la Société générale du financement, la Caisse de dépôt et placement, Sidérurgie québécoise, and an expanded Hydro-Québec.[10] The common denominator since then has been the use of the provincial state as an instrument for the socio-economic advancement of Francophones.

A very different approach to language policy, based on a conception of French and English Canada that cuts across provincial borders, has been pursued by successive federal governments since the 1960s. Responding to the new assertive nationalism of the Quiet Revolution, the signs of which ranged from Quebec's demands for greater taxation powers and less interference by Ottawa in areas of provincial constitutional responsibility to bombs placed in mailboxes and public monuments, the Liberal government of Lester Pearson established the Royal Commission on Bilingualism and Biculturalism. As Eric Waddell writes, 'The federal government was facing a legitimacy crisis in the 1960s and 1970s and had the immediate task of proposing a Canadian alternative to Quebec nationalism.'[11] The B&B Commission was a first step towards the adoption by Ottawa of a policy of official bilingualism. This policy was intended to defuse the *indépendantiste* sentiment building in Quebec, especially among young Francophones, in part by opening Ottawa as a field of career opportunities to rival the Quebec public service.

The alternative Ottawa offered, expressed in the federalist philosophy of Pierre Trudeau, was of a Canada in which language rights would be guaranteed to the individual and protected by national institutions. In practical terms this meant changing the overwhelmingly Anglophone character of the federal state so that Francophones would not have grounds to view it as an 'alien' level of government from which they were largely excluded. These changes have been carried out on two main fronts. First, what Raymond Breton refers to as the 'Canadian symbolic order' has been transformed since the 1960s.[12] Through a new flag, the proclamation of 'O Canada' as the official national anthem, new designs for stamps and currency, and the language neutering of some federal institutions, documents, and celebrations (for example, Trans-Canada Airlines became Air Canada, the BNA Act is now officially titled the Constitution Act, and Dominion Day is now called Canada Day), a deliberate attempt has been made to create symbols that do not alienate French Canadians by reminding them of the colonial past and British domination. Second, the passage of the Official Languages Act (1969) gave statutory expression to the policy of bilingualism set in motion under Prime Minister Lester Pearson. This Act established the Office of the Commissioner of Official Languages as a watchdog agency to monitor the three main components of language equality set forth in the Act:

- the public's right to be served by the federal government in the official language of their choice;
- the equitable representation of Francophones and Anglophones in the federal public service;
- the ability of public servants of both language groups to work in the language of their choice.

The situation the Official Languages Act was intended to redress was one where Francophone representation in the federal state was less than their share of the national population. Francophone underrepresentation was greatest in managerial, scientific, and technical job categories (see Figure 9.1). Moreover, the language of the public service—the language that officials worked in and, in most parts of the country, the language that citizens could realistically be expected to be served in—was English. In view of these circumstances, Ottawa's claim to represent the interests of Francophones lacked credibility.

Among the main actions taken to increase the bilingual character of the federal bureaucracy have been the designation of an increasing share of positions as bilingual, language training for public servants, and the creation of the National Capital Region as the office blocks of the federal government spread into Hull, Quebec, during the 1970s. In view of the fact that two of the objectives of the Official Languages Act have been to increase the number of Francophones recruited into the public service and to improve Francophones' opportunities for upward mobility within it, the designation of positions according to their linguistic requirements has been the most significant feature of Ottawa's language policy. As of 1996, about 38 per cent of positions in the public service were designated either bilingual or French (31.4 per cent bilingual; 6.4 per cent French essential). The popular perception that one must be bilingual to be hired by the federal public service is quite simply wrong. As Figure 9.2 shows, outside the Ottawa-Hull region and Quebec, comparatively few positions in the federal bureaucracy require mastery of both French and English.

Evidence on recruitment to the federal public service and upward mobility within it demonstrates that the linguistic designation of positions *has* worked to the advantage of Francophones. A clear majority of appointments to bilingual positions are filled by Francophones. This is true both for new appointments to the public service (66 per cent of these went to Francophones in 1995–6) and for reappointments with the federal bureaucracy (72.5 per cent to Francophones). But as the Commissioner of Official Languages has regularly observed, increased representation of Francophones should not be taken as an indication that the French and English are approaching greater equality as *languages of work* in the federal state. Outside of federal departments and agencies located in Quebec, the language of work remains predominantly

FIGURE 9.1
Anglophone and Francophone Representation in the Federal Public Service as a Whole, in the Management Category of the Public Service, and in the Canadian Population, Selected Years

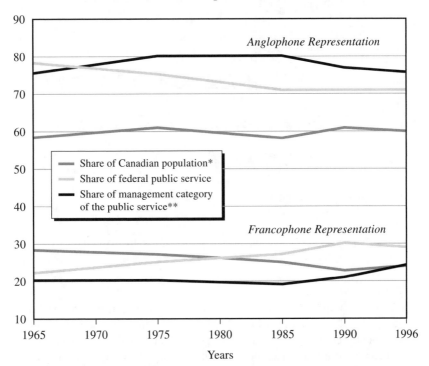

* Data for the representation of French and English language groups in the Canadian population are taken from the censuses for 1961, 1976, 1986, 1991, and 1996. The question refers to mother tongue, and therefore the figures do not add up to 100 per cent.

** The 1965 survey used to determine the language of those in the management category asked respondents to indicate their mother tongue; 5.2 per cent indicated a language other than English or French.

SOURCES: Figures provided in various annual reports of the Commissioner of Official Languages, *Canada Yearbook*, and *Report of the Royal Commission on Bilingualism and Biculturalism*, vol. 3A (Ottawa: Queen's Printer, 1969), 215, table 50.

English. Former Commissioner of Official Languages D'Iberville Fortier summarized the situation this way:

> The fact of the matter is that, in the bilingual regions, French is not used in communications between public servants to anything like the extent or anything like the freedom or regularity that the numerical presence of

FIGURE 9.2
Public Service Positions Designated
Bilingual Imperative, by Region, 1996

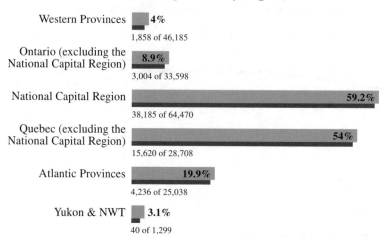

Western Provinces 4%
1,858 of 46,185

Ontario (excluding the National Capital Region) 8.9%
3,004 of 33,598

National Capital Region 59.2%
38,185 of 64,470

Quebec (excluding the National Capital Region) 54%
15,620 of 28,708

Atlantic Provinces 19.9%
4,236 of 25,038

Yukon & NWT 3.1%
40 of 1,299

SOURCE: Commissioner of Official Languages, *Annual Report 1996*, 61.

Francophone public servants would lead one to expect. If one were to judge the official status of French, for instance, from its use in interdepartmental committees or at meetings of deputy heads, one would be hard pressed not to conclude that it has no status to speak of whatsoever.[13]

The domination of English as the *lingua franca* of the bureaucracy persists even in the National Capital Region. This led D'Iberville Fortier to conclude that French had become a valuable attribute from the standpoint of career advancement without becoming a working language on a par with English.[14]

Ottawa's language policy acquired two additional thrusts in the 1970s. The first of these has involved financial assistance to organizations and individuals seeking to defend or expand the rights of official-language minorities and to local Francophone cultural organizations outside of Quebec. This included financial support for court challenges to provincial laws affecting language rights. Among the challenges financed by Ottawa were Supreme Court decisions in 1979 and 1985 that established the official status of French in the province of Manitoba[15] and successful challenges to the restrictions on education and public signs and advertising contained in Quebec's Bill 101.[16] Until 1985, language rights cases were the only ones supported by Ottawa under its Court Challenges Program.[17]

A second thrust of federal policy to promote bilingualism in Canadian society has been through financial assistance for second-language instruction and minority-language schools controlled by the provinces, including French immersion schools throughout Canada, and support for summer immersion programs based mainly in Quebec. The number of elementary and secondary schools offering French immersion programs increased from 237 in 1977–8, with 37,881 students enrolled, to 2,146 schools and 312,057 students in 1996–7. About half of these schools and almost half of all immersion students in Canada are in Ontario.[18]

The popularity of French immersion education continues to grow as non-Francophone parents perceive that bilingualism will give their children an edge in the future competition for good jobs. This perception of greater opportunities for bilinguals, at least in the private sector, remains to be substantiated. Indeed, a 1980s study of bilingual job opportunities by the Commissioner of Official Languages answered the question, 'Do immersion graduates make good use of their French after high school?' with 'Yes, they do—in Ottawa.'[19] Despite the rapid growth of immersion education, one should not assume that Canada is on the fast track to becoming a nation of polyglots in the manner of some of the small Western European democracies. The 1991 census showed that about 22 per cent of Canadians between the ages of 15 and 24 claimed to be able to carry on a conversation in both French and English. The percentage for young Canadians living in Quebec was about three times greater than for their counterparts elsewhere in Canada.[20] Moreover, studies of immersion graduates demonstrate that the experience tends to produce 'receptive' bilinguals—people who neither initiate conversations in French nor consume French-language newspapers, radio, or television after leaving immersion. Bilingualism becomes in some sense a badge of social distinction rather than a part of their lifestyle. This has led some to comment on the incidental effects of immersion on social class distinctions. Eric Waddell writes:

> There is much to suggest that the current fascination for French language education is more an expression of class (and indirectly of ethnic class) interests than of a concern to forge a new national identity. French immersion schools give the impression of constituting an élite system of education functioning within the public system. The state, through federal intervention, is in the process of elaborating a dual system, one for tomorrow's leaders and one for the followers. For this 'new' class, the bilingualism that mastery of the French language confers constitutes something profoundly Canadian in the sense of being sophisticated and more 'European'. Hence it serves increasingly to demarcate this class from other social classes and, strikingly, from our southern neighbours.[21]

To conclude this section let us summarize the main distributional effects of language policy in Canada. They include the following:

1. Official bilingualism at the national level has increased the value of French-language proficiency for entry into and mobility within the federal

bureaucracy. Francophones have been the main beneficiaries of the increased importance attached to language skills. Official bilingualism has not, however, resulted in the equality of French and English as working languages in the federal state. English remains the principal language of communication, a fact that is most marked at the senior levels of the bureaucracy.

2. Quebec's policy of promoting the use of the French language in both the public and private sectors of that province has helped to establish French as a 'necessary and useful language' in Quebec society. The main beneficiaries of provincial language policy have been middle-class Francophones who have gained greater access to the economic structure of Quebec, not to mention almost exclusive control over the provincial state.

3. The failure of language policy to have any appreciable impact on the private sector outside of Quebec—specifically the economy and popular culture—has meant that the rate of francophone assimilation continues to be high in every province except Quebec.[22] Thus, the demographic basis for identifying French Canada with Quebec has become even stronger over time (the proportion of Canadian Francophones residing in Quebec has increased from 78 per cent in 1921 to about 90 per cent today).

4. If Ottawa's policy of official bilingualism was intended to increase the affective loyalties of French-speaking Quebecers to Canada by providing a field of career opportunities to rival the Quebec state, the policy has been only partly successful. Francophones residing outside of Quebec have received more than their share of benefits from the bilingualization of the federal public service. Although they constitute just over 10 per cent of all Francophones in Canada it is estimated that they account for 40 per cent of all French-language employees of the federal bureaucracy.[23] Within Quebec, young highly educated Francophones continue to be among the groups most supportive of separatism.

5. French immersion, touted by former Language Commissioner Max Yalden as possibly 'the most important educational development in the linguistic affairs of our country over the last twenty years or more',[24] appears to have as an incidental effect the reinforcement of class divisions. This is due to a self-selection process whereby the children of middle-class professionals are the main consumers of these programs. The product of immersion may not be a new generation of functional bilinguals so much as a new dimension to élitism in Canada.

Multicultural Policy

1. Introduction

One of the platitudes of Canadian popular sociology and history is that Canadian society is more tolerant towards ethnic and cultural diversity than is the highly individualistic society of the United States. Thomas Berger writes that 'We in Canada do not share the American goal, often reiterated . . . , of integration and assimilation. We believe that diversity is not inconsistent with a common citizenship.'[25] The familiar metaphors of the Canadian 'mosaic' and the American 'melting pot' are intended to convey this difference in the pressures on the members of minority ethnic groups to discard their distinctive cultures.

There is no doubt that official policy in the two countries suggests significant differences in the approach to minority cultures. Khayyam Paltiel has documented the existence of a long tradition in Canada of according official recognition—including special rights and entitlements—on the basis of group membership.[26] At the constitutional level the Canadian Charter of Rights and Freedoms makes explicit reference to Canada's multicultural heritage (s. 27) and guarantees minority language educational rights (s. 23), and another section (s. 35) of the Constitution Act, 1982, includes provisions regarding the rights of Aboriginal peoples. These features stand in contrast to the exclusive concern with the rights of the individual as set forth in the American Bill of Rights. In 1971 the Canadian government adopted a policy of official 'multiculturalism', and from 1973 to 1993 the cabinet position of Minister of State for Multiculturalism existed, until the responsibilities associated with this post were absorbed in the portfolio of the new position of Heritage Minister. Such a policy, if adopted in the United States, would almost certainly be attacked as socially divisive and politically fractious. But despite these differences in policy it is not at all clear that ethnic cultures are more viable in Canada than in the United States.

What is 'culture' for purposes of multicultural policy? The term connotes membership in a group that is marked off from others by its origins. In practice, this meaning of culture is identical to ethnicity, evoking the traditional beliefs and practices of a biological descent group. As Harold R. Isaacs writes, 'It is the identity made up of what a person is born with or acquires at birth',[27] an inheritance whose most important features are language, religion, and the characteristic ways of perceiving and evaluating experience that are the product of the group's history. Culture in the sense of ethnic group is exclusionary, demarcating one tribe and its idols from another.[28] Contrary to the expectations of modernization theory, these ethnic identities persist despite the homogenizing pressures of global communications, modern technology, and urbanization. Indeed, it is popular among students of ethnicity to speak of the resurgence of ethnic cultures and attachments. This resurgence is attributed by many to the inability of individuals to find personal fulfilment in modern societies whose icons—McDonald's arches, the plastic credit card, television, and the Internet, to mention a few—glorify uniformity of experience.

Reaction against the alienating quality of modern life may explain why a growing number of people are receptive to the appeal of tradition, including ethnic origins. It does not, however, explain why individuals would carry their ethnic identity into politics or why the state would become involved in the protection or promotion of ethnic group cultures. To understand the politicization of ethnicity one must identify the ways in which state action affects the distribution of valued symbols and material benefits among ethnic groups. Official status for the language a group speaks provides an obvious illustration. Those who do not speak the group's language—which is also the language of the state—are faced with a choice of either learning it or being effectively excluded from public affairs.

Conferring official status on a group's language or devoting public revenue to teaching its children the language of their forebears provides these groups with obvious material benefits. But as Raymond Breton observes, 'public institutions and their authorities are involved in the distribution of symbols as well as material resources.'[29] He continues:

> They dispense recognition and honour. They allocate possibilities for identification with purposes that have significance beyond an individual's limited experience. They distribute opportunities for meaningful social roles. . . . Accordingly, a well developed symbolic/cultural system can be perceived as inadequate by particular linguistic or ethnocultural groups, in the sense that they feel disadvantaged relative to other groups as far as possibilities of identification, meaningfulness and recognition are concerned.[30]

In other words, public policy and the very structure of the state may reinforce the self-esteem of members of an ethnocultural group by providing them with a reflection of themselves. The ways this may be accomplished range from the appointment of group 'representatives' to highly visible positions within the state system to incorporating the group's traditions into such public events as Canada Day celebrations.

While not denying the psychological significance of the state's symbolic character, the possibility that multicultural policy may degenerate into mere tokenism and ethnic folk dances is great. The increased representation of minority ethnic groups in the celebrations and institutions of public life may promote their sense of being a part of the society. But this is not the same as reducing the barriers to their fuller participation in that society and in its economy. The difference between symbolism and material conditions is dramatically illustrated by the gap between Ottawa's integration of the symbols of Aboriginal culture into public celebrations and even the structure of the state, on the one hand, and, on the other, the continuing exclusion of Native Canadians from the economic benefits of this society. Soapstone carvings given to foreign dignitaries and constitutional conferences on Aboriginal issues have not been accompanied by significant improvement in the living standards of Aboriginal Canadians or the resolution of issues relating to land claims and self-government. A cynic might suggest that the concern with symbolic distribution may even act as a substitute for more substantive policy.

2. Official Multiculturalism: Symbolism and Substance

It is generally agreed that Ottawa's adoption in 1971 of an official policy of multiculturalism was a direct response to the concerns expressed by ethnic organizations to the 'two nations' vision of Canada that had preoccupied the B&B Commission, a vision implied in the policy of official bilingualism. As Raymond Breton puts it, these concerns 'reflected status anxiety—fear of being defined as second-class citizens, marginal to the identity system being redefined'.[31] At the same time as official multiculturalism met the symbolic concerns of ethnic group leaders, it also was a clear refutation of the 'two nations' view of Canada advocated by the supporters of special status or independence for Quebec.[32] Thus, the policy was symbolically important on two fronts. It allocated *recognition* to the claims of ethnic organizations at the same time as it deprived Quebec nationalists of the legitimacy that a policy of biculturalism would have bestowed on their particular vision of Canadian pluralism. Interestingly, two studies within three years of the policy's adoption found that only about one in five 'ethnic' Canadians was even aware that such a policy existed, and that the idea of using public money for the promotion of multiculturalism was rejected by most.[33] In view of this low level of both popular awareness and support for multiculturalism, it would appear that the main beneficiaries of the symbolic recognition of non-French, non-British cultures were the ethnic organizations that received status and funding under the policy.

Symbolism aside, it is hard to escape the conclusion that Ottawa's multiculturalism policy, in substantive terms, has been little more than the 'song and dance affair' its critics have charged. Material benefits can take the form either of money devoted to the promotion of goals held by ethnocultural groups or of special rights or entitlements enjoyed by members of designated groups. On the second count, the Charter of Rights and Freedoms includes an express prohibition against discrimination based on race, national or ethnic origin, colour, or religion (s. 15[1]), thus appearing to rule out the possibility of special rights based on membership in a designated ethnic group. But as s. 15(2) of the Charter indicates, this anti-discrimination provision does not preclude programs of affirmative action for disadvantaged groups. Apart from this constitutional sanction for group rights, the only other section of the constitution that makes reference to the special status of cultural communities—other than the guarantees for French and English language rights—refers to the rights of the Aboriginal peoples of Canada (s. 35). The provision stating that 'This Charter shall be interpreted in a manner consistent with the preservation and enhancement of the multicultural heritage of Canadians' (s. 27) appears too nebulous to have material significance, although it is a clear symbolic affirmation of official multiculturalism.

In 1988 the Canadian Multiculturalism Act was proclaimed. It commits the federal government to the recognition and promotion of the cultural and racial diversity of Canadian society. More specifically, the Act declares that all institutions of the federal government shall:

(a) ensure that Canadians of all origins have an equal opportunity to obtain employment and advancement in those institutions;

(b) promote policies, programs, and practices that enhance the ability of individuals and communities of all origins to contribute to the continuing evolution of Canada;

(c) promote policies, programs and practices that enhance the understanding of and respect for the diversity of the members of Canadian society;

(d) collect statistical data to enable the development of policies, programs and practices that are sensitive and responsive to the multicultural reality of Canada;

(e) make use, as appropriate, of the language skills and cultural understanding of individuals of all origins; and

(f) generally, carry on their activities in a manner that is sensitive and responsive to the multicultural reality of Canada.[34]

While many Canadians are unfamiliar with Ottawa's policy of multiculturalism, there is evidence to show that a clear majority of Canadians support the idea of cultural diversity. Their support is not, however, unqualified. A recent study of federal multicultural policy prepared for Heritage Canada summarized these reservations as follows:

> There appears to be a growing feeling that immigrants should make more effort to assimilate into mainstream society. Few Canadians are concerned about issues such as inter-racial marriage or multiracial neighbourhoods. A significant number of Canadians are concerned about minority demands for rights and power, about possible competition for employment, and about possible strains on social services. A majority of Canadians are concerned about immigration-related violence, turbans in the RCMP, multiple spouses, and women's rights in ethnic groups. It appears that visible differences may be an important factor in determining attitudes toward members of minority ethnic groups—the more 'visible' the minority, the more concern it seems to cause.[35]

With regard to state expenditures, the amounts spent on multicultural programs are paltry. Most of these programs are financed through the budget of Heritage Canada, whose total spending of about $2 billion in 1996 represented only slightly more than 2 per cent of all program spending. Only a small portion of this money was devoted to programs intended to promote multiculturalism, including annual funding for national ethnocultural organizations, the establishment and operation of multicultural associations, centres, and events, language and other instruction for immigrants, language instruction in heritage-language programs administered by some provinces, support for university teaching and research in ethnic studies, assistance to ethnic writers, publishers, and the performing and visual arts, and advertising to promote popular acceptance of ethnic and racial diversity. The fact that final approval of all grants administered under Ottawa's Multiculturalism Program lies with Cabinet, instead of with an independent agency as is the case with most other areas of cultural support, leaves open the possibility that funding decisions may be influenced by partisan considerations. Even in the absence of obvious political interference, it is clear that the existing system of funding ethnocultural organizations and activities contains a built-in bias towards established ethnic organizations that have received funding in the past and towards those groups that are the most articulate and well organized.

A full accounting of government spending on multiculturalism must go beyond the grants channelled to ethnic organizations. Both CBC radio and television programming include productions intended to reflect the ethnocultural diversity of Canadian society. As well, multiculturalism is subsidized through National Film Board productions on themes related to the experience of ethnic groups in Canada, through grants from the Canada Council for the performing arts, and through the collection and research of the National Museum of Civilization. All totalled, these additional sums spent on the promotion of multiculturalism are relatively small. Moreover, the fact that much of this money finances activities and productions that are not in the native language of the ethnic community certainly makes them accessible to a wider public, but arguably this has the effect of presenting these ethnic cultures as museum curiosities rather than as part of the current reality of Canadian cultural life.

Forms of financial support for ethnocultural groups similar to those provided by Ottawa are also common at the provincial level. These range from grants for such purposes as the construction of ethnic community centres and the publication of books on provincial ethnic communities to the provision of some provincial services in the language of immigrant communities. One of the more publicized developments in provincial multicultural policy has been the expansion of heritage language instruction in the schools. Ontario accounts for more than half of all heritage language pupils in the country, and in Metro Toronto heritage language classes are a required part of the elementary school curriculum. In British Columbia, where native speakers of Punjabi and Mandarin outnumber Francophones by a large margin, the province's Education Department decided in 1996 that, along with French, Japanese, Mandarin, and Punjabi would qualify as the second language needed by BC students to graduate from high school. Previously, the second language requirement had to be French.

3. Multiculturalism and Visible Minorities

The fact that multiculturalism is part of the lexicon of Canadian politics reflects the ethnically diverse character of Canadian society. The share of the population with neither British nor French origins has increased steadily since the post-World War II wave of immigration to Canada, from about one-fifth in 1951 to around one-third today. This has resulted from the changing mix of immigration and, more recently, the higher birth rates among 'new' Canadians in comparison to those of British and French origins. One of the most striking aspects of immigration over the past two decades has been the dramatic increase in the share of those with non-European origins. Whereas immigrants from the UK, the US, and Europe accounted for 80 per cent of all immigration between 1962 and 1967, they accounted for 56 per cent during the 1968–76 period and even became a minority of total immigration (42 per cent between 1980 and 1982) during the years when there was a heavy influx of refugees from Vietnam. Countries such as India, the Philippines, China, Vietnam, Lebanon, and Jamaica have been among the main sources of recent immigration to Canada (see Table 9.1). This has led to an increase in the size of this country's 'visible minorities'. In response to incidents of interracial tension in some of Canada's major urban centres—particularly Toronto and Vancouver, where much of the non-European immigrant population has located—and to studies suggesting that racist attitudes are widespread in Canada,[36] the federal government and some provincial governments have made

Table 9.1
Top 10 Countries of Birth for All Immigrants and
Recent Immigrants*, 1991

All Immigrants			*Recent Immigrants*		
Country of Birth	*Number*	*%*	*Country of Birth*	*Number*	*%*
1. United Kingdom	717,745	16.5	1. Hong Kong	96,540	7.8
2. Italy	351,620	8.1	2. Poland	77,455	6.3
3. United States	249,080	5.7	3. People's Republic		
4. Poland	184,695	4.3	of China	75,840	6.1
5. Germany	180,525	4.2	4. India	73,105	5.9
6. India	173,670	4.0	5. United Kingdom	71,365	5.8
7. Portugal	161,180	3.7	6. Vietnam	69,520	5.6
8. People's Republic			7. Philippines	64,290	5.2
of China	157,405	3.6	8. United States	55,415	4.5
9. Hong Kong	152,455	3.5	9. Portugal	35,440	2.9
10. Netherlands	129,615	3.0	10. Lebanon	34,065	2.8
Total	4,342,890		Total	1,238,455	

*Immigrants who came to Canada between 1981 and 1991.

SOURCE: Statistics Canada, *Canada's Changing Immigrant Population*, cat. no. 96–311E, Table 1.1.

the elimination of racial discrimination a major component of multicultural policy.

Unlike the policy of official multiculturalism adopted by Ottawa in 1971, policy on racial discrimination aims to provide both material and symbolic benefits to visible minorities. The emphasis is less on cultural expression than on removing the barriers to the equal participation of racial minorities in the economy and in society. In practice this means that the private sector is a major target of this more recent thrust of multicultural policy. Human rights legislation that prohibits discrimination on grounds of race in such matters as employment and accommodation is one of the instruments for dealing with racial inequality in the private sector. This is, however, an *ex post facto* remedy in that it is only brought into play after an alleged incident of discrimination has taken place. In relying on the possibility of legal penalties against those who are found guilty of racial discrimination, this approach does not address the fundamental problem of racist attitudes that cause such behaviour. The pervasiveness of racism in grosser or subtler forms in societies across the world suggests that such attitudes are not easily changed and that public spending on media campaigns to promote racial harmony probably has a marginal impact at best. As in the case of state subsidies to ethnocultural organizations, spending on television advertisements, posters, and other visual portrayals of a multiracial society is best understood as an investment in symbolic politics, intended to affect the distribution of symbolic rather than material benefits in society.

Following the long-standing American practice of affirmative action for racial minorities, both Ottawa and some provincial governments have adopted a policy of increasing the representation of visible minorities in the public service. At the federal level this policy is administered through the Public Service Commission. During the 1980s, affirmative action was pursued mainly through a system of employment *targets* and *incentives* for departments to meet rather than through *mandatory quotas* on group representation.

Governments in Canada continue to use targets and incentives, but some of them now use mandatory quota systems (generally labelled 'employment equity' policies). For example, an RCMP memo came to light in 1991, indicating that all new hirings should be of women and targeted minorities. The Metro Toronto police force has in place a similar policy. It is well known that some governments have followed such policies, as in Ontario under the NDP government of 1990–5, even though they denied that they had mandatory affirmative action policies that discriminated against White males. Parapublic institutions like colleges and universities and private-sector companies that do business with the federal government have adopted affirmative action policies partly in response to the requirements of the Federal Contractors' Program. This requires organizations receiving federal contracts to develop a census of their workforce, indicating such things as gender and visible minority representation, and to implement affirmative action programs under federal supervision.

But what is a 'minority', and which groups should be targeted for preferential treatment? Although there is no universally agreed-upon definition, the following one captures the main lines of contemporary thinking about minorities:

> We may define a minority as a group of people who, because of their physical or cultural characteristics, are singled out from others in the society in which they live for differential and unequal treatment and who therefore regard themselves as the objects of collective discrimination.[37]

'Physical' and 'cultural' are key words here. These are characteristics over which the bearer has little or no control. But the term 'minority' has acquired broader connotations than this, to also include groups whose distinguishing characteristic is their lifestyle or characteristics associated with stages in the life cycle (for example, being a child, elderly, or pregnant). The working definition of minority status used by human rights commissions and other organizations with a rights mandate has four main characteristics:

- identifiability;
- differential power;
- differential and pejorative treatment;
- group awareness.[38]

Thus, alongside more traditional minorities defined by race, ethnicity, and religion have emerged gays and lesbians, the poor, convicted criminals, drug abusers, and others whose minority status is based on the claim that they are victimized by the law and/or society and therefore deserve protection.

This broadened conception of minorities has had important consequences for multicultural policy. The earlier emphasis on ethnic origins has been overshadowed by more recent preoccupations with race and non-cultural badges of minority status like gender, sexual orientation, and social condition. Official multiculturalism has given way to a new state-sponsored pluralism in which ethnic, racial, and religious characteristics—along with language, the traditional indicators of cultural distinctiveness—are only some of the features defining minorities. The human rights commissions that exist in most of the provinces and territories, as well as federally, have played a key role in generating this broader conception of minorities. This is not surprising. As Thomas Flanagan observes:

> There is no reason to think that human rights agencies are less motivated by self-interest or ambition than the rest of us, and their self-interest is served by amplifying their mandate. . . .

> In short, the commissions are not neutral agencies of enforcement. They are active centres for promoting human rights, which has meant adding ever more criteria to the legislation. They continue to lobby in this direc-

tion and, without exception, they feel themselves to be without adequate resources to enforce anti-discrimination law in its present restricted form.[39]

Human rights commissions have not been alone in pushing for an ever wider conception of minorities. Other state agencies and some political parties, particularly the NDP, have also supported the shift from traditional multiculturalism to a pluralism that recognizes minorities on the basis of claims that they are disadvantaged. Programs administered by the federal Secretary of State, for example, were oriented in the early 1970s mainly towards cultural retention for traditional (i.e., chiefly European) ethnic groups. Since then, there has been a reorientation of activities and funding in the direction of social issues, particularly racism.[40] To a large extent this shift merely reflects the changing character of Canada's 'ethnic' communities. First-generation Canadians are today much more likely to be non-White and non-European than in the past. But this reorientation also reflects the political ascendancy of the broader conception of minorities discussed earlier, and it provides the ideological basis for a more intrusive state role in promoting the opportunities of those groups defined as minorities.

Chapter Ten

Environmental Policy

There is something fundamentally wrong in treating the Earth as if it were a business in liquidation.

—Herman Daly, economist, World Bank[1]

Governments have long been in the business of defending their territory and making war against their neighbours; building roads, canals, aqueducts, airports, and the other apparatus of ancient and modern commerce; taxing citizens and organizations that fall within their jurisdiction; protecting or suppressing the rights and practices of religious, ethnic, racial, and linguistic groups; and even promoting the arts. They are relative newcomers, however, to matters that concern the environment. Indeed, the very idea that the environment should be the subject of government action is of recent origin. The triggering event was the 1962 publication of Rachel Carson's best seller, *Silent Spring*.[2] Carson's passionate and scientifically solid documentation of the environmental ravages and risks to human health created by the use of agricultural chemicals—the 'elixirs of death', as she evocatively called them—led directly to the appointment of an American presidential commission to study their use and effects and eventually to the banning of carcinogenic DDT. The environment had been transformed from a biological concept to a political one.

Since then, public concern and government action regarding environmental matters have ebbed and flowed in response to ecological crises and the prominence of other public issues, such as the state of the economy. But despite the uneven attention paid to environmental issues, the clock cannot be turned back to the era of general apathy and ignorance, an era whose illusions of innocence were smashed forever by *Silent Spring*. The consequences of human activities for the environment are today far too great and public awareness of environmental issues too deeply entrenched (if often poorly informed) for this to happen. Moreover, the last couple of decades have seen the proliferation of a complex network of laws and programs whose goals range from the control of toxic chemicals to the preservation of wilderness areas and that aim at regulating the effects of human activity on the environment. Environmental policy, we will see, is not housed neatly in a single department or agency. Nor is it primarily the responsibility of one level of government in Canada.

What Is the Environment?

For some people, the word 'environment' evokes images of green forests, clear streams, and abundant wildlife, images of an unspoiled natural world beyond the corrupting influence of humankind and industry. Others think of belching smokestacks, dead fish on a littered beach, and cancer-causing chemicals. In both cases the environment is associated with the world of nature and with those influences that pollute and corrupt it. But the environment can be conceived more broadly than this. The environment may be thought of as all those conditions that sustain life and affect the health of human beings. Viewed from this perspective, overcrowded living conditions, excessive noise levels, choked freeways, and the build-up of military weapons would all qualify as environmental problems. By this definition the environment includes the natural world and the world created by human activity, both of which affect the quality and viability of human life. This way of conceptualizing the environment is, however, criticized by some as being anthropocentric—placing human beings and their needs above other forms of life. The radical fringe of the environmental movement, called 'deep ecology', makes no distinction between man and nature, between human and other forms of life. It offers a third way of conceptualizing the environment, viewing it as the entire interrelated chain of life in which no species is morally superior to others.

Policies and ideas are linked. Assumptions about the environment, what it is, whether and why it matters, and how environmental values relate to other values—especially economic ones—will affect the way individuals, organizations, and governments treat the environment. A publication of Environment Canada identifies five competing approaches to environmental management.[3] As Table 10.1 shows, each is based on a rather different set of assumptions about the environment. In most industrialized societies, Canada included, the *resource management* model dominates, although the rhetoric of governments often leans heavily on the *green society* and *sustainable development* models.

Table 10.1
Five Models of Environmental Management

Model 1   Frontier economics
  • little thought to the environment
  • environment as an infinite supply

Model 2   Resource management
  • subjugate the environment to economics
  • polluter pays
  • environmental mitigation and assessment

Model 3   Green society
  • subjugate the economy to the environment
  • environmentally friendly products
  • environmental preservation and planning

Model 4   Sustainable development
  • society, economics, and environment part of a mutually
    supporting system
  • long-term consideration of the environment and economy seen
    as inseparable
  • healthy environment essential for healthy economy

Model 5   Deep ecology
  • little thought to the economy
  • environmental supplies limited

SOURCE: Adapted from Environment Canada, *The State of Canada's Environment—
1991* (Ottawa: Supply and Services, 1991), 1–7. The label of model three has been
changed here from 'selective environmentalism' to 'green society'.

The Environmental Conundrum

In mainstream economics, selfishness is generally counted a virtue. As Adam
Smith explained in *The Wealth of Nations*, it is not the charity of the baker that
ensures our daily bread. The baker expects to enrich himself by selling bread,
but in doing so also contributes to the general well-being of society by offering for sale something that is valued by others. Economists since Smith have
argued that a society in which people are free to buy and sell as they like,
greedily pursuing their individual self-interest, will produce the greatest welfare for all. There is, they maintain, nothing incompatible between individual
selfishness and the good of the community.

What may be true for economics is not necessarily true for the environment.

Garret Hardin illustrates this through the parable of the 'tragedy of the commons'.[4] Hardin explains how the logic of marketplace behaviour left the common pastureland of England increasingly less capable of sustaining grazing. Acting in accordance with his own self-interest, it made perfect sense for each individual farmer to add another head of livestock when he could afford to do so. After all, this farmer would reap all of the benefits from the additional animal, but would bear only a small fraction of whatever costs were generated on the common pastureland. But if all farmers behave in this way, the result will ultimately be collapse of the environment on which they all depend for their livelihood. An overstressed commons, incapable of sustaining the demands placed on it, is undesirable from everyone's standpoint. Yet this appears to be the inevitable outcome of a market system that allows individuals to capture all of the benefits of their actions while spreading the costs associated with individual behaviour across the entire community.

The broader relevance of this parable should be clear. Substitute consumers, corporations, car owners, tourists, high-tech farmers, suburbanites with lush lawns, or some other group whose behaviour imposes stress on the environment and the dynamic remains the same. Consumers who enjoy the convenience of overpackaged products and plastic bags in which to carry them home impose a burden on the environment through the waste this generates; but the social costs generated by this behaviour are not apparent to most until the regional landfill shuts down or the local council proposes the construction of a garbage incinerator near their homes. Likewise, a corporation that pollutes the air, water, or soil has no particular incentive to act differently so long as it does not bear the burden of the costs associated with this polluting behaviour. Why does the market, generally effective when it comes to ensuring the most efficient distribution of economic resources and producing the greatest level of material affluence for society, fail to work as well when it comes to environmental efficiency?

The answer has to do with how prices are determined, which in turn is influenced by what can only be described as ideological-ethical presumptions (with apologies to the economists who are rendered apoplectic by this no longer uncommon charge). In a market economy, prices reflect what buyers are willing to pay for a good or service. They represent what economists call the marginal utility derived from the use of that which is purchased. The fact that poor information on the part of sellers or buyers or a lack of real competition may distort price levels is irrelevant. Prices, within these limits, basically are set according to the marginal utilities that *individual* buyers *currently* in the market expect to enjoy from purchasing goods and services.

'Individual' is one of the key terms here. Prices in a market economy are set impersonally, through the unorchestrated behaviour of buyers and sellers. But as the tragedy of the commons demonstrates, individual decision-makers may have no incentive to consider the collective implications of their individual choices. The social costs that may be associated with a particular good or service generally are not captured in its price because their impact is felt so diffusely, or elsewhere, or at a later point in time. Economists use the term 'externalities' to refer to these costs that are not reflected in the price paid for a good or service. But whatever one calls them, they are costs just the same and the failure to take them into account means that the goods and services in question are underpriced.

'Currently' is the other key term. Prices reflect the utilities of buyers in the market at a particular point in time. These utilities seldom take account of how future generations will be affected by current behaviour. The market does not automatically register the preferences of these later generations. Indeed, it shuts them out and gives them no voice. This would not be true if individual buyers, whether persons or organizations, gave thought to those who will succeed them when considering how much something is worth. If, for example, consumers believe that the emissions from gasoline-powered automobiles are leaving future generations a legacy of accumulated carbon dioxide in the atmosphere, which in turn is contributing to global warming, and if—a very big if!—they believe that the current price of gasoline should include the costs that future generations will bear, then the retail price of gasoline would be much higher than it is currently. Such thinking however, is uncommon. *Après nous, le déluge* better captures the implicit mind-set of most buyers.

Most people, most of the time, think locally and for the short term. Relatively few people regularly reflect on the global impacts of their behaviour, nor do they have a time perspective that extends beyond their own and possibly their children's lifetimes. Utopians and millennialists aside, we may chalk this up as part of the human condition. Unhappily for human beings, the environmental consequences of their actions are not always limited to their neighbourhood, region, or country; nor are they always limited to the generation responsible for them.

Although short-termism and localism are almost certainly rooted in the human condition, there is also a cultural dimension to space and time perspectives. Some people do think globally and for the long term, and some cultures do appear to be more sensitive to the interests of future generations. This brings us back to the claim that prices in a market economy are influenced by ideological-ethical presumptions. It is neither biologically determined nor divinely ordained that prices reflect only the utilities of those currently in the marketplace. If people are aware that certain costs are not captured by conventional pricing practices and if they believe that these are real costs that should be reflected in the price of fossil fuels, plastic packaging, disposable diapers, industrial emissions, etc., then this is a starting point for a very different price system from the one that currently predominates in market economies. Is there evidence that this is happening? Yes and no. For various reasons, individual buyers and sellers are unlikely to adjust their expectations very much to take into account the long-term and collective consequences of the things they produce and buy. But there is evidence that they are sometimes willing to accept taxation and regulating policies that increase prices when governments justify these higher prices on environmental grounds.

Is Environmental Policy Different?

Environmental problems possess many of the characteristics of other sorts of modern public policy issues. They are often highly technical, requiring an understanding of specialized scientific information and complicated interrelationships. They often have an intergenerational dimension, with the benefits and burdens of current behaviour falling unequally on current and future generations. They frequently have an interjurisdictional dimension, as ecosystems and the consequences of human actions do not respect political boundaries.

It cannot even be said that the subject of environmental policy is always unique. Energy policy—including the choice of energy sources, how they are priced, and the technologies used to exploit and conserve them—shares some of the same turf as environmental policy (although environmentalists typically have had to fight hard to get these matters recognized as environmental issues). Is the build-up of nuclear arms a strategic defence issue or an environmental issue (given the obviously devastating consequences that even a limited nuclear war would have on living ecosystems)? The answer is, of course, that it is both. Are urban congestion, inner-city decay, and suburban sprawl environmental issues? Certainly: but they are more likely to be recognized by policy-makers as social, crime, transportation, or housing problems. A widely used reader on environmental issues includes sections on the value of wilderness, the protection of endangered species, population growth, air quality, nuclear power, the use of pesticides in modern agriculture, hazardous waste, municipal trash, ozone depletion, and the possible relationship between industrial chemicals and cancer, among other topics.[5] What links these apparently diverse matters is the fact that they all concern the relationship between human behaviour and the conditions that sustain life and affect its quality. This is a very broad umbrella. The 1987 report of the World Commission on Environment and Development (hereafter referred to as the Brundtland Commission) made clear just how broad when it identified the environmental challenges facing the world's governments.[6] They included the following:

- global population growth;
- food supplies;
- preserving species and ecosystems;
- energy;
- industrial production;
- urbanization;
- the threat of nuclear and other military conflict.

But the very breadth of the 'environmental problem', which is really not a single problem but a diverse set of issues that have in common a relationship to the quality and sustainability of human life, tends to cripple attempts to deal with it. There are two reasons for this. First, the political constituency that can be called on to support environmental policy is fragmented, and is often weak and difficult to mobilize. Citizens who are alarmed at the prospect of a land-fill near their homes may care nothing about the impact of carbon dioxide emissions on global climatic change. A city dweller who cares passionately about the poisoning of the Beluga whale's native habitat may give no thought whatsoever to how his or her groceries are packaged, much less how they have been produced. It is sometimes said that all politics is local. The truth of this adage is brought home by the fact that it is generally much easier to mobilize citizens around an issue like the quality of municipal drinking water than around something like ozone depletion or the relationship between the lifestyles of affluent societies and pressures on the global ecosystem.

A second way in which the sheer scope of the environmental issue under-mines efforts to deal with it involves the shortcomings of existing political institutions. Quite simply, environmental problems tend not to 'fit' the policy-making and representative structures currently in place. The Brundtland Commission referred to this as the problem of *institutional gaps*.[7] In a world characterized by interdependence, not simply of nations but of human activi-ties and the consequences they generate, it is a stubborn fact that the structures for dealing with transnational problems are not up to the job. There are, in fact, two distinct institutional gaps that impede progress on environmental issues.

Gap 1: Local and national governance versus transnational problems. This is the dilemma mentioned above. The chief 'containers' for political decision-making are national and subnational governments. Not surprisingly, these gov-ernments will be more responsive to the concerns and demands of citizens and interest groups within their borders than to those of outsiders. This would be fine were it not for the fact that environmental problems often spill over these political boundaries, requiring co-operation in order to deal with them. Transnational institutions capable of resolving environmental issues in an authoritative way, backed up by sanctions, are rare. Co-operation between jurisdictions is usually not easy to achieve because of the unequal benefits and burdens it may impose on the co-operating parties. For example, much of the damage inflicted on vegetation, lakes, and buildings by the sulphur dioxide emissions that produce acid rain occurs in jurisdictions outside the major sources of this pollution. Measures to limit these emissions will provide clear benefits for these affected jurisdictions, but the costs will be borne by the pol-luting jurisdiction(s). Why should they pay? The answer is 'They won't.' Some combination of external threats and/or incentives and domestic pressure is usually needed to persuade the offending jurisdiction to change its ways.

Gap 2: New problems and old structures. All modern state systems are complex organizations comprised of dozens or even hundreds of administra-tively separate units that perform different functions or serve different regions or clienteles. These administrative structures have emerged over time to deal with particular issues and interests. Taken together, they represent a sort of institutional status quo whose strength is reinforced by the bureaucratic interests tied to existing programs and budgets, and by the societal groups that benefit from this status quo. Environmental policy—a relatively new policy field—does not fit neatly into the existing structures of the modern state. The usual response of governments has been to create a new agency to deal with environmental matters, such as the federal Department of the Environment, provincial ministries of the environment, and the Environmental Protection Agency in the United States. But the mere creation of such an agency does not guarantee that it will have clout. Indeed, it is almost certain to encounter resistance from other departments and agencies representing such traditional policy fields as energy, agriculture, fisheries, industrial development, health, public works, and so on. The bottom line is this: environmental issues do not fit neatly into the existing institutional machinery of government. Any attempt to create a policy space for these issues is likely to be resisted to the extent that this would encroach on the turf of existing administrative agencies and threaten the interests that depend on their policies.

Getting and Staying on the Agenda

When a public opinion poll taken in 1990 showed that about a third of Canadians named the environment as the most pressing issue facing the country, this was widely heralded as a breakthrough for environmental awareness. Within a year, however, the percentage of respondents naming the environment as problem number one had slipped to under 5 per cent. Economic recession weighed too heavily on the minds of most Canadians for them to give more than a passing thought to the environment. Pollsters, who only a year earlier had made statements like 'The Greening of Canada has almost reached the state of a social movement',[8] were suddenly pontificating on the shallowness of public concern with the environment and Canadians' unwillingness to put the environment before jobs and the state of the economy.

The truth is that public concern over the environment has seldom been very great. Brief bursts of attention, triggered by a bunching of ecological disasters, have been separated by long stretches of indifference (see Figure 10.1). Indeed, public awareness of the environment as a public policy issue really only dates from the 1960s. Even then, surveys showed that Canadians seldom mentioned the environment as being a pressing national concern. The fact that the environment was not something on which pollsters regularly questioned Canadians just confirmed the subject's pre-political character.

Before *Silent Spring* thrust the pesticide issue onto the public agenda and a couple of major oil spills in the United States aroused public concern over eco-disasters, the environmental issue was defined mainly in terms of wilderness and wildlife conservation. There were some cases, such as the 'killer smogs' that periodically descended on London, where the public was aware

FIGURE 10.1

Percentage of Canadians Naming the Environment/Pollution as the Most Important Problem Facing the Country, Selected Years*

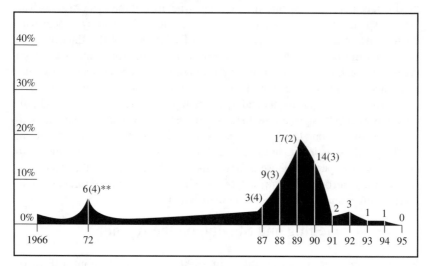

*The years shown are those when the environment/pollution received enough mentions to be listed as one of the country's major problems.

**The numbers in parentheses signify the environment's ranking.

SOURCE: Canadian Institute of Public Opinion, *The Gallup Report* (Toronto).

that human activity produced dangerous environmental conditions and policy-makers were prepared to act. The approximately 4,000 deaths attributed to the smog of December 1952 led, in fact, to the adoption of Britain's Clean Air Act, possibly the world's first comprehensive air pollution law.

More often, however, the environment was not perceived as an issue of urban-industrial society but as a matter of conserving nature. Indeed, the roots of environmentalism in North America go back to the nineteenth century, when opposition to some of the more destructive techniques of exploiting natural resources, such as clear-cutting forests, was first organized. Organizations like the Sierra Club (1892) and the Audubon Society (1895) advocated these reforms and were instrumental in the creation of national parks and the passage of the first forest management laws in the United States. The conservationists had allies in the associations of hunters and fishermen who, motivated by rather different concerns, also advocated wilderness preservation. However, they faced formidable opposition in the form of the forestry, mining, and agricultural interests that generated thousands of jobs and millions of dollars from the activities that the conservationists proposed to restrict.

Moreover, the conservation movement was far from being united in its goals. As Glen Toner observes, 'Conservationism has been and still is characterized by an internal tension between the wise use or management of resources and the preservation of wilderness areas.'[9] Groups like the Canadian Forestry Association viewed conservation as the more responsible harvesting of renewable natural resources (the fact that Canada's forestry industry has had a pitiful reforestation record is another matter), thus linking conservation principles to accepted business values. They certainly did not support the idea of making wilderness areas off limits to commercial exploitation. But others in the conservation movement did. Naturalists who drew their inspiration from the American writers Henry David Thoreau and Ralph Waldo Emerson and Canadians Ernest Thompson Seton and Charles G.D. Roberts, and from the work of such early conservationists as John Muir and Thomas Audubon, were much more sceptical about the ability of industry and nature to coexist. Through organizations like the Canadian National Parks Association they opposed the commercial exploitation of wilderness areas.

Despite their differences, both factions within the conservation movement defined the environmental problem as one that involved man's activities in the wilderness. The preservation of species and their habitats and how best to exploit natural resources were the key issues within this first phase of environmentalism. Conservationism did not challenge the fundamental values and practices of industrial capitalism. Aside from the occasional poetic soul, those in the conservation movement paid virtually no attention to the lifestyles of affluent societies. Many of the issues that have been at the centre of environmentalism over the last few decades—overpopulation, industrial pollution, toxic chemicals, global warming, modern agricultural practices, to mention only a few—were entirely absent from environmentalism's earlier phase.

What happened to change this? How was environmentalism transformed from an issue with very low political visibility into the stuff of headlines and speeches by political leaders? What explains the enormous transformation that took place in the concerns and character of the environmental movement that emerged in the 1960s, compared to those of its predecessor?

John Kingdon's model of the agenda-setting process suggests the answers. According to Kingdon, an issue may reach the political agenda through three processes: problems, policies, and politics.[10] These categories can be applied to the environmentalism that emerged in the 1960s.

1. Problems

A dramatic event or imminent crisis is often the trigger for increased public awareness of some condition. A cluster of such events, and dark forebodings of such crises, occurred during the 1960s. A couple of major oil spills, one in the English Channel in 1967 and the other off the coast at Santa Barbara, California, in 1969, the spectacle of fire on the oily Cuyahoga River at Cleveland, reports that the lower Great Lakes were 'dead', and evidence of mercury accumulation in the bodies of fish and other animals were among the factors that combined to raise the public's level of awareness about environmental problems. At the same time, the dire predictions of the late British economist, Thomas Malthus, about population growth began to be taken seriously. The world's population increased by about one billion, or 40 per cent, between 1950 and 1970, and was expected to reach about 7 billion by the year 2000 (it will fall a bit short of this predicted level). This spawned fears that the problems of malnutrition and famine in developing countries would be exacerbated and that the world's cities, growing even more rapidly than the global population, would be unable to cope with the strains on their physical infrastructure, economies, and social systems. *The Population Bomb*, the title of a book by biologist Paul Ehrlich,[11] and the Club of Rome's apocalyptic predictions of global collapse in *The Limits to Growth*[12] were among the more prominent alarms that a population crisis was imminent.

These were conditions that could not be ignored. Their magnitude and the fact they were bunched together in the mid- to late 1960s made it inevitable that the environment would be defined as a problem requiring government action. Not only was the environment catapulted to the centre of public attention, but the predominant character of the issue was transformed. The previous conservationist focus was swamped by concern over the physical and social costs of industrial society and by Malthusian fear of global scarcity. This was a far more sweeping conception of the environmental issue that encompassed a much broader range of government action than had environmentalism's conservationist phase.

2. Policies

Even before the attention of policy-makers and the public was captured by what some interpreted as the portents of eco-catastrophe, a body of specialized knowledge had accumulated on pollution, population growth, industrial chemicals, and the other items on the new environmental agenda. The most prominent example, of course, was Rachel Carson's carefully documented attack on environmental contamination caused by chemicals used in industry and agriculture.

It is important to realize that the data in *Silent Spring* were not new. Carson drew on scientific studies that were already on the public record—in many cases they had been carried out by agencies and departments of government. It was less a matter of the impact of chemicals on the environment being understudied than of this impact being fully recognized by the public and policy-makers. Carson's best seller was instrumental in making this information better known, but it is unlikely that *Silent Spring, The Population Bomb, The Limits to Growth*, or any of the other specialist-written advocacy books of the era would have pushed environmental issues towards the centre of the political agenda without the cluster of conscious-raising events discussed previously or without the political changes that were unfolding at the same time.

3. Politics

The new environmentalism that emerged in the 1960s focused on issues and proposed reforms that challenged some values and institutions that previously had been taken for granted by all but a few. Belching smokestacks and the murky lagoons and rivers near factories might not be pretty, but they were viewed as signs of economic prosperity. Sprawling freeways, dams for hydro-electric power and irrigation, the herbicides and pesticides that made possible enormous increases in agricultural yields, denuded forests, a 'right' to cheap petroleum, and plastics adapted to all sorts of new uses were among the many phenomena that comprised the socially dominant idea of progress in the post-World War II years of steady economic growth.

The unprecedented affluence produced by postwar expansion—in the developed capitalist world, at least—nurtured a generation of people for whom what have been called 'post-materialist' values had political appeal.[13] Accustomed to material affluence, more educated than their fathers and mothers, and the first generation to be raised in the 'global village' created by electronic mass communications, the values of those who entered adulthood during the 1960s appear to have been less materialist than those of their predecessors. Ronald Inglehart labelled this the 'silent revolution'. 'The values of Western publics', he argues, 'have been shifting from an overwhelming emphasis on material well-being and physical security toward greater emphasis on the quality of life.'[14] Included in this bundle of post-materialist values was a concern for environmental beauty. (In Inglehart's survey of Americans, this item read 'Protect nature from pollution'. In the other nine countries of his study this item referred to 'More beautiful cities and countryside'.)

In fact, Inglehart found only a weak and somewhat ambiguous relationship between attitudes regarding environmental beauty and the other values that made up the post-materialist cluster.[15] None the less, many have argued that the environmental movement of the 1960s and the 'Green Parties' that eventually came onto the political scene in Western Europe in the late 1970s have their roots in the post-materialist value system. For example, Toner maintains that 'the first wave of environmentalism was related to the broader counter-culture critique of materialist-industrial society of the late 1960s and early 1970s.'[16] Jurg Steiner observes that the 'Greens are united in their emphasis on postmaterial values.'[17] If the post-materialist argument is correct, the emergence of the environment as an important political issue during the 1960s was facilitated by a more receptive climate of public opinion than had existed in the past. Politics, in this case the value shifts occurring in so-called postindustrial societies, helped push this issue onto the agenda.

Public concern over the state of the environment waned during the mid-1970s. This probably was due to the growing sense of economic insecurity that spread throughout most of the industrialized democracies. Indeed, it became common to speak of the 'crisis' of capitalism, the decline of the US-dominated postwar economic order, and the ungovernability of modern democracies. Particular developments like the OPEC oil embargo of 1973, rampant inflation and mounting unemployment during the late 1970s, the recession of the early 1980s, and the loss of manufacturing jobs to Japan and the low-wage NICS (newly industrializing countries) conspired to push environmental issues to the margins of public attention and low on the scale of government priorities.

Eclipsed by the economic pessimism of these years, environmental issues assumed a low profile from the mid-1970s to the middle of the 1980s, despite the fact that ecological disasters and near-disasters continued to happen throughout this period. Miscarriages and deformities caused by the toxic waste dump at Love Canal in Niagara Falls, New York; the accident at the Three Mile Island nuclear generation plant in Pennsylvania; accumulating scientific evidence on atmospheric damage caused by chloro-fluorocarbons (CFCs); a number of major oil spills throughout the world; the derailment of tanker cars carrying deadly chlorine and the evacuation of 225,000 people from Mississauga, Ontario; lakes and forests ravaged by acid rain: the list of internationally publicized eco-crises was a long one. Incidents and developments like these certainly captured the public's attention, but they did not generate and sustain the level of concern that existed during the previous decade. One should not overgeneralize, however. Green politics actually gained momentum in some societies, like West Germany, where a major recycling effort, the 'Blue Angel' program, was launched in 1979 and the Green Party elected members to parliament for the first time in 1983.

Despite the lower political profile of environmental issues, the environment's place on the policy agendas of industrialized democracies was secure. There were two reasons for this.

First, environmentalism no longer meant simply nature conservation. Overpopulation, pollution, industrial and agricultural chemicals, nuclear power, and many of the other issues that comprised the agenda of environmentalism's first wave were matters that related to industrial society and the sustainability of human activities in the face of what the Club of Rome called 'the limits to growth'. Conservation was still part of the agenda, but environmentalism had been reconceptualized as something far broader and of greater immediate relevance to the lives and lifestyles of those in urbanized societies.

Second, the evidence of environmental deterioration had reached a point where it could no longer be ignored. Quite simply, the magnitude of some of the problems on the environmental agenda—pollution, the accumulation of toxic wastes, deforestation, soil erosion, population pressures, and so on—had never been greater. Moreover, all indications were that they would quickly become worse. The Club of Rome's pessimistic best seller, *The Limits to Growth*, helped popularize a fact that was well known to specialists, namely, that growth is often an *exponential process*. This means that a quantity (accumulated garbage, toxic chemicals, human population, or whatever) increases by a constant percentage over a given time period. The significance of this may be seen in Figure 10.2, which shows the increase in the earth's population over the last few centuries and projects this increase into the future. A constant level of growth will, in the early stages, produce small increases in the total size of a given quantity. A point will eventually be reached, however, when the increase in the absolute size of the quantity becomes much sharper. The curve that plots the increased size of the quantity appears to 'take off', rising steeply. The 'take-off' stage had clearly been reached by the 1960s in the case of many factors believed to threaten the environment and, ultimately, the viability of human life.

It was possible to ignore or at least to evade the implications of exponential growth for several years. Its meaning was brought home to laypersons, however, when bursting landfills started to close and the disposal of garbage became a crisis for many cities, when several unusually warm years during the 1980s served to popularize the 'greenhouse effect' (i.e., global warming as a result of accumulating carbon dioxide emissions), and when rapidly accumu-

FIGURE 10.2
World Population Growth

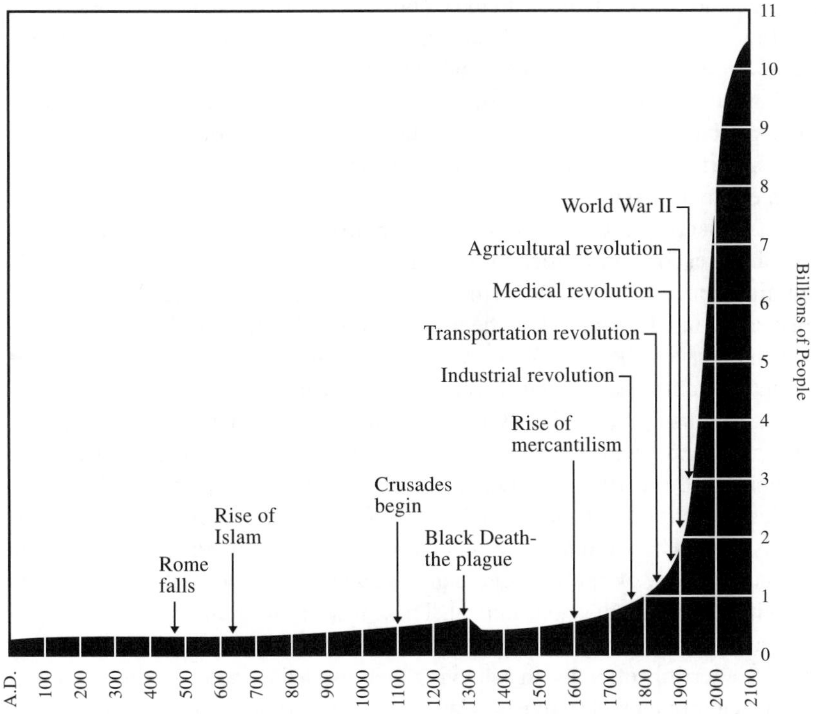

SOURCE: Global Tomorrow Coalition, *The Global Ecology Handbook* (Boston: Beacon Press, 1990), 25.

lating CFCs appeared to be eating holes in the atmosphere's ozone layer, thereby letting in more of the sun's ultraviolet rays that can cause skin cancer and eye cataracts. The gloomy forecasts of the Club of Rome, marginalized by other concerns and dismissed by many as alarmist, once again became fashionable in the 1980s. But this time the predictions could not be ignored because their effects were already being experienced.

Environmental issues were kept on the agenda by the public institutions and private organizations spawned during the first wave of environmentalism. In the United States, the National Environmental Protection Act (NEPA) became law in early 1970 and the Environmental Protection Agency (EPA) was created a few months later. The NEPA required all federal agencies to prepare a 'detailed environmental statement to accompany proposals for legislation and other major federal actions significantly affecting the quality of the human environment'.[18] This 'action-forcing' mechanism acquired enormous significance in the hands of environmental groups, providing them with a legally enforceable lever to challenge all sorts of development projects. Other legislative measures spawned by the first wave of environmental concern in the US included amendments to the Clean Air Act (1970), with timetables for compliance and precise specification of what pollutants had to be reduced by what percentage; the Federal Environment Pesticide Control Act of 1972; and the Federal Water Pollution Control Act Amendments of 1972. All of these laws were administered by the newly created EPA, making it a sort of 'super-agency' whose writ and authority cut across more conventional policy fields. It should be noted that similar institutions were established in many American states, in some cases, particularly California, imposing far greater restrictions on polluters than did federal regulations.

In Canada, the Department of the Environment was created in 1970. It acquired responsibility for those resource management programs previously administered by other departments like Energy, Mines and Resources, Fisheries, and Transport. But the goals set down in the department's enabling legislation went beyond these traditional conservation functions to include pollution control, assessing the environmental impacts of development projects, facilitating federal-provincial co-operation in environmental projects, and public education. A number of environmental laws were passed at the beginning of the 1970s, including the Canada Water Act and Arctic Waters Pollution Act of 1970 and the federal Clean Air Act of 1971.

As in the United States, the first wave of environmentalism bequeathed to Canada a legacy of new agencies and laws whose goals were the regulation of activities affecting the environment. These institutions remained in place after the public concern responsible for their creation had faded. Even when they were not terribly effective in achieving their ostensible goals—which, according to environmental activists, was most of the time—they helped to keep environmental issues on the policy agenda by virtue of their existence and ongoing activities. Environmentalism had become institutionalized in the politics of Canada and other advanced capitalist societies as a result of government responses to the movement's first wave.

Kept alive by the policy community that had developed between the late sixties and early seventies, environmental issues lost much of their *cachet* during the decade that followed. Complacency replaced the alarmed concern that crested with the first Earth Day, celebrated on 22 April 1970. In the United States, the tables turned to such an extent that environmentalism actually came under attack with the election in 1980 of Ronald Reagan. The Reagan administration viewed environmental regulation as just another instance of excessive government interference in the affairs of business.

While Canadian governments continued to express their support for the goals of environmentalism, their actions spoke louder than their words. The position of Minister of the Environment continued to be a very junior Cabinet post, a stepping-stone up or down in one's career, but hardly a power base. Until the appointment of Lucien Bouchard to the Environment portfolio in 1989, no Minister of the Environment had ever been a member of the influential Priorities and Planning Committee of Cabinet. As Ottawa's finances worsened, Environment Canada became one of the chief targets for cuts to what was already a comparatively small budget. The first Progressive Conservative budget of November 1984 announced a $46 million spending reduction for Environment Canada, or a rollback of about 6 per cent. The government's Task Force on Program Review recommended cuts of about $40 million over the years 1985–9.[19] Although cuts were recommended and implemented in other policy fields as well, it was clear that environmental issues did not have the public prominence, nor the environmental bureaucracy the political clout, to protect these programs from the Treasury Board's scalpel.

No single development turned things around for environmentalists. Instead, a cluster of eco-events during the latter half of the 1980s refocused world attention on the vulnerability of the environment and mankind to human activities, just as oil spills, toxic chemicals, and fears of overpopulation had a decade and a half earlier. These events included the chemical leak at a Union Carbide plant in Bhopal, India, that killed over 10,000 and maimed hundreds of thousands more (1984); the discovery of a hole in the ozone layer over Antarctica (1985); the partial meltdown of the nuclear reactor at Chernobyl (1986); a mounting crisis of 'homeless' garbage; unusually warm temperatures, droughts, and other climatic changes that many scientists attributed to the 'greenhouse effect'; the rapid deforestation of the Amazon (and, for that matter, other parts of the world's tropical and temperate forests); and the massive oil spill of the *Exxon Valdez* off the coast of Alaska. By the time the twentieth anniversary of Earth Day arrived, the environment was once again at the centre of public attention.

By the end of the 1980s, environmentalism had acquired what seemed to be an unstoppable momentum. The United Nations World Commission on Environment and Development issued its report, *Our Common Future*, in

1987, and suddenly the term 'sustainable development' was heard everywhere. The Montreal Protocol, an international agreement on limiting and eventually phasing out the production of ozone-destroying CFCs, was signed in 1988. In the wake of some of the most blistering summers on record, the Toronto Conference on the Changing Atmosphere was held in 1989, although it did not produce an international agreement on how to manage global warming. International pressure mounted on Brazil and some other tropical states to limit deforestation. 'Green Parties' and environmental interest groups enjoyed a resurgence, and the 'greening' of business—businesses tailoring their products, production processes, and marketing to the environmentally conscious consumer—became widespread. The world's nations set their sights on the 1992 'Earth Summit', the United Nations Conference on Environment and Development, held in Brazil.

In Canada, the signs of environmentalism's ascendance were everywhere. Ontario introduced 'blue box' recycling in 1985. The media were bristling with reports of conflicts between industry and environmentalists over old-growth forests like those of Temagami (Ontario) and South Moresby (BC), pollution by pulp and paper companies, global warming, toxic chemicals, mountains of garbage, and other eco-stories. 'Can we save this planet?' was the headline of a *Globe and Mail* special report that ran to several pages.[20] Southam papers ran a series of articles on the environment in the autumn of 1990, including the results of a specially commissioned Environics poll on the environment. George Hoberg calculates that the number of stories on the environment in Canadian newspapers ranged from 600 to 800 per year between 1983 and 1988, but exploded to about 1,300 in 1989.[21] Television documentaries on environmental issues were chock-a-block during 1989–90, when media coverage of these matters peaked.

Governments responded to the undeniable evidence of public concern with policies. Consultations among industry, environmental groups, and government began in 1986, marking an important shift in policy-making style in this policy sector. Ottawa's 1989 decision to phase out leaded gasoline was a (belated) response to undeniable evidence of lead's toxic effects. Amidst much ballyhoo Ottawa introduced its Green Plan in 1990, earmarking $3 billion over five years to the policies it comprised. Environmental assessments and delays of major development projects became standard, and Ottawa introduced a new environmental assessment law in 1990. Similar developments were unfolding in many of the provinces.

But then the environmental bandwagon stalled, its momentum slowed by the economic recession that deepened in 1990–1. The polls showing enormous public concern over environmental problems looked like a statistical blip by 1991, as the percentage of Canadians naming the environment as the most important issue facing Canada fell back to the very modest levels of the late 1970s and early 1980s. The explanation appeared to be simple enough: anxiety over the state of the economy had eclipsed the public's fears about the deteriorating environment, the implication being that economic recovery would be accompanied by a recovery of public attention to environmental issues. Perhaps. But the vertiginous rise of public concern over the environment and the even more precipitous fall in the public prominence of this issue certainly said more about the media's influence on the public agenda and the fickleness of public opinion than about the deeply rooted values of Canadians. If environmental issues could be pushed to the margin of public attention so quickly by economic recession, the confident talk about a revolution in public attitudes was certainly premature.

Prediction is a perilous enterprise, perhaps best left to seers, horoscope writers, and fools. None the less, it is probably reasonable to expect that concern over environmental issues, and support for the regulation and costs necessary to deal with them, will fluctuate widely over the next several years. But even when the level of public concern appears to be low, as has been the case since the recession of 1991–2, environmental concerns will retain a secure foothold on the public agenda of Canada and other industrialized democracies. The sheer unprecedented scale of the risks and ecological damage ensures this. Moreover, public awareness of these issues—not the same as understanding or concern—is not something that an international crisis or an economic recession can obliterate. There exists, therefore, a constituency of support for environmental reforms that is wider and deeper than ever before, a constituency that can be mobilized and can push governments to act, given the right configuration of conditions.

Environmental Policies in Canada

When the federal Task Force on Program Review undertook a one-time inventory of government programs in 1985, it identified 34 that fell under the authority of the Minister of the Environment. The range of these programs was broad. They included the heritage and conservation activities of Parks Canada; climatic, meteorological, and air quality monitoring and research; environmental assessment; activities relating to toxic chemicals, commercial and industrial chemicals, and waste management; flood control and water quality programs; wildlife conservation and public education.[22] Together, these activities accounted for $766.5 million in spending, or less than 1 per cent of the federal budget. By 1992, the Ministry of the Environment's budget was up to $1,135.5 million, which was still less than 1 per cent of Ottawa's total spending. This, it must be said, was *after* the federal government's much trumpeted Green Plan, which promised to add $3 billion over five years to the environment budget. Where did this money go?

First, spending on the Green Plan initiatives was slower than projected. Indeed, only one year after the plan's introduction the period over which the $3 billion would be spent was extended from five years to six. Then, the 1992 federal budget cut Green Plan spending by $150 million for the years 1992–4, but with the promise that this money would be reallocated later. This did not happen. The Liberal government's 1995 budget targeted the Ministry of the Environment for major cuts. It was to lose about one-third of its budget between 1995 and 1998. Many other programs with an environmental component, but administered by some other department or agency, were also scheduled to take significant hits. By the 1996–7 fiscal year the budget of Environment Canada had fallen to $546 million.

It must be kept in mind, however, that the budget of Environment Canada provides only a partial picture of environmental spending by Ottawa. Many environmental programs, and much of the money the Progressive Conservative government designated under the Green Plan, fall under the authority of other departments. For example, the Department of Fisheries and Oceans administer the Total Allowable Catch program, the Canadian Climate Program, the Canadian Global Change Program, and the Fisheries Resource Conservation Council. The Canadian International Development Agency requires environmental impact assessments for projects that it finances. Forestry Canada generates numerous programs that are targeted at environmental management, such as reforestation measures through Tree Plan Canada.

The federal government has maintained that this dispersion of responsibility for environmental policy is a strength. The environment, the 1991 Green Plan argued, 'must be a forethought, not an afterthought, in decision-making throughout the government,'[23] a position that appears to be consistent with the philosophy and recommendations of the Brundtland Commission. On the other hand, some argue that decentralized authority for the environment, parcelled out among numerous departments and agencies—to say nothing of the intergovernmental division of authority regarding environmental matters—cripples attempts to deal with environmental issues. In the words of Harold Harvey, a biologist and acid rain activist who worked for the Department of Fisheries in the 1960s, 'there were three layers of bureaucrats between me and the deputy minister [in the 1960s]. Since that time, they've added another eleven.'[24] David Israelson, environmental writer for the *Toronto Star*, agrees that the bureaucracy of environmental policy-making is a problem. He argues that ministers and senior officials are often more concerned with protecting their turf and taking credit for programs than they are with the problems that these programs are ostensibly intended to address.[25] If the responsibility for environmental policy continues to be dispersed among several departments and agencies and the Green Plan initiatives and budget are doled out among them, this almost certainly has more to do with jealous bureaucracies and Cabinet ministers than it does with a rational strategy for managing environmental issues.

In some circumstances process may be policy. The dispersion of authority for environmental matters across agencies and departments of the federal government may reasonably be interpreted as a major aspect of federal environmental policy. But whereas the government's official explanation is that this decentralized process is intended to ensure that all parts of the administrative machine are sensitive to environmental concerns, there is another possible— perhaps more plausible—interpretation of the policy significance of this process. When the environment is the responsibility of many agencies and departments whose programs and clienteles *do not* have environmental protection as their chief concern, this may be the same as admitting that the environment is a second-rate policy issue. How likely is it that environmental concerns will trump the other interests and objectives of a well-established department like Agriculture, Energy, Mines and Resources, or Transport Canada? To this one might respond that the idea is not to 'trump' other legitimate policy goals but simply to ensure that environmental concerns are adequately taken into account. Yet, in the absence of either incentives that provide bureaucrats and their political masters with clear pay-offs for doing so or coercive measures requiring them to do so, it seems more reasonable to expect that the environmental implications of policies and programs will usually take a distant back seat to other considerations.

On the other hand, it cannot be assumed that a more centralized system of environmental policy-making automatically shifts the balance of interests in favour of environmental concerns. In the United States, the setting and enforcement of environmental regulations is chiefly in the hands of the EPA. During its first decade of operation it seemed that the EPA was indeed a sort of environmental super-agency whose authority cut across the interests and jurisdictions of other parts of the bureaucracy. This changed, however, with the 1980 election of Ronald Reagan to the White House. It quickly became apparent that the powers of the EPA could be reined in by a determined executive. Budget cuts, the choice of agency director, and changes to the EPA's enforcement policy combined to reduce its stature as environmental watchdog. It is not clear, therefore, that centralizing environmental authority in a single agency necessarily elevates the status of environmental concerns over what it is under a more decentralized system of environmental policy-making.

A fair picture of environmental policies in Canada must cover all three levels of government. Indeed, authority over some of the most important environmental matters, including waste management, conservation and recycling, electrical power, forest management, and industrial pollution, lies chiefly in the hands of provincial and local governments. Although a full account of what governments in Canada do in the name of environmental policy is beyond the scope of this chapter, we will examine some of the major issues of recent years. These are environmental assessment, pollution, and transboundary environmental problems.

1. Environmental Assessment

Environmental assessment involves the attempt to identify the likely consequences that a development will have on the environment. The 'environment' in question usually is understood to be the natural environment, but sometimes is defined to include social and cultural effects as well. Environmental assessments are carried out by all levels of government. At the local level, zoning by-laws and other land-use planning regulations constitute a form of environmental assessment. Exemptions from these regulations require special approval by a committee of adjustment, a process that typically involves public hearings and consideration of how an exemption would affect the land-use goals that underlie existing regulations. Any major urban project—a sports complex, a convention centre, waterfront development, a new shopping mall, a freeway—is certain to be examined for its effects on such things as local traffic, storm and sanitary sewers, and the character of the surrounding area.

In some provinces, impact studies are required by law for projects and activities expected to have environmental effects that are undertaken by departments or agencies of the province or that will take place on land that falls under provincial control. Examples of such projects would include a dam, pipeline, electricity transmission corridor, landfill, garbage incinerator, new mining or logging on Crown lands. It should be emphasized that provincial laws are very uneven. In some provinces environmental assessment is not required by law, occurring only when political pressures force government's hand. Ontario's environmental assessment law requires that the social and cultural effects of projects be taken into account, along with the expected impacts on the natural environment. Even in those provinces where environmental impact studies and public hearings are required, environmentalists often charge that their concerns are typically brushed aside by economic and political considerations. For instance, BC's Ministry of Forests Act and Forest Act require that a number of uses and values be considered in managing that province's forests. Critics maintain that the impact assessments and public hearings carried out in compliance with this legislation do more to legitimize timber industry interests than to protect rival claims on the BC wilderness.[26]

Federally, a formal environmental assessment process has been in place since 1973. Following the American lead, Ottawa introduced the Environmental Assessment and Review Process (EARP) as a Cabinet directive to departments and agencies. But unlike the NEPA passed in the United States, EARP did not impose non-discretionary duties on the federal government. The fact that EARP was not embodied in law meant that its legal status was questionable. In 1984 the original EARP Cabinet directive was replaced by a Guidelines Order issued under the authority of the Government Organization Act. While spelling out quite clearly the scope of its application and the process of environmental assessment, it remained unclear whether the new EARP guidelines were legally binding on the federal government. Critics believed they were not. The issue was resolved, however, by a series of court decisions between 1989 and 1991. Three Federal Court rulings determined that the 1984 EARP Guidelines Order had the status of law and must be complied with in matters coming under Ottawa's jurisdiction.[27] Indeed, a 1991 decision of the Federal Court ruled that the government could not, by Order in Council, exempt a project from environmental assessment required by EARP.[28] Any doubt was removed when a 1992 Supreme Court decision ruled that EARP was legally binding. Under the Canadian Environmental Assessment Act, passed by the Liberal government in 1994, the Canadian Environmental Assessment Agency is assigned responsibility for the assessment function.

The scope and process of federal environmental impact assessment are similar to those at the provincial level. Federal guidelines require that projects be screened for their environmental implications in the following cases:

- the project is to be undertaken by a federal department or agency, for example, renovations to a federal harbour or building a new runway at a federally owned airport;
- the project may affect the environment in an area that falls under federal responsibility, such as a dam that will flood federal lands or affect waters falling under Ottawa's jurisdiction;
- the project is one in which the federal government has a financial commitment;
- the project is located on lands or offshore controlled by the federal government.

This initial screening is done by the department or agency that initiates the review process. In 9 out of 10 cases the process stops here and the project is approved, sometimes with modifications to mitigate damaging effects on the environment. In only 10 per cent of cases is a proposal sent on for further study, and only rarely will a proposal be referred to the Minister of the Environment for review by an independent environmental assessment panel, including public hearings.

According to most environmentalists, environmental assessment is not very effective. There have certainly been some spectacular failures. Foremost among these was the construction of the Rafferty and Alameda dams on the Souris River in Saskatchewan. Ottawa's approval of the project without a federally conducted assessment was successfully challenged in court by the Canadian Wildlife Federation. The federal government responded by carrying out an assessment and again approving the dams' construction. The Canadian Wildlife Federation challenged this reapproval on the grounds that the assessment process set down in EARP was not properly followed. The Federal Court agreed once more, ordering the Minister of the Environment to establish an independent review panel and hold public hearings. Ottawa complied, but in the meantime construction of the Rafferty dam continued. At this point a major federal-provincial conflict erupted. Ottawa attempted to halt construction pending the results of its review process, while the Saskatchewan government, the province's power corporation, landowners who stood to benefit from the dams, and majority public opinion in Saskatchewan saw this as yet another case of Ottawa meddling in the affairs of the province. While all of this was happening, the project was approaching completion. Ultimately, the dams were completed with very little change from the plan proposed in 1986 when the project began. Faced with powerful economic interests and a government committed to a development project, it did not appear that environmental assessment stood much of a chance.

One should not conclude, however, that nothing stands in the way of development projects having the potential to harm the environment. Environmental impact assessments may not derail such projects, but they can certainly add to their costs and lead to long construction delays. This is not true only in Canada. The head of Hamersley Iron, Australia's largest iron ore producer, recalls that in the 1960s his company was able to put in a mine, a railway, and a port and build two towns around them in western Australia, all within about 18 months. Today, he observes, it would take that long just to get approval for such a project, and then only if the company was extremely lucky![29] Canadian corporate executives tell similar stories.

2. Pollution

The first wave of environmentalism focused mainly on pollution. Oil spills, toxic chemicals in the air, water, and land, hazardous wastes and what to do about them: these were among the lightning rods of the movement. Governments responded by passing a spate of laws whose ostensible goal was the control of these polluting activities. In Canada, these laws included the Clean Air Act, the Canada Water Act, the Canada Shipping Act, the Arctic Waters Pollution Prevention Act, the Environmental Contaminants Act, and amendments to the Fisheries Act, among others. The International Boundary Treaties Act between Canada and the United States, directed at pollution in the Great Lakes basin, was another important initiative. Provincial governments were also busy passing new pollution laws, and indeed most air and land pollution, and a good deal of water-polluting activities, fell under provincial jurisdiction.

Where Ottawa has sole jurisdiction, as in the case of federally controlled lands, the Great Lakes, or offshore waters, the federal government both establishes pollution standards and is responsible for their enforcement. Divided jurisdiction is more typical, however. Under the Clean Air Act, for example, the federal government would establish national emission standards that were not legally binding on polluters, but which were adopted by most provincial governments in establishing and enforcing air pollution regulations. Provinces rely on a permit system in regulating air and water pollution, requiring companies whose operations will release contaminants into the environment to apply for a pollution permit before starting construction and to conform to provincial guidelines once in operation.

The flexibility of these guidelines has always been notorious. Sudbury's Inco smelting operations, the single largest source of acid rain pollution in North America, has been granted lenient extensions of the provincially set targets for reducing its sulphur dioxide emissions since these targets were first set in the 1970s. Throughout the 1980s, the *daily* amount of pollution that Inco's permit allowed was about double the amount that was released into the atmosphere by the peak of the Mount St Helens volcano eruption in the state of Washington.[30] When pollution fines have been levied, they have seldom been heavy enough to act as a deterrent to polluters. For example, Dow Chemical received a fine of $16,000 in 1985 after pleading guilty to the accidental release into the St Clair River of a 'blob' of toxic dry-cleaning fluid that also contained the deadly chemical dioxin. Moreover, the acceptable defence of 'due diligence'—that a company took reasonable care to avoid causing pollution—makes conviction difficult.

It must also be said that governments are themselves among the worst offenders when it comes to pollution. Sewage from municipalities has long been a major source of water pollution, contributing to the eutrophication of lakes. Many municipalities, particularly in Quebec and the Atlantic provinces, pour untreated waste into rivers and lakes. In other cases, treatment facilities are often old and inadequate to cope with the volume of sewage they are required to handle. Provincially owned electricity generation plants are important sources of air pollution, many of them relying on carbon dioxide-producing fossil fuels. Nuclear power, which accounts for almost half of all electrical power generated in Ontario, is relatively non-polluting while in operation. But before reaching the operating stage, a nuclear facility produces an enormous amount of carbon dioxide pollution because of all the fossil fuels used up in its construction. And then, of course, there is the problem of disposing of the radioactive waste generated by a nuclear power station. Even hydroelectric power generation is not without its pollution downside. The flooding of thousands of square kilometres of land in northern Quebec has produced increased levels of lead in the fish that live in the rivers and streams of the region and has generated greenhouse gases from the decomposition of the forests and other vegetation flooded for hydroelectric dams. One should not imagine, therefore, that private industry is the only culprit when it comes to pollution.

Two years before unveiling its Green Plan, the Progressive Conservative government introduced a new law that replaced several existing laws, including the Clean Air Act and the Environmental Contaminants Act. The Canadian Environmental Protection Act (1988) was heralded by government spokespersons as a 'cradle-to-grave' approach to managing pollutants and an environmental 'bill of rights'. On the first count, it is not clear that passage of CEPA has had much of an impact on the regulation of industrial pollutants. Depending on whose estimates one believes, there are between about 35,000 and 100,000 chemicals in commercial use in Canada, but only a minuscule fraction of these are on the Priority Substance List of closely regulated substances. During the first few years of its operation, formal petitions to add chemicals to the Priority Substance List were rare and very few investigations had been launched into violations of CEPA regulations.[31]

On the second count, the claim that CEPA creates an environmental 'bill of rights', it is true that the Act goes beyond previous federal legislation in providing formal opportunities for citizens or groups to request that substances be added to the Priority Substance List or that alleged violations of CEPA regulations be investigated. Moreover, the Act provides a basis for legal action by anyone suffering loss or damage as a result of such violations. This approach resembles the legalistic policy style that has been characteristic of environmental policy in the United States. So far, however, individuals and groups have made relatively little use of the rights that CEPA extends to them and the corresponding obligations placed on environmental officials. It should be added that CEPA does not interfere with government's discretion in deciding what substances should be placed on the Priority Substance List.

3. Transboundary Environmental Problems

One of the distinctive features of the second wave of environmentalism that gained momentum in the 1980s was its concern with global issues. These included acid rain, ozone depletion, global warming, and the growing world trade in garbage and hazardous waste. Problems whose causes and consequences spill across national boundaries require solutions based on international co-operation. But co-operation is usually difficult to achieve for reasons explained earlier by the parable of the commons. When an individual country receives all the benefits from an activity but bears only a portion of the costs it generates, the incentive to behave differently will probably be weak. The greater the gap between the benefits and the costs, the less likely it is that a country will be prepared to change its behaviour. The jobs and economic benefits associated with, say, clear-cutting rain forests in Malaysia or Brazil, or relatively cheap energy prices in Canada and the United States that encourage consumption, are readily appreciated by policy-makers and those who elect them. On the other hand, the effects of the greenhouse gases produced by both of these activities appear much less tangible to most people and are shared with one's neighbours rather than being limited to their producer's backyard.

Unless a country experiences more of the costs than the benefits associated with some environmentally damaging activity, what incentives exist to make its policy-makers control that activity? If altruism was the only answer, the world would certainly be in serious trouble. Self-interest is usually a more reliable basis for action. Unfortunately, experience has shown that transboundary environmental problems must usually have achieved crisis dimensions before those countries that are net beneficiaries from some activity are willing to take serious measures to control it.

Acid rain provides a classic illustration of this. The phenomenon of acid rain has been known for over a century.[32] Its potentially adverse effects on human health were first identified several decades ago.[33] By the 1970s the environmental costs of acid rain, if not its consequences on human health (still a more controversial issue), were becoming undeniable. Despite a sharp jump in the Canadian public's awareness of acid rain as a problem, virtually nothing was done to limit the increase of sulphur dioxide, produced through the burning of fossil fuels, and nitrogen oxides, generated from vehicles, electricity generation, and other combustion processes, let alone decrease existing levels of these emissions. Sulphur dioxide emissions did decline marginally during the 1980s, but most of this reduction was attributable to higher energy costs that encouraged more fuel-efficient and therefore less-polluting vehicles. Emissions actually increased slightly during the last half of the decade,[34] at a time when the Canadian government was taking credit for being a world leader in the fight to control acid rain.

Even slower to act, however, was the United States. Indeed, before passage of the Clean Air Act of 1990, the American government's policy was essentially to deny that the scientific data established a conclusive link between activities like mineral smelting and coal-fired electricity generation, on the one hand, and dying forests and lakes, on the other. This reluctance to act had important consequences for Canada, given that an estimated 50 per cent of sulphur dioxide deposition in Canada comes from American sources.[35] Without American action to restrict the sources of acid rain, Canadian efforts to deal with the problem can only achieve limited success. Likewise, international efforts to control the problem require the co-operation of many governments. This co-operation is made difficult by the fact that some of the worst offenders—countries such as those of Eastern Europe, where coal accounts for a large proportion of electricity generation—are less able to afford the costs of conversion and abatement than some other countries, and because some of the main victims of acid rain—such as the Scandinavian countries, whose forest industries are important sources of national income—generate comparatively little in the way of acid deposition.

Just as it has become commonplace to remark that national economies are more interdependent today than at any time in the past, the same is true of 'national' environments. In fact, the very concept of a 'national' environment is somewhat absurd. While it is true that some environmental problems involve strictly local effects, many have transboundary and even global dimensions. Three of the six major 'current issues' featured in Environment Canada's second *State of the Environment* report—climatic change, stratospheric ozone, and acidic deposition—are clearly international in scope. The other three—toxic chemicals, solid waste disposal, and protecting wilderness and wildlife—have important international dimensions. Is there reason to believe that these transboundary problems can be managed?

There are both positive and negative signs. On the positive side, the governments of Canada and many other countries have entered into agreements on a number of transboundary issues. These include the following:

- *Ozone depletion.* The Montreal Protocol on Substances that Deplete the

Ozone Layer (1987) committed signatories to a 50 per cent reduction in CFC use by 1998 and limits on halon use to 1986 levels by 1992. The Protocol also restricted trade in ozone-depleting chemicals.

- *Global warming.* The World Conference on the Changing Atmosphere, held at Toronto in 1988, recommended that developed countries cut their emissions of greenhouse gases by 20 per cent from 1988 levels by the year 2005. This was followed by the Kyoto conference in 1997, which produced an agreement committing 38 developed countries to reductions in their greenhouse gas emissions from 6 to 8 per cent below 1990 levels by the year 2012.

- *Acid rain.* In 1985, Canada and several European governments signed the Helsinki Protocol, committing them to a 30 per cent cut in sulphur dioxide emissions by 1994.

- *Species and habitat preservation.* Through commercial exploitation, hunting, and habitat destruction, many of the world's animal populations have been endangered. International agreements to ban imports of ivory, stop commercial whaling, and end drift-net fishing provide examples of successful international co-operation to protect endangered species. The Convention on the Protection of the World Cultural and Natural Heritage (UNESCO, 1972) and the Convention on the Conservation of Wetlands of International Importance (1971) are two of the main international agreements aimed at habitat preservation.

- *Water pollution.* The international Law of the Seas, the London Dumping Convention, and the UN Environment Program Montreal Guidelines respecting land-based sources of marine pollution are examples of international co-operation to deal with transboundary water pollution. In the Great Lakes basin, the Canada-US International Joint Commission monitors water pollution, identifies areas of concern, and commits Ontario and the eight states bordering the lakes to the development of remedial action plans.

This is only a partial list of the international initiatives that have been taken to deal with transboundary environmental issues. But before concluding that governments are willing and able to co-operate on these issues, the limits of their co-operation must be examined. These limits are due to three main factors: conflicting interests, inadequate decision-making and enforcement machinery; and the nature of the policy instruments used to tackle transboundary environmental issues. The first factor is the most intransigent, and is one we have touched on already. It may be illustrated with a couple of examples:

Example #1: Why should China, which in 1987 produced about 0.4 tonnes of carbon dioxide emissions per capita, agree to carbon dioxide restrictions favoured by Canada, which on a per capita basis was ten times as polluting?[36] For that matter, why should industrialized France or Japan agree to the same cuts as Canada or the United States when their per capita carbon dioxide emissions are only about half those of the latter two countries? Developing countries, including China, account for less than one-third of carbon dioxide emissions. Not surprisingly, they tend to be irritated when the governments of developed countries call for reductions in the pollutants associated with industrialization. International agreements like the Montreal Protocol and the Toronto Convention acknowledge their concerns and use a combination of less stringent targets for developing countries and cash transfers to them from industrialized ones to encourage/bribe them into compliance.

Example #2: It was no accident that Brazil was selected as the site for the UN's 1992 Earth Summit. That country has been the tilting ground for sometimes violent clashes between developers, on the one hand, and environmentalists, Aboriginal peoples, and small landholders, on the other. The rapid pace of deforestation in Brazil's Amazon basin has become an international symbol of the clash between economic and environmental values. The Amazonian rain forest represents about 30 per cent of the world's tropical rain forest and is estimated to hold close to half of the world's plant and animal species. Amazonia is Brazil's own version of North America's western frontier, attracting colonists from other parts of the country who rip into nature and traditional communities to build an economy based on exploitation of the region's natural resources.

But Brazil is not alone. Southeast Asian countries such as Indonesia, Thailand, and Malaysia have for years been active in exploiting their own tropical forests, usually employing clear-cutting methods. The lumber industries of these countries are more important than that of Brazil, where most deforestation is to clear land for agricultural use. Moreover, some industrialized countries, including Canada, continue to exploit commercially more of their forests than is regenerated each year.[37]

Leaving aside the arguments about the loss of species diversity, the impact on traditional forest-dwelling peoples, and the aesthetic and ecological effects (for example, soil erosion) of clear-cutting forests, deforestation contributes to the greenhouse effect. It does so through the release of carbon dioxide from burning or rotting trees and other vegetation and from the loss of forests that absorb carbon dioxide from the atmosphere as part of the photosynthesis process. Environmentalists argue that deforestation of the lush tropical rain forests is an important source of global warming and therefore should be limited. The obsessive concern among northern environmentalists with preserving the tropical forests of the Southern hemisphere has been labelled 'tropical chic' by Peter Swire. He notes:

> There is one problem with all of this. Backers of the rain forest movement are mostly in the United States or other modern industrialized countries. The rain forests are not. They're mostly in developing countries, which face other, more pressing issues, such as feeding their grow-

ing populations. So two questions must be answered. First, why is it our business to tell Brazil, Indonesia, and other forested countries what to do with their forests? And, assuming there's an answer to that question, how can we in developed countries convince the forested countries they should listen to us?[38]

The answer is, 'It isn't easy!' In the eyes of the developing countries where deforestation contributes to economic growth, the developed countries lack credibility on this issue. On a per capita basis, both Canada and the United States release about as much greenhouse gases as does Brazil, and twice the amount of Indonesia.[39] Moreover, these developed countries have already cleared much of their original growth forest for agriculture, settlement, and commercial exploitation. Their demands that developing countries refrain from doing what they themselves have done is not unreasonably viewed as self-serving hypocrisy by the governments of many developing countries.

The second factor that impedes international co-operation on environmental issues involves the inadequacy of transnational institutions. Despite the existence of a large number of bilateral and regional organizations established to deal with transboundary environmental issues and a clutch of United Nations agencies concerned with environment protection, international decision-making tends to be feeble. The basic problem is, of course, that participating countries are generally unwilling to give up any part of their political sovereignty to an international agency. In recent years we have seen that this obstacle can be overcome to some extent on matters regarding international security and economics. The UN Security Council was able to take concerted action against Iraq after that country invaded Kuwait, and it supported Anglo-American demands that Libya turn over two of its citizens to be tried for the terrorist bombing of a Pan-Am jet. On economic matters, the World Trade Organization sometimes is able to impose sanctions on members who violate its restrictions on protectionist policies. Regional free trade agreements like the European Union, the Canada-United States Free Trade Agreement, and NAFTA impose certain restrictions on national sovereignty in matters of trade and investment. But when it comes to environmental matters, international agencies still have not progressed very far beyond their research, monitoring, and 'talking shop' functions. Part of the reason for this is that international environmental issues still are not considered as vital to national interests as economic and security matters.

Given the realities of national sovereignty, the tendencies towards short-termism to which governments are subject, and their preoccupation with domestic affairs, can this institutional gap be bridged? This brings us to the third limit on international action, the problem of enforcement. International agreements on transboundary environmental issues typically rely on targets and voluntary compliance by member states. The 1997 Kyoto Protocol on greenhouse gases is typical in this respect. The Protocol failed to include enforcement mechanisms, stating simply that the determination of 'appropriate and effective' ways of dealing with non-compliance would be dealt with at a later meeting. The result is predictable. Targets are not met, or not met on time; some countries balk at being asked to comply with the same guidelines that apply to less efficient or more polluting countries; and some countries just do not want to co-operate at all.

Sanctions and inducements are needed to achieve what goodwill cannot. These already exist to some degree. For example, the International Monetary Fund and its lending arm, the World Bank, the Inter-American Development Bank, and other development agencies consider the environmental impacts of the development projects they are asked to finance. One of the consequences has been that many fewer dams are built in developing countries. India and China, whose production of ozone-destroying chemicals is increasing more rapidly than in the developed countries, refused to agree to the Montreal Protocol on CFCs unless developing countries were given longer to restrict their production and developed countries agreed to contribute to the costs of replacing CFCs with ozone-friendly substitutes. At the 1997 Kyoto conference on global warming the gap between developed and developing countries proved unbridgeable. Countries such as China—quite understandably, from their point of view—refused to be bound by the same limits on greenhouse gas emissions as were agreed to by developed countries. The possibility of rich countries paying poorer countries to pollute less was raised, as it often is, but the scale of the payments required to buy an appreciable change in the behaviour of developing countries is beyond what is politically saleable in most developed countries (and certainly beyond the political pale in the United States, which, with about 4 per cent of the world's population, generates about one-fifth of global greenhouse gases and would be expected to meet a large part of the bill for any such scheme).

It is worth noting that virtually all the sanctions and inducements that currently exist run in one direction—from developed to developing countries. In the case of wealthy industrialized countries, their compliance still depends on goodwill and a sense of responsibility to their own future generations and the global community. These may not be enough. In 1995, only seven years after the Toronto conference on global warming, the Canadian government admitted that greenhouse gas emissions had in fact increased and were expected to be about 13 per cent higher in the year 2000 than they had been in 1990. Then, at the second Earth Summit, in 1997, Prime Minister Chrétien acknowledged that the target Canada agreed to at Rio de Janiero in 1992 would not be met. Ottawa blames the provinces for this failure, provincial co-operation being necessary to regulate the sources of carbon dioxide emissions. And while it is certainly true that the federal division of powers complicates environmental policy-making and may prevent Ottawa from being able to follow through on international commitments, federalism may also provide a convenient excuse for Ottawa to pass the buck for environmental matters to the provinces.[40]

This is particularly true since the Supreme Court's 1997 ruling in *R. v. Hydro-Québec*. This case involved the alleged dumping of PCBs by Hydro-Québec into a river. Hydro-Québec was charged pursuant to the Canadian Environmental Protection Act. The constitutionality of those parts of the Act under which it was charged was challenged by Hydro-Québec and the Quebec government on the grounds that they did not fall within the ambit of any federal power set out in s. 91 of the Constitution Act, 1887. Relying on a generous and flexible interpretation of Ottawa's constitutional authority to make criminal law, five of the court's nine judges upheld the validity of regulations made under the Canadian Environmental Protection Act. In so doing, the Court seems to have extended significantly the scope of Ottawa's authority over the environment. Nevertheless, although the feds may have the constitution on their side, the hard realities of politics, including the political costs associated with appearing to meddle in provincial affairs to the detriment of its economy, make passing the buck a tempting option.

A Non-Malthusian Case for Environmentally Friendly Policies

As Mark Sagoff observes, the problem of environmental deterioration is often framed as a problem of overconsumption.[41] Roughly one-fifth of the world's population, those living in the economically developed countries, accounts for about 80 per cent of global consumption. Given the earth's finite resources and its limited capacity to tolerate the increasing amounts of waste and pollution that accompany ever higher levels of production and consumption, the over-consuming lifestyles of the world's wealthier countries cannot be sustained indefinitely. The idea that the size of the global economic pie can continue to expand so as to pull the developing world up to the consumption standards considered normal in the developed world is, in Paul Ehrlich's words, 'basically a humane idea made insane by the constraints nature places on human activity.'[42]

Books like Ehrlich's *The End of Affluence* and the Club of Rome's *The Limits to Growth* popularized the idea that scarcity would eventually send the prices of crucial natural resources skyrocketing and that these shortages would bring to a halt the era of constant growth in production and consumption. In fact, however, the exploitable stocks of most of these raw materials have become more rather than less abundant and their real prices have fallen. Sagoff offers three reasons for this:

- In the case of subsoil reserves, technological advances have increased the ability of industry to locate new reserves and maximize the exploitation of these resources.
- The substitution of plentiful for scarcer, more expensive resources has

reduced the importance of shortages in what previously were crucial raw materials.

- Industry's ability to use materials more efficiently continues to increase. Studies have shown that the 'materials intensity' of production—i.e., the total material input required for a constant unit of output—has been falling. Economist Robert Solow asks, 'Why shouldn't the productivity of most natural resources continue to rise more or less steadily through time, like the productivity of labour?'[43] His answer is that the natural resource requirements of industry, per unit of production, are likely to continue to decline.

Sagoff argues that technology has enabled us to avoid critical shortages, contrary to the neo-Malthusian predictions of those who claim that the world, especially the wealthy parts of the world, consumes too much. He examines energy resources, food, and timber, and concludes that in each case supply is abundant. As he says of energy, 'The global energy problem has less to do with depleting resources than with controlling pollutants.'[44] But even this potential limit to growth is one that Sagoff believes can be managed through new energy technologies and resource substitution.

'Can' and 'should' have very different meanings. Sagoff makes the case that neo-Malthusians like Ehrlich have been shown to be wrong in their predictions of global scarcity due to overconsumption. The world can, Sagoff argues, continue to consume at increasingly high levels. Those who base their case for less consumption of the world's resources on economics are bound to lose, he argues, because history shows that technology is generally successful in overcoming scarcity.

That consumption can continue to grow does not mean, however, that it should do so. 'The question before us', he writes, 'is not whether we are going to run out of resources. It is whether economics is the appropriate context for thinking about environmental policy.'[45] Sagoff suggests that it is not. Arguments that the extinction of a particular species of plant or animal life, or the deterioration of some specific habitat, will have calamitous results for the ecosystems on which mankind depends are, he notes, seldom even remotely credible. Very few species are, in biologist David Ehrenfeld's words, 'vital cogs in the ecological machine'.[46] But if arguments rooted in economics and the sustainability of human life fail to convince, why should anyone care about the effects of consumption on the environment?

The answer, according to Sagoff, has to do with our sense of moral purpose. 'In defending old-growth forests, wetlands, or species,' he says, 'we make our best arguments when we think of nature chiefly in aesthetic and moral terms.'[47] The quality of life rather than the standard of living must become the compass that guides our thinking about the environment. There is, of course, abundant evidence of precisely this sort of moral challenge to the high-consumption society. The David and Goliath court battle between the fast-food chain

McDonald's and two British environmental activists during the mid-1990s raised ethical and lifestyle issues. The now commonplace confrontations between North American and European activists, on the one side, and forestry companies and public authorities, on the other, over the fate of old-growth temperate rain forests in British Columbia represent another such challenge. But so far the general public seems to be little moved by arguments about the putative sacredness of forests or the great chain of being (although there are significant cross-national variations in popular beliefs). Until such time as there are more votes in conservation than consumption, it is unrealistic to expect policy-makers—most of them, anyway—to use the language of morality in making the case for the environment.

Notes

Chapter 1

1. Thomas R. Dye, *Understanding Public Policy*, 3rd edn (Englewood Cliffs, NJ: Prentice-Hall, 1978), 3.
2. Murray Edelman, *Constructing the Political Spectacle* (Chicago: University of Chicago Press, 1988), 12
3. Statistics Canada, cat. no. 13–888.
4. Richard M. Bird, *The Growth of Government Spending in Canada* (Toronto: Canadian Tax Foundation, 1970), 288, table 43.
5. Based on estimates in Economic Council of Canada, *Responsible Regulation* (Ottawa: Supply and Services, 1979), and the Task Force on Program Review, *Regulatory Programs* (Ottawa: Supply and Services, 1986).
6. Economic Council of Canada, *Minding the Public's Business* (Ottawa: Supply and Services, 1986), II.
7. Statistics Canada, *Income after tax distributions by size in Canada*, cat. no. 13–210.
8. Constitution Act, 1982, section 36(2).
9. Thomas J. Courchene, 'Towards a Protected Society: The Politicization of Economic Life', *Canadian Journal of Economics* 13 (Nov. 1980).
10. Task Force on Program Review, *Economic Growth: Services and Subsidies to Business*, 15.
11. Raymond Breton, 'Multiculturalism and Canadian Nation-Building', in Alan Cairns and Cynthia Williams, eds, *Politics of Gender Ethnicity and Language* (Toronto: University of Toronto Press, 1986), 30.
12. *The Economist*, 'The Myth of the Powerless State', 7 Oct. 1995, 15.
13. Neil Nevitte, *The Decline of Deference: Canadian Value Change in Cross-National Perspective* (Peterborough, Ont.: Broadview Press, 1996).
14. See 'Scénarios de la mondialisation', *Le Monde diplomatique* (nov. 1996): 6.
15. For a discussion of this possible linkage, see Nevitte, *The Decline of Deference*, 28–41.
16. Office of the Prime Minister, 'Notes for Remarks by the Prime Minister at the Harrison Liberal Conference', Harrison Hot Springs, BC, 21 Nov. 1969, 7.

Chapter 2

1. J.M. Keynes, *The General Theory of Employment, Interest and Money* (London: Macmillan, 1936), 383.
2. These three characteristics of theoretical perspectives are used by Robert Alford and Roger Friedland to distinguish between political theories. See *Powers of Theory* (Cambridge: Cambridge University Press, 1985), esp. ch. 1.
3. Leo Panitch, 'Elites, Classes and Power in Canada', in Michael Whittington and

Glen Williams, eds, *Canadian Politics in the 1980s*, 2nd edn (Toronto: Methuen, 1984), 239.

4. See, for example, Christian Bay, 'Politics and Pseudopolitics: A Critical Evaluation of Some Behavioral Literature', *American Political Science Review* 59, 1 (Mar. 1965): 39–51.

5. Richard Simeon, 'Studying Public Policy', *Canadian Journal of Political Science* (hereafter *CJPS*) 9, 4 (Dec. 1976): 566. Emphasis added.

6. Michael Atkinson and Marsha Chandler, eds, *The Politics of Canadian Public Policy* (Toronto: University of Toronto Press, 1983), 3–5.

7. See G. Bruce Doern and Richard W. Phidd, *Canadian Public Policy* (Toronto: Methuen, 1983), chs 1, 6.

8. See Robert I. Jackson and Doreen Jackson, *Politics in Canada* (Toronto: Prentice-Hall, 1990), esp. 585–602.

9. E.E. Schattschneider, *The Semi-Sovereign People* (New York: Holt, Rinehart and Winston, 1960), 35.

10. Richard J. Van Loon and Michael S. Whittington, *The Canadian Political System*, 4th edn (Toronto: McGraw-Hill Ryerson, 1987), 13.

11. Joseph A. Schumpeter, *Capitalism, Socialism and Democracy* (New York: Harper & Brothers, 1943).

12. Robert Dahl, *A Preface to Democratic Theory* (Chicago: University of Chicago Press, 1956).

13. See Anthony King, 'Ideas, Institutions and the Policies of Governments: A Comparative Analysis', *British Journal of Political Science* 3, 3 (July 1973): 291–313, and 3, 4 (Oct. 1973): 409–23; H. Heclo, 'Toward a New Welfare State?', in Peter Flora and Arnold Heidenheimer, eds, *The Development of Welfare States in Europe and America* (New York: Transaction Books, 1981), 383–406; Ira Sharkansky, *Whither the State* (New York: Chatham House, 1979).

14. Robert L. Heilbroner, 'The View from the Top: Reflections on a Changing Business Ideology', in Earl F. Cheit, ed., *The Business Establishment* (New York: Wiley, 1964), 12.

15. Charles Lindblom, *Politics and Markets* (New York: Basic Books, 1977), esp. chs 13–16.

16. Theodore Lowi, *The End of Liberalism* (New York: W.W. Norton, 1979), 280.

17. Charles Lindblom, 'The Market as Prison', in Thomas Ferguson and Joel Rogers, eds, *The Political Economy* (Armonk, NY: M.E. Sharpe, 1984), 3–11.

18. Ibid., 6.

19. Michael J. Trebilcock et al., *The Choice of Governing Instrument* (Ottawa: Supply and Services, 1982), 21.

20. James M. Buchanan and Gordon Tullock, *The Calculus of Consent* (Ann Arbor: University of Michigan Press, 1965).

21. Ibid., vi.

22. In Hobbes's words, 'during the time men live without a common power to keep them all in awe, they are in that condition which is called war, and such a war as

is of every man against every man.' See *Leviathan* (New York: Bobbs-Merrill, 1958), 106.

23. Trebilcock et al., *Choice of Governing Instrument*, 27–9.

24. James Buchanan, 'Why Does Government Grow?', in Thomas E. Borcherding, ed., *Budgets and Bureaucrats* (Durham, NC: Duke University Press, 1977), 4–5.

25. Mark Sproule-Jones, 'Institutions, Constitutions, and Public Policies: A Public-Choice Overview', in Atkinson and Chandler, eds, *The Politics of Canadian Public Policy*, 127.

26. Ibid., 144.

27. See Fred Block, 'The Ruling Class Does Not Rule: Notes on the Marxist Theory of the State', in Ferguson and Rogers, eds, *The Political Economy*, 32–46.

28. These categories were introduced in James O'Connor, *The Fiscal Crisis of the State* (New York: St Martin's Press, 1973), 6.

29. This argument is associated with the French Marxist Nicos Poulantzas. See *Classes in Contemporary Capitalism* (London: New Left Books, 1975).

30. Block, 'The Ruling Class Does Not Rule', 40.

31. Ralph Miliband, 'State Power and Capitalist Democracy', a paper delivered at Carleton University, Ottawa, July 1984, 6.

32. Quoted in Thomas S. Kuhn, *The Structure of Scientific Revolutions*, 2nd edn (Chicago: University of Chicago Press, 1970), 151.

Chapter 3

1. G. Bruce Doern, Leslie A. Pal, and Brian W. Tomlin, eds, *Border Crossings: The Internationalization of Canadian Public Policy* (Toronto: Oxford University Press, 1996), 5.

2. Ibid., 5.

3. For a good summary of the approach, see Seymour Martin Lipset, *Continental Divide: Values and Institutions of the United States and Canada* (New York: Routledge, 1990).

4. Kenneth McRae, 'The Structure of Canadian History', in Louis Hartz, ed., *The Founding of New Societies* (New York: Harcourt, Brace and World, 1964), 219–74; Gad Horowitz, 'Conservatism, Liberalism, and Socialism in Canada: An Interpretation', *CJPS* 32 (1966): 143–71.

5. See George Woodcock, *Confederation Betrayed* (Madeira Park, BC: Harbour Publishing, 1981).

6. Philip Resnick, *Parliament vs. People* (Vancouver: New Star Books, 1984).

7. Ibid., 25.

8. Ibid., 38.

9. Alan C. Cairns, 'The Governments and Societies of Canadian Federalism', in Douglas E. Williams, ed., *Constitution, Government, and Society in Canada: Selected Essays by Alan C. Cairns* (Toronto: McClelland & Stewart, 1988), 141–70.

10. With the passage of the Constitution Act, 1982, the BNA Act of 1867 and all of its

amendments have been renamed the Constitution Act, with the date of their passage by the British Parliament.

11. I assume that the readers of this text are familiar with the basic features of Canada's constitution. Those who are not should consult the appropriate chapter of any introductory text on Canadian government.

12. Cairns, 'Governments and Societies', 144.

13. Ibid., 151–2.

14. F.R. Scott, *Essays on the Constitution* (Toronto: University of Toronto Press, 1977).

15. For rather different interpretations of the influence that the JCPC has had on Canadian federalism, see Alan Cairns, 'The Judicial Committee and Its Critics', *CJPS* 4, 3 (Sept. 1971): 301–45.

16. This principle was established by the Judicial Committee of the Privy Council in the *Labour Conventions Case*, 1937. See Peter H. Russell, *Leading Constitutional Decisions*, 3rd edn (Ottawa: Carleton University Press, 1982), 122–30.

17. See Richard Simeon, *Federal-Provincial Diplomacy: The Making of Recent Policy in Canada* (Toronto: University of Toronto Press, 1972).

18. Alan C. Cairns, 'Citizens (Outsiders) and Government (Insiders) in Constitution-Making: The Case of Meech Lake', in Cairns, *Disruptions: Constitutional Struggles, from the Charter to Meech Lake* (Toronto: McClelland & Stewart, 1991), 136.

19. F.L. Morton, 'The Charter Revolution and the Court Party', *Osgoode Hall Law Journal* 30, 3 (Fall 1992): 630.

20. Ibid., 649.

21. Statistics Canada, *Canada's International Investment Position 1994* (Ottawa: Statistics Canada, 1995).

22. Elizabeth Smythe, 'Investment Policy', in Doern et al., eds, *Border Crossings*, 192.

23. Claude Morin, *Quebec versus Ottawa: The Struggle for Self-government 1960–1972* (Toronto: University of Toronto Press, 1976).

24. See the argument set out in Cairns, 'Governments and Societies', 141–70.

25. See Roger Gibbins, *Regionalism: Territorial Politics in Canada and the United States* (Toronto: Butterworths, 1982), ch. 7.

26. See J.C. Morrison, 'Oliver Mowat and the Development of Provincial Rights in Ontario: A Study in Dominion-Provincial Relations, 1867–1896', in Ontario Archives, *Three History Theses* (Toronto, 1961).

27. Constitutional amendments in 1951 and 1964 assigned legislative authority over old age pensions and supplementary benefits to Ottawa, but with the proviso that provincial authority remained paramount.

28. This interpretation of why Canadian federalism is characterized by a comparatively high degree of decentralization follows Alan Cairns's argument in 'The Governments and Societies of Canadian Federalism'.

29. See Jeffrey Sachs, 'Nature, Nurture and Growth', *The Economist*, 14 June 1997, 19.

30. Doern et al., *Border Crossings*, 3.

31. Sachs, 'Nature, Nurture and Growth', 22.

32. *Le Monde diplomatique* (Paris), nov. 1996, 9, my translation.

33. Quoted ibid., 7, my translation.

34. Doern et al., *Border Crossings*, 19–24.

35. Andrew Cooper and Leslie Pal, 'Human Rights and Security Policy', in Doern et al., *Border Crossings*, 227. The three groups were the Charter Committee on Poverty Issues, the National Anti-Poverty Organization, and the National Action Committee on the Status of Women.

36. Doern et al., *Border Crossings*, 23.

37. G. Bruce Doern and John Kirton, 'Foreign Policy', in Doern et al., *Border Crossings*, 263.

38. Leslie A. Pal, *Beyond Policy Analysis* (Toronto: Nelson, 1997).

Chapter 4

1. See the seminal article by Woodrow Wilson, 'The Study of Administration', *Political Science Quarterly* 2 (June 1887).

2. *The Oxford Universal Dictionary* (Oxford: Oxford University Press, 1955).

3. Martin Albrow, *Bureaucracy* (London: Macmillan, 1979), ch. I.

4. Robert T. Nakamura and Frank Smallwood, *The Politics of Implementation* (New York: St Martin's Press, 1980), 9.

5. Bank of Canada Act.

6. James Q. Wilson, *Bureaucracy: What Government Agencies Do and Why They Do It* (New York: Basic Books, 1989), 34.

7. Broadcasting Act.

8. Leslie A. Pal, *State, Class and Bureaucracy: Canadian Unemployment Insurance and Public Policy* (Montreal and Kingston: McGill-Queen's University Press, 1988), 103–18.

9. Jeffrey Pressman and Aaron Wildavsky, *Implementation* (Berkeley: University of California Press, 1984).

10. Ibid., 93.

11. Ibid., 134.

12. Richard E. Neustadt, *Presidential Power: The Politics of Leadership* (New York: Wiley, 1960).

13. This section relies heavily on Pressman and Wildavsky, *Implementation*, and Wilson, *Bureaucracy*.

14. Wilson, *Bureaucracy*, 5.

15. K. Meier and Lloyd D. Nigro, 'Representational Bureaucracy and Policy Preferences: A Study in the Attitudes of Federal Executives', *Public Administration Review* 36 (1976): 406–67.

16. Robert K. Merton, 'Bureaucratic Structure and Personality', *Social Forces* 17 (1940): 560–8.

17. Marc Tipermas, 'Jurisdictionalism: The Politics of Executive Reorganization', Ph.D. thesis (Harvard University, 1976), 35, 76–81, as quoted in Wilson, *Bureaucracy*, 180.

18. Philip Selznick, *Leadership in Administration* (Evanston, Ill.: Row, Peterson and Co., 1957), 121.

19. Marver Bernstein, *Regulating Business by Independent Commission* (Princeton, NJ: Princeton University Press, 1955).

20. Wilson, *Bureaucracy*, 91.

21. Selznick, *Leadership*, ch. 2.

22. Sandra Gwyn, 'The Great Ottawa Grant Boom (And How It Grew)', *Saturday Night* 87 (Oct. 1972): 22.

23. Stewart Goodings, quoted in Leslie A. Pal, *Interests of State* (Montreal and Kingston: McGill-Queen's University Press, 1993), 161.

24. Ibid., 154.

25. Alan Freeman, 'The Department That Counts', *Globe and Mail*, 1 June 1992, A5.

26. Ibid.

27. Ibid.

28. See the summary in Wilson, *Bureaucracy*, 350–2.

29. Task Force on Program Review, *Introduction to the Process of Program Review* (Ottawa: Supply and Services, Mar. 1986), 23.

Chapter 5

1. These proposals are not explicitly advocated in John Maynard Keynes, *The General Theory of Employment, Interest and Money* (London: Macmillan, 1936), but are spelled out in other writings of Keynes both before and after the publication of that book.

2. See the discussion in Doug Owram, *The Government Generation: Canadian Intellectuals and the State 1900–1945* (Toronto: University of Toronto Press, 1986), 307–14.

3. Quoted in Maurice Lamontagne, *Business Cycles in Canada* (Ottawa: Canadian Institute for Economic Policy, 1984), xxiv.

4. Figures from *The Economist*, 22 Sept. 1984, 48.

5. Quoted ibid., 49.

6. The following discussion of monetarism draws heavily on Rudiger Dornbusch and Stanley Fischer, *Macroeconomics* (New York: McGraw-Hill, 1978), and on the interview with Karl Brunner in Arjo Klamer, *Conversations with Economists* (Totowa, NJ: Rowman & Allanheld, 1984), 179–99.

7. Quoted in Dornbusch and Fischer, *Macroeconomics*, 546.

8. See the interviews with Robert Solow, Alan Blinder, Karl Brunner, and James Tobin in Klamer, *Conversations*.

9. Lucas is quoted ibid.

10. Karl Brunner, quoted ibid., 194.

11. Alan Blinder makes this argument in *Economic Policy and the Great Stagflation* (New York: Academic Press, 1979).

12. Klamer, *Conversations*, 101.

13. See Lamontagne, *Business Cycles in Canada*; Paul Anthony Samuelson, *Economics* (Toronto: McGraw-Hill Ryerson, 1984), ch. 14.

14. Milton Friedman and Anna Schwartz, *Monetary History of the United States 1867–1960* (Princeton, NJ; Princeton University Press, 1963).

15. Samuelson, *Economics*, 255.

16. Joseph Schumpeter, *Business Cycles* (New York: McGraw-Hill, 1939).

17. Alvin Hansen, *Fiscal Policy and Business Cycles* (New York: W.W. Norton, 1941). While Hansen's focus was on cycles of shorter duration, he did provide dates for periods conforming to Kondratieff's theory of long-term movements.

18. Quoted in Lamontagne, *Business Cycles in Canada*, 131.

19. Ibid., 125–6.

20. Bruno S. Frey, *Modern Political Economy* (New York: John Wiley & Sons, 1978), ch. 11.

21. Samuelson, *Economics*, 836.

22. Quoted in J.L. Granatstein, *The Ottawa Men* (Toronto: Oxford University Press, 1982), 167.

23. Quoted in Robert Lekachman, 'The Radical Keynes', in Harold Wattel, ed., *The Policy Consequences of John Maynard Keynes* (Armonk, NY: M.E. Sharpe, 1985), 36.

24. Quoted in Robert L. Ascah, 'The Deficit Debate: A Survey and Assessment', paper presented to the Canadian Political Science Association annual meeting, Winnipeg, 8 June 1986, 1.

25. *Report of the Royal Commission on Banking and Finance* (Ottawa: Queen's Printer, 1964), 398.

26. Economic Council of Canada, *First Annual Review* (Ottawa: Queen's Printer, 1964).

27. Liberal Party of Canada, *Creating Opportunity: The Liberal Plan for Canada* (Ottawa: Liberal Party of Canada, 1993), 15.

28. Jim Stanford, 'The Economics of Debt and the Remaking of Canada', *Studies in Political Economy* 48 (Autumn 1995): 132.

29. Mancur Olson, 'How Ideas Affect Societies: Is Britain the Wave of the Future?', in Institute of Economic Affairs, *Ideas, Interests and Consequences* (London: Institute of Economic Affairs, 1989), 39.

30. Andrea Boltho, ed., *The European Economy* (Oxford: Oxford University Press, 1982), ch. 1.

31. Quoted in Lamontagne, *Business Cycles in Canada*, xxii.

32. This interpretation is David Gordon's, in Klamer, *Conversations*, 208.

33. Ernest Mandel, *Long Waves of Capitalist Development* (Cambridge: Cambridge University Press, 1980), 100.

34. Figures cited in John Sargent, ed., *Post-War Macroeconomic Developments*, vol. 20 of the research studies for the Royal Commission on the Economic Union and Development Prospects for Canada (Macdonald Commission) (Toronto: University of Toronto Press, 1985), 61.

35. Quoted ibid., 60.

36. Bank of Canada, *Annual Report 1973* (Ottawa: Queen's Printer, 1974), 7.

37. See the brief survey in Craig Riddell, ed., *Dealing with Inflation and*

Unemployment in Canada, vol. 25 of the research studies for the Macdonald Commission (Toronto: University of Toronto Press, 1985), 52.

38. Quoted in John Sargent, ed., *Fiscal and Monetary Policy*, vol. 21 of the research studies for the Macdonald Commission (Toronto: University of Toronto Press, 1985), 232.

39. Gordon Thiessen, 'Uncertainty and the Transmission of Monetary Policy in Canada', lecture delivered at York University, 30 Mar. 1995, 17.

40. The meaning of 'excessive' in this context is described by John Bossons as a perception 'that a seemingly chronic government deficit may indicate that the current set of government tax, transfer, and expenditure programs is not sustainable over the long run.' In Sargent, ed., *Fiscal and Monetary Policy*, 92.

41. David A. Wolfe, 'The Politics of the Deficit', in G. Bruce Doern, research co-ordinator, *The Politics of Economic Policy*, vol. 40 of the research studies for the Macdonald Commission (Toronto: University of Toronto Press, 1985), 141.

42. Ibid., 149–50.

43. Department of Finance, *Quarterly Economic Review 1990*.

44. Maureen Appel Molot and Glen Williams, 'The Political Economy of Continentalism', in Michael Whittington and Glen Williams, eds, *Canadian Politics in the 1980s*, 2nd edn (Toronto: Methuen, 1984), 94.

45. This fourth economic stance is relevant to understanding the colonial activities of France and Britain in pre-Confederation Canada and to understanding some of the nineteenth-century tensions in the relationship between the United States and British North America.

46. Richard Pomfret, *The Economic Development of Canada* (Toronto: Methuen, 1981), 69.

47. Arthur Lower has described the 1879 tariff as 'a frank creation of vested manufacturing interests living on the bounty of government.' See ibid., 91–4, for Lower and for a survey of interpretations of the 1879 tariff.

48. J.L. Granatstein, 'Free Trade: The History of an Issue', in Michael D. Henderson, ed., *The Future on the Table: Canada and the Free Trade Issue* (Downsview, Ont.: York University, 1987), 5.

49. See the discussion in Richard Harris, *Trade, Industrial Policy and International Competition*, vol. 13 of the research studies for the Macdonald Commission (Toronto: University of Toronto Press, 1985), 39–40.

50. Keith Banting, 'Social Policy', in Doern et al., *Border Crossings*, 52.

51. See ibid., 38–9, for the analysis of surveys demonstrating the gap between the values of élites and those of the general public.

52. Hugh G. Thorburn, *Planning and the Economy* (Ottawa: Canadian Institute for Economic Policy, 1984), 245.

53. Banting, 'Social Policy', 38.

Chapter 6

1. This is the title of the report prepared by the federal New Democratic Party Policy Review Committee, Halifax, June 1991.

2. James O'Connor, *The Fiscal Crisis of the State* (New York: St Martin's Press, 1973).

3. United Nations Development Program, *Human Development Report 1996* (Oxford: Oxford University Press, 1996).

4. Statistics Canada, *Income After Tax Distribution by Size in Canada,* 1990.

5. An absolute measure of poverty, defined as the income needed to pay for the basic needs of a household of a given size, is used by some organizations, such as the Social Planning Council of Metropolitan Toronto.

6. E. Sabatini, *Welfare—No Fair: A Critical Analysis of Ontario's Welfare System (1985–1994)* (Vancouver: Fraser Institute, 1996), 197.

7. Quoted ibid.

8. Thomas Courchene, *Social Policy in the 1990s* (Toronto: C.D. Howe Institute, 1987).

9. National Council of Welfare, *Pension Reform* (Ottawa: Supply and Services, Feb. 1990), 52.

10. Department of Finance, *The Canada Pension Plan: Keeping It Financially Healthy* (Ottawa: Supply and Services, 1985), 4.

11. *Report of the Royal Commission on the Economic Union and Development Prospects for Canada,* vol. 2, 611–19.

12. *Report of the Royal Commission on Unemployment Insurance,* 115–19.

13. Paul Martin Jr, *Budget Speech 1995* (Ottawa: Department of Finance, 1995), 16.

14. See the summary of these studies in Sabatini, *Welfare—No Fair,* 182–4.

15. Doug Allen, 'Welfare and the Family: The Canadian Experience', *Journal of Labour Economics* 11, 1 (Jan. 1993): 220.

16. See M. Taylor, M. Stevenson, and P Williams, 'Sociological Perspectives on Canadian Medicare', in David Coburn et al., eds, *Health and Canadian Society* (Toronto: Fitzhenry & Whiteside, 1987); Stevenson and Williams, 'Physicians and Medicare: Professional Ideology and Canadian Health Care Policy', *Canadian Public Policy* 11, 3 (Sept. 1985): 504–21.

17. See V.R. Fuchs, *Who Shall Live?* (New York: Basic Books, 1975); Aaron Wildavsky, 'Doing Better and Feeling Worse: The Political Pathology of Health Policy', *Daedalus* 1 (Winter 1977): 105–23.

18. David K. Foot, *Boom, Bust, and Echo* (Toronto: Macfarlane Walter & Ross, 1996), 168.

19. Giles Grenier, 'Health Care Costs in Canada: Past and Future Trends', in François Vaillancourt, *Income Distribution and Economic Security in Canada,* vol. 1 of the research studies for the Macdonald Commission (Toronto: University of Toronto Press, 1985), 270.

20. Canadian Medical Association, *Report of the Task Force on the Allocation of Health Care Resources* (Ottawa: Canadian Medical Association, 1984), 58.

21. Foot, *Boom, Bust, and Echo,* 164.

22. Quoted in Emmett M. Hall, *Canada's National-Provincial Health Program for the 1980's* (Ottawa: Supply and Services, 1980), 10.

23. National Council of Welfare, *Funding Health and Higher Education: Danger Looming* (Ottawa: Supply and Services, Spring 1991), 20.

24. Department of Finance, *Budget 1995,* unpaginated.
25. *Western Report*, 3 Apr. 1995, 19.
26. W. Irwin Gillespie, *The Redistribution of Income in Canada* (Ottawa: Carleton University Press, 1980), 173.
27. See the survey in B.G. Dahlby, 'The Incidence of Government Expenditures and Taxes in Canada: A Survey', in Vaillancourt, *Income Distribution*, 129–35.
28. Separate studies by Gillespie and D. Dodge reach this conclusion. See ibid., 139–43.
29. Gillespie, *Redistribution of Income*, 160. The same conclusion is arrived at by D. Dodge, 'Impact of Tax, Transfer and Expenditure Policies of Government on the Distribution of Personal Incomes in Canada', *Review of Income and Wealth* 21 (1975): 1–52, Table 9.
30. Irwin Gillespie, Arndt Vermaeten, and Frank Vermaeten, 'Who Paid the Taxes in Canada, 1951–1988?', *Canadian Public Policy* 21, 3 (Sept. 1995): 317–43.
31. Ibid., 333.
32. Constitution Act, 1982, section 36(2).
33. Robin Boadway and Frank Flatters, *Equalization in a Federal State: An Economic Analysis* (Ottawa: Economic Council of Canada, 1982).

Chapter 7

1. 'The Family: Home Sweet Home', *The Economist*, 9 Sept. 1995, 25.
2. Margrit Eichler, *Family Shifts: Families, Policies, and Gender Equality* (Toronto: Oxford University Press, 1997), 6.
3. Ibid., 159.
4. *Canadian Social Trends*, vol. 2 (Toronto: Thompson Educational Publishing, 1994), 209–12.
5. National Council of Welfare, *Child Benefits: A Small Step Forward* (Ottawa: Supply and Services Canada, 1997), 2.
6. Hillary Rodham Clinton, *It Takes a Village, and Other Lessons Children Teach Us* (New York: Simon and Schuster, 1996).
7. Ibid., 13.
8. June Callwood, 'Citizens' Shame', *Homemaker's* (May 1997): 92.
9. Clinton, *It Takes a Village*, 76.
10. Ibid., 99.
11. Ibid., 107.
12. Ibid., 39.
13. Jean Bethke Elshtain, 'Suffer the Little Children', *New Republic*, 4 Mar. 1996, 33–4.
14. Richard Weissbourd, *The Vulnerable Child: What Really Hurts America's Children and What We Can Do About It* (New York: Addison-Wesley, 1996).
15. Ibid.
16. Clinton, *It Takes a Village*, 41.
17. Eichler, *Family Shifts*.
18. Ibid., 148–9.

19. Ibid., 164.

20. Ibid., 159.

21. Ibid., 95.

22. Ibid., 74–5.

23. This is the title of Elizabeth Fox-Genavese's review of Weissbourd's *The Vulnerable Child*, which appeared in *New Republic* 3 June 1996, 41–4.

24. David Popenoe, 'The Family Condition of America: Cultural Change and Public Policy', in Henry Aaron, Thomas Mann, and Timothy Taylor, eds, *Values and Public Policy* (Washington: Brookings Institution, 1994), 96.

25. Barbara Dafoe Whitehead, 'Dan Quayle was Right', *Atlantic Monthly* (Apr. 1993): 47.

26. Quoted ibid., 62.

27. Sara McLanahan and Gary Sandefur, *Family Background, Race and Ethnicity, and Early Family Formation* (Madison: University of Wisconsin, Institute for Research on Poverty, 1990), 51.

28. Dafoe Whitehead, 'Dan Quayle was Right', 74.

29. Judith Wallerstein and Sandra Blakeslee, *Second Chances: Men, Women, and Children a Decade After Divorce* (New York: Ticknor and Fields, 1989).

30. Deborah A. Dawson, 'Family Structure and Children's Health: United States, 1988', National Center for Health Statistics, *Vital and Health Statistics*, series 10, no. 178 (Hyattsville, Md: Department of Health and Human Services, June 1991).

31. James Q. Wilson, 'Culture, Incentives, and the Underclass', in Aaron, Mann, and Taylor, eds, *Values and Public Policy*, 63.

32. Sara McLanahan and Gary Sandefur, *Uncertain Childhood, Uncertain Future* (Cambridge, Mass.: Harvard University Press, 1996).

33. Nicolas Zill and Charlotte Schoenborn, 'Developmental, Learning, and Emotional Problems: Health of Our Nation's Children, United States, 1988', in National Center for Health Statistics, *Advance Data*, no. 190, 16 Nov. 1990.

34. See the summary of these studies in Dafoe Whitehead, 'Dan Quayle was Right', 66–7.

35. Amitai Etzioni, *The Spirit of Community: Rights, Responsibilities, and the Communitarian Agenda* (New York: Crown, 1993).

36. Quoted in 'The Family', *The Economist*, 9 Sept. 1995, 29.

37. Eichler, *Family Shifts*, 74–5.

38. 'The Family', *The Economist*, 29.

39. Quoted in Dafoe Whitehead, 'Dan Quayle was Right', 77.

40. Ibid., 71.

41. Popenoe, 'The Family Condition of America', 96.

42. McLanahan and Sandefur, *Uncertain Childhood, Uncertain Future*.

43. Dafoe Whitehead, 'Dan Quayle was Right', 72.

44. Cited ibid.

45. Cited ibid.

46. William Mattox Jr, 'Running on Empty: America's Time-Starved Families with

Children', Working Paper 5 (New York: Council on Families in America, Institute for American Values, 1991).

47. Popenoe, 'The Family Condition of America', 100–1.

48. McLanahan's arguments are summarized in Dafoe Whitehead, 'Dan Quayle was Right', 82.

49. Ibid., 84.

50. See Cindy Silver, 'Family Autonomy and the Charter of Rights: Protecting Parental Liberty in a Child-Centred Legal System', Discussion Paper 3 (Gloucester, Ont.: Centre for Renewal in Public Policy, 1995).

51. Reform Party of Canada, *Blue Book, 1996–1997* (Calgary: Reform Party of Canada, 1996), 31.

52. *Egan v. Canada* (1995) 2 S.C.R. 513; 124 D.L.R. (4th) 609.

53. Clinton, *It Takes a Village*, 223.

54. Danielle Crittenden, 'The Mother of All Problems', *Saturday Night* (Apr. 1995): 44–54.

55. House of Commons, *Hansard*, 29 May 1996, Motion 30, 3155–8.

56. Clinton, *It Takes a Village*, 221.

57. France is not the only European country to have such a system. Belgium and Italy are among the other countries that operate publicly funded preschools.

58. Clinton, *It Takes a Village*, 228.

59. Popenoe, 'The Family Condition of America', 102.

60. Ibid.

61. Details and a critical analysis can be found in National Council of Welfare, *Child Benefits: A Small Step Forward.*

62. Frances Woolley, Judith Madill, and Arndt Vermaeten, 'Credits in Crisis: Evaluating Child Benefit Reform in Canada', in Meg Luxton, ed., *Feminism and Families* (Halifax: Fernwood Publishing, 1997), 74.

63. Canada, Department of Finance, *Budget Plan, 1997* (Ottawa: Supply and Services, Feb. 1997), 107–8.

Chapter 8

1. *Regina v. Howson* (1894), 1 Terr. L.R. 492 (S.C.N.W.T.), 494.

2. Peter A. Cumming and Neil H. Mickenberg, eds, *Native Rights in Canada* (Toronto: General Publishing, 1972), 9.

3. *Reference Re: Whether Eskimo are Indians*, C.L.R. (1939): 104.

4. Harvey McCue, 'Indian Reserve', *The Canadian Encyclopedia*, vol. 2 (Edmonton: Hurtig, 1988), 1056.

5. Indian leader James Gosnell, quoted in Michael Asch, *Home and Native Land: Aboriginal Rights and the Canadian Constitution* (Vancouver: University of British Columbia Press, 1993), 29.

6. Quoted in Melvin H. Smith, *Our Home or Native Land?* (Toronto: Stoddart, 1995), 97.

7. Ibid., 143.

8. Donald Purich, *Our Land: Native Rights in Canada* (Toronto: James Lorimer & Company, 1986), 46.

9. George Erasmus and Joe Sanders, 'Canadian History: An Aboriginal Perspective', in Diane Engelstad and John Bird, eds, *Nation to Nation: Aboriginal Sovereignty and the Future of Canada* (Concord, Ont.: House of Anansi Press, 1992), 6.

10. Ibid., 8.

11. Cumming and Mickenberg, eds, *Native Rights in Canada*, 41.

12. Smith, *Our Home or Native Land?*, 47.

13. For example, *St Catherine's Milling and Lumber Company v. The Queen* (1888), 14 A.C. 46 (JCPC); *Regina v. White and Bob* (1965), 50 D.L.R. (2d) 613; *Calder et al. v. Attorney-General of British Columbia* (1973), S.C.R. 313, 4 W.W.R. 1.

14. Quoted in Cumming and Mickenberg, eds, *Native Rights in Canada*, 17.

15. Ibid., 18. Emphasis added.

16. See excerpts from this ruling in David De Brou and Bill Waiser, eds, *Documenting Canada: A History of Modern Canada in Documents* (Saskatoon: Fifth House Publishers, 1992), 158.

17. Quoted ibid., 572.

18. Ibid.

19. Ibid., 595.

20. Ibid., 665. Section 35(1) of the Constitution Act, 1982, recognizes and affirms Aboriginal and treaty rights existing as of 1982.

21. Ibid., 666.

22. Cumming and Mickenberg, eds, *Native Rights in Canada*, 55.

23. Ibid.

24. Erasmus and Sanders, 'Canadian History', 3.

25. Ibid., 4.

26. Cumming and Mickenberg, eds, *Native Rights in Canada*, 58.

27. Quoted ibid., 61–2.

28. Quoted in Purich, *Our Land*, 110.

29. Cumming and Mickenberg, eds, *Native Rights in Canada*, 53.

30. Roger Gibbins and J. Rick Ponting, 'Historical Overview and Background', in J. Rick Ponting, ed., *Arduous Journey: Canadian Indians and Decolonization* (Toronto: McClelland & Stewart, 1988), 30.

31. Purich, *Our Land*, 109. Emphasis added.

32. These examples are taken from a long list found in Smith, *Our Home or Native Land?*, 110–11.

33. Department of Indian Affairs and Northern Development, *Basic Departmental Data 1996* (Ottawa: Supply and Services Canada, Jan. 1997), 93.

34. Ibid., 122.

35. Thomas R. Berger, *Northern Frontier, Northern Homeland: The Report of the Mackenzie Valley Pipeline Inquiry*, vol. 1 (Ottawa: Minister of Supply and Services, 1977), 118.

36. See, for example, Murray Angus, *And the Last Shall Be First: Native Policy in an Era of Cutbacks* (Toronto: NC Press, 1991).

37. Canada, Department of Indian Affairs and Northern Development, 'Statement on Claims of Indian and Inuit People', press release, Aug. 1973.
38. Quoted in John Greenwood, 'This Land', *The Financial Post Magazine* (Mar. 1993): 17.
39. The recommendations of this task force are summarized in Angus, *And the Last Shall Be First*.
40. These are the words used in the James Bay and Northern Quebec Native Claim Settlement Act, 1977.
41. Harold Cardinal, *The Unjust Society* (Edmonton: Hurtig, 1969), 1.
42. See Leslie A. Pal, *Interests of State* (Montreal and Kingston: McGill-Queen's University Press, 1993).
43. See De Brou and Waiser, eds, *Documenting Canada*, 540.
44. Pierre Trudeau, *Federalism and the French Canadians* (Toronto: McClelland & Stewart, 1969), 151.
45. Pierre Trudeau and Thomas Axworthy, *Towards the Just Society: The Trudeau Years* (Toronto: Viking, 1990), 364.
46. Frank Cassidy, ed., *Aboriginal Self-Determination* (Halifax: Institute of Research on Public Policy, 1991).
47. Renée Dupuis and Kent McNeil, *Canada's Fiduciary Obligation to Aboriginal Peoples in the Context of Accession to Sovereignty by Quebec*, vol. 2, *Domestic Dimensions* (Ottawa: Minister of Supply and Services Canada, 1995), 57–8.
48. Ibid., 66.
49. Ibid., 65.

Chapter 9

1. The *Fontana Dictionary of Modern Thought*, p. 150, provides this anthropological definition of culture: 'The "social heritage" of a community: the total body of material artifacts . . . of collective mental and spiritual "artifacts" . . . and of distinctive forms of behaviour . . . created by a people (sometimes deliberately, sometimes through unforeseen interconnections and consequences) in their ongoing activities within their particular life-conditions, and (through undergoing kinds and degrees of change) transmitted from generation to generation.'
2. Royal Commission on Bilingualism and Biculturalism, *The Cultural Contribution of the Other Ethnic Groups*, Book IV of the Final Report (Ottawa: Queen's Printer, 1970).
3. Duplessis's policy was in fact one that invited this domination, especially by American capital, through low taxation of resource-based corporations and legislation hostile to labour unions.
4. Victor Barbeau, *Mesure de notre taille* (1936); Jacques Melançon, 'Retard de croissance de l'entreprise canadienne-française', *L'Actualité Économique* (jan.-mars 1956): 503–22.
5. Lois du Québec, 1974, c. 6.
6. Lois du Québec, 1977, c. 5.
7. See *Attorney-General of Quebec v. Blaikie* (1979), in Peter H. Russell, *Leading*

Constitutional Decisions, 3rd edn (Ottawa: Carleton University Press, 1982), 460–8.

8. *Ford v. Attorney-General of Quebec* (1988), Supreme Court of Canada.

9. Calvin Veltman, 'Assessing the Effects of Quebec's Language Legislation', *Canadian Public Policy* 12, 2 (June 1986): 314–19. Veltman observes that the effectiveness of Bill 101 in promoting the use of French among the children of immigrants varies considerably among ethnic groups.

10. See the discussion of these economic initiatives in Kenneth McRoberts, *Quebec: Social Change and Political Crisis*, 3rd edn (Toronto: McClelland & Stewart, 1988), 132–5.

11. Eric Waddell, 'State, Language and Society: The Vicissitudes of French in Quebec and Canada', in Alan Cairns and Cynthia Williams, eds, *The Politics of Gender, Ethnicity and Language in Canada*, vol. 34 of the research studies for the Macdonald Commission (Toronto: University of Toronto Press, 1985), 97.

12. Raymond Breton, 'The Production and Allocation of Symbolic Resources: An Analysis of the Linguistic and Ethnocultural Fields in Canada', *Canadian Review of Sociology and Anthropology* 21, 2 (1980): 129.

13. Commissioner of Official Languages, *Annual Report 1985* (Ottawa: Supply and Services, 1986), 50. Emphasis added.

14. 'Francophones in the National Capital Region represent over 35 per cent of the Public Service population but, on average, they work more than 60 per cent of their time in English. In bilingual areas of Ontario the corresponding figures are 23 per cent and 66 per cent; roughly one-quarter of all employees are thus working two-thirds of their time in their second language.' Ibid., 54.

15. *Attorney-General of Manitoba v. Forest* (1979), 2 S.C.R. 1032; *Reference on the Constitution Act, 1867, and the Manitoba Act, 1870*, 13 June 1985 decision of the Supreme Court.

16. *Attorney-General of Quebec v. Quebec Association of Protestant School Boards* (1984), 10 D.L.R. (4th) 321, judgement rendered on 26 July 1984; January 1985 decision of the Quebec Superior Court.

17. In 1985 the Progressive Conservative government broadened the scope of this program to include more of the areas covered by the Charter of Rights and Freedoms, with an emphasis on the Equality Rights section. The program later was cancelled by the Tory government for a few years, but it has since been reinstituted.

18. These figures are from the Commissioner of Official Languages, *Annual Report 1985*, 227–8, App. B.4.

19. Ibid., 172.

20. Ibid., 167, Table V.4.

21. Waddell, 'State, Language and Society', 101.

22. R. Beaujot, 'The Decline of Official Language Minorities in Quebec and English Canada', *Canadian Journal of Sociology* 7, 4 (Fall 1982): 373–5.

23. Cited in Waddell, 'State, Language and Society', 97.

24. Max Yalden, 'French Immersion: A Canadian Experience', *Language and Society* 12, 3 (Winter 1984).

25. The Honourable Thomas R. Berger, 'Towards the Regime of Tolerance', in Stephen Brooks, ed., *Political Thought in Canada* (Toronto: Irwin, 1984), 84.

26. Khayyam Paltiel, 'Group Rights in the Canadian Constitution and Aboriginal Claims to Self-determination', in Robert Jackson, Doreen Jackson, and Nicolas Baxter-Moore, eds, *Contemporary Canadian Politics* (Toronto: Prentice-Hall, 1987), 26–43.

27. Nathan Glazer and Daniel P. Moynihan, eds, *Ethnicity* (Cambridge, Mass.: Harvard University Press, 1975), 30.

28. This function of culture is described in Harold R. Isaacs, *Idols of the Tribe: Group Identity and Political Change* (New York: Harper and Row, 1975).

29. Raymond Breton, 'Multiculturalism and Canadian Nation-Building', in Cairns and Williams, eds, *Politics of Gender, Ethnicity and Language*, 30.

30. Ibid., 30–1.

31. Ibid., 49.

32. John Jaworsky, 'A Case Study of the Canadian Federal Government's Multiculturalism Policy', MA thesis (Carleton University, 1979), 59.

33. The studies are cited in Breton, 'Multiculturalism and Canadian Nation-Building', 45–6.

34. Multiculturalism and Citizenship Canada, *The Canadian Multiculturalism Act: A Guide for Canadians* (Ottawa: Minister of Supply and Services, 1990).

35. Heritage Canada, Corporate Review Branch, *Strategic Evaluation of Multiculturalism Programs: Final Report* (Ottawa: Heritage Canada, Mar. 1996), 50.

36. See the studies done for the Special Parliamentary Committee on Visible Minorities in Canadian Society, 1984.

37. Public Service Commission, *Annual Report 1991*.

38. Anthony G. Dworkin and Rosalind J. Dworkin, *The Minority Report* (New York: Praeger, 1976), 17.

39. Thomas Flanagan, 'The Manufacture of Minorities', in Neil Nevitte and Allan Kornberg, eds, *Minorities and the Canadian State* (Oakville, Ont.: Mosaic Press, 1985), 119.

40. See the discussion in Leslie A. Pal, *Interests of State* (Montreal: McGill-Queen's University Press, 1993), ch. 7.

Chapter 10

1. Quoted in Walter H. Carson, *The Global Ecology Handbook* (Boston: Beacon Press, 1990), 1.

2. Rachel Carson, *Silent Spring* (Boston: Houghton Mifflin, 1962).

3. Environment Canada, *The State of Canada's Environment—1991* (Ottawa: Supply and Services, 1991), 1–7.

4. Garret Hardin, 'The Tragedy of the Commons', *Science* 162 (1968): 1243.

5. Theodore D. Goldfarb, *Taking Sides: Clashing Views on Controversial Environmental Issues*, 4th edn (Guilford, Conn.: Dushkin Publishing Group, 1991).

6. World Commission on Environment and Development, *Our Common Future* (Oxford: Oxford University Press, 1987).

7. Ibid., 9–10.

8. Angus Reid, commenting on the results of the poll done for the Southam Environment Project, autumn 1990.

9. Glen Toner, 'The Canadian Environmental Movement: A Conceptual Map', Carleton University, unpublished paper, 1991, 4.

10. John Kingdon, *Agendas, Alternatives, and Public Policies* (Boston: Little, Brown, 1984).

11. Paul R. Ehrlich, *The Population Bomb* (New York: Ballantine Books, 1969).

12. Dennis L. Meadows et al., *The Limits to Growth* (New York: New American Library, 1972).

13. The post-materialist hypothesis was first laid out in Ronald Inglehart, *The Silent Revolution* (Princeton, NJ: Princeton University Press, 1977).

14. Ibid., 3.

15. Ibid., 43–50.

16. Glen Toner, 'Whence and Whither: ENGOs, Business and the Environment', unpublished paper, Oct. 1990, 3.

17. Jurg Steiner, *European Democracies* (New York: Longman, 1986), 40.

18. Richard Liroff, *A National Policy for the Environment* (Bloomington: Indiana University Press, 1976), 12.

19. Task Force on Program Review, *Environment* (Ottawa: Supply and Services, 1985), 27.

20. *Globe and Mail*, 15 Apr. 1989, section D.

21. George Hoberg, 'Representation and Governance in Canadian Environmental Policy', paper presented at McMaster University, 26 Oct. 1991, 5.

22. Task Force on Program Review, *Environment*.

23. Environment Canada, *Canada's Green Plan: The First Year* (Ottawa: Supply and Services, 1991), 1.

24. Quoted in David Israelson, *Silent Earth: The Politics of Our Survival* (Toronto: Viking, 1990), 212.

25. Ibid. Israelson provides examples of this throughout his book.

26. Jeremy Wilson, 'Wilderness Politics in BC: the Business-Dominated State and the Containment of Environmentalism', in William D. Coleman and Grace Skogstad, *Policy Communities and Public Policy in Canada* (Toronto: Copp Clark Pitman, 1990), 154–62.

27. *Canadian Wildlife Federation v. Canada (Minister of the Environment)* 4 C.E.L.R. (NS) I; *Friends of the Oldman River Society v. Canada (Minister of Transport)*, Federal Court of Appeal, 13 March 1991; *Canadian Wildlife Federation et al. v. Minister of the Environment*, 4 C.E.L.R. (NS).

28. Patricia Lusk, 'Full Review Ordered on $1-Billion Project', *Globe and Mail*, 17 May 1991.

29. 'Survey of Australia', *The Economist*, 4 Apr. 1992, 10.

30. Israelson, *Silent Earth*, 169.

31. Hoberg, 'Representation and Governance in Canadian Environmental Policy', 21–7.

32. The phenomenon was first labelled by a British chemist, Robert Angus, who published a voluminous study of the effects of industrial pollution in Manchester, England, on precipitation in that area.

33. M. Firket, 'The Causes of Accidents which Occurred in the Meuse Valley During the Fogs of December 1930', cited in Jon. R. Luoma, 'The Human Cost of Acid Rain', *Audubon* (July 1988): 17.

34. Environment Canada, *The State of Canada's Environment—1991* (Ottawa: Supply and Services, 1991), 24–8, figure 24.4.

35. This estimate is cited in Environment Canada, *The State of Canada's Environment —1991*, 24–7.

36. Figures according to the World Resources Institute, cited in 'The World through Green-tinted Specs', *The Economist*, 19 May 1990, 52.

37. Environment Canada, *The State of Canada's Environment—1991*, 10–15.

38. Peter P. Swire, 'Tropical Chic', in Steven Anzovin, ed., *Preserving the World Ecology* (New York: H.W. Wilson, 1990), 164.

39. According to estimates from the World Resources Institute, Washington, DC, cited in 'Green Diplomacy', *The Economist*, 16 June 1990, 17.

40. See Kathryn Harrison, *Passing the Buck: Federalism and Canadian Environmental Policy* (Vancouver: University of British Columbia Press, 1997).

41. Mark Sagoff, 'Do We Consume Too Much?', *Atlantic Monthly* (June 1997): 80–96.

42. Quoted ibid., 92.

43. Quoted ibid., 87.

44. Ibid., 90.

45. Ibid., 96.

46. Quoted ibid.

47. Ibid.

Index

Note: Page numbers followed by 'f' denote a figure.
Page numbers followed by 't' denote a table.

Aboriginal policy, 183–217; comprehensive claims, 202–5; defining 'Indian', 184–6; dependency and assimilation, 206; integration and equality, 206–10; landownership, 189–200; language and culture, 187–8; and the law, 189–200; as paternalistic, 184, 188–9, 207; population size, 186–8, 187f; principles underlying, 205–14; and Quebec, 214–16; reserve system, 188–9; rights, 62; self-government, 205, 213–14; sovereignty, 189–200; specific claims, 200–2; treaty land entitlements, 200. *See also* Indian Act; Royal Commission on Aboriginal Peoples; White Paper (1969)
accumulated federal debt, 108; criticisms of, 108–9
accumulation policies, 34
Agenda for Jobs and Growth: Improving Social Security in Canada (Liberal government), 133
Allen, Doug, 137
American Library Association, 163
Amiel, Barbara, 153
Anderson, Elijah, 172
Angus, Murray, 202
Arctic Waters Pollution Prevention Act, 252, 260
Atkinson, Michael, 25
Audubon, Thomas, 247
Audubon Society, 246
'automatic punishing recoil', 28, 34
Auto Pact, 118

Baker Lake et al. v. Minister of Indian Affairs (1980), 195
balance of payments, 111–13
Bank of Canada, 99, 105–6
Banting, Keith, 117
Beenstock, Michael, 104
Berger, Thomas E., 203–4, 228
Berger Inquiry, 203–4

bilingualism: official, 227–8, 231–3; in the public service, 224–6, 225f, 226f; in society, 226–7. *See also* language policy
Bill 101 (Quebec), 221–2, 226
Bill 178 (Quebec), 13, 222
Blinder, Alan, 92
Bliss, Michael, 54
Block, Fred, 36
Boadway, Robin, 148
Boltho, Andrea, 102
Boom, Bust, and Echo (Foot), 156
Boothe, Paul, 144
Bouchard, Lucien, 253
Bouey, Gerald, 106
Bradshaw, John, 160
Breton, Raymond, 5, 13, 223, 230, 231
British Columbia, Ministry of Forests Act and Forest Act, 258
British North America (BNA) Act, 1867, 45, 47–8, 59, 185, 220
Bronfenbrenner, Urie, 173
Brundtland Commission, 243–4, 253–4, 256
Brunner, Karl, 90
Buchanan, James M., 28, 29, 32
Buchanan, Pat, 153
bureaucracy, role of, 69–70
bureaucratic personality, 78–9
business cycles, 87, 93–7; intermediate, 87, 93–4; long, 93, 94–6; political, 94, 97; short, 93–4
business power, 28
Byfield, Ted, 153

Cairns, Alan, 42, 49, 50–1, 57
Calder et al. v. Attorney-General of British Columbia (1973), 191, 194–5, 204
California Children of Divorce, 171
Callwood, June, 162
Camp Ipperwash, 183–4
Canada Assistance Plan. *See* Canada Health and Social Transfer program
Canada Health Act, 138, 144

Canada Health and Social Transfer program, 132, 135, 143
Canada Pension Plan/Quebec Pension Plan (CPP/QPP), 128–9
Canada Shipping Act, 260
Canada-US Free Trade Agreement. *See* FTA
Canada-US International Joint Commission, 264
Canada Water Act, 252, 260
Canadian Climate Program, 256
Canadian Environmental Assessment Act, 1994, 259
Canadian Environmental Protection Act, 1988, 261–2, 268
Canadian Forestry Association, 247
Canadian Global Change Program, 256
Canadian International Development Agency, 256
Canadian Medical Association, Task Force on the Allocation of Health Care Resources, 1984, 142
Canadian Wildlife Federation, 259
Capitalism, Socialism and Democracy (Schumpeter), 26
capitalist system, 35–6, 104; Marxist theory, 33–6
capital markets, and policy-making, 55
Cardinal, Harold, 207, 209
Carson, Rachel, 238, 248
CBC (Canadian Broadcasting Corporation), 57, 233
Chandler, Marsha, 25
Charlottetown Accord, 1992, 5, 52; Aboriginal peoples, 215; referendum, 51
Charter of Rights and Freedoms: Aboriginal policy, 185, 192, 196; Bill 178, 13, 222; and family policy, 165; multiculturalism, 229, 231; and policy making, 50–2
Child Tax Benefits, 181
Choice of Governing Instrument, The, (Trebilcock), 31
Chrétien, Jean, 220, 267
Clean Air Act: Canada, 252, 260–1; Great Britain, 246; United States, 252, 263
cleavages, 26
Clinton, Hillary Rodham, 162, 163–5, 177, 179
Club of Rome, 248, 250, 252, 268
collectivist ideology, 9
communication gap, and world-view, 40
comparative advantage, theory of, 114–15
complexity of joint action, 77
constitution, 47–52

Constitution Act, 1867. *See* British North America (BNA) Act, 1867
Constitution Act, 1982, 47, 186, 202, 215, 229
contextual influences, on policy-making, 43–65, 43t
Convention on the Conservation of Wetlands of International Importance, 264
Convention on the Protection of the World Cultural and Natural Heritage, 264
Cooper, Andrew, 63
Cooper ruling, 199
co-optation. *See* policy implementation
corporate head offices, distribution of, 59t
Courchene, Thomas, 13, 129
'Court Party', 51
Crittenden, Danielle, 177
Crow, John, 106
cultural policy, 15; *See also* language policy; multicultural policy
cultural sovereignty, 118
culture: Aboriginal, 187–8; Americanization of, as global phenomenon, 56–7; definition of, 218; and multiculturalism, 229; organizational, 80–2; political, 80–2
Cumming, Peter A., 185, 192, 198, 199
currently, and market prices, 241, 242
cyclical deficit, definition of, 107

Dafoe Whitehead, Barbara, 153, 162, 170, 171, 173, 175, 180
Dahl, Robert, 26–7
Daly, Herman, 238
Daly, Martin, 173
Darwin, Charles, 22–3
deep ecology, environmental management model, 239, 240t
Delgamuukw v. Attorney-General of British Columbia, 196–7
demand economy. *See* market economy
Department of Fisheries and Oceans, 256
Department of Foreign Affairs and International Trade (DFAIT), 63–4
Dion, Léon, 42
Divorce Act, 128, 156
Dodge, D., 145
Doern, G. Bruce, 25, 42, 60–1, 62, 64
Duplessis, Maurice, 219, 220
Dupuis, Renée, 215
Dye, Thomas, 2

EARP. *See* Environmental Assessment and Review Process (EARP)

Earth Summit 1992, 254, 265, 267

Easton, David, 24; model of politics, 24t, 42

Economic Council of Canada, 98

economic efficiency: family policy, 169; public choice theory, 32

economic policy, and globalization, 17

economic stabilization policy. *See* macroeconomic policy

Economist, The, 15, 153, 172

Edelman, Murray, 5

Egan v. Canada, 176–7

Eggebeen, David, 170–1

Ehrenfeld, David, 269

Ehrlich, Paul, 248, 268

Eichler, Margrit, 153, 155, 165, 167–9, 172, 175

Eisenhower, Dwight D., 77

Elshtain, Jean Bethke, 164

embedded state, 42

Emerson, Ralph Waldo, 247

employment insurance (EI), 128, 132; net transfers by industry, 133f

Emson, H.E., 141

End of Affluence, The, (Ehrlich), 268

environment: definition of, 239–40; as public policy issue, 245–6, 246f

Environmental Assessment and Review Process (EARP), 258; Guidelines Order, 258–9

Environmental Contaminants Act, 260–1

environmentalism: Amazon deforestation, 253; Bhopal, India chemical leak, 253; Chernobyl meltdown, 253; Earth Day, 253; *Exxon Valdez* oil spill, 253; greenhouse effect, 253; Green Parties, 249–50, 254; green society model, 239–40; homeless garbage, 253; ozone layer over Antarctica, 253; resource management model, 239; sustainable development model, 239–40; world population growth, 251f. *See also* environmental policy

environmental policy, 238–70; environmental assessment, 257–60; management models, 240t; politics, 249–55; pollution, 260–2; problems, 243–8; Task Force on Program Review 1985, 84–5, 253, 255; transboundary environmental problems, 262–8. *See also* Brundtland Commission; environmentalism; Environment Canada; Green Plan

Environmental Protection Agency (US), 245, 252

Environment Canada, 245, 252, 253, 255–6, 263

Erasmus, George, 191, 192, 198, 209, 213

Established Programs Fiscal Arrangements Act (EPF), 142–3

Etzioni, Amitai, 172

executive federalism, 50

exhaustive expenditures, definition, 9

externalities, definition of, 242

Fabian socialism, 16

family: definition of, 156–7; size of, 157

family income, 158–60; index of, after tax, 148f; index of, before transfers, 147f

family policy, 152–83; backlash, 152–3; in Canadian society, 156–60; child poverty, 170–1; collectivist model, 161–9; common-law households, 157, 158; day care versus home care, 177–9; and divorce, 179–81; economic goals, 155; family structure, 160–75; guaranteed income, 181–2; individual responsibility model, 165, 166–7t, 167; infant health, 163; marriage breakdown, 163–4; nuclear family, 169–70; options, 175–82; and parenting, 163; patriarchal family, 165, 168t; personal responsibility model, 169–75; same-sex couples, 176–7; single-parent families, 156, 157, 170, 172; and social conservatism, 153; social responsibility model, 166–7t, 167; step-families, 173; traditional and nontraditional, 157, 165; working mothers, 158

Federal Contractor's Program, 235

federal government: accumulated debt, 108–9; deficit 1980–96, 109f

federalism, 49–50, 59

Fisheries Act, 260

Fisheries Resource Conservation Council, 256

Flanagan, Thomas, 236

Flatters, Frank, 148

Flavel, Blaine, 213

Fontaine, Phil, 190

Foot, David, 142, 156

foreign investment, US, in Canada, 53–5

foreign ownership, in Canada, 54–5

foreign policy, definition, 63–5

Forestry Canada, 256

Forget Commission, 1986, 132–3

Fortier, D'Iberville, 225–6
fragment theory, 44
Freeman, Alan, 82
free trade, arguments for and against, 115–19
Frey, Bruno, 97
Friedman, Milton, 88, 89–90, 92, 93, 106
frontier economics, environmental
    management model, 240t
Frum, David, 153
FTA (Canada-US Free Trade Agreement),
    55–6, 62, 114, 116–17, 119, 266
Fuchs, Victor, 173

Galbraith, John Kenneth, 105
GATT (General Agreement on Tariffs and
    Trade), 55, 118
Gendron Commission, 1972, 221
General Agreement on Tariffs and Trade. *See*
    GATT
*General Theory of Employment, Interest and
    Money* (Keynes), 87
Gillespie, W. Irwin, 144, 145
Glendon, Mary Ann, 16, 180
globalization, 14–17, 43, 60–5; and
    economic policy, 17; information and
    culture, 15; of investment capital, 54–5;
    technology and culture, 61
global village, 249
Globe and Mail, The, 254
Goods and Services Tax (GST), 145
Gordon, David, 95
Gosnell, James, 190
government: and business confidence, 34–5;
    and control of policy agenda, 7; and
    subordinate classes, 36
governmentalizaton of society, 42
Government Organization Act, 258; criticism
    of, 258–9
Great Depression, 91, 98
Green Party, Germany, 250
Green Plan: Canada 1990, 254, 255–6, 261.
    See also environmental policy
green society, environmental management
    model, 239, 240t
Guaranteed Income Supplement (GIS), 128–9
Gwyn, Sandra, 81

Hall, Emmett, 195
Hansen, Alvin, 95
Hardin, Garret, 241
Hart, Betty, 163
Hartz, Louis, 44
Harvard Institute for International

Development, 60
Harvey, Harold, 256
health policy, 140; national standards, 143–4;
    public share in total expenditure, 139t
Heilbroner, Robert, 27
Helms-Burton law, 54
Helsinki Protocol, 264
Hobbes, Thomas, 31
Hoberg, George, 254
Horowitz, Gad, 44
House of Commons, Standing Committee on
    Finance, Trade, and Economic Affairs,
    106

immigrants, countries of birth, 234t
implementation. *See* policy implementation
income distribution, for families, 150t
income redistribution, and tax system, 12
Indian Act, 185, 186, 187, 199; definition of
    reserves, 188–9; proposed revisions,
    212–13
individual, and market prices, 241
individual choice: public choice theory, 32;
    theory of, 28
Inglehart, Ronald, 249
institutional fairness, public choice theory,
    32
Inter-American Development Bank, 267
International Boundary Treaties Act, 260
internationalization, 43; of policy discourse,
    62–3
International Monetary Fund, 267
Irwin, Ron, 212
Isaacs, Harold R., 229
Israelson, David, 256
*It Takes a Village, and Other Lessons
    Children Teach Us* (Clinton), 162

Jackson, Doreen, 25
Jackson, Robert, 25
Johnson, Lyndon, 125
Judicial Committee of the Privy Council, 49,
    192, 194

Kaldor, Nicholas, 100
Kalecki, Michael, 97
Keynes, John Maynard, 16, 20–1, 87
Keynesianism, 16–17, 20–1, 89–92, 99;
    challenges to, 89–91; paradigm, 89
Kindleberger, C.P., 100
Kingdon, John, 247
Kirton, John, 64
Kondratieff, Nikolai, 95

Kondratieff long waves, 95
Kyoto Protocol, 1997, 264, 266–7

labour force participation, and families with children, 159f
Lamarck, Jean, 20
Lamontagne, Maurice, 95–6
language policy, 8, 178, 218, 219–28; demographic trends, 221; French immersion education, 227–8; origins of, 219–20; in Quebec, 220–3. *See also* bilingualism; Bill 101; Bill 178
left-versus-right ideological debate, 9
legitimation policies, 34
Leontief, Wassily, 89
Lesage, Jean, 223
Lewis, W. Arthur, 100
Liberal government, 99, 133
liberal ideology, and socialization, 35
Liberal Party, Red Book 1993, 99
liberal-pluralism, 25
Lichter, Daniel, 170–1
Limits to Growth, The, (Club of Rome), 248, 250, 268
Lindblom, Charles, 27–8, 34
Living Treaties: Lasting Agreements, 205
Lowi, Theodore, 27
low-income cut-off lines (LICOs), 126, 128
Lucas, Robert, 91

McCue, Harvey, 189
Macdonald, Sir John A., 59, 114
Macdonald Commission, 1985, 132–3
McLanahan, Sara, 170, 171, 173, 174
McNeil, Kent, 214–15
McRae, Kenneth, 44
macroeconomic policy, 86–119; and budget deficits, 98; critics of, 99; deficit and the economy, 107–11; definition of, 86–7; economic conditions 1970s–90s, 100–11; economic growth and government spending 1950–79, 103f; external dimensions, 111–13; goals of, 97–111; international context, 113–19; inventory cycle, 93–4; Keynesianism, 16, 87–9; Keynesian stabilization policy, 97–8; monetarism, 89–91, 92, 105–6; new classical economics, 91–2; protectionism, 114–15; tariffs, 114; and trade, 111–13; trends in OECD economies, 101–2t. *See also* business cycles
Madill, Judith, 181
Malthus, Thomas, 248

Mandel, Ernest, 102
market economy: characteristics of, 27–8; and Marxism, 33–4
'Market as Prison, The', (Lindblom), 27
Marshall, John, 193–4
Martin, Paul, Jr, 134, 143, 178
Marx, Karl, 22–3, 33
Marxist theory, 25; capitalist system, 33–6; and class conflict, 22, 33, 37; critics of, 23, 33; of policy formation, 33, 35; world-view, 22, 33
mass media, and policy discourse, 6–7
Meech Lake Accord, 1987, 5; failure of, 13–14, 51–2; and Quebec, 13
Mendel, Gregor Johann, 20
Mercredi, Ovide, 191, 202, 209, 212
Merton, Robert K., 78–9
methodological individualism, 29
methods, and theories of public policy, 23–4
Mickenberg, Neil H., 185, 192, 198, 199
microeconomic theory, 28–9
Miliband, Ralph, 36
minority: definition of, 236. *See also* multicultural policy
Modegliani, Franco, 92
Molot, Maureen Appel, 113
Monde diplomatique, Le, 61
monetarism. *See* macroeconomic policy
Montreal Protocol, 254, 263, 265, 267
Morin, Claude, 57
Morton, Ted, 51–2
Mowat, Oliver, 59
Moynihan, Daniel Patrick, 153, 161, 172
Muir, John, 247
Mulroney government, 98
multiculturalism, and visible minorities, 233–7
Multiculturalism Act, 1988, 231
multicultural policy, 228–37; and Charter of Rights and Freedoms, 229, 231; criticisms of, 232; and employment equity policies, 235; federal financing of, 232–3; and politicization of ethnicity, 229–30; and symbolism and substance, 230–3

NAFTA (North American Free Trade Agreement), 55–6, 62, 116–17, 119, 266
Nakamura, Robert, 71
National Child Care Survey, 158
National Child Development Study (Great Britain), 173
National Council of Welfare, 127, 143, 145, 160, 175

National Film Board, 57, 233
National Museum of Civilization, 233
National Parks Association, 247
Native Rights in Canada (Cumming and Mickenberg), 192
Nevitte, Neil, 15
new classical economics. *See* macroeconomic policy
New Framework for Economic Policy, A, (Liberal government), 99
Newsweek magazine, 61
North American Free Trade Agreement. *See* NAFTA
Nunavut agreement, 202, 204–5, 214

OAS (Old Age Security), 128
O'Connor, James, 121–2
OECD (Organization for Economic Co-operation and Development), 88
Official Languages Act, 1969, 221, 223–4
Oka crisis, 183–4
Old Age Security (OAS), 128
Olson, Mancur, 100
Organization for Economic Co-operation and Development (OECD), 88
Our Common Future (Brundtland Commission), 253–4
Our Home or Native Land? (Smith), 192

Pal, Leslie A., 63, 65, 76, 81–2
Paltiel, Khayyam, 229
patriarchal ideology, family policy, 165, 168t
Pearson, Lester, 223
pension programs, 130–1t
Perot, Ross, 116
Phidd, Richard, 25
Phillips, A.W., 88
Phillips Curve, 88
Planck, Max, 41
Plato, 154–5
pluralism, 25–8, 37; critics of, 27; and world-view, 22, 29
policy, definition of, 2–3, 68
policy discourse, 6–8; internationalization of, 62–3
policy implementation, 69–77; administrators of, 78–9; bureaucractic rationality, 74; client agencies, 80; communication, 74–6; co-optation, 80; definition of, 67–9, 69; and delivery problems, 76–7; democratic dilemmas, 69–70; efficiency dilemmas, 70–1; evaluation of, 82–5;

instrument choice, 71, 72–4; and organizational culture, 80–2; political rationality, 73–4; problems of, 77–85; rational-hierarchical model, 71–2, 72f; and special interest groups, 80; technical expertise system, 70–1; technical rationality, 73; turf and autonomy, 79
policy instruments: changing mix of, 64–5; choice of, 10–11; tax system as, 10–11
policy-makers, 17; decline of deference, 15; and social policy, 122–3
policy-making: and Cabinet, 50; contextual influences on, 43–65; economic characteristics, 52–60; élitist style, 15–16; foreign and domestic, 63–5; interest groups, 63; political culture, 43–7; regionalism, 44–5; social characteristics, 52–60; stages of, 68f. *See also* Charlottetown Accord; Meech Lake Accord
policy objectives, and public policy, 11
policy process, and public choice, 30f
policy sciences movement, 16
political agenda, 5–6
political culture, 43–7
political economy. *See* public choice theory
Politics and Markets (Lindblom), 27
politics of recognition, 14
pollution: environmental policy, 260–2; as public policy issue, 246f
polyarchy, 52; democracy as, 26–7
Popenoe, David, 162, 169–70, 173, 174, 180
Population Bomb, The, (Ehrlich), 248
post-materialism, 16
poverty: definition, 125–6; feminization of, 127
poverty line, 160; defined by Statistics Canada, 126; income by family type, 160f; single-parent families, 170; welfare income as percentage of, 1996, 127t
poverty trap, definition of, 137
power, as transactional property, 31
PPPS. *See* purchasing power parities (PPPS)
Pressman, Jeffrey, 76–7
Priorities and Planning Committee, 253
Priority Substance List, 261–2
programs. *See* policy implementation
progressivism, 16
protected society, 13
protectionism, 114–15, 118
provincialism, in policy-making, 57–60
proximate influences, on policy-making, 43t
Public Accounts of Canada, 8, 13

public choice theory, 24, 25, 28–32; ideology in, 32; individualism as criterion of, 28; institutional fairness, 32; and policy process, 30f; world-view, 29
public pension programs, 130–1t
public policy: agenda and discourse of, 5–8; definition of, 2–3; determination of, 3–4; methods of studying, 23; quantitative and qualitative approaches, 23; relevance of studying, 17–18; scope of, 8–10; theories of, 19–41. *See also* policy-making
public-sector debt, 108; as percentage of GDP and OECD average 1980–96, 110f
Public Service Commission, 235
purchasing power parities (PPPs), 123; health spending in, 141f; per capita OECD countries, 1994, 124f
Purich, Donald, 191, 200

quality of life (QOL), 123, 269–70
Quayle, Dan, 153
Quebec: identification of French Canada with, 220–1; referendum, 1995, 214; sovereignty and Aboriginal policy, 214–16
Quebec Royal Commission of Inquiry on the Position of the French Language and Language Rights in Quebec. *See* Gendron Commission
Quebec vs. Ottawa (Morin), 57
Quiet Revolution, 219, 220–1, 223

rational expectations school. *See* new classical economics
rational-hierarchical model: communication, 74–6; delivery, 76–7; instrument choice, 72–4; of policy-making, 71–2, 72f
rattrapage, ideology of, 220–1
Reagan, Ronald, 253, 257
redistribution of wealth: among individuals, 12; between regions, 12; function of the state, 9; social policy, 144–9; and tax system, 12
Reed, Ralph, 153
Regina v. Cooper (1969), 199
Regina v. Sparrow (1990), 195–6
regionalism, in policy-making, 44–5, 57–60
Reich, Robert, 61
Report of the Mackenzie Valley Pipeline Inquiry. *See* Berger Inquiry
Report of the Royal Commission on Banking and Finance, 98
Resnick, Philip, 45–6

resource management, environmental management model, 239, 240t
Riel, Louis, 190
'rights talk', 16, 51
Risley, Todd, 163
Roberts, Charles G.D., 247
Royal Commission of Inquiry on Unemployment Insurance. *See* Forget Commission (1986)
Royal Commission on Aboriginal Peoples, 209, 211–14, 215
Royal Commission on Banking and Finance, 98
Royal Commission on Bilingualism and Biculturalism, 218, 223, 231
Royal Commission on the Economic Union and Development Prospects for Canada. *See* Macdonald Commission (1985)
Royal Proclamation, 1763, 191–2, 194; excerpts from, 216–17

Sachs, Jeffrey, 61
Sagoff, Mark, 268–9
St Catherine's Milling and Lumber Company v. The Queen, 192, 194
Samuelson, Paul, 93, 94, 97
Sandefur, Gary, 170, 171
Sanders, Joe, 198
Schattschneider, E.E., 26
Schoenborn, Charlotte, 171
Schumpeter, Joseph, 26, 95
Sechelt Indian Band Self-Government Act (1986), 213
Selznick, Philip, 79, 80
service-sector employment, 128, 137
Seton, Ernest Thompson, 247
Sierra Club, 246
Silent Spring (Carson), 238–9, 245, 248
Simeon, Richard, 24, 50
Smallwood, Frank, 71
Smiley, Donald, 52
Smith, Adam, 240
Smith, Melvin, 192, 201–2
Smythe, Elizabeth, 54
social assistance, 128, 134–6, 143; caseloads of working-age population, 136f
social policy, 120–51; health care system, 138–44; health spending per person in PPPs, 141f; income security system, 127–37; public spending on health, 139–41; redistribution, 144–9; social need, 125–7; spending on, 128. *See also* welfare state

social spending, 121; cuts to, 118; unemployment insurance, 121; working-age transfers as percentage of GDP 1992, 122f
Solow, Robert, 269
South Moresby, British Columbia, 254
Sparrow ruling, 195–6
special interest politics, 51
Sproule-Jones, Mark, 32
stagflation, 88
Stanford, Jim, 99
State of the Environment (Environment Canada), 263
statism: definition of, 45–6; and welfare state, 46
Steiner, Jurg, 249
structural changes, 88
structural deficit, definition of, 107
subordinate classes, and government, 36
Supreme Court of Canada: Aboriginal policy, 185, 191, 195–7, 198, 199; environmental policy, 259, 268; family policy, 176; language policy, 13, 221–2, 226
sustainable development, 254; environmental management model, 239, 240t
Swire, Peter, 265
symbolic order, of society, 5, 14
systemic bias, definition of, 8
Szabo, Paul, 178

Task Force on Program Review (1985), 84–5, 253, 255. *See also* environmental policy
tax system, as policy instrument, 10–11
technology, and health-care costs, 141–2
Temagami, Ontario, 254
Thatcher government, 89
Theissen, Gordon, 106–7
theoretical perspectives: compared, 36–41; examples of, 21–2; on policy formation, 38–9t
theory, definition of, 19–21
Thorburn, Hugh, 119
Thoreau, Henry David, 247
Tobin, James, 89, 92
Toner, Glen, 247, 249
Toronto Conference on the Changing Atmosphere 1989, 254
Toronto Star, 256
Total Allowable Catch program, 256
trade, and policy-making, 53
'tragedy of the commons', 241
transfer payments, 9, 60; to provinces and

territories, 149t; redistributive, 12. *See also* distribution of wealth
Transitional Adjustment Assistance Plan, 133
treaties, and policy-making, 55–7
Trebilcock, Michael, 31
Tree Plan Canada, 256
Trudeau, Pierre, 17, 56, 125, 143, 223; Aboriginal policy, 201–2, 204, 207–10
Truman, Harry S., 77
Tullock, Gordon, 29

Uncertain Childhood, Uncertain Future (McLanahan and Sandefur), 171
unemployment and social assistance caseloads, working-age population, 136f
unemployment insurance. *See* employment insurance (EI)
Unemployment Insurance System, evolution of, 135t
United Nations: Conference on Environment and Development 1992, *see* Earth Summit; Declaration on the Granting of Independence to Colonial Countries and Peoples, 197; human development index, 1–2, 124; Security Council, 266
United States: Bill of Rights, 229; Federal Environment Pesticide Control Act, 252; Federal Reserve Board, 106, 107; Federal Water Pollution Control Act Amendments, 252; National Environmental Protection Act (NEPA), 252; Supreme Court, 193

Vanier Institute of the Family, 175
Vermaeten, Arndt, 145, 181
Vermaeten, Frank, 145
Vulnerable Child, The, (Weissbourd), 164

Waddell, Eric, 223
Wallerstein, Judith, 171, 173
Wealth of Nations, The, (Smith), 240
Weissbourd, Richard, 164–5
welfare. *See* social assistance
welfare state, 120–1; comparative perspective, 123–5; definition, 11–12; erosion of, 149–51; redistributive effect, 36. *See also* public policy; social policy; transfer payments
White Paper, 1969, 201–2, 204, 205; critics of, 210; integration and equality, 206–10
'Why Does Government Grow?' (Buchanan), 32
Wildavsky, Aaron, 76–7

Williams, Glen, 113
Wilson, James Q., 75, 78, 80, 83, 162, 171
Wilson, Margo, 173
Wilson, Michael, 98
Wolfe, David, 109–10
Woolley, Frances, 181
Worcester v. Georgia, 193
World Bank, 267
World Commission on Environment and Development. *See* Brundtland Commission
World Conference on the Changing Atmosphere (Toronto 1988), 264, 265
world population growth, 251f
World Trade Organization. *See* WTO
world-view: and communication gap, 40; Marxism, 33; pluralism, 29; theoretical perspectives, 22
WTO (World Trade Organization), 55–6, 62, 119, 266

Yalden, Max, 228
Yukon agreement, 214

Zill, Nicolas, 171–2, 173